THE QUEST OF THE HISTORICAL GOSPEL

Mark, John, and the origins of the gospel genre

Lawrence M. Wills

London and New York

First published 1997
by Routledge
11 New Fetter Lane, London EC4P 4EE

Simultaneously published in the USA and Canada
by Routledge
29 West 35th Street, New York, NY 10001

© 1997 Lawrence M. Wills

Lawrence M. Wills has asserted his moral right under the Copyright, Designs and
Patents Act, 1988, to be identified as the author of this work

Typeset in Garamond by M Rules

Printed and bound in Great Britain by Mackeys of Chatham Plc, Chatham, Kent

British Library Cataloguing in Publication Data
A catalogue record for this book is available from the British Library

Library of Congress Cataloguing in Publication Data
Wills, Lawrence M. (Lawrence Mitchell)
The quest of the historical gospel: Mark, John, and the
origins of the gospel genre / Lawrence M. Wills.
p.   cm.
Includes bibliographical references and index.
1. Bible. N.T. Mark—Criticism, Form.   2. Bible. N.T.
John—Criticism, Form.   3. Aesop—Biography—History
and criticism.   I. Title.
BS2585.2.W56   1997
226′.066—dc21   97–3706
CIP

ISBN 0–415–15093–0

THE QUEST OF THE
HISTORICAL GOSPEL

The question of John and the synoptics should evoke a consideration, or reconsideration, of the question of gospel genre, particularly as it relates to the origin of gospels. Was the writing of gospels a break with tradition rather than its natural culmination?

(Dwight Moody Smith)

CONTENTS

Acknowledgments		vi
List of abbreviations		vii
1	THE GOSPEL GENRE	1
2	THE *LIFE OF AESOP* AND THE HERO CULT PARADIGM IN THE GOSPEL TRADITION	23
3	A SYNOPSIS OF MARK AND JOHN	51
	Part One *Mark 1: 1–3: 30/John 1: 1–7: 20*	52
	Part Two *Mark 5: 21–10: 52/John 4: 46–11: 57*	76
	Part Three *Mark 11: 1–16: 20/John 12: 12–20: 23*	104
4	CONCLUSION	156
	Appendix English translation of the Life of Aesop	180
	Notes	216
	Bibliography	255
	Index of ancient sources	267
	Subject index	279
	Index of modern scholars	281

ACKNOWLEDGMENTS

I have engaged many people in conversation on the issues that are covered in this book, and am indebted to all of them. Several people have been especially generous with their time and input, and have greatly aided the progress of the study: Gregory Nagy, Richard Pervo, Kimberley Patton, and Adela Yarbro Collins. I only wish I could have exploited their suggestions as much as they deserved, but the conversation will doubtless continue. Others whom I would like to thank for support, suggestions, and critical comments include Richard Burridge, Allen Callahan, Joanna Dewey, Georgia Frank, Niklas Holzberg, Richard Horsley, Jon Levenson, Dennis MacDonald, Paul Mirecki and my research assistants, Maryse Levy and James Skedros. Richard Stoneman, Anne Owen and Pauline Marsh of Routledge, have been a pleasure to work with, as have all the other staff members of the press. I would also like to thank two "corporate bodies," both of which prove that intellectual endeavors are not carried out in a vacuum: the faculty, students, and staff at Episcopal Divinity School, and the members of the Ancient Fiction Group of the Society of Biblical Literature, who heard some of these theories discussed in an earlier version. And last, I would like to thank my family, Shelley, Jessica, and Daniel, for their constant support and good humor.

Lawrence M. Wills
December 1996

ABBREVIATIONS

ANRW	Hildegard Temporini and Wolfgang Haase (eds), *Aufstieg und Niedergang der römischen Welt*, Berlin/New York: De Gruyter
CBQ	*Catholic Biblical Quarterly*
HSCP	*Harvard Studies in Classical Philology*
HTR	*Harvard Theological Review*
JAOS	*Journal of the American Oriental Society*
JBL	*Journal of Biblical Literature*
JQR	*Jewish Quarterly Review*
JR	*Journal of Religion*
JSJ	*Journal for the Study of Judaism in the Persian, Hellenistic, and Roman Period*
JSNT	*Journal for the Study of the New Testament*
JSOT	*Journal for the Study of the Old Testament*
JTS	*Journal of Theological Studies*
NT	*Novum Testamentum*
NTS	*New Testament Studies*
RB	*Revue biblique*
TDNT	*Theological Dictionary of the New Testament*, ed. Geoffrey W. Bromiley, Grand Rapids, Mich.: Eerdmans, 10 vols, 1964–76.
ZNW	*Zeitschrift für die neutestamentliche Wissenschaft*

1

THE GOSPEL GENRE

Modern readers in the Christian tradition feel comfortable with the gospel genre. It is a category of literature which seems to have been destined to come into being, its special character often identified with God's unique revelation. But historians of literature cannot presume a doctrine of divine causation, and must ask, Where did the gospel come from? Is it like other literature of the ancient world, or is it a new and revolutionary form? If one tries to examine the gospels anew, without the guides born of familiarity, one finds that there are several strange things about them. We may note, first of all, that they are not proportionally structured. Martin Kähler stated in 1896 that Mark was "a passion story with a long introduction."[1] If Mark was the oldest gospel, then we find from the beginning an uneven emphasis on certain aspects of Jesus' life and death, and very little teaching, except in parables – and even these are meant to be misunderstood by most people (Mark 4: 11–12). Furthermore, unlike Matthew and Luke, Mark and John do not contain any infancy narrative, or any account of Jesus' life before his baptism by John the Baptist. There is little explicit analysis of Jesus' thoughts or character, and no sense of psychological development; our modern preconceptions of "biography" are thereby violated. Unlike Albert Schweitzer's concern in *The Quest of the Historical Jesus*,[2] which was to rediscover the "real" Jesus of the gospels who had been obscured by nineteenth-century romantic sensibilities, the raising of these sorts of questions in twentieth-century scholarship reflected a different concern, a concern for the composition of the gospel rather than its content. Thus began the modern genre criticism of the gospels.

The study of the genre of the gospels is necessarily based on assumptions about the literary relationship among them; that is, a decision about the genre has depended upon scholarly views of how one gospel may have utilized another. There is at the end of the twentieth century a large measure of consensus about the relations of the four canonical gospels. Matthew, Mark, and Luke in large part tell the same story and include many of the same episodes, sometimes with wording that is very close. Because their contents can be viewed together side by side, they are referred to as "synoptic" gospels. The similarity of the wording also indicates that one of the gospels was used as a written source for the other two, and the majority opinion of scholars is that Mark was that source. Mark is generally considered the oldest because it is shorter and simpler in style, and also because it lacks some of the most impressive passages of the other gospels.[3] It is difficult to imagine, for example, Mark intentionally omitting the moving infancy narratives that are found at the beginning of Matthew and Luke, or editing out the many sayings of Jesus that are contained in Matthew and Luke but not found in Mark. Matthew and Luke thus probably used Mark as a source, and working independently, supplemented it by the additions of narratives, such as the infancy narratives at the beginning and the resurrection narratives at the end, and by a great deal of sayings material. The sayings which Matthew and Luke have in common, but which are lacking in Mark, are attributed by most scholars to a hypothetical sayings source called Q, for German *Quelle*, or "source." Matthew and Luke therefore probably had two sources in common, Mark and Q. The so-called two-source hypothesis can be represented in this way:

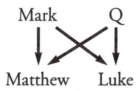

With this diagram in mind, we can see how two primary areas of gospel research in this century have taken shape. Mark, as the earliest narrative gospel of the three (Q has very little narrative material), has become the focus of much analysis of narrative style and of the question of the origin of the gospel genre. Q has also been reconstructed with some success from a comparison of Matthew and Luke, and its theology, its social context, and even its stages of development have been plumbed. What has generally, and surprisingly, received less attention is the investigation of what any observer would agree must be one of the most important questions: What is the relationship of Mark and John? Despite many parallels to the synoptic gospels, John has been seen as relatively independent, interesting mainly for the internal evidence of sources and development, and for its more speculative and cosmological theology. Yet, although the style of Mark and John are often very different, they have the same overall structure. They both contain, in roughly the same order, the baptism of Jesus by John the Baptist and the ministry and miracles of Jesus, followed by his trial, crucifixion, and resurrection (even though the last element is only announced in Mark). Here, then, as well, there must be some discernible relationship between Mark and John, just as there was between Mark, Matthew, and Luke. There are four possibilities to explain this relationship: (1) John knew Mark; (2) Mark knew John; (3) John and Mark, using smaller pieces of the primitive gospel traditions, independently strung them together in a similar order – in effect, a biographical order; and (4) John and Mark both used a previously existing gospel narrative as a source.

Some would argue quite cogently that John read Mark. The similar structure is thus explained, and the differences are attributed to the unique style of John, who has molded the outlines of Mark to a new theological program. Norman Perrin made a programmatic statement to this effect, and has been followed by some of his students and others.[4] There are difficulties with this solution, however. Time and again, those elements in Mark that scholars agree are characteristic of that author are lacking in John (see chapter 3 for a full discussion). The scarcity of such Markan elements in John indicates to many scholars that John could not have received the gospel genre through Mark, directly or indirectly. A few discrepancies may be briefly mentioned here. Mark and John both interpret John the Baptist as the forerunner of Jesus, but in different ways.[5] Mark and John both critique the triumphalistic miracles of their source, but in different ways: Mark with the characteristic "messianic secret" (which is not found as such in John[6]) and John with ironic discourses on the meaning of signs (which is not developed in Mark). Mark and John both introduce the theme of the obtuseness of the disciples, but it is presented in different ways.[7] Mark and John both evidently "demote" Peter (Mark 8: 33; John 1: 40; 20: 4), but in completely different ways; there is no intersection between the two gospels' approaches here. The concern in both gospels over Peter's role likewise appears to have arisen for different reasons: in Mark, a Pauline-influenced opposition to the memory of Peter's stance toward the law, and in John, a geographical or sectarian opposition to Peter's rising authority, which has nothing to do with Paulinism and little to do directly with the law. Mark's and John's anti-Jewish polemics have little in common. John in general does not quote the same scripture as Mark; Matthew and Luke add scripture quotations to Mark, but John uses different scripture. To assert, therefore, that John used Mark, one would have to argue that John systematically extirpated every piece of evidence, certainly every clear piece of evidence, of Markan redaction. As Dwight M. Smith stated, "[W]e can discern a purpose and pattern in Matthew's or Luke's use of Mark, but not in John's."[8] Admittedly, those who hold that John knew Mark tend to see Mark's redaction in some of the parallel elements, but none of these examples is so convincing as to persuade a majority of scholars that Mark's redactional touches can be found in John.

The opposite possibility, that Mark knew John, is quite unlikely, and has been advocated by few scholars. John's Gospel is so dominated by lofty theological assertions, couched in such striking poetic language, that it is difficult to believe that a writer like Mark could recreate a gospel from John without retaining some of the tell-tale signs of Johannine style. This is not to say that John does not contain traditions about Jesus that are in some cases earlier than Mark's – this was John A. T. Robinson's real intention in arguing that John was early[9] – but simply that Mark did not come by them from reading the Gospel of John.

The independence of John from Mark was argued forcefully in 1938 by Percival Gardner-Smith,[10] which then led to the remaining two possibilities. It is often held that neither author read the other, but both utilized many pre-existing, independent narratives, and strung them together following a biographical model. Scholars who have emphasized form criticism of individual passages, such as Rudolf Bultmann and two of his students, Helmut Koester and James Robinson, have favored this approach, as has David E. Aune.[11] That the two authors Mark and John simultaneously but independently hit upon the idea of stringing primitive material together in a biographical framework may at first appear far-fetched, but Robinson makes the very interesting point that two other authors, Matthew and Luke, also simultaneously and independently came to the same new formulation of gospel materials by incorporating Q into the structure of Mark, and adding infancy and resurrection narratives as well. Thus the theory of independently composed biographies remains a distinct possibility, *if* there was no pre-existing structure that had already included all of the pieces together in one narrative. However, it is likely that the connection of the materials was made before Mark and John wrote, as I shall try to show. The fourth possibility above is therefore likely the correct one: Mark and John both utilized an independent gospel narrative tradition.

As noted above, there are specific reasons why the relationship of Mark and John is more difficult to discern than that of Matthew, Mark, and Luke. In the case of Matthew and Luke, the likely source document, Mark, is available to us, and Matthew and Luke followed it closely as a written source. This is not true for Mark and John. Although every scholar must acknowledge the similarities between Mark and John at numerous points, it is quite striking that the wording in the parallel passages is almost never the same. Mark and John often use different Greek words for the same thing. (Contrast the material that Matthew and Luke have in common that is assigned to the hypothetical source Q; the source is probably a written source, and the agreement is sometimes nearly word for word.) Only occasionally do Mark and John have a sentence that uses the same words, and in those cases the words are usually memorable lines that are very stable: "Rise, take up your bed and walk" (Mark 2: 11/John 5: 8); "The poor you will always have with you" (Mark 14: 7/John 12: 8); "Rise, let us be going" (Mark 14: 42a/John 14: 31b); and "Do you want me to release for you the king of the Jews?" (Mark 15: 9b/John 18: 39b).

There are several possible explanations for the divergences in wording. First, the narrative traditions in common could be oral traditions that were very fluid. To be sure, orally transmitted traditions are not *by necessity* unfixed, but popular, orally transmitted prose narratives generally are. It is also possible, however, that the differences in the wording result from the transmission of unfixed written texts.[12] We who live in a highly literate culture tend to equate the written medium with stability and fixity, but it was not generally so in the ancient world for most genres. To judge from our manuscript evidence, popular narratives in the Greco-Roman period were altered freely by each copyist. Each text-witness reflects an individual "performance" of the narrative, altered to fit the pressing concerns of the copyist. This is evident in the case of literature contemporary with the gospel: ancient Jewish novels (consider the text history of Esther, Daniel, Tobit, or *Joseph and Aseneth*), or early Christian acts (consider the textual variants of Acts of the Apostles or the apocryphal Acts), or ancient Greek novels (consider the textual instability of the *Alexander Romance* or *Life of Aesop*). All of these texts were transmitted and copied in written form, even where there was an oral tradition as well, and they remained extremely fluid.[13] This phenomenon also carries over to the Christian gospels: Matthew and Luke are variant versions of Mark, and Mark itself circulated in several editions. Still, although an unfixed *written* tradition behind Mark and John is not impossible, we would have to account for the very great divergences between Mark and John in the wording of the parallel passages. The evidence of other unfixed written traditions indicates that words, phrases, even entire paragraphs are often retained, while other sections are completely rewritten.[14]

It is also necessary, however, to investigate a broader notion of "unfixed narrative tradition." Whether the core narrative that lay behind Mark and John was written or oral is ultimately not as important here as the structure and content of the tradition. We shall never know the precise nature of any hypothetical source, some "proto-gospel," but here I shall posit a narrative complex as a heuristic device, a postulate for the explanation of the present development of Mark and John. It will be argued that it includes some motifs and themes and excludes others. More important, it can be stated that it has one narrative structure, and not another. Folklorists have raised another question, however, that bears on the reconstruction of a "stable" core narrative. Alan Dundes has noted that legends of a cultural hero generally recount different parts of the hero's life story; no one narrative tells the whole.[15] In regard to the multivalency of oral traditions, John Miles Foley also argues that we should not expect oral narrative traditions to be full renditions of a commonly agreed upon "agenda" of events:

> In primary oral tradition, there simply is no such thing as an omitted story-part, or flawed episode, or misnomer. Since the primary oral performance draws its meaning not only from the present event but equally from the diachronic and pan-geographic tradition of which it is only an instance, the process of generating meaning proceeds via metonomy, *pars pro toto*. Our text recalls numerous others by synecdochy, just as one phrase or scene is always embedded conceptually in the word-hoard, in the experience of tradition. Under such conditions the oral reality of Jesus conjured for its audience not simply its present, discrete story-shape, but all story-shapes that oral tradition had gathered about this central figure.[16]

5

For Edmund Leach, the differences between narrative tellings are not a problem for the researcher; rather, variety is necessary to bring different facets and local renderings to the reflection on the deeply held truths of a group, that is, to the group's myth.[17] Myth can only be myth if there are differing, even contradictory, narrative tellings. The best example of this variegated tradition that Leach can put forward is the Christian gospels. It is because they differ, he says, that they are myth. Mark and John are thus closely related by-forms, part of a multivalent tradition; their common source is not a single written text, and presumably not a single fixed narrative.

To clarify these issues, we may turn to a distinction that has been used in genre criticism in other fields. The literary critic Frederic Jameson divides recent theories of genre definition into two distinct approaches: a *semantic* approach, which defines genres based upon the separate motifs that appear in a text, and a *syntactic* approach, which focuses more on the relationships between motifs.[18] For Jameson, the quintessential semantic theorist is Northrop Frye, and the quintessential syntactic theorist is Vladimir Propp. Rick Altman has applied this distinction very successfully to the study of film genres as well, where he argues that semantic elements which we encounter are often quite varied, but that new syntactic structures come into being which, because they fulfill a certain function, are stable for a time, and are replaced later by other syntactic structures when their function has become obsolete.[19] The relations between motifs create expectations and narrative tensions that must be resolved in a satisfactory way. Although Foley's warning about the danger of trying to determine which motifs are present or absent in a tradition can apply both to semantic and syntactic variations, here I would argue that some syntactic structures achieve enough stability to be "mapped," as a result of their coalescence around a particular social location and function.

Although the Jesus tradition as developed over the course of the first two centuries C.E. is certainly quite varied, within the timeframe of the first half-century of the Jesus movement, the narratives were likely limited to a few types, depending upon their function. Q and the *Gospel of Thomas* likely reflect a teaching setting, miracles collections likely reflected a missionary preaching function, and the narrative complex that lies behind Mark and John is likely a cult narrative. As a result, although the earliest tellings of the life of Jesus that are of the same type as Mark and John, and that pre-existed Mark and John, may have included or omitted different episodes, and told the same episodes in different ways, they did not likely include, for example, the miraculous birth or remarkable childhood of the hero.[20] Variety does not mean that there is no structural core to be found. The cultic narrative included the necessary information for the establishment of a cult: the call of the hero, the benefactions, the barbed teaching that incenses the leaders, the resultant execution, and the resolution of the separation from God.

Judging from the evidence of Mark and John given in chapter 3 below, it appears that there were variations in the narrative tradition – some of the miracles, the teachings, the resurrection appearances – but a common core narrative existed nevertheless. What constituted this core would be indicated by the presence of certain motifs in the same or nearly the same order, such as baptism by John the Baptist, miracles, controversies with opponents (especially Pharisees), a plot on Jesus' life by the chief priests and others, and so on, but the core might also be described structurally as the development of a positive relation declared between Jesus and God, a negative relation developing between Jesus and the Jewish authorities (and with God?), and the resolution of this dramatic opposition through execution and cult. A text, or an entire genre, is identified as much by the tensions it creates as by its individual motifs. Propp's advance was simply to place more emphasis on the *relations between* motifs in a narrative than on the isolated events themselves. An interdiction in a fairytale, for example, soon gives rise in the narrative to a violation of the interdiction. But this can be stated more strongly: the relations can often be seen as *tensions*, great or small, that create the need either for further complication or for resolution. A structural description of the tensions and resolutions in Mark and John (as well as Matthew and Luke) may appear more stable than a listing of separate episodes, and our analysis may allow a reconstruction of a pre-Markan and pre-Johannine version of this core narrative.

Two examples will illustrate the point being drawn. First, one can postulate a popular narrative tradition that exhibited a stable structure, even though there were variations of motifs. The various renditions of Esther provide an instructive case in point, as some parts of the drama are expanded in the different editions that have come down to us. In a second example, however, Judith, who is always depicted in ancient Judaism and early Christianity as a positive, triumphalist avenger (whether in literature or visual art), experiences a reversal in the early modern period.[21] With the gradual emancipation of women, Judith evidently becomes a threatening presence (again, in both literary and visual representations), in some retellings raped by Holofernes, after which she is aroused to fury and executes him in a bloodbath of sexual revenge. The audience's sympathies are shifted from Judith's point-of-view to Holofernes'. From this point on, Judith's actions are often condemned by critics. It is not just that a few motifs in the story have changed; the structure itself has changed, seen precisely in the fact that the tensions have changed. This woman, who before was seen as wielding her sword "for us," becomes a woman who may secretly harbor threatening designs "against us," that is, against the male perspective reader or viewer. Thus two different structures can be seen in the history of the Judith narrative, a pre-1600 structure and a post-1600 structure. Each is stable for the duration of its own period, but both are ultimately replaced by new structures. Analogously, the structure we are seeking in the forebears of Mark and John is relatively stable, as long as it functioned in a particular way, but would soon change into the new structures required by the church.

APPROACHES TO GENRE

Before proceeding to a consideration of past research on the identification of the gospel genre, it would be helpful at this point to state some of my operating assumptions of how genres function in the reading process. The second half of this century has witnessed the production of a rich literature on the nature of genres, but rather than reviewing this body of scholarship in detail, I shall simply emphasize several points that seem to me relevant for the following discussion.[22]

1. I assume that genres are not simply subjective categories that we impose by convention on an infinitely variable world, but that they really do correspond to "types" of texts. There is a general agreement among literary critics that genres are ways of identifying real similarities among texts, and that there is an unexpressed set of expectations set up between author and readers within a particular culture, whereby the readers bring to the text an understanding of the conventions of the genre. It is common to hear the reading process referred to now as a "contractual" or even "covenantal" relationship between author and reader.[23]

2. Genre classifications cannot be established on the basis of a small set of criteria, such as common motifs, common themes, a common function and social setting, the overall literary form (poetry or prose), or any other partial criteria. So many factors enter into our reception of a text that any conceivable aspect could provide clues as to genre, from the common visible "envelope," that is, the material and production of a text (vellum versus papyrus, scroll versus codex, and so on),[24] to the minutiae of rhythm or sentence structure. Genre classifications are perceived by the reader on the basis of all the impressions that a text presents. Ludwig Wittgenstein's asseveration that all definitions operate on the basis of the "family resemblances" among members of a set was appropriately taken over into genre definition by Alastair Fowler,[25] and it is by means of the family resemblances that the contract between author and reader is perceived.

3. Having said that, one must still recognize that in dealing with ancient texts, only a fraction of the generic clues will become clear to us. Although we must proceed by identifying as many significant markers as possible, not restricting ourselves to any single category, we are still limited in our ability to decode all of the data that are available to us, and are further hampered by being deprived of many of the data that once existed.

4. Genres, as they function in society, are not neat and mutually exclusive groupings. Difficulties of classification of ancient genres often lead to the conclusion that there is something wrong with genre classification as such. Although genre designations by their very nature tend to minimize differences and deny the specificity of texts in order to group them, it is important to recall that genres are malleable, overlapping and changeable, and that they can be grouped and regrouped in different "legitimate" ways, depending upon

what criteria are being applied. This is not simply a result of our distance from and ignorance of the ancient world; it is true for all genres and subgenres. If a group of modern novels were sitting on a table before us, we might group them and regroup them differently depending upon what criteria were invoked. Some novels might be placed in each of the following categories: detective novels, apocalyptic novels, first-person narratives, novels with female protagonists, and so on. None of these categories is totally definitive of the work, because other questions might provoke other rearrangements. The relevant question thus becomes, What concerns are brought to bear *at this point* in grouping literary works?

5. Because readers bring expectations to the reading of any work of literature — expectations engendered by their identification of the genre's conventions — elements that violate these expectations may challenge the audience, and may present them with a need to reevaluate the usual experience. Such variations, however, do not "destroy" the genre; they in fact may reaffirm the "essence" of the genre by showing the consequences of the unexpected. Jonathan Culler affirms the value of the unexpected in the reading experience:

> [T]he most interesting features of a text . . . become those by which it asserts its otherness, its difference from what is already dealt with by the cultural models of literature as an institution.[26]

Encountering the unexpected must thus be viewed as a normal part of the reading experience, whether the unexpected elements are minor, or result in a full-blown satire. Satirical texts help us to define the genre just as effectively as do the more straightforward texts, by attempting to destabilize what elsewhere has been stabilized.

6. The name of a genre is quite often irrelevant for identifying it or describing it; genres generally function without being named, and are often named only when they have become obsolete. The name of a genre is not often important because the genre is "a mode of discourse which a culture takes as natural."[27] Therefore it should not surprise us that the word "gospel" was not used of written texts in first-century Christianity; it refers only to the oral preaching about Jesus.[28] A corollary to this is that when genre names do appear, they are often overly inclusive or inappropriate for modern scholarly purposes. The Hebrew *mashal*, for example, includes both what we would call "proverbs" and "parables," and other forms as well. The term "gospel" was not precise when it did come to be applied to Christian writings in the second century, but was applied to both "Mark-type" (narrative) gospels and "Thomas-type" (sayings) gospels.

7. This brings us to our next thesis: a theory of genre *evolution* is as necessary as a theory of genre *distinctions*. We do not live in a world of static genres, but a world of changing genres, and so all of the texts we analyze exist in a context of growth, change, obsolescence, and the creation of new genres.

Alastair Fowler proposes that we think of the growth and change of genres in three stages: (1) an innovative combination of old and new elements that communicates a new theme; (2) a realignment of elements that brings about a classic unity and develops the full potentialities of the genre; and (3) a baroque period in which the classic structure is embellished, inverted, or satirized.[29] The comparisons of texts and the assignment of genre designations must take the element of change into consideration.

8. It is important to distinguish "genre" from words that are sometimes taken to mean the same thing, such as "theme" or "mode." Certain literary or dramatic effects can be found in gospels and in other literature, or indeed in other media, but no matter how much they may *influence* the gospels or *be expressed by* the gospels, they do not constitute the same *genre* unless they are taken up and used in approximately the same way in society.[30] Ironically, it is necessary here to emphasize the important difference in meaning between genre and theme because in this study I also point out an interesting *convergence* of genre and theme. The Gospels of Mark and John, the *Life of Aesop*, and perhaps some other works all occupy the same *genre*, the aretalogical biography – that is, an account of the great deeds of a god or hero – which is attached to a cult, and they develop the same *theme* of the opposition of the protagonist to his people (and perhaps to his god, or at least his temple), the antagonism that results from this opposition, and the resolution of this antagonism through an expiatory death. I shall point out in the course of this study how this theme had been prepared for in a number of works – aretalogies, Jewish wisdom and apocalyptic works – and how the genre that here expresses it had been prepared for in various other genres as well: historiography, biography, Greek and Jewish novelistic works, and so on. In other words, the content and the form may have evolved along separate paths, but converged in this genre. To be sure, Mark and John may begin at times to move away from their origins, and the authors perhaps even feel the need to critique this soteriology, but that should not surprise us either. Matthew and Luke move even further away, until they are in effect something else, a different kind of biography.

THE INVESTIGATION OF THE GOSPEL GENRE

In summarizing the history of the investigation of the gospel genre, Robert Guelich divides modern theories into two groups: analogical and derivational.[31] Analogical theories compare the gospels to contemporary genres of the Greco-Roman or Jewish literature, such as one or another subdivision of biography. The derivational theories reconstruct a development of the gospel from within early Christianity, usually from the *kerygma*, or proclamation of the significance of Jesus and his death. Each approach has its origin around the turn of the century. The analogical approach found an early champion in Johannes Weiss, who argued that the gospels were, as Justin Martyr had indeed referred to them, the *apomnemoneumata* or memorabilia of the apostles.[32] It was Clyde Weber Votaw, however, who in 1915 first compared the gospels to Greco-Roman biographies and established the classic argument for the analogical approach. He distinguished between "historical biographies" and "popular biographies," a division based largely upon modern historiographical criteria of logic and connectedness.[33] Votaw likened the gospels to the latter only, a category which also included Arrian's *Discourse of Epictetus*, Plato's *Apology*, Xenophon's *Memorabilia*, and Philostratus' *Apollonius of Tyana*.

Other analogs have also been explored, though none is so durable as biography. Some have sought the essence of Mark, or of the gospel in general, in categories that are not on the surface comparable. Perrin likened Mark to apocalypses, Werner H. Kelber proposed "parable" as a description of Mark's literary activity, Philip Carrington and Michael Goulder the midrashic lectionary, David L. Barr the Socratic dialogues, Gilbert G. Bilezikian tragedy, Dan O. Via, Jr. tragicomedy, and H. Fischel the *chreia*, or short narrative culminating in a profound or witty saying.[34] Although many of these analogies seem to stretch the possibilities of genre "relatedness," they should perhaps be seen as *partial* analogies that call attention to one aspect or another of the gospel genre.

Two other scholars have proposed analogs that, like biography, are closer in outward form to the gospel. First, Mary Ann Tolbert introduces a broad treatment of the Greek novels and notes that Mark conforms to some of their most salient characteristics: the novels are entertaining prose narratives written in a less elevated style than the histories, biographies, and philosophical works of the aristocratic class.[35] The gospels arose at a time when a revolution was taking place in the applications of prose narrative to create fictitious works for a broader, more literate audience. There is still a distance between the social level and literary attainments of the Greek novels and the Gospel of Mark, however. Her arguments would have been stronger had she made reference to the novels from a lower, more indigenous social level, which are shorter and written in a style much closer to Mark. The fact that Gospels seem to lie "between" several genres simply reflects the innovations that can be seen in popular literature. Greek history and biography had already witnessed the introduction of novelistic techniques (Xenophon's *Cyropaedia*, Pseudo-Callisthenes' *Life of Alexander, Ninus and Semiramis*), and older Jewish narratives were already being expanded into novels (Greek Esther, Greek Daniel, Tobit, Judith, and *Joseph and Aseneth*). The novelistic techniques that would soon be exploited in the Christian apocryphal Acts were already being utilized in the gospels.[36]

Second, Adela Yarbro Collins asserts that Mark is an "apocalyptic historical monograph."[37] Although not many scholars have picked up on her suggestion, it may contribute toward a solution to the genre problem. There are two parts to her genre designation, "apocalyptic" and "historical monograph," and they should be considered separately. "Historical monograph" was a term used in the ancient world to describe a history that deals with a circumscribed subject, as opposed to a "universal" or "general history," which covered the entire history of a particular people. Hans Conzelmann and Martin Hengel had earlier argued that Acts was a historical monograph, and Aune had argued that Luke and Acts together were a universal history.[38] To Collins, Mark is a historical monograph also, covering the circumscribed period of history that involves Jesus' ministry and death. This historical monograph is also governed throughout, however, by the eschatological time-scheme of God's plan in history. The similarity to historical writing is thus noted, and the dissimilarity to biography is argued.

There is an important element in the theories of Tolbert and Collins that will ultimately figure in the determination of the genre of the gospels. The relation of the gospel to the novel is mainly in the area of technique, in the description of the individual, character, and psychology, as Erich Auerbach saw fifty years ago.[39] History and biography, interestingly enough, are actually rather weak on these points. The novel, or more precisely, the indigenous novelistic literature of the ancient world, is what prepared the way for the gospel. Yet the gospel is not fiction, in the sense of an invented world that is recognized as such by both author and reader, but a cult narrative, and similar in some ways to the "historical novel." In this connection, the very surprising thesis of G. W. Bowersock must be mentioned. He argues that the gospel narrative, rather than being influenced by the rise of the Greek novel, is instead the wellspring of the development of this literature.[40] He ignores the earlier existence of the *Ninus Romance*, and insists that the *Scheintod*, or "apparent death" motif, is the *sine qua non* of the novel, and must have been a Greek response to the dramatic depiction of the death of Jesus in the gospels. His exclusive emphasis on the *Scheintod*, I believe, has skewed the discussion away from the much broader body of literature developing throughout the Greco-Roman world. The description of the gospel and of texts like *Aesop* as novels *and* cult narratives also calls to mind the theories of Reinhold Merkelbach and Karl Kerényi, who saw in the Greek novels allusions to the mystery cults of Isis and Dionysus.[41] Their theories in their specific assertions no longer have many followers, since the novels were not likely encoded with references to the mysteries, but the general role of the myth of salvation in the novels does have an analogy in the contemporary mysteries, as Niklas Holzberg affirms:

> Initiates who pass successfully through cult trials can expect their god to keep them from harm on earth and free them spiritually from troubles and fears, and they can look forward to eternal bliss after death. For the heroes of novels a similar fate is in store. . . . What we have in both cases is a myth, an idealistic vision of man's journey through life – the one a religious, the other a profane myth of salvation.[42]

And whereas the gospel is a "novelization" of the cult narrative, in relation to Collins' thesis, it must also be said that it differs from *Aesop* and *Secundus*

12

in its seriousness of purpose, both regarding its eschatological urgency and, in the case of Mark, its lack of humor. John introduces the humor of dramatic irony, and Luke–Acts will later exhibit further novelization, losing at times the urgency and adding humor, but Mark retains an unusual level of intensity. Collins thus reminds us once again of the overlapping nature of genre characteristics, and the difficulty in subsuming an eschatological gospel under the biographies, which are generally non-eschatological. I find the analogies of both the novel and the apocalyptic historical monograph helpful, but ultimately not compelling enough to dislodge the biographical model *when rightly understood.*

Derivational theories of the origin of the gospel genre grew up in opposition to the analogical theory of biography proposed by Votaw and others. Karl Ludwig Schmidt first rejected comparisons of the gospels with Greco-Roman biographies by arguing that the New Testament should be seen as "folk literature" (*Kleinliteratur*), not in any way comparable to the "elite literature" (*Hochliteratur*) of the educated upper classes.[43] Schmidt's challenge reflects a different approach to the categorization of the gospel genre, which takes it to be essentially unique, a creation of early Christianity, and only vaguely similar to the biographies of antiquity. Corresponding to the rise of the view that the gospel genre was unique is the emphasis on the origin of the gospel in the *kerygma* or proclamation of the early church. The Protestant emphasis on the word of God as revelation found a welcome home in a theory that posited the preaching of the good news as the crucible of the gospel narrative. Even scholars as distinct in their conclusions as C. H. Dodd in England and Rudolf Bultmann in Germany could perceive an innate genius in the early Christian preaching that could account for the apparent uniqueness of the literature that resulted.[44]

The gospel-as-*kerygma* has a compelling logic to it that has proved resilient, despite challenges. The formula of the *kerygma*, found in numerous New Testament passages (for example, 1 Cor 15: 1–5; Rom 1: 3–4; 8: 31–34; and the missionary speeches in Acts 2: 22–36; 3: 13–21; 10: 37–43; and 13: 23–33) indicates a common narrative framework, around which the fuller account of the gospel could be structured. This approach could be extended beyond the core narrative of the passion to other events in the life and after-life of Jesus, as Dodd attempted to do. The *kerygma* developed into a narrative telling of events within the missionary program of the early church, in a state relatively isolated from more elite Greco-Roman genres. Since this traditional development was seen as having no "literary" concerns or inclinations from the outset – and even disdained such pretensions – and since the materials developed out of the requirements of the church's mission, the end product, the gospel, was viewed as standing without literary parallel. This is possible, however, only in a derivational theory that allows for a huge gap between one stage and the next. The *kerygma* as isolated by these scholars is bare bones, no longer than a creedal statement, and not capable by itself of generating a larger narrative. Richard Burridge rightly emphasizes the difficulty of defining a genre of 10,000–20,000 words in terms of a genre of 50–100 words.[45] Dodd tried to explain this development across the gap as a written *explication* of the *kerygma*, rather than an internal evolution,[46] and indeed, some relationship between the gospel and the *kerygma* must have existed. As Koester has pointed out, the additions to the gospel narrative in the first and second centuries correspond in content precisely to the additions that were made to the creedal statements during the same period. For example, birth narratives are added to the gospels at the same time that the virgin birth is added to the creedal statements, and so on.[47] This relationship does not by itself define the genre, however, only the background of the genre, or perhaps at best the theme of the genre. The derivational approach also inevitably gave rise to a sharp distinction between *kerygma* and *didache* or teaching. If the gospel was originally a narrative explication of the *kerygma* only, then teaching was extraneous to this and entered in only later, when Matthew and Luke combined the sayings of Q with the gospel structure of Mark.

Another derivational model, which has not received the attention that it deserves, is that of Anitra Bingham Kolenkow, who believes that the gospel evolved from the tradition of healing controversies found in Mark and John.[48] Convinced that John was independent of Mark, she noted the parallel motifs between Mark 2: 1–12 and 3: 1–6 on the one hand and John 5: 1–18 on the other (see chapter 3), and also between these controversies and the passion narrative. Kolenkow suggests, following Bultmann, that the healing controversies arose as defenses of early Christian healing practices, practices which might have brought on the threat of death at the hands of Jewish authorities, and that this influenced the development of the passion narrative from a political trial to a model martyrdom of the healer. Whether she is correct in the specifics of her argument, she highlights one crucial issue: the conflict story encapsulates the essence of the gospel, much more than the parable does, and she can present a plausible theory of how it may have given rise to the gospel as a whole. Mark and John are not derived from accounts of the religious leader and his disciples, but of the religious critic and his opponents. Kolenkow also undercuts the popular theory of Robert T. Fortna that the Gospel of John consisted of miracles-plus-passion (see below). We shall have reason to return to Kolenkow's theory again.

Although the derivational view held sway through much of this century, comparisons with Greco-Roman popular biography have recently begun to influence the discussion again, and have forced a paradigm shift away from the doctrine of uniqueness back to a view akin to Votaw's, that is, from a derivational to an analogous approach once more. Some have pressed anew the parallels in Greco-Roman biography, making, in some cases, cautious and somewhat vague comparisons (Albrecht Dihle), or in other cases, closer and more ambitious ones (Richard Burridge).[49] Dihle notes the general similarity between the biographical interest of the gospel and Greek and Roman biographies, but offers little encouragement for a finer delineation of the relationship. The Greek and Roman biographies are simply too varied, often carrying a particular or *ad hoc* application, and lacking in the cosmic–metaphysical–eschatological interests of the gospels. Dihle notes drily, however, that although New Testament students are routinely warned in introductory classes that the gospels should *not* be read as biographies of Jesus, this is precisely how they have been read through almost the entirety of Christian history. Dihle also argues that they *should* be read as biographies, provided that we are careful about precisely what this means. In Diogenes Laertius' *Lives*, for example, Dihle grants that some of the accounts (for example, that of Empedocles) are similar to Mark in structure: they place the teaching of a sage, his relation with his disciples, and the events of his life in a framework that begins with the origins and youth of the sage, and concludes with the death, testament, and burial tradition. Dihle is surely correct about the variety of Greek and Roman biographies in terms of form, content, and moral application or function, but he is too negative about the possibility of discerning relevant subcategories. Burridge goes further and presents the most detailed and comprehensive consideration of the genre "biography" and its application to the gospels, and offers valuable correctives to the near-misses of his colleagues. Particularly helpful is his consideration of the interrelation of genres, and the necessary overlapping of categories that the genre-hunter must negotiate. Burridge also notes the variety of forms of biographies, and points out that the gospels do not differ from biographies any more than biographies differ from each other.

Others have also promulgated particular subcategories of the ancient biography as more exact and instructive parallels, such as the biography of the sage who founds a school (Charles Talbert), or the encomium type of biography (Philip Shuler).[50] Talbert divides the Greco-Roman biographies into four types based on function, and assigns Mark and John to type B, which aim to "dispel a false image of the teacher and to provide a true model to follow." Closely related to the category of biography is also that of aretalogy, or an account of the great deeds of the divine man, which Morton Smith and Moses Hadas have proposed as a parallel to the gospel.[51] They connect the aretalogy to the *vita* or biography of the philosopher in antiquity, as opposed to the warrior (see also chapter 2). Some scholars, such as Howard Clark Kee and David Tiede, have chafed at the use of this term,[52] since there is no clear model of an "aretalogy" labeled as such in the ancient world, but the problem is partly terminological. The word "aretalogy" is also applied to the inscriptions placed at sacred sites that describe the great deeds of the god or hero. This is hardly similar to a gospel; one is an inscription in stone, perhaps a hundred words long, the other a book, containing about 15,000 words. But the idea and the impulse to create an aretalogical biography is what Smith and others have focused on as similar, and there are in the Greek tradition various Lives of the poets, centered like aretalogies around shrines, which tend toward the biographical, and also emphasize the sacrificial nature of the poet's relationship to the gods. The Lives of Archilochus, Hesiod, Homer and Pindar vary in length and scope, but reflect a common concern to depict aspects of the poet's life and death, and their status as a "*therapon* (ritual substitute) of the Muses."[53] These traditions are longer than most aretalogies and shorter than most biographies, but a further-developed vehicle for this theme is the *Life of Aesop*, composed probably in the first or second century C.E. As I shall argue in chapter 2, it is the missing link between popular, aretalogical biographies in Greco-Roman culture and the gospel tradition.

Dieter Georgi also takes up this same combination of aretalogy and philosopher's *vita*, and makes provocative suggestions about the genre of Mark by describing its likely source, an aretalogical collection which stretched from the baptism to the ascension. (Georgi follows many others in seeing the transfiguration in 9: 2–8 as the original ascension scene, retrojected into the life of Jesus.) Mark has critically transformed a *theios aner* ("divine man" or miracle worker) christology into a Suffering Son of Humanity christology, using the model of philosopher's *vita*:

> The taking over of an aretalogy, the incorporation of controversy stories, the inclusion of speeches (ch. 4 and ch. 13), the strong emphasis on the disciple motif, and the increase of redactional references to Jesus as itinerant teacher, all these features speak for closeness to the milieu of philosophical schools and their literary production. My thesis actually is that Mark consciously presents the record of Jesus in analogy to the philosopher-*vita* – still close enough to the aretalogical *vita* to compete with it.[54]

Klaus Berger, judging Schmidt's distinction between folk literature and elite literature too simplistic, also sought finer nuances in the different types of Greco-Roman biography. He divided them into four types, one of which shades into popular literature at a lower social level, the "popular, novelistic" type. In this category he includes, at the upper end of the scale, Xenophon's *Cyropaedeia*, but also, at a middle and lower level, the *Life of Secundus the Silent Philosopher* and the *Life of Aesop*.[55] Aune also discusses popular biographies such as these, as well as Pseudo-Hesiod, *Life of Homer* and "Herakles" in Apollodorus, *Library* 2.4.6–2.7.8, and concludes:

> Gospels form a recognizable subtype of Hellenistic biography, distinctive because the *content* is Jewish and Christian, while the *form* and *function* is Hellenistic. The Gospels themselves reflect the syncretistic world within which they arose.[56]

Perhaps the solution lies in focusing on this subset of biography, the popular, novelistic biography of the extraordinary person. A "canon" of such writings can be assembled, most of which appear in both the list of aretalogies of some scholars, and the lists of biographies of others: Philo's *Life of Moses*, the anonymous *Life of Aesop* and *Life of Secundus the Silent Philosopher*, perhaps even the

Onias III traditions now incorporated into 2 Maccabees. The shorter aretalogies need not be seen as exact members of the same genre, but as part of the body of traditions that influenced it.

Another fruitful adaptation of the gospel-as-biography theory, however, is that of Klaus Baltzer, taken up also by Dieter Lührmann, Detlev Dormeyer, and Helmut Koester.[57] Here we find the exploration of a theory that is both analogical and derivational. In addressing the question of the biography of the prophet in ancient Israel, Baltzer distinguished between Greco-Roman biographies that emphasized the individuality of the person's life (and explicitly or implicitly, of the author as well), and Hebrew Bible biographies of the prophet that emphasize not the individual traits but the "typical": the prophet is not great or even important in himself, but only insofar as God has called him into an office for service (only the male prophets have call narratives). The Greco-Roman biography emphasizes the *bios* or life of the important personage, and often a conversion to *arete* or virtue, while the Israelite prophet, when called to office, is not depicted as a better person, but is a mouthpiece for God's message. Mark, as the representative gospel, conforms to the Israelite, not the Greco-Roman, pattern: there is no miraculous birth or remarkable youth, but the gospel begins with a call of Jesus to the "office" of Son of God (Mark 1: 11), and ends with the recognition that Jesus was the Son of God (15: 39). The cult of the risen Jesus at the tomb, an important motif of the Greco-Roman heroic biography, is rejected by Mark; we find instead a summons to proceed to Galilee. Lührmann also assimilates the prophetic biography of Baltzer to an "ideal biography," based on the servant of God in Isaiah 42–53.[58] Although the differences are rightly noted by Guelich[59] – Mark, unlike Isaiah, involves a concrete depiction of a clearly named figure and his problematic relation with his disciples – it is important to note the evolution of the paradigm of the suffering righteous person in ancient Judaism, as witnessed especially in Wisdom of Solomon and *Testament of Joseph*. George W. E. Nickelsburg argues convincingly that there is a thematic development in the various depictions of the suffering righteous person that includes the Gospel of Mark; specifically, he points out that *Testament of Joseph* combines the narrative motif of the persecuted righteous with interpretive allusions to Psalms of the persecuted righteous, just as the passion narratives do.[60]

The comparison of the gospels to Greco-Roman biographies on the one hand and aretalogies on the other is suggestive, but in both cases one is left wondering whether at best we see the *kinship* of genres, and not an actual identity of genre. When we recognize the shadings of biographies and aretalogies, however, the kinship becomes much closer. Burridge's observation (see above) that the differences between the gospels and some of the biographies are no greater than the differences among the biographies is quite apt and is also stated by Aune.[61] Thus the comparison of the gospels with biographies does not require an adjustment of what we mean by "gospel" (as was once believed), but may entail an adjustment of what we mean by "biography."

Reviewing the two types of genre theories concerning the gospels, we can see upon reflection that derivational theories tend to be diachronic, as they postulate a development across time, usually with origin-points and end-points. Analogical theories, on the other hand, tend to be synchronic, seeking to isolate the nature or essence of the gospel genre by comparison with other known genres. There is in analogical theories little consideration of origins. It is also important to note, however, the inevitable tendency of derivational theories to be historically and sociologically oriented, and analogical theories to be grounded in literary criticism. There is also a general, but not absolute, tendency of the derivationists to utilize Jewish background and parallels, and the analogists to use Greco-Roman. This divergence could not be more dramatic than Joel B. Green's derivational approach to the death of Jesus tradition, which does not mention Greco-Roman literature, and Burridge's, which lacks any significant reference to Jewish literature.[62] The separate mindsets of the two approaches can thus give rise to dramatically different depictions of the world of the gospels. In these recent discussions of the genre of the gospel, however, the best theories are both derivational and analogical; that is, they emphasize the internal development of a narrative that is parallel to, if not inspired by, the *kerygma*, the paradigm of the persecuted righteous person, eschatological perspectives, and so on, and yet they also emphasize the parallels between these developments and biographies as they most likely existed at a less aristocratic level of society, whether popular aretalogical biographies or Jewish biographies of the prophet. At any rate, here I shall argue that the gospels are "biographical" in this sense: they are parallel to these popular biographies that have a strong sense of cult or reverence of the extraordinary hero, a reverence that goes beyond admiration or didacticism.

POSSIBLE SOURCES OF MARK AND JOHN

There have been many attempts to detect sources in Mark and John, and any attempt to reconstruct an older narrative that was used by both of these gospels must take into consideration the most important of these. For Mark, it is first of all often suggested that the passion narrative derived from a separate source that was developed in the earliest years of the Christian movement.[63] (See discussion in chapter 3.) Not only does the special character of the passion narrative suggest this to some scholars, but so also does the fact that Mark and John appear to be much closer to each other in this section. Disagreements over which verses derive from the source and which from Mark's redaction, however, have created a somewhat murky picture, and a number of scholars now argue that Mark's own redaction accounts for much of the structure that was once considered pre-Markan.[64] Other than these theories concerning the passion narrative, however, there have been few attempts to posit a substantial connected narrative behind Mark. C. H. Dodd attempted to find in the geographical notices in Mark an earlier itinerary of

18

the gospel story, to which narratives were added.[65] This theory has rightly been criticized, and is not widely accepted. Likewise, smaller sources or collections of particular kinds of traditions have been posited: the "little apocalypse" of Mark 13, the parables collection of Mark 4, the two "miracle catenae" or chains of Mark 5–8, and the collection of controversy stories in Mark 2: 1–3: 6.[66] All of these sections are composed of distinct kinds of material – apocalyptic discourse, parables, controversies – and the theories, while quite plausible, assume that material composed of a certain form circulated orally and was passed on in short collections, not composed or collected into one section by the redactor Mark. B. S. Easton goes so far as to suggest that the exorcisms in Mark that are now separated in the gospel (Mark 1: 21–28; 5: 1–20; 7: 24–30; 9: 14–29) may have been derived from a single collection.[67] There is also evidence of slightly different versions of Mark in circulation in the first century, one which was used by Matthew and Luke (so-called *Ur-Markus*), and Secret Mark, which contained passages depicting esoteric instructions, but these slightly different editions do not affect the question of a substantial, connected source.

None of these theories provide evidence of a substantial source; they would indicate at best that there existed a series of building blocks, which Mark the redactor assembled into a connected narrative; indeed this is the way Mark's compositional activity has been viewed by many scholars. Others would simply deny the existence of any significant source, and argue instead that Mark is responsible for the gospel structure and much of its content.[68] Under the latter theory, the gospel genre is Mark's creation, and John took over this genre from Mark. Thus, a theory that holds that Mark did utilize an extensive narrative source would have to counter both the building-blocks approach to Markan construction and the Mark-as-creator theory of gospel origins.

The reconstructions of sources in John has proceeded in general quite independently of any consideration of sources in Mark. Bultmann in 1941 proposed that John depended on three separate sources, which were heavily redacted and rearranged: a passion narrative (which differed in many respects from Mark's), a special discourse, elevated and heavily laden with symbols, called the Revelation Discourse, and a collection of miracles called a Signs or Semeia Source (*semeia* is the Greek word for signs).[69] Each of these three suggestions has experienced a separate fate, but the last has at least been kept very much alive by a number of scholars, most notably Robert T. Fortna, W. Nicol, Dwight Moody Smith, Howard M. Teeple, and Urban C. von Wahlde.[70] They rendered Bultmann's general suggestion into a quite ambitious source theory. Although there are not as many miracle stories in John as there are in the other gospels, the few that there are seem to shine more brightly as a result. They are in several cases interpreted very symbolically with the same dualistic symbols that appear in the Revelation Discourse sections of John; in fact, in some cases they become discourses. Two of them, however, have an unusual notation at the end. At 2: 11, the miracle at the wedding in Cana, where Jesus turned the water into wine, concludes, "This was the first of his signs which Jesus did at Cana in Galilee, and manifested his glory; and his disciples believed in him." At 4: 54, after Jesus has healed an official's son (also in Cana), it says, "This was now the second sign that Jesus did when he had come from Judea to Galilee." Other miracles, however, are not similarly numbered, and at John 2: 23 there is also a reference to "the many signs which he did," even though sign number two has not yet occurred. It has been argued that the numbered miracles may simply refer to the order of the miracles in Cana of Galilee, although the significance of this would be obscure, and there is no amplification of this theme later in the gospel (but see chapter 4 below). Fortna argues that it is more likely that these, and perhaps other miracles, were derived by the author from a collection of miracle stories which focused on the word "signs," and the stories may even have been numbered in an attempt to emphasize their significance. This is partially confirmed by the fact that the theology of the numbered signs appears to stand in disagreement with the redactor's own view: elsewhere in John's Gospel it is stated that faith based on the witnessing of miracles is an inadequate faith (4: 48; 14: 11). One would wonder why only the enumerations of two of the miracles remain, if others were also taken from this source, but the process of opening up the other miracle stories to Johannine discourses presumably involved the removal of the original conclusions. As a result, Fortna could propose that the Signs Source consisted of these miracle stories (several displaced from their original locations):

1. The water changed to wine (2: 1–12)
2. An offical's son healed (4: 46–54)
3. A miraculous catch of fish (21: 1–14)
4. The feeding of the five thousand (6: 1–15)
   Interlude: Walking on the water (6: 16–21)
5. The raising of Lazarus (11: 1–45)
6. A blind man healed (9: 1–8)
7. A man healed at the pool of Bethzatha (5: 1–9).

He goes on to suggest that the call of the first disciples and the passion narrative were also part of the original Signs Source.

As plausible and appealing as Fortna's reconstruction is, I cannot agree with it in full, or with the other Signs-Source theorists, although many of their observations will find corroboration in my analysis (see discussion in chapter 3). In simple terms, Fortna assumes that the miracles are the key to the main narrative source in John, and that the source includes the passion story and the introduction (although his arguments based strictly on the numbered signs would not entail this). He has rightly been criticized for presuming too much when he says that the passion and introduction are part of the Signs Source, and for presuming that other parts of the gospel were not part of this source. For example, Fortna maintains that the Signs Source contained no teaching material, no concerns of the social organization of the church, no sacraments, no prediction of the passion, no Son of Humanity sayings or filial relation of Jesus and God, and no eschatology. Just as Dodd's distinction above between *kerygma* and *didache* (narrative proclamation and teaching) has ill served Mark, so Fortna's distinction between narrative and teaching here has ill served John. The criticism of Barnabas Lindars is compelling, that Fortna has jumped from small pieces of evidence concerning a few miracle stories to a grand recovery of an entire gospel.[71] For my own theory, however, the numbered signs are not the key to the main narrative source of John, but perhaps only the key to a minor source, a small collection of miracles (see chapter 4). Although my proposed source is extensive, and in fact partly overlaps with Fortna's, it is argued on completely different criteria, and does not prioritize the numbered signs.

Other scholars do not emphasize a small number of sources and a single, creative redactor, but rather an evolution of material in a continuous tradition. The difference is one of emphasis: the former approach emphasizes a few written sources, the latter many source traditions, often oral; the former emphasizes discontinuity, the latter continuity; the former argues no direct connection with disciples, but the latter often argues for some reliable connection with the first disciples. Raymond Brown represents this evolutionary approach, and sees a community that was founded by "the disciple whom Jesus loved" mentioned in John 13: 23, whose words have been passed on and developed by a changing sect. Bent Noack presses it even further, and sees the entire development of the Johannine tradition as the expansion of freely circulating oral traditions.[72] Some scholars, however, who advocate evolutionary approaches perceive quite complicated source-and-redaction, or source-and-multiple-redaction, or multiple-source-and-multiple-redaction theories for the development of John. These will not be analyzed closely here, as their complexity makes it difficult to evaluate them within the compass of this book. A source theory that is overly complicated is impossible to refute; it is also impossible to believe. The most influential source theories have actually been quite simple.

THE PLAN OF THIS STUDY

Two different theses will be argued here: (1) Mark and John have both utilized an extensive gospel narrative, identifiable and, to some extent, recoverable through a comparison of those sections of Mark and John that contain parallel motifs; (2) This older narrative was of a type that was not uncommon in the eastern Mediterranean, influenced by both Jewish and pagan tradition: the cult narrative of the dead hero. It is important to note that the two major theses argued here are interrelated, but not interdependent; that is, either could be true while the other is false. These theses cannot be argued simultaneously; they will be considered separately. Thesis (2) will be argued first, in chapter 2, where I shall consider the question of the genre and function of gospel-like writings, specifically, Mark, John, and the *Life of Aesop*, and their relation to cults of the revered dead. Thesis (1) will be argued in chapter 3, where I shall present a synopsis of the parallel sections of Mark and John, with a short discussion of each passage, and argue that John does not reflect a knowledge of Mark, and that there is present here evidence of an earlier narrative tradition. This core narrative I attempt to reconstruct in part, although speculation on the precise form of such a document is avoided. What must also be shown in order to posit the existence of a core narrative is that (1) neither Mark nor John show evidence of literary dependence on the other gospel; (2) the parallel material in Mark and John is in the same or nearly the same order; and (3) this order cannot be explained by recourse to a pattern, such as a prophetic biography pattern, that each author could have imposed independently upon the varied narrative materials available. Chapter 4 will summarize the findings of the synoptic comparison of chapter 3, noting how it relates to the question of a cult narrative of the revered dead. Finally, I have included an appendix that contains the text of the *Life of Aesop*. The latter is not readily available, and its inclusion here will allow a better consideration of the thesis argued in chapter 2.

2

THE *LIFE OF AESOP* AND THE HERO CULT PARADIGM IN THE GOSPEL TRADITION

As we saw in the previous chapter, the origin of the gospel genre must be sought in both analogical and derivational models. Partial analogies to the gospels can be found in many genres, from novels to parables to apocalypses, but the closest analog is the popular, novelistic biography that is related to the cult of the hero. On the derivational side, the gospel also appears to have developed from the Jewish ideal of the suffering righteous person, influenced as well by the growth of the Christian *kerygma*, or proclamation of the death and resurrection of Jesus and the conflictual nature of the controversy stories. In this chapter we shall examine this conclusion more closely, to see how these seemingly disparate influences might have coalesced quite naturally in the Gospels of Mark and John.

The most important novelistic biography for the comparison with the gospel genre is the anonymous *Life of Aesop*. The tradition of Aesop as a teller of barbed fables – more barbed and satirical than one might expect from the stereotyped view of Aesop the "moralist" – is found as early as the fifth century B.C.E., and the account of his life, which circulated in multiple versions, may derive from narrative traditions that are as old.[1] The extant versions, however, are dated to about the turn of the era, that is, roughly contemporary with the gospels, and these are what draw our attention. Its importance for the study of popular literature was noted years ago by Ben E. Perry and others, and it has recently been taken up once again.[2]

Aesop is introduced in the *Life* as an ugly and misshapen slave who is in the beginning unable to speak. He is devoted to Isis, however, and after he shows kindness to one of her priestesses, falls into a sleep and is granted by the goddess the power of speech. This gift he uses to the utmost – he never stops talking, but with an acid wit skewers the pretensions of his new owner, a philosopher, and also the owner's wife and fellow philosophers. In this section of the *Life* we find a series of satirical and sometimes bawdy episodes, constituting what we may call "teaching," if we understand this in a satirical, inverted way, that is, the theme of the Cynic preacher played out in a narrative form. Through his cleverness he manages to help both his master and the citizens of Samos, and ultimately attains his freedom. Once free, however, he

23

soon runs foul of the citizens of Delphi, and rebukes them with his sharp-pointed fables. They condemn him to death on a trumped-up charge, and he is executed. When a plague strikes the city, they consult an oracle of Zeus and learn that they must expiate their sin through sacrifice.

The Life of Aesop, on the surface at any rate, reflects less the viewpoint of the ruling class than do the other Greek and Roman novels, and is written in a correspondingly lower style, much closer to that of the gospels. It does not partake of many of the intellectual pretensions of ancient biography, or of the mock-biography which Lucian cultivates, but like the biographies, focuses from beginning to end on the important life-events of a single character. It overlaps with the same genres as do the gospels – novel, biography, aretalogy – and we can consider it along with the gospels as a "biographical novel." Aesop is very primitive in some of the main areas of accomplishment of novelistic art; it is episodic, with little clear plot development over the middle section of the novel, and the characters are little more than one-dimensional. It is still not without its interest from the literary point of view. Niklas Holzberg rightly defends the style of Aesop on the grounds that it is intentionally ironic and satirical, in contrast to the pretensions of contemporary rhetoric and philosophy. Holzberg perceives in the novel a five-part structure, in which can be discerned an important thematic development:[3]

1 Introduction (1–19)
2 Aesop and his master Xanthos, whom he eventually helps (20–91)
3 Aesop helps the Samians (92–100)
4 Aesop helps King Lykoros of Babylonia (101–23)
5 Aesop in Delphi, where he cannot help himself (124–42).

Within each of the sections Aesop uses a particular kind of discourse:

1 Aesop is mute, but uses gestures with positive effect
2 Aesop uses direct, barbed instruction and wisely solves problems
3 Aesop uses fables with positive effect
4 Aesop uses direct, barbed instruction and wisely solves problems
5 Aesop uses fables with negative effect.

Further, the novel reflects parallels to Attic drama; the five sections, indeed, call to mind the five acts of Attic drama. Holzberg also emphasizes that the motif of the "world turned upside down," found also in New Comedy, does not imply that Aesop should be viewed as a comedy. Rather, it is like tragedy: just as Oedipus helps the Thebans and becomes their king, but cannot save himself, Aesop the true philosopher can help others, but in the end cannot help himself. In the latter case, however, it is also satirical: the pathetic mute slave can save himself with hand gestures, but Aesop the emancipated philosopher of the end of the work cannot save himself with pungent words and fables. The Life thus develops a sustained plot-interest and theme – the ironic contrast of Aesop's outer fortunes and his inner worth – and maintains a consistency of style throughout.

It would be tempting to see in the pages of this novel a satirical art form created and transmitted by members of Aesop's own class, that is, by literate slaves. The *Life*, however, was more likely written for the entertainment of the wealthy – compare the "Hellenistic grotesques" in the private art of the wealthy, decorative sculptures that included both slaves and the "misshapen" as subjects, the two markers of Aesop's social position.[4] There is sometimes also among intellectuals an aristocratic fascination with lower classes, even sympathy, in the sense that a Stoic, who believed that all people might equally rise above the vicissitudes of their existence, would romanticize slaves, or that a Cynic, who tried to dissolve the bonds of social distinctions, would laugh at a satire of the respectable class. Keith Hopkins considers the possibility that the audience may have been mixed, but then gives impressive arguments for an interpretation of *Aesop* as an aristocratic fantasy: "The story allowed repressed fears and erotic attributions to rise briefly to the surface, gave fantasy a short airing, and then blocked off the imaginary transgressions . . . by mocking them away as comic fictions" (p. 22).[5]

Perhaps, then, the narrative of *Aesop* offered up the experience of a temporary release through entertainment, a Mardi-Gras sense of the carnivalesque. Mikhail Bakhtin analyzed this sort of literary experience in his *Rabelais and his World*, arguing that in some satires there is a spirit of liberation lurking within the descent into the scatological and sexual, an aesthetic that he labels "grotesque realism":

> The essential principle of grotesque realism is degradation, that is, the lowering of all that is high, spiritual, ideal, abstract; it is a transfer to the material level, to the sphere of earth and body in their indissoluble unity.[6]

Annabel Patterson has taken up Bakhtin's analysis and applied it to the reception of Aesop in European history,[7] arguing that the scatological obsession of the *Life* is an example of grotesque realism, which presents Bakhtin's "material bodily principle" as a populist form. The descent into the body is what Bakhtin calls the rediscovery of the "collective ancestral body of all the people," and for Patterson it becomes a "philosophical reconsideration of the mind/body liaison," "a test of civilized thought." She remarks on the variety of ways that the narrative focuses on bodily processes. From the first, vomiting, urinating, and defecating are interwoven into the story, along with Aesop's special dinner of tongue that gives all the guests diarrhea. Patterson thus seems to affirm the power of texts such as the *Life*, when attached to a culturally recognized figure such as Aesop, to undercut class and deconstruct it. She argues the following theses:

1 Literature, in its most basic form, has always spoken to unequal power relations.

2 Those without power in those relations, if they wish to comment upon them, must encode their commentary.
3 Writing is authorized by authorship, texts needing a name to cling to if they are to acquire cultural resonance.
4 Wit (literary ingenuity) can emancipate.
5 Basic issues require basic metaphors; when, as in the fable, the role of metaphor is to mediate between human consciousness and human survival, the mind recognizes rock bottom, the irreducibly material, by rejoining the animals, one of whom is the human body.[8]

But it remains difficult to determine whether this outsider's perspective actually deconstructs class privilege, or merely provides a release from the burden of maintaining decorum and the rigid distinctions of class.[9]

At any rate, we can perceive how this satire is carried out. From the beginning there is played out in the text an ironic contrast between the brilliance of Aesop's true character and the loathsomeness of his condition, as he receives the stigma of every conceivable disability:

> Aesop, the story teller and composer of fables, great benefactor of humanity, was born in Amorium of Phrygia, as fate would have it, a slave. He was truly horrible to behold: worthless, pot-bellied, slant-headed, snub-nosed, hunchbacked, leather-skinned, club-footed, knock-kneed, short-armed, sleepy-eyed, bushy-lipped – in short, an absolute miscreant.

This ironic contrast of the great benefactor who is an ugly creature is hardly new to Aesop; it is the stock treatment in Greek culture of the satirical outsider, or what John Winkler calls the Grotesque Outsider, the antisocial miscreant who, as a result of his or her marginal position, has a higher, penetrating understanding of humanity. This figure is found in the *Iliad* as Thersites, who criticizes Achilles and is killed as a result, and Plato's depiction of the death of Socrates is shaped by the *vita* of the outcast poet.[10]

The satire thus probably comes from the pen of an aristocrat who finds humor in turning the world upside down. This is what we find in the plays of Plautus, and even more to the point, in the Roman novels *Satyricon* and *The Golden Ass*, as Winkler emphasized. The importance of the satirical novel in the ancient world is being increasingly recognized among scholars. In addition to the *Satyricon* and *The Golden Ass*, Bruce D. MacQueen sees in Longus' *Daphnis and Chloe* and Achilles Tatius' *Leucippe and Clitophon* satirical reflections of the more earnest Greek novels. Richard Stoneman likens the *Alexander Romance* to the trickster tales rather than to strictly heroic legends, and among Jewish novels the *Testament of Abraham* may be a satirical novel as well.[11] Just as Michael McKeon can argue for the coeval origins and dialectical relationship between the satirical and earnest novels in England,[12] so should we see the play between the satirical and earnest novels in antiquity.

The satirical novel should by no means be excluded from comparison with its earnest counterpart on the grounds that it has turned the genre upside down; rather, satirical novels play upon the preconceptions of the earnest versions, and presume the same structural codes. As Keith Hopkins has said of *Aesop*, "The very tactic of inversion implies its opposite. Disorder implies order."[13] Francisco R. Adrados has also made much of the high moral intent behind the low, seemingly amoral comedy:

> We have . . . the story of the anti-hero from the lower steps of society who laughs at his master and wins everyone's respect because of his ingeniousness. It is a picture of a "world turned upside-down," like that of the Comedy, in which the slave overcomes his master . . . the philosophers, the private citizen, kings and whole cities . . . In short, he is always working to gain his own salvation, and that of others. Indeed we could say he is fighting for justice.[14]

Aesop's ironic fight for justice was generally recognized in the ancient world, where he was considered one of the Seven Sages of Greek tradition. One tradition, Diogenes Laertius, *Lives*, Chilo 2, notes that when Chilo asked Aesop what Zeus was doing, Aesop replied, "He is lowering what is high, and exalting what is low," calling to our minds the Song of Hannah (1 Sam 2: 1–10) and the Magnificat (Luke 1: 46–55). Behind the humor and satire of the episodes, then, is a serious teaching, in outer form similar to the episodic narratives and teachings of the gospels.

Although Aesop begins and ends the story with Isis and the Muses on his lips, there is a more important and ambivalent relationship between Aesop and Apollo, "the leader of the Muses." When Aesop saves the citizens of Samos and a shrine is established, he snubs Apollo by sacrificing to the Muses, and in addition, erects a statue of himself.[15] Apollo exacts his revenge when Aesop makes his way to Delphi. Aesop attacks the leading citizens publicly, and they, with the help of Apollo, connive to convict him falsely of theft. Even though Aesop calls upon Apollo to avenge him, he is nevertheless executed by the Delphians, and the story ends abruptly by noting that a plague is brought upon the city as a result, and thus Aesop is ultimately avenged against them. Other Aesopic traditions note that Apollo proclaims that, in order to avert disaster, the Delphians must expiate their guilt by establishing a cult of Aesop.[16]

It was the suggestion of Perry that Aesop's reverence for Isis and the Muses reflected a popular disenchantment with Apollo and the class he was identified with, the slave-owning class of the pretentious aristocratic philosopher. Gregory Nagy, however, argues that Apollo is throughout the patron deity of Aesop; the latter becomes estranged from the god, only to be reunited in death. This estrangement, in fact, is typical of hero cults in ancient Greece, where there is, according to Nagy, "antagonism in myth, symbiosis in cult":

> By losing his identification with a person or group and by identifying

himself with a god who takes his life in the process, the hero effects a purification by transferring impurity.[17]

Nagy has also demonstrated that the cults of the poet as hero are as significant as the warrior cults.[18] The poet-heroes are not "heroic" in stature: Archilochus, Thersites, and Aesop are specifically and relentlessly described as ugly, even grotesque, but they constitute a favorite type in Greek tradition.[19] It is really only the genre containing the three figures that differentiates them: Thersites is a figure in epic, Archilochus is a poet, and Aesop alone is "hymned" in a novel. For Nagy, there is an identification of Archilochus, Aesop, and other poetic figures who have an ambivalent relationship with the Muses and with Apollo as head of the Muses: the poet is sacrificed as a ritual substitute (*therapon*), and is then honored in cult and identified with the god through death. By extension, and by reference to the traditions about the poets, Nagy argues that Homer and Hesiod are identified as "*therapon* of the Muses" as well. The ironic contrast of the ignominy of some of these figures and their status as heroes of cult reflects a deeply embedded drama that is played out in Greek religious sensibilities. The experience of calumny which they receive, even to the point of a humiliating death at the hands of others, results in impurity, but this impurity is expiated through cult. As Nagy argues, this is at least as clear, if not clearer, in the Aesop tradition than in the other, more famous cults:

> [W]e see from the *Life of Aesop* tradition that the poet's death results in purification. The immediate result from the death itself is impurity, but the ultimate result is eternal purification by way of propitiating the hero in cult – as ordained by Apollo himself. Moreover, the mode of Aesop's death is itself a purification, in that he dies like a *pharmakos* "scape-goat."[20]

One fragment of the Aesop tradition, in summarizing the establishment of his cult, recounts how the Delphians have a practice of distributing sacrificial meat in such a way that the person who provided the meat often goes away empty-handed. When Aesop mocks them for this, they become angry, set upon him, and kill him. A pestilence descends upon their city, and when they consult the oracle of Apollo, they are told to make a sacrifice to Aesop.[21] In just a few lines in this fragment, we are told several things that are more dispersed in the novel: as a result of the poet's blame of the people for an offense in their temple sacrifices, they become angry, kill him, and as a result incur pollution, which is only expiated by establishing a cult of the victim. The relationship of blame, violent reaction, impurity, expiation, and immortality of the hero are drawn closely together.

Similarities to the expiatory death of Jesus can be seen here, especially if we begin to consider the latter in terms of an ambivalent relationship with his people, that is, to Jews, Israel, or Jerusalem. We may repeat the quotation of Nagy above, this time with Jesus in mind: "By losing his identification with a person or group and by identifying himself with a god who takes his life in the process, the hero effects a purification by transferring impurity." Further: "In such a hero cult, god and hero are to be institutionalized as the respectively dominant and recessive members of an eternal relationship."[22] Nagy is speaking strictly of the Greek models, but what he says might apply also to early Christian cult, or at least to some strands of it. The mythical dynamic of the Greek hero cult that animates the *Life* thus provides the basis for very suggestive parallels with the Jesus tradition.

In its length *Aesop* is a bit longer than Mark and John, about the same length as Matthew and Luke, but in structure it remains closer to Mark and John. A treatment of the life of the protagonist, it begins not with an account of the birth of the figure, or with his growth and development, but with a crucial point in the adult life. An account of the birth of the protagonist is thus as unnecessary for the *Life* as it is for Mark and John. At the beginning of the *Life*, Aesop, still dumb, chooses an idyllic spot to rest, a sacred grove, as it were: "He chose a pleasant spot, green and secluded, a shaded grove of trees surrounding a blanket of green grass and all sorts of flowers, encompassed by a brook." There he has an experience that amounts to a baptism and a declaration from heaven:

> The brook echoed the rustling of the branches of the trees round about. As a sweet, gentle wind began to blow, the verdant limbs were gently moved and wafted over him a cool breeze, creating in the many-blossomed wood a fresh and restful spot. The hum of cicadas in the branches filled the air, and the chorus of many different kinds of birds could be heard. . . . And Echo, the imitator of voices, uttered her responsive sounds in harmony. All of these voices conspired to lull Aesop into a deep and blissful sleep. Our lady, the goddess Isis, then made her appearance, together with the nine Muses, and said, "You see here, my daughters, the very image of true piety, a man who may be ill-proportioned on the outside, but is above all reproach in regard to his inner spirit. He once gave guidance to my servant when she had lost her way, and now in your presence I shall reward him. I myself shall restore his voice, while you bestow upon that voice the most noble ability in speaking." When she had said this, Isis removed from Aesop's tongue the impediment that had prevented him from speaking, and gave him back his voice. She also persuaded each of the Muses in turn to grant Aesop something of her own gifts. They bestowed upon him the power to compose and elaborate Greek tales.
>
> (6–7)

This scene, reminiscent in some respects of the introduction to Hesiod's *Theogony* on the one hand, and to the Muses' bestowal of poetic powers on Archilochus on the other,[23] is also similar to the openings of Mark and John. The account of the great benefactor is begun, not with the birth, but with a

29

crucial, defining event in adulthood. In Mark the narrative of John's baptism (1: 9–11) is recounted with as few details as possible, but is like the *Life* in specifying the special relationship of the protagonist with God. In John we see a more positive depiction of the scene of baptism (even though the baptism itself is pointedly omitted), along with the descent of the spirit as a dove, and shortly thereafter a reference to angels ascending and descending upon Jesus (1: 51). The tone in John is in some ways more similar to the *Life* than is Mark, but the overall similarities of all three are clear enough.

The long central section of the *Life*, as noted above, is a "teaching" section, a "ministry" section if you will. Anecdotes of Aesop's cynical wit are recounted one after another, which despite their satirical indirection, do carry a didactic point: the social order, built upon appearances, elevates dunces and fails to recognize the true philosopher. Parallels to the Socratic tradition can be drawn, for example, Aesop's prison scene (chs 129–33) and his claim to know nothing (ch. 25), as well as to the Cynic tradition: Aesop's general lack of social restraint, his quest for someone who minds his own business (chs 57–64), and his anecdote about finding true men in the baths (ch. 66).[24] In terms of the overall structure of the *Life*, one notes that humorous episodes dominate the first sections, but give way in the last to a more serious discourse, consisting of fables that have a negative effect, and the ineluctable movement toward Aesop's death in Delphi. Apuleius' *Golden Ass* also shifts near the end from the broadside to the serious, and it is appropriate to compare the analogous shift in Mark and John from ministry to passion. Aesop's ability to speak, bestowed upon him late in life by a goddess, takes on an increasingly serious aspect. During the last section, when the comic episodes have fallen away and Aesop wields clout as an adviser to kings, he tells a fable in which a cicada (representing the position of Aesop) says, "You will find nothing in me but my voice" (ch. 99, W version). Nagy, in fact, analyzes the speech acts of Aesop, specifically his fables, in terms of parallels to the much loftier poetry of Archilochus and others. The fables constitute a specific language of judgment, or in the language common to ancient Greek rhetoric, of "blame." "Praise of the noble" and "blame of the base" were considered equally important themes for the poet in ancient Greece, beginning as early as the Homeric epics, and perhaps in Indo-European tradition as well.[25] Holzberg also discerns a correspondence between the structure of the *Life* and the three-part structure of the Aesopic fables: someone does something right, and someone does something wrong, which finally brings about his own end.[26] The satirical nature of the *Life*, therefore, should not obscure the weighty theme that is developed, the power of Aesop's fables, or the "evangelical" fervor of the author. At a number of points the theme of the power of speech is explored in droll and fascinating ways, reminding one of George Bernard Shaw's *Pygmalion*. Aesop is considered remarkable precisely because he is like an inanimate object who, by some miracle, also possesses the power of speech (ch. 21), or alternatively, like a "bird that can talk" (ch. 26; compare chs 13–14), and it is this power of speech, abstracted from an inferior body, that elevates him to a higher vantage point, the level of the true philosopher. At ch. 99, for example, he says, "My worthless body is my instrument, by which I utter wise sayings to benefit the lives of mortals." In this context it should also be noted how the form of the novel plays out this theme: a huge percentage of the story consists of dialogue and interior monologue.

The fables at the end of *Aesop* find striking parallels in Mark and John. When Aesop arrives at his final destination in the narrative, Delphi, he utters fables that are even more caustic than before, and that condemn the citizens of Delphi and accuse them of being descended from slaves (chs 125–26). We are reminded, first, of Mark's use of the parable of the wicked tenants near the end of the gospel, in ch. 12. Unlike most of the other parables, it is a full-blown allegory that specifically condemns the Jerusalem authorities.[27] Its length and tone are almost identical to that of Aesop's allegorical fables at the end of the *Life*. We are also reminded of John 8, where Jesus accuses the Judeans of being offspring of Satan. Richard Pervo rightly compares theories of Mark as a "gospel in parable" to *Aesop* as a "gospel in fable."[28] Further, the city officials in the *Life*, we are told, "decided to kill Aesop by treachery (*dolo*)" (127). This reaction of the city officials is very similar to that of the opponents in Mark when they hear the parable of the wicked tenants, or more to the point, it is similar to Mark 14: 1, where the chief priests and scribes were "seeking how to arrest him by treachery (*dolo*) and kill him."[29] Further, the movement in *Aesop* from Samos to Delphi – that is, from the periphery to the center, especially the center as far as the god Apollo is concerned – is similar to the movement in Mark and John from Galilee to Judea (compare especially *Aesop* 124 with Mark 10: 32–34 and Luke 9: 51), and in both cases the narrative action of the conflict will come to revolve around a temple, where the god's deliverance will become problematic.

Similarities with Mark can also be found in terms of literary technique. One aspect of Mark's style that has been taken as characteristic, if not unique, to that gospel is the sandwiching of one episode within another to provide a subplot while maintaining continuity. This is alternately seen as an innovation of Mark and an important sign of that author's style, or as a lingering indicator of oral composition. It is also found, however, in the Greek novels of the period,[30] as well as in the *Life*. At chapter 65, when Aesop is sent to the baths on an errand for his master, he has a witty encounter with the governor on his way; when this is concluded, the story resumes with Aesop's errand. Although Mark is particularly fond of this technique, it is clearly not unique to that gospel, and it does not have any apparent value for oral transmission in the *Life*. It is perhaps, rather, a somewhat primitive trait of popular novelistic works, in which the author is searching for some means to elongate and suspend the narrative by the use of subplots.[31]

LIFE OF AESOP AND ANCIENT HERO CULTS

The parallels in generic traits between the *Life* on the one hand and Mark and John on the other also give rise to the further and equally pressing question of the similarity of cult behind them. Throughout this study, we shall be addressing directly or indirectly the problem of the relation of cult to narrative. Specifically, the *cult* of the *dead* hero is related to a *narrative* about the hero's *life and death*. The *Life of Aesop*, for example, evidently reflects a real cult of a "heroic" figure.[32] Although the phrase "hero cult" may evoke images of a valiant warrior, such as Achilles or Theseus, who attains immortality through a fight to the death, this is much too one-dimensional a view to do justice to the actual cults of the Greco-Roman world. In a certain sense, all reverence for the dead that is intended to obtain a salutary effect for the living can be grouped together; hero cult is a subset of cult of the dead. For practical purposes, however, I shall be drawing some necessary working distinctions in order to specify which subset of reverence for the dead is reflected in the early gospel tradition, and which parallels are most instructive.

Turning first to ancient Greece, we see that the background of the hero cult, according to most scholars, lay in the reverence for dead ancestors.[33] From the general cultic remembrance of dead ancestors, it was a small step to venerating the one truly remarkable benefactor as someone who, after death, attained immortality and a potence that approached that of the gods. It was also only a minor alteration to locate this veneration at shrines of the heroes, so that the practice of the cult was carried out at a particular place. From about the eighth century B.C.E., the important elements of the Greek cult of *particular* heroes came to prominence as the *generalized* cult of the dead receded. The latter was mainly a family cult, but now reverence of the hero could be embraced by the people as a whole. This cultic development was paralleled in the epic tradition, where the stories were now dominated by the heroes. The significance of this change can hardly be overestimated; it corresponds with the rise of the city-state as the common institution of Greek life, subsumed under a truly panhellenic spirit.[34]

Yet the figure of the hero in ancient Greece is not easily systematized. The categories of divine and semi-divine beings in Greco-Roman culture was enormously complex; we should perhaps think of a "Great Chain of Being" which allowed for a large number of modes of being between the divine and the human (sky gods versus earth gods, gods versus heroes, divine figures versus *daimones*, and so on) or for becoming divine ("divine men," divine parentage on one side, or heroization of a person born mortal). Ancient authors could distinguish between gods and humans (Pindar, *Nemean* 6), gods, mortals, and heroes (Arrian, *Anabasis of Alexander* 4.11.2–4, Quintus Curtius, *History of Alexander* 8.5.15–19) or between Olympian gods and earth gods (Plato, *Laws* 828c), but there are many subcategories of divinity and divinization.[35] Likewise there are differences between the classical and late Hellenistic period in Greece with regard to heroes. Many of the heroes of early Greek tradition are conceived of as figures from an ancient past, for example, Herakles (who in effect joins the Olympian gods), Perseus, and Asclepius. These three are interesting because Justin Martyr notes the similarities between them and Jesus (*Apol.* 1.54, *Dial.* 69). The relation of non-Olympian gods to the heroes is fascinating, and constitutes a gray area in the pantheon of divine and semi-divine figures. Some heroes are born of gods, such as Herakles, yet he still earns immortality, and was revered both as a god and as a hero. Dionysus also does not begin as a member of the Greek pantheon, but is elevated and joins them. He remains, however, always a new and slightly alien "Olympian." Heroes may also gain or lose some of their status. While Philostratus debunks the legends of many heroes, he reelevates Protesilaus (*Heroicus* 9.141.6); people pray to his cult-statue and he cures ailments. He also aids lovers and opposes adulterers, which gives us some insight into the moral world of those petitioning the hero.[36] In the Hellenistic and Roman periods, however, a larger number of figures from the *recent* past attain a heroic cult status, whether that includes those who were sometimes considered to have one divine parent (Alexander the Great, Augustus, or Apollonius of Tyana), or mortals who have no divine parentage, especially philosophers and kings (such as Empedocles, Lysander, or Cleomenes of Sparta).[37] It is important to note that these figures are not simply the subjects of learned discussion, but received actual cult veneration. Many philosophers, such as Plato, Aristotle, Pythagoras, and Apollonius of Tyana received such veneration, which often included the construction of temples and shrines.[38] There were many heroine cults as well, usually associated with male figures, but sometimes independent. The expiatory death of a woman, a concomitant of cult, was also a common literary and dramatic motif.[39]

The increasing importance of the hero cult from the classical period on and the steadily enlarging group of divine dead also resulted in some protest by satirists. In Lucian's *The Passing of Peregrinus*, the self-immolation of the protagonist and resultant "apotheosis" are viewed with derision. Pseudo-Seneca, *Apokolokyntosis*, (*The Pumpkinification of Claudius*) 9 states that "once it was a great thing to become a god; now you have made it into a farce." The satire by elite intellectuals only serves, however, to prove the vitality of the process of heroization on the popular level. Thus we may pause to take a closer look at Lucian's *Peregrinus* as a satire that sheds light on the more straightforward hero-cult narratives of the period. It is not a novel that defends a true philosopher, but a satire that is included by Hans Dieter Betz as an accusation against the false philosopher.[40] It is still quite relevant, however, precisely because of this reversal. That is, in narrating the accusation against the false philosopher, it inverts the usual tragic elements of the defense of the true philosopher. Beneath the counter-values of Lucian the narrator we can still detect the believer's values of the followers of Peregrinus.

Lucian's account of Peregrinus' duplicity consists largely of a story within a story, supposedly told to Lucian by one who has observed Peregrinus closely, although the voice of the observer should probably be understood as Lucian's own. This section constitutes an inverted gospel, a story of the ministry, passion (actually more an extended social protest), death, and resurrection of Peregrinus, all told as a parade of examples of his shameless hucksterism. The period of "ministry" consists, first, of various misdeeds, including Peregrinus' murder of his own father, and the taking up of a new, irrational cult – that is, Christianity – while he defrauds his gullible followers of their few pennies. He is excommunicated from the company of Christians, and turns next to Cynicism. He then proceeds to Rome, where, playing the typical Cynic preacher, he upbraids the leading citizens, including the emperor himself. At Olympia he also upbraids a leading citizen and benefactor of the games – none other than the famous rhetorician Herodes Atticus – and after barely escaping with his life, announces that at the next Olympiad he will burn himself to death on a pyre. As he approaches his end, Peregrinus constantly associates himself with gods and heroes. According to his followers, his apotheosis is predicted by the Sibyl, and at his tomb there will be miraculous cures and oracles (chs 27–29). After his immolation there are resurrection appearances to his faithful followers (ch. 40).

Although reconstructing the "gospel message" of the historical Peregrinus from Lucian's satire is an uncertain enterprise, there are a few points worth noting concerning genre. It is Peregrinus' activity as a Cynic, not his Christian phase, that brings about his end, so our attention should focus there. This activity as a Cynic consists of upbraiding the citizens of several cities in Italy and Greece – for what we are not told, but the word for upbraid, *loidoreomai*, is used several times here as though it were a fixed term. At the climax of this inversion of events, the satirist has sufficient confidence in his craft that he can give a straightforward presentation of Peregrinus' own reason for his immolation. Peregrinus wanted to return to Olympia and burn himself in order – and here is one of the few places where Lucian gives a direct quotation of Peregrinus' words – "to benefit humankind by showing them the way in which one ought to despise death" (ch. 33). This is very similar to *Aesop* 99, quoted above: "My worthless body is my instrument, by which I utter wise sayings to benefit the lives of mortals." Peregrinus' biting social criticism, which has already landed him in trouble numerous times, now brings him to the ultimate sacrifice for the sake of humanity. Although Peregrinus is not killed by the powers-that-be, but must mastermind his own execution – an irony surely not lost on Lucian – his death is directly related to his stance as a Cynic preacher and a social critic. Thus, even within Lucian's *Passing of Peregrinus*, which satirizes the pretensions of the would-be Socrates, it is clear that Peregrinus' role as critic is presumed. And it is accounts such as these, earnest and satirical alike, that recount the death and divinization of figures from the recent past that will most concern us.

The connection of the gospel tradition with the hero paradigm was argued by Moses Hadas and Morton Smith in 1965 in their joint work *Heroes and Gods*, a book which posits the existence in the ancient world of a genre of reverential biography called "aretalogy," an account of the great deeds of a god or divinely inspired person. Although no single model of aretalogy exists from early antiquity, there are numerous reverential accounts of the life and death of great religious reformers from Socrates to Cleomenes the Stoic to Eleazar the Jewish priest. The lack of a single model for these accounts has lessened the impact of this and similar studies, but the rich material that Hadas and Smith rightly bring to the discussion should not be dismissed. While Nagy examines the death of the warrior in relation to the death of the poet, Hadas and Smith move from the warrior to the philosopher. Still, the treatment of poet and philosopher will overlap a great deal in our study. Although the heroic warrior in epic and tragedy is sometimes presented as a social monster – Achilles abandons his comrades, while Ajax is brutal and headstrong – in death they ultimately save the very people from whom they were alienated. This ambivalence of the hero toward fellow human beings, as well as the ambivalence of a god toward a hero, appears to be a constant theme in the hero paradigm, although it is often significantly altered in the stories regarding philosophers. There the philosopher seldom rejects other people, but is instead rejected by them.[41] The philosopher dies because of his love of humanity, as Socrates, the quintessential martyr to truth, dies witnessing to the obligation to live a just life. There were others as well in the earlier periods of Greek history – Orpheus, Empedocles, Pythagoras – but the model of Socrates came to proliferate and predominate. Although Hadas's and Smith's quest for a single literary genre came up short, as many have asserted, the larger pattern which was identified seems to inform every presentation of the significant death of a philosopher or religious reformer. Hadas's and Smith's summary of the import of the life and death of Socrates, for example, is worth quoting in some detail:

> Socrates was a strikingly ugly man, trained as a stone carver, who went about Athens, in a peculiar waddling gait, humbly dressed and shoeless, asking questions and provoking discussions chiefly on ethical problems. He was followed and admired by a group composed for the most part of upper-class youths. He might be spoken of as a Sophist by a comic poet, but he differed from the Sophists obviously in that he took no regular pupils and received no pay. He believed in his own mission to question people, chiefly to the end of convincing them that an unexamined life is not worth living. Sometimes he went into a sort of trance while pondering a thought. In his discourse he habitually employed homely images drawn from the daily life of artisans, but he was not cowed by persons of superior wealth or social position. The upshot of his doctrine was that the world of our senses lacks reality and that man must aspire to union with true goodness and beauty, which are beyond the

sensible world. In 399 B.C., at the age of seventy, he was tried and condemned to death on the charge of disbelieving in the gods of the state
and persuading others to his disbelief.[42]

Nagy's advance over Hadas and Smith was to transfer the search for a single
genre over to a search for mythic patterns, emphasizing the ambivalent relation
of hero and god, and the reverence that exercises people long after the hero is
dead. Hadas and Smith (p. 9) had referred to one of the ancient reverential
writings broadly as "hagiography for a cult," and this is the issue that seems
most pertinent: they did not identify a single genre, but a more general mythical topos concerning the life and death of a great person. Not all of the
supposed elements of this topos – remarkable birth, brilliance and goodness,
supernatural abilities, adversarial relation with a monarch, noble death, resultant cult – are found in each case, and some do not detail the establishment of
an actual cult. Hadas and Smith do, however, include one rationalized account
that is very interesting for our purposes. Tacitus relates the death of the
Republican Cremutius Cordus in a way that is reminiscent of the cult patterns. This is suggested, first of all, by Cremutius' last words: "To every man
posterity gives his due honor, and if a fatal sentence hangs over me, there will
be those who will remember me as Cassius and Brutus." The attempt by the
Senate to extinguish his memory then backfires:

> He left the Senate and ended his life by starvation. His books, so the
> Senators decreed, were to be burnt by the aediles; but some copies were
> left that were concealed and afterwards published. And so one is all the
> more inclined to laugh at the stupidity of men who suppose that the
> despotism of the present can actually efface the remembrances of the
> next generation. On the contrary, the persecution of genius fosters its
> influence; foreign tyrants and all who have imitated their oppression
> have merely procured infamy for themselves and glory for their victims.
> (*Annals* 4.34–35)

What Tacitus emphasizes is that, despite all the efforts of Cremutius' opponents, his memory could not be extinguished, but rather, it grew and
redounded to his praise. The praise and blame that are to be apportioned are
also significant. Cremutius' memory, along with that of Cassius, Brutus, and
others, will be magnified, and the proper individuals will be blamed. We do
not have to posit an actual tomb cult of Cremutius; a "cult of remembrance"
fulfills the same function.

Also closely related to the hero cult in Greece and Rome is the tradition of
the scapegoat. It may in fact be the case that the Greek *pharmakos* and *therapon* of the hero cult is an elaborated subset of the scapegoating process. Here
we note the examples of scapegoating where one figure becomes a ritual sacrificial victim to restore balance or safety to the community, or one figure is
exiled into the "abyss" outside the city's borders in order to take impurity and

danger away from the community. The examples are widespread in the ancient world, from the *pharmakos* and ostracism in Athens, the self-sacrifice of kings and maidens in Greek tragedy, and the *devotio* of the sacrificial Roman soldier, to scapegoat rituals in Hittite sources. In some, the sacrificed victim is an ugly or repulsive citizen, in others a marriageable woman, a slave posing as a king, a king posing as a slave, or an animal substitute (as in the scapegoat of the Yom Kippur ceremony in Israel; see below). In some cases the victim is killed, in others chased away into the forbidden chaos of the world outside the city, or into the enemy camp to visit a plague upon those who would threaten the city. Common to these is the ritualized *designation* of the victim, the "selection, investiture, and expulsion of the victim to be 'accepted' and destroyed by some hostile force," even if it is often the community itself that in many cases actually performs the killing. Two fascinating observations emerge from Walter Burkert's investigation of these materials.[43] First, the pattern isolated is reflected more in *myths* and *legends* in Greece, but in *rituals* in Hittite and Roman sources. Further, the narrative versions in myth and legend emphasize more the *victim's* experience, the rituals more the *community's* experience. It will be important, therefore, to keep in mind as we proceed that the typological pattern may not appear in a "complete" form in every instance, nor will the narrative of sacrifice always be directly attached to a ritual.

What seems at first to be an inexplicable and virtually unique episode in Philo becomes clearer in light of Burkert's description. At *Flaccus* 6.36–39, Philo recounts the circumstances surrounding an Egyptian riot that occurred when the Jewish king Agrippa I arrived in Alexandria. A crowd opposed to the Jewish king picked out an insane man named Carabas and fawned over him and greeted him as if he were the Judean king Agrippa I. The similarity of the name Carabas to Jesus' "twin" in the passion, Barabbas, has been noted, suggesting the possibility that there is behind both a scapegoating ritual in which one man is installed as mock-king, and he (or another man) is then executed. Paul Wendland suggested in 1898 that the mock-king ritual of the Roman Saturnalia had influenced the mocking and scourging of Jesus in the passion narrative,[44] but James Frazer responded by arguing that a better parallel than the mock-king of the Saturnalia festival is that of the Babylonian Sacaea.[45] Here a prisoner condemned to death is "installed" as king, with robes, rule of the court, and access to the concubines for the period of the festival, after which he is stripped, scourged, and crucified. It is not necessary here to posit a historical connection between the Sacaea and Judea; the parallels to such a mock-king ritual are common enough to allow for the influence of some such pattern at the time of the composition of the gospels.

THE REVERED DEAD IN ANCIENT JUDAISM

The hero cult in Greek and Roman culture was so central that it can be studied in its full history in some detail. It now remains to investigate whether there is any evidence of a similar cult in the popular religion of ancient Judaism. Contrary to the common assumption that in Judaism such notions would be anathema, evidence can be adduced that suggests that similar practices existed here as well. In discussing this evidence, it is wise to proceed by distinguishing various aspects of the cult of the dead: (1) veneration of graves, and offerings for the well-being of dead ancestors, specifically veneration of a special individual (not necessarily a direct ancestor) who would be revered for his or her achievements; (2) a marked grave, especially as a pilgrimage site; (3) prayers and petitions made to a person after death, especially where they result in benefits for the living; (4) a narrative account of the antagonism of the person with his or her own people, especially if the antagonism results in the revered person's death; and (5) the belief that the death of the hero or heroine, which resulted from hero/people antagonism, was later understood as a sacrifice that effected expiation. This last element of the veneration of the hero is clearly the most important for a comparison with Mark, John, and *Aesop*.

Reverence for the dead is found in ancient Israel and later Jewish tradition as well, although some of its various manifestations were suppressed by the kings of Judah, or passed over in silence by the principal biblical authors. The "high places" (*bamot*) were early sanctuaries that may have arisen from ancestor cults, though this remains uncertain. Afterlife in the Hebrew Bible, as in archaic Greece, is often depicted as a vague state of shade-existence (Ps 88: 11–12; Eccles 9: 10; Isa 29: 4; Job 14: 22), but necromancy (consulting the spirit of a dead person through a medium) is encountered (1 Sam 28); it is condemned at Lev 19: 31; Num 6: 6–7; 19: 11–22; and Deut 18: 11, likely as a result of the centralization of the cult in Jerusalem in the eighth–seventh centuries B.C.E. under kings Hezekiah and Josiah. This centralization of the cult likely swept away much evidence of popular practices that would have fallen under the category of cult of the ancestors. There is archaeological evidence of the veneration of the dead: provisioning of the dead at family burial plots with food, weapons, spices, and figurines (perhaps of Asherah).[46] The shadowy *teraphim*, or family gods, may have originally been connected with ancestor worship, perhaps later identified with a mother goddess, used by women in fertility and child-bearing (Gen 31: 19; 35: 4; 1 Sam 19: 13).[47] When the dead Samuel is called back from the grave by the woman at Endor (1 Sam 28: 13), he is referred to as *elohim*, variously translated as "god," "gods," "spirits," or "spirits of the dead." Reverence of the dead certainly enters into Israelite culture in the *marzeah* festival that is celebrated by Israelites as a festival for the residents of Sheol (Jer 16: 5–9), but condemned by Amos (Amos 6: 7) and discouraged in Leviticus (Lev 19: 28; 21: 1–5, 10–11). Attested elsewhere in the ancient Near East, it was practiced for centuries, down into the Roman period.[48] Discussions can also be found in Jewish tradition of the bones of the ancestors, the need to deposit them in the proper burial site and protect them from being disturbed later. Abraham, for example, purchases land from the Hittites for Sarah's grave (Genesis 23), and later he, Isaac, Jacob, Rebecca, and Leah are also buried there, with much attention to the identification of the family members with that spot (Gen 25: 7–10; 35: 27–29; 49: 31; 50: 13). It is known as the cave of Machpelah near Hebron (Kiriath-arba). Already a major southern sanctuary at the beginning of the monarchy, from which David chose Zadok as the Aaronid priest to come to Jerusalem, it has remained an important holy site for Jews and Muslims until today. The embattled nature of this site in today's newspaper headlines attests to its enduring significance. There is also a reference to the *massebah* that is erected at Rachel's tomb (Gen 35: 20).

The veneration of dead ancestors evidently involved cultic acts, invocations, necromancy, and beliefs in the fecundity and healing powers of the remains, just as it did in many other cultures. We should not attempt to minimize or rationalize the ancient Israelite and Jewish beliefs, based upon the limitations placed upon the cult of the dead in later legislation. Various ideas of reverence for the dead appear to be reflected in a number of passages. Just as the site of Hebron became a local center for the reverence of the patriarchs, the burial sites of the judges – or better, "heroic leaders" of the pre-monarchic period – are often noted in the book of Judges (Judg 8: 32; 10: 2, 5; 12: 7, 10, 11, 15; and perhaps 16: 31). Although there is no explicit reference to any special reverence or pilgrimage, it is stated at Judg 2: 17–18 that God saved the people *because* of the judges. The book of Judges may in fact derive from a collection of stories about the judges, their miraculous deeds, and their burial places, in order to promulgate a connection of their stories with reverence at the burial sites. And in this same book we find the sacrifice of Jephthah's daughter (Judges 11), which is ritually reenacted annually by young women. A close parallel in Pausanias 9.17.1 only serves to confirm that this troubling passage reflects an early cultic celebration commemorating the sacrifice.

A general notion of the reverence for the dead, especially at family sepulchers, is found in Israel, but is there a special veneration of the dead *hero*? Many of these references are ambiguous, and some scholars press a distinction between veneration of the dead in Israel and the resurrection or heroization of the dead.[49] Certainly Abraham and Moses were accorded special honors, and Solomon's name became associated later with the power to heal.[50] But was there a *cult* of these people, that is, special offerings and veneration on a ritual level? Were they perceived as enjoying a special status after death, even as immortals? Did they render any benefits to the living? Early evidence is intriguing but ambiguous. The prophet Samuel, for example, is treated as a special hero of the past. The prophetic circles that are largely responsible for the deuteronomistic history revere Samuel as a "founder" of the prophetic guild, or at least a transitional figure between the judges and the prophets. Samuel does not just act with authority; he has a miraculous birth and childhood (1 Sam 1–3), he intervenes for his people (1 Sam 12), and he speaks from the grave to Saul (1 Sam 28). The story of Samuel contains many of the motifs of the hero as isolated by Lord Raglan. The prophetic guild was also

39

likely responsible for collecting the cycle of legends concerning the prophets Elijah and Elisha (1 Kgs 17–2 Kgs 10). Whereas for the "writing prophets" we have pages of oracles but little narrative, regarding Elijah and Elisha we have pages of narrative but few oracles. The oral stories of their deeds and words were collected, most likely by their followers in the prophetic guild. Joseph Blenkinsopp notes that like Anthony the Hermit, Hanina ben Dosa, and Apollonius of Tyana, Elijah is fed by birds (1 Kgs 17: 2–7) and by angels (19: 5–8), controls the weather (17: 1), multiplies food (17: 8–16), raises the dead (17: 17–24), levitates (18: 12, 2 Kgs 2: 1–12, 16), and demonstrates super-human endurance (1 Kgs 18: 46, 19: 8).[51] The guild of prophets preserved the memory of their heroic predecessors, and also invested their memory with supernatural significance: Elijah achieves a kind of immortality when he ascends to God in a chariot of fire (2 Kgs 2: 9–12), but more important, Elisha's bones become powerful relics: they are capable of bringing a dead man back to life on contact (2 Kgs 13: 20–21). These signs – especially the last – are the hallmarks of a revered, dead hero in other cultures.

The *pharmakos* of Greek tradition finds a parallel in Israel in the scapegoat ritual of Yom Kippur, for which our English word "scapegoat" was coined. The ritual itself may have originated in the expulsion of an older forest deity. In the biblical legislation for the Yom Kippur ritual, two goats are chosen, on one of which the high priest transfers the sins of Israel, and it is "sent to Azazel" (Lev 16: 20–22; compare also Lev 14: 6–7; 17: 7), but in Mishnah *Yoma* 6: 6 the goat is hurled off a cliff.[52] The fourth "Servant Song" of Isaiah 52–53 also develops this theme of the expiation of the sins of the people through the slaying of a sacrificial animal. René Girard has developed a comprehensive theory of the scapegoating mechanism, the process by which the group identifies a single member as a bearer of impurity that must be expelled or sacrificed.[53] The Greek hero cult, with its hero/people antagonism and the resolution of antagonism through sacrifice and reverence after death, is obviously a prime example of Girard's broad "scapegoating" category, but he also finds many examples in the Hebrew Bible. Many of the deaths, expulsions, sacrifices, and near-sacrifices of the Hebrew Bible, such as those of Adam and Eve, Abel, Isaac, Joseph, or the Suffering Servant of Isaiah 42–53, involve "victim-age," and are related as foundation myths to the creation of new communities or new movements within Israel's history. Girard's theory is especially percep-tive in illuminating the relationship of the group to the scapegoated member, and the extent to which the reality of the violent process of victimage is obscured and transformed to create a positive "myth of origins."[54]

In the Greco-Roman period there are a number of Jewish figures who attained special status in death, based on their special deeds in life. Judith, at the end of her story, receives adoration that approaches that of a reverential cult. After saving her people, she withdraws to a life of asceticism, is buried in her husband's tomb, and is proclaimed a benefactor who protected Israel *even after her death* (16: 25). Although there was no heroine/people antagonism in her case, she was forced to upbraid her people (8: 11–27), a common motif in the hero narratives, and she does live out the motif of the lonely hero/heroine, always separated from her people and incapable of being integrated.[55] Similarly, at *Testament of Moses* 9.7 (first century C.E.) the death of the martyrs effects atonement for the people's sins.

It is likely that pilgrimages to the graves of revered figures played an important role in Jewish popular religion of this period. Strong traditions developed that included pilgrimages on Lag ba-Omer to the grave of Simeon bar Yochai at Meron, and on the second Passover of 14 Iyyar to the grave of Meir Baal Ha-Nes at Lake Kinneret. The latter included offerings and legends of miracles associated with the grave. Pilgrimage to the tombs of Christian saints likely reflects many parallels and influences from these Jewish pilgrimages.[56] The role of pilgrimage to the tombs of the rabbis is thus attested in the Judaism of the first few centuries C.E., but it is difficult to determine how widespread tomb-pilgrimages were during the first century. The graves of kings had long been given special treatment (1 Kgs 2: 10; Ezek 43: 7–9, and Neh 3: 16), and Josephus also mentions the tomb of the high priest Eleazar, son of Aaron (compare Josh 24: 33), whose grave is marked by a monument and a sepulchre (*mnemeion kai taphos, Antiquities* 5.1.29 §119), and shows interest in the pyramids consecrated to the memories of the Maccabean martyrs (*Antiquities* 13.6.1 §211–12). He also refers to the tombs of the "children of Abraham" at Hebron (*Jewish War* 4.9.7 §532; compare the "tower of Abraham" in *Jubilees* 29: 16–19). These references are crucial for establishing the existence of a strong concern for the graves of revered people in first-century Judaism, but they do not indicate directly what *kind* of reverence existed for the dead.

An answer to this question has been sought in the *Lives of the Prophets*, a collection of short biographical sketches of the prophets that at first seems to lack any conceivable literary purpose: the sketches are short, have no dramatic or narrative qualities, and read like a checklist of the famous men of old. However, the burial sites of many of the prophets are given, and what narrative there is seems only to establish that the person merited some special status. The text was likely a summary of the canonical list of prophets that pointed out the pilgrimage sites that were known to the author. Here we see some indication of the *significance* of the burial sites to contemporary Jews: the post-death benefits of the prophets are emphasized. Isaiah is the local "saint" of Siloam, where his prayers keep the water flowing, while Jeremiah, at his burial site, renders the soil effective for healing asps' bites. The problem with utilizing this text to investigate Jewish practices contemporary with Jesus is the disagreement over its dating. Although Joachim Jeremias and others have assumed a date in the first century C.E., David Satran has pointed out that there is little evidence for this date, and some of the sections appear to be the developed Christian ascetical theology of a later century.[57] This is certainly the case with the information on Daniel, but the material in *Lives of the Prophets* may come from different periods. However, to establish the date of tomb cults, we are forced back on the other evidence, which remains somewhat meager.

Hero/people antagonism, which is not emphasized in *Lives of the Prophets*, is certainly an old tradition,[58] and in Q is found linked to the concern for the graves of the prophets: "You build the tombs of the prophets whom your ancestors killed!" (Luke 11: 47). For early Christians, veneration of the prophets was viewed from the perspective of the rejection of the latest prophet, but Q gives evidence also of a more positive Jewish attitude. We may compare here also the whitewashed graves of Matt 23: 27, likely the graves of revered people. The concern with burial places implies a reverence of these figures, and possibly pilgrimage as well.

There are a variety of ways, then, that certain figures in Israel intervene with God and grant salutary effects on behalf of their people, even after death, and some are quite ancient. There is other evidence in the later period, down to and beyond the period of Jesus, of even more emphasis on expiatory motifs. It is possible that the death of the *maskilim*, the "wise" who are mentioned in Dan 11: 33; 12: 3 among the persecuted, is also seen to be propitiatory; through their death they make the *rabbim* (the Jewish people) righteous, although this is not clear from the text. However that may be, the sacrificial aspect of the near-death of the three young Jews is emphasized in the Prayer of Azariah 16–17 (Additions to Daniel in the Apocrypha).[59] There are perhaps traces in 2 Maccabees of a "hero novel" concerning the high priest Onias III, whose unjust execution in the days of the Maccabean Revolt is followed by his appearances to the Jewish guerrillas.[60] The sage can become the sacrificial means of the salvation of the world in Wisdom of Solomon 6: 24, and in Philo Moses takes on more qualities of the divinized hero (Philo, *Life of Moses* 2.51.2 §288; Josephus, *Antiquities* 4.8.48 §326). In the *Manual of Discipline* from Qumran it is said that twelve men and three priests will "expiate iniquity" (*ratzot 'avon*) among the members (1QS 8: 3), "to offer expiation for the earth (*lekaper be'ad ha'aretz*, 8: 10; compare also 9: 4)."

Fourth Maccabees, a Jewish martyrological document of the first century C.E., has also been adduced as an important source for Jewish notions of expiatory death.[61] Two passages are especially interesting for our purposes. As the elderly Eleazar is tortured to the point of death by the Seleucids, he prays (6: 29): "Render my blood an expiation (*katharsion*) for your people, and receive my life as a ransom (*antipsychon*) for theirs!" Also, the Jewish martyrs are said to "become as though a ransom (*antipsychon*) for the sins of the people. Through the blood of these pious ones and the expiation (*hilasterion*) of their death, divine Providence saved Israel" (17: 21–22). The parallels between 4 Maccabees and Greek funeral orations has often been noted, and the possibility that it is an early cult narrative for the graves of the Maccabean martyrs should not be overlooked.

Honi ha-Me'aggel ("the Circlemaker"; first century B.C.E.) also provides important parallels to the hero tradition. One of the few miracle workers described in rabbinic literature, he is often compared by modern scholars to Jesus because of his powers.[62] It is often overlooked, however, that there is connected with him the motif of hero/people antagonism, just as there is with the Greek hero. To be sure, in the Talmud (*b Taanit* 23a) the theme of hero/people antagonism is only suggested; Honi fails to receive the honor from the people that is due him and prays for death (though compare *Aesop* 124!). In Josephus, however (*Antiquities* 14.2.1–2 §22–28), his ending is more dramatic. In a power struggle for the throne of Jerusalem, one party demands that he curse the other; when he refuses, they stone him. Josephus states that God soon took vengeance on the perpetrators of this outrage by sending a scorching wind that lasted for a year, creating a widespread drought. The similarity to the resolution of *Aesop* and other Greek hero narratives is quite strong.

JESUS' DEATH AS HERO'S DEATH IN EARLY CHRISTIANITY

With this survey of the reverence for the dead in Greco-Roman and Jewish tradition in mind, it is easy to perceive a similar strain in the early Christian *cultus*: the benefactor Jesus is executed at the hands of the authorities in Jerusalem (presumably a decision of the Roman rulers), and in this process effects a sacrifice that takes away sins. This is already expressed in Paul's letters as "Christ died for our sins" (1 Cor 15: 3), "as an expiation (*hilasterion*) by his blood" (Rom 3: 25; compare 4 Macc 17: 22 above), or "Christ, our paschal lamb, has been sacrificed" (1 Cor 5: 7) – all probably pre-Pauline formulations; in Hebrews as "making expiation (*hilaskomai*) for the sins of the people" (2: 17), and in Mark as "giving his life as a ransom (*lytron*) for many" (10: 45).[63]

As in the *Life*, so in Mark, the execution of Jesus is triggered by a prophetic reproach within the precincts of the temple, the so-called "cleansing" scene. Jesus' act of overturning the moneychangers' tables occurs just at the beginning of the passion week, and one may wonder if this was what motivated the series of legal reactions which actually resulted in Jesus' execution. (Recall also that in one tradition Aesop is executed for opposing the way sacrificial offerings are administered by the Delphians.) E. P. Sanders, in fact, argues that the prophetic action at the temple, meant to prophesy its imminent destruction, is a historically accurate tradition about an event in the life of Jesus. Only in this way, argues Sanders, can we explain how an action in Jesus' ministry could have given rise to the charge of insurrection and the ironic title "King of the Jews."[64] The questions at the trial concerning Jesus' threat to the temple also reflect very early Christian tradition, because, according to Sanders, it was obviously an embarrassment for early Christians that Jesus had prophesied against the temple, a fact clumsily passed over in the trial scenes. This is, indeed, one of the strongest arguments for the historical reliability of the tradition: it was something well known that required an explanation and defense, even though no adequate response is offered. Whether Sanders is correct in all of his argumentation, the centrality and importance of the temple pronouncement as a prophetic action, from an early stage in the gospel tradition, seems clear, along with its connection to the trial and execution of Jesus. Although we are not in the present study concerned with the historical Jesus, confirming an event in the life of Jesus would perforce establish it as an early tradition, and in this case, one that is parallel to Aesop: Jesus reproaches Jerusalemites in their temple precincts, is hated for it, and is executed. Further, there is a common motif in the Greek and Roman traditions in question that the sacrifice of the hero is demanded or predicted by an oracle, often the oracle of Delphi.[65] At John 11: 50 the curious prophecy of the high priest Caiaphas may provide an exact analog: "It is expedient that one man should die for the people, so that the whole nation not perish." Despite certain Johannine elements that can be found in the surrounding verses, at the base of this passage probably lies a fragment of pre-Johannine tradition. The verse as quoted implies that Jesus will die for the Jewish people only, and only in verse 52 is it broadened to others.[66] The latter is likely Johannine redaction, while the earlier verse attests an association of Jesus' death with expiation for the Jewish people, and more specifically, the temple.

It could be objected that, unlike the Greek and Roman examples, Jesus is killed at the instigation of one group, the Jews (or the Romans with Jewish cooperation), but becomes the cult figure of another, the first Christians. However, the separation of Christians from Jews is something that only occurs over a period of decades, and is not present in the earliest Christian traditions. Even Paul's critique of Judaism (or critique within Judaism) does not really separate out the Christian cult from Judaism.[67] The analogous argument that the sins of the executioners is not removed, but rather only the sins of those who approach Christ through the *cultus*, may also read the sensibilities of later decades back into the first decades of the movement. Among the early Christians there was an emphasis on the expiation of the guilt of Israel. Jesus' action in the temple was not to establish a "new" religion, or to purify an old one, but to prophesy against the practices at his own temple, the center of the Jewish people. This would certainly be within the prophetic tradition of the Hebrew Bible, where we find many vocal critics of Jerusalem cult practices. Sanders also reminds us of another prophet contemporary with Jesus (ironically, also named Jesus) who, according to Josephus, went through the streets wailing, "A voice from the east, a voice from the west, a voice from the four winds; a voice against Jerusalem and the sanctuary, a voice against all the people" (*Jewish War* 6.5.3 §301). In the latter case it is significant that there is, in effect, an identification of Jerusalem, the temple, and the people. Jesus of Nazareth was probably remembered as being focused in the same way on an idealized "Israel," while his followers thought of themselves as the "true Israel." He was no more "anti-Jerusalem" in principle than was the other prophet Jesus, or than Socrates was "anti-Athens." In addition, Martin Hengel makes an observation that may bear on this question. Mark, unlike the other gospels, appears to place the guilt of misunderstanding Jesus, if not executing him, on *all* the *dramatis personae:* Pilate, the soldiers, the chief priests, the Pharisees, Judas, the disciples, Peter, even the women who flee at the end.[68] If he is correct in this judgment, then it may be that in Mark's view, the sin of the world, not simply the "people of Jesus," is expiated by his execution, and here we may compare John 3: 16 as well.

Although there are many ways in which we can speak of the cult of Christ in the early church, we need not assume that a cult narrative of the hero will clearly and explicitly refer to him in cultic terms. Nagy notes that despite the fact that the *Iliad* and the *Odyssey* arose in a context in which the hero cult was very important, ritual matters pertaining to the cult are surprisingly absent.[69] Nagy adds, however, that the death of the hero Patroklos in *Iliad* 16.791–92; 18.28–31, 175–77 shares a number of details with the description of the sacrifice of a bull in *Odyssey* 3.447–55. Thus, the relation between the death of the hero and sacrifice is drawn, though hardly commented on. And indeed, there are several places in the early Christian traditions where we may press the cultic connection. To be sure, despite the passages noted above that suggest that Jesus' death was viewed as a sacrifice or expiation, it is surprisingly weakly attested in the gospels. Mark 10: 45 expresses it – "For the Son of Humanity also came not to be served but to serve, and to give his life as a ransom (*lytron*) for many" (quoted above) – but it is merely repeated by Matthew (20: 28), and dropped altogether by Luke (compare 22: 27).[70] It is present in the tradition, however, and just as Paul can refer to Jesus as "our paschal lamb" (1 Cor 5: 7, quoted above), in both Mark and John there is also an intentional association of Jesus' death with the Passover lamb. John 19: 36 even places the hour of Jesus' death at the precise moment when the Passover lambs were to be slaughtered in the temple.[71] Although Paul himself does not seem particularly interested in *developing* this notion, he does transmit what must have been a common christological confession, that Jesus' death was a sacrifice.[72] Paul can even use the language of a purifying sacrifice in regard to his own actions at 1 Cor 4: 13, though this does not usually come through sufficiently in the English translation: *perikatharma* and *peripsema* both mean "offscouring," but also "propitiatory sacrifice."

Concerning the ambivalent relationship of the hero with the deity – in the Greek tradition we even hear of the *menis* or wrath of the god against the hero – we note the words of Jesus on the cross: "My Lord, my Lord, why hast thou forsaken me?" (Mark 15: 34). The words are taken from Psalm 22, a favorite mine for passion references, but in this context it still implies an abandonment by God, a theological difficulty for some early Christians, alleviated by Luke's alteration: "Father, into thy hands I commit my spirit!" (23: 46), or the triumphal "It is finished!" of John 19: 30. Although it certainly evokes the tone of lament of Psalm 22, a temporary estrangement from God is not out of the question, nor is it out of the question to see Jesus' role of

45

victim at the hands of God-the-sacrificer as part of a process of estrangement and reconciliation through ritual, as Jon Levenson has argued.[73]

Regarding the hero's relationship to the city, it could be argued that Mark and John are not parallel to hero-cult narratives because Jerusalem does not take up the veneration of Jesus. However, many of the earliest Christians probably maintained a close association with Jerusalem, sacrificing in the temple and observing Jewish law. It is quite possible that in the early decades of the Christian movement, Jesus' death was seen more precisely as an expiation for the city's guilt for having executed him, as Caiaphas' prophecy implies (whether Jewish leaders, the Roman governor Pilate, or the two in concert were responsible). Although the motif of inculpating the Jews for Jesus' death, while exculpating the Romans, is often rightly considered a later trend in the synoptic tradition, it is not a unilinear development, but rather, a variegated process. The same dynamic is not likely taking place in each gospel. The Gospel of John, as it now stands, appears to render the Jews (or perhaps the "Judeans") as the "Other," a thoroughly separate group who are everywhere to be distinguished from the evangelist's own group, but it is significant that Matthew, the gospel that most explicitly inculpates the Jews, is also by scholarly consent the most "Jewish" gospel. Interreligious divisions between the bulk of Jews and Matthew gave rise to a very sharp polemic in the latter, but more than likely it is aimed at a group that is still, in Matthew's mind, part of the same "religion." A different sense of the locus of the divine drama could have obtained in the earliest gospel tradition, which had not yet separated off the Roman officials for exoneration, or yet separated off the Jews-as-Other for condemnation. It is possible that the change that occurs in the history of the synoptic tradition is from "Our city has killed Jesus" – in much the same way that Plato would have said "Our city has killed Socrates" – to "Their city has killed Jesus," that is, "the Judeans' city" in John, or "the *other* Jews' city" in Matthew.

Still, what we would like to see for a connection to the hero cult would be the ambivalent relationship of the deity to the hero, and a veneration of Jesus that expiates the sin of the city, Jerusalem, or perhaps of the people of Israel. Suggestions of these motifs can be found, but in an inchoate manner. It is possible that they were clearer at an early stage, a stage that corresponded to the creation of the gospel genre, a stage paralleled by the *Life of Aesop*, but that they were obscured in subsequent versions. The hero cult, after all, is one of the few paradigms for reflection on the significance of the death of a figure that *requires* a narrative of the person's life. And there is also one point at which a "cult of remembrance," posited above regarding Cremutius Cordus, coincides here with the actual Christian *cultus*: the eucharist. Remembrance is an explicit part of the words of institution of the eucharist in some texts: "Do this in remembrance of me" (1 Cor 11: 24; Luke 22: 19; lacking in Mark 14: 22–25 and Matt 26: 26–29).[74] To be sure, the very earliest traditions of the Lord's Supper were not likely associated with the death of Jesus, or with the

Passover, but looked forward to an eschatological in-gathering of the faithful and a "messianic banquet" with Jesus (*Didache* 9–11).[75] Still, when this tradition is attached to the gospel narrative it takes on an association with the death of Jesus.[76] Thus in Mark the telling of the story reenacts the sacrifice of Jesus, just as the eucharist may have also. The relationship between ritual, reading, and reenactment has been noted by scholars in other contexts as well.[77]

The strongest evidence of the cult of remembrance, however, may perhaps be found outside of an actual ritual, in the missionary origins of the gospel traditions. We find the relevant passages in the various endings of Mark and John. The first passage in John that is of interest is 20: 30–31:

> And there were many other signs (*semeia*) which Jesus did in the presence of the disciples, which have not been written in this book, but these have been committed to writing in order that you may come to believe that Jesus is the Christ, the son of God, and that by believing you may have life through his name.

The passage recommends the gospel to the reader not just for "remembrance," but in order that the reader "believe" (*pisteuo*). This sounds like a fitting conclusion for the gospel, and although there is an entire chapter which follows, many scholars believe that chapter 21 was added later (see chapter 3 below). The conclusion of John 21 is still quite interesting for our purposes. It is not unlike John 20: 30–31, and may have been composed in imitation of it:

> This one [the "beloved disciple" just mentioned] is the disciple witnessing concerning these things, and committing them to writing, and we know that his testimony is true. And there are also many other things which Jesus did; if they were all written down, I myself doubt that the world could hold the books.

Believing as a theme is only implied here, but there is an even greater sense of the expansion of the reputation of the revered hero than in the case of Cremutius mentioned above.

In the case of Mark, a similar ambiguity exists concerning the final form of the conclusion. A nearly universal agreement among scholars holds that the traditional ending, Mark 16: 9–20, was added after the composition of the gospel as a whole. As a result, these verses do not appear in the text of many modern translations, but are included only in a footnote (see chapter 3). The shorter ending of Mark, 16: 1–8, does not clearly bespeak a cult of remembrance or a cult of any kind; it does not describe the resurrection, and undercuts the whole idea of a cult. It only proposes a hopeful sign in the voice of a messenger dressed in a white robe, who tells the disciples that they will find Jesus risen in Galilee. This ending will be of little help to us in understanding the cultic significance of Jesus' death. The longer ending, however, is more "typical" and voluble on this subject, and has been too quickly dismissed as a later fabrication. Even though the longer ending contradicts the shorter one (Mark 16: 1–8), and did not likely coexist with it as the conclusion of Mark, there is no reason to assume that it is significantly later than the rest of Mark. It could be an equally early, independent tradition, perhaps even earlier than the rest of Mark. The longer ending is rather unrestrained in its development of several themes, especially miracle working (both Jesus' and the disciples') and the importance of faith. It is thus very similar to the early layers of John that emphasize signs, *semeia*. Significantly, it ends by saying "the Lord worked with them by confirming the word through accompanying signs (*semeia*)." The cult of remembrance in the longer ending of Mark, as in John 20–21, is more a cult of believing (*pisteuo*), of faith (*pistis*), not in the sense of Pauline faith, which is set in contrast to works of law, but faith that certain signs – *semeia* – signal the true prophet or Messiah. The result, then, is a cult of faith, a faith which sustained the early Christians and was instrumental in the formation of their group identity. One is reminded of the question which launched Hans Jonas's life-long investigations into Gnosticism: Why did the early church choose faith, *pistis*, over knowledge, *gnosis*? As obvious as it seems, it is important to emphasize that early Christianity was marked by faith, and the Gospels of Mark and John testify to that.[78] The cult of remembrance in this case is a cult of faith, that is, a missionary cult.

And yet we return to a crucial element of the Greek hero typology absent in Mark and John. The "missing body" of the gospel resurrection accounts would seem to preclude the possibility of the cult of the dead hero. This motif can be interpreted in a number of ways, however; its function in each case must be noted carefully. Elias Bickerman, for example, distinguishes sharply between rapture or ascension into heaven in the Greco-Roman context, and resurrection from the dead and reappearance on earth.[79] The empty tomb for Bickerman is intended to confirm the rapture of Jesus, not his reappearance on earth in bodily form. For instance, Josephus spoke of Enoch, Moses, and Elijah as disappearing and being translated into heaven, but not reappearing on earth (*Antiquities* 1.3.4 §85, 3.5.7 §96, 9.2.2 §28).[80] David Aune, however, refined these distinctions, differentiating between ascension into heaven, which implies apotheosis and a change of status; ascension in Luke–Acts, which implies only a change of "location and mode of presence," and not a change of status; resurrection of the body, which is a confirmation of a miraculous victory over death; and the *ambiguous* motif of the missing body.[81] For Aune, the latter is no guarantee of the divinization of the hero in the Greco-Roman world; rather, the missing body can be taken as a means of *denying* the divinization of a human being (see, for example, Strabo 9.2.11 regarding the missing body of Amphiaraos). As it happens, however, the missing body motif is not an anomaly in the hero tradition; it is quite common. In Raglan's list of hero narratives, we find that the body is missing or the burial place uncertain for eight of nine of the Greek heroes (narratives of Olympian gods and non-Greek heroes were not counted). Although a missing body *may* be a problem for the establishment of an actual cult practice, it is not an unusual aspect of the *narrative* accounts of the death of a revered figure; in fact, the presence of the body would be striking. The unknown location of Oedipus' body at the end of *Oedipus at Colonus*, for example, introduces a very compelling *lack* of resolution, a negative capability, as it were. The ultimate resolution of the problem will be found in the fact that Theseus carries with him the secret knowledge of the location of Oedipus' body which is passed on to future generations.[82] And as Adela Yarbro Collins puts it in regard to the missing body in Mark:

> Even if the location of the tomb of Jesus was unknown to the author of Mark, and even if there were no cultic observances at the site of the tomb, it would still be important as a *literary* motif in characterizing Jesus as herolike.[83]

The variety of reactions to the missing-body problem, then, indicates not a lack of tangible evidence of divinization, but an indeterminacy of status for the hero that is meant to be provocative and suggestive. Regarding the resting place of the body of Amphiaraos, Strabo merely capitalizes on the uncertainty, and we see that the two possibilities, a real disappearance and a faked disappearance, are two sides of the same conception, like prophecy and false prophecy. In Pindar's *Nemean Odes* 9.23–26, for example, Amphiaraos's body is not consumed by fire, but swallowed up in the earth by Zeus.[84]

In addition, the Greek conception of ascension is quite different from Jewish or Christian resurrection of the body.[85] Divinization of a dead hero in Greek culture is accomplished by the burial of the body and the ascension of the spirit. Both parts are considered important, the former ideally to insure proper cult. Jewish and Christian resurrection of the body assumes that at the Endtime, all people will be resurrected in bodily form to face judgment. Such a notion was abhorrent to Greek sensibilities, and is even a problem in certain Jewish and Christian texts (Philo, *Life of Moses* 2.51 §288, 1 Cor 15), but for our purposes, what is interesting is the way that the two views are reconciled in the gospel narratives. The empty tomb implies the bodily resurrection of Jesus, a resurrection seen as the "first fruits" of the eschatological resurrection of all Christians (1 Cor 15: 20). The dramatic problem of his absence in the gospels is solved, for example, with Jesus' resurrection appearances at John 20, or alternatively, with the *promise* of a resurrection appearance at Mark 16: 1–8. The reappearance of a dead hero, either as a material being or as a ghostly leader, is also encountered elsewhere.[86] In Greek, Jewish, and Christian cultures, the missing body serves a "legendary" function, especially in a cult that does not have or does not want a central pilgrimage site: it emphasizes that the body is absent in flesh, but present in cult, wherever the cult may be. And just as the local hero narratives of Greek tradition are dissociated from ritual as they become panhellenic in spirit,[87] so Christians had no single cult *site*, and thus no need for a body, precisely because the sect was moving beyond the bounds of Galilee and Jesualem. The cult of Christ was becoming panhellenic as well.

Ultimately, the strongest arguments against the influence of the hero paradigm do not concern the presence or absence of certain details, since the paradigm is so varied; they have to do with larger questions of genre. First, *Aesop* is unlike Mark and John in one important respect: it is satirical, and possibly (though not likely) to be read as fiction. And yet, it is like Mark and John in *telling the story* that establishes the cult. Whether *Aesop* is satirical or fictitious seems shockingly irrelevant for determining its genre, or for determining whether it is of the same genre as the two gospels: they accomplish the same ends by using the same sort of narrative. We find a similar, but not quite identical situation with Lucian's *Peregrinus*, which is satirical but does not establish the cult. However, even here, the fact that it attempts to *disestablish* the cult is significant. Lucian overturns the genre to undermine its would-be beneficiary. Second, the elements of the hero-cult pattern are not *explicitly* attested in the early Christian texts. Although this is quite true, neither does *Aesop* explicitly refer to the cult, and as we noted above, the *Iliad* and the *Odyssey* do not mention the hero cult that was so central to their social world. One must also remember that it is very difficult to advance any *single* paradigm of the interpretation of Jesus' death as constitutive of the early Christian texts.[88] There is no one paradigm that is strongly attested in the earliest witnesses. Even if a single paradigm were discernible in the letters of Paul – and this is not as easy to isolate as one might think – our main concern is with the paradigm that is pre- or extra-Pauline, and which gives rise to the earliest gospel tradition. In chapter 1, it was argued that the conflict-and-resolution pattern is the best way of characterizing the structure of the gospel genre as a whole, and the best "theological correlative" for this pattern is the hero paradigm. As the various "classical" explanations for the background of the concept of the saving role of Jesus are called into question, such as Suffering Servant, Suffering Son of Humanity, and mystery-religions savior,[89] the heuristic value of the hero paradigm may increase.

3

A SYNOPSIS OF MARK AND JOHN

In this chapter, parallel sections of Mark and John are presented side by side, followed by commentary that addresses the importance of the similarities and differences between them for the issues under discussion here. I have made the commentary as brief as possible, focusing only on some of the main points of the debate.[1] It is my hope that this synopsis will make the outlines of the argument clearer, and allow the entirety of the proposed primitive gospel narrative to be considered at once, even if the details of the reconstruction are not presented. The significant discrepancies in the order of the two gospels in the first section can also be more easily seen, and possible reasons for some of these variations will be given.

Specifically, the synopsis allows for a consideration of the question of Markan influence on John. If clear examples of Mark's redaction can be detected in John, then the latter is directly or indirectly influenced by Mark. However, in the following commentary, I argue that both Mark and John have made use of an older gospel narrative tradition, and that John is not familiar with Mark's composition of the gospel narrative. In omitting the hundreds of detailed arguments for Mark's redaction in John that have been proffered by scholars, I am deliberately choosing to privilege the "forest" over the "trees." The question I address is this: Is the *general* case for a separate, early gospel narrative more plausible than the alternative explanations? I believe that it is, and all the arguments of detail fail to convince me otherwise. The debate over detailed examples will surely continue, but my goal here is to prove the explanatory power of a thesis that posits a pre-existing, "complete" narrative tradition, whether oral or written, relatively fixed or unfixed. The thesis proposed in this chapter and that proposed in chapter 2 are not mutually dependent – either can rise or fall separately from the other – but the interlocking nature of the two arguments is noted. Just as the discovery of a complete text of the *Gospel of Thomas* strengthened the arguments for the existence of Q, the comparison of the *Life of Aesop* and related texts aids in the description of a function and *Sitz-im-Leben* for the proposed early gospel narrative.

The following works are referred to often in the commentary: C. K. Barrett,

THE QUEST OF THE HISTORICAL GOSPEL

The Gospel According to St. John, 2nd ed., Philadelphia: Westminster, 1978; Raymond Brown, *The Gospel According to John*, 2 vols, Garden City, N. Y.: Doubleday, 1964–70; Rudolf Bultmann, *The Gospel of John*, Philadelphia: Westminster/Oxford: Basil Blackwell & Mott, 1971; *idem*, *History of the Synoptic Tradition*, New York: Harper & Row, 1963; C. H. Dodd, *Historical Tradition in the Fourth Gospel*, Cambridge: Cambridge University Press, 1963; Robert T. Fortna, *The Gospel of Signs: A Reconstruction of the Narrative Source Underlying the Fourth Gospel*, Cambridge: Cambridge University Press, 1970; Howard Clark Kee, *Community of the New Age: Studies in Mark's Gospel*, Philadelphia: Westminster, 1977; Helmut Koester, *Ancient Christian Gospels: Their History and Development*, Philadelphia: Trinity Press International, 1990; Dieter Lührmann, *Das Markusevangelium*, Tübingen: Mohr (Paul Siebeck), 1987; Burton Mack, *A Myth of Innocence: Mark and Christian Origins*, Philadelphia: Fortress, 1988; Willi Marxsen, *Mark the Evangelist: Studies on the Redaction History of the Gospel*, Nashville: Abingdon, 1969; D. E. Nineham, *Saint Mark*, Harmondsworth: Penguin, 1963; and E. P. Sanders, *Jesus and Judaism*, London: SCM, 1985.

Part One   Mark 1: 1–3: 30/John 1: 1–7: 20

MARK 1: 1/JOHN 1: 1

Mark 1: 1   **John 1: 1**

[1]The beginning of the good news of Jesus Christ, the son of God . . .

[1]In the beginning was the Word . . .

Commentary on Mark 1: 1/John 1: 1

The fact that Mark and John both open their gospels with the word *arche*, "beginning," is not likely coincidental.[2] The same root also occurs in important recitations of events in Luke 24: 47, Acts 1: 22; 10: 37, and also in Ignatius of Antioch's *Letter to the Ephesians* 19.3, a hymn of the advent of the redeemer: "What was ordained by God received its beginning." The term, then, likely came to be associated with both hymnic and prose narrative descriptions of the advent of the redeemer. The traditional gospel narrative must have been introduced with a description of how the drama unfolded, using the word *arche* or the same root.[3] This would correspond to what is often found in Greek and Latin histories: the positing of origins using *arche* or an analogous root.[4]

Cross-cultural studies of the legend of the hero indicate that miraculous birth stories could easily be part of the narrative, as they are in Matthew and Luke, but here we are dealing with a subset of the hero legend genre, one that

52

is more concerned with the life of the hero as it relates to his death. What is associated with the "beginning" is thus not the same in Mark and John; the timeframe is very different. In Mark, Acts 1, and Acts 10, it is the beginning of Jesus' ministry, but in John it is Jesus' primordial origins. It is likely that Mark reflects the earlier gospel narrative tradition in associating the beginning with Jesus' ministry, while John has placed this back into a mythical prehistory. John the Baptist must have been introduced early, however, for he stands there in Mark, John, and Acts 10. This issue will be addressed below.

MARK 1: 2–6/JOHN 1: 6–8, 19–24, 3: 23–24

Mark 1: 2–6

2As it is written in Isaiah the prophet, "Behold, I am sending my messenger before you, who will prepare your way. 3The voice of one crying in the wilderness: Prepare the way of the Lord, make straight his paths."
4John the baptizer appeared in the wilderness, proclaiming a baptism of repentance for the forgiveness of sins.

5And all the Judean countryside and all the Jerusalemites went out to him, and they were baptized by him in the Jordan River, confessing their sins. 6John was clothed in camel hair and a leather belt around his waist, and he ate locusts and wild honey.

John 1: 6–8, 19–23; 3: 23–24

(compare John 1: 23 below)

6There appeared a man, sent from God, whose name was John. 7He came as a witness in order to testify concerning the light, so that all might believe through him. 8He was not the light, but in order to witness concerning the light.

(compare John 3: 23 below)

19This is the testimony of John, when the Judeans sent priests and Levites from Jerusalem to him to ask him, "Who are you?" 20He confessed and did not deny, but confessed, "I am not the Christ." 21And they asked him, "What then? Are you Elijah?" and he said,

(compare Mark 1: 3 above)

"I am not." "Are you the prophet?" And he answered, "No." 22Then they said to him, "So that we may give an answer to those who have sent us, tell us, who are you? What do you say about yourself?" 23He said, "I am the voice of one crying in the wilderness: make straight the way of the Lord," as Isaiah the prophet says.

3: 23–24

(compare Mark 1: 5 above)

23And John was baptizing in Aenon near Salim, because water was abundant there, and they came there and were baptized, 24for John had not yet been thrown into prison.

Commentary on Mark 1: 2–6/John 1: 6–8, 19–23; 3: 23–24

We move immediately after the opening into a section that is the most complicated in the entire synopsis of Mark and John. It is unfortunate that our discussion must address these complexities at such an early point in the synopsis, but it will nevertheless become clear here that there is considerable material paralleled in Mark and John, and that common source traditions can be posited for the two gospels.

After the opening line, Mark commences the gospel with the biblical quotation as an overture, and not as the words of John the Baptist. The Baptist is introduced immediately afterward, indeed as the fulfillment of Isaiah's prophecy: "As it is written in Isaiah the prophet . . . John the baptizer appeared . . ." The Gospel of John, on the other hand, places the quotation in the mouth of the Baptist, a few verses later in the gospel. It could be argued that John has altered the Markan tradition by "historicizing" this utterance and incorporating it into the narrative. The other alternative, however, that John represents the order of the earlier gospel narrative and that Mark has altered it, is equally plausible. Mark would have redactional warrants for moving the quotation from its position as reflected in John as the first preaching of the Baptist, and placing it foremost in the gospel. This can be seen more clearly when we look at the contents of the quotation.

Mark's quotation, unlike that in Matthew, Luke, and John, consists of Mal 3: 1 in addition to Isa 40: 3, even though the quotation is attributed to Isaiah alone. It could once again be argued that John corrected this inaccurate ascription to Isaiah by omitting the Malachi verse, as Matthew and Luke have evidently done. On the other hand, John's source may not have included the quotation from Malachi. The two sayings in Mark both have the word "way" (*hodos*) figuring prominently in them, and Mark was likely responsible for bringing the two together as a biblical witness to the importance of the term "way." At three other crucial points in Mark's Gospel, the passion prediction passages of 8: 27; 9: 33; and 10: 52, "way" also appears as a central term. This word was one of the earliest terms used to refer to the new sect of Christianity, and Mark has probably changed the contents of the quotation, made it independent of any speaker, and altered its position in the narrative to create an overture to the entire gospel on the theological meaning of "way."[5]

In the section above the possibility was considered that *arche* was the theme of the early gospel introduction, but beyond this one word, the comparison of Mark and John did not suggest much about this section. Here, however, we find some indicators of how the primitive gospel narrative likely began. John begins with a hymn (1: 1–18), but this hymn probably had an independent existence, and therefore did not introduce John's source. Both Mark and John, however, place John the Baptist very early, and if we extract the John the Baptist material from John's hymn, we see that some of these verses may quite plausibly reflect the introduction of the first actor in the gospel tradition, as several scholars have suggested.[6] We may consider, for example, John 1: 6–7a,c: "There appeared a man, sent from God, whose name was John. He came as a witness in order . . . that all might believe through him." John the Baptist is introduced with the same word in Mark and John, "appeared" (*egeneto*), and in both gospels characteristic redaction by the authors can account for some of their differences: "in the wilderness" in Mark (absent in John) is probably redactional,[7] and in John the reference to light in verse 7 is likely redactional, along with all of verse 8, since they carefully subordinate the Baptist to Jesus in a way typical of John. Perhaps redactional in Mark is the ascetic image of John the Baptist in verse 8, reminiscent of Elijah (compare 2 Kgs 1: 8). Although the Elijah motif is strong in John, that particular tradition is lacking at this point. There are thus many verbal similarities between the two gospels, yet nothing which they have in common is distinctively Markan, and Mark's distinctive redactional elements are lacking in John.

Mark introduces Jesus as coming from "Nazareth of Galilee" (1: 9). The title "Jesus of Nazareth" also appears in the recital of gospel events in Acts 10: 38, and in a slightly altered form, "Jesus, son of Joseph, from Nazareth," at John 1: 45. It is likely that this identification appeared early in the gospel tradition, but there is no interest at this point in the birth of Jesus on the part of Mark or John (or Acts 10), beyond this vaguest of ascriptions. The birth narratives of Matthew and Luke thus do not reflect the earliest interests of the church, but retroject concerns of the second or third generation back onto the birth of the redeemer, after the gospel tradition had already been established.[8]

Mark 1: 5 has parallels at two points in John's narrative: John 1: 19b and 3:

22–24, although the position of the Baptist tradition in John 3 is very awkward. M.-E. Boismard has also suggested that John 3: 23–24 should be placed at the beginning of his reconstruction of the source material that John used,[9] and here I agree, although it is hardly necessary for the present reconstruction. When John is compared with Mark 1: 5, we detect parallel language: "they appeared and were baptized" (*pareginonto kai ebaptizonto*) in John is similar to the two words at the beginning and end of Mark's parallel phrase (*exeporeueto, ebaptizonto*).

The scenes in Mark 1: 5 and John 1: 19 are similar – the procession of Judeans out to see John the Baptist – but the reason they come in each case is different. In Mark, the people come out to John to be baptized, while in John, it is priests and Levites who come out to question him. The similarities in wording at first appear to be minor,[10] but the motif of people coming out to Jesus from Jerusalem is perhaps significant; it occurs also at Mark 3: 22 and 7: 1, and in the peculiar notation at John 1: 24. It is important to distinguish, where possible, those places where the people coming out are positive (Mark 1: 5; John 3: 23) and those places where they are negative (Mark 3: 22; John 1: 19 by implication at 1: 26). John's version of events here is somewhat ambiguous, but the fact that John 3: 23 appears to be out of place, and may have been originally associated with the beginning of the narrative, indicates that John's source treated the coming out as positive. Since Mark has probably rearranged the introduction of the Baptist by moving the Isaiah quotation earlier, it is possible that Mark's source also initiated John the Baptist's witness as a response to the question of those who came out to see him. Certainly, the words used to describe those who came out are parallel in Mark and John, whatever the people might have said when they arrived.

The Johannine passage here presents a number of literary difficulties which have provoked various theories of redactional layers, summarized very well by Brown, *John*, 1.67–71. Most of these difficulties are relatively minor, the same sort of things one encounters in many places in John, with its repetitive, meditative style. Some, however, are worth noting: (1) the sayings which are parallel to Mark are interwoven into other sayings more characteristic of John's discourses; (2) verse 21 could quite logically be followed by verse 25, and the fact that the same line occurs in both ("and they asked him") indicates that a seam might have been formed where a redactor paused, added material, and then continued with the same line that occurred before the break; indeed, between the two parts of this seam appear the closest parallels to the synoptic tradition. Bultmann (*John*, p. 85) isolates a coherent account by eliminating the material between the two parts of this seam and attributes them to the "Ecclesiastical Redactor," a later editor who has inserted material – including synoptic sayings – in order to bring the gospel into the fold of the emerging Great Church. Doublets are thereby also neatly explained. In addition to what many other scholars would assign to the Ecclesiastical Redactor, such as the eucharistic references at 6: 51b–59, Bultmann here wants to include all the

56

parallels with the synoptic tradition.[11] However, as conceptually satisfying as this hypothesis is, it has problems, and has yielded to other possibilities. There is no reason why the parallels to Mark would not more likely represent the source which John the evangelist has redacted to arrive at its present character. In favor of this view, we note that John often opens up source material and inserts sayings and discourse material (compare, for example, the prologue, chs 5–7, and ch. 9). This has often resulted in a confusing latticework of layers and disjunctions, and it evidently has here as well.

J. Louis Martyn[12] also provides an ingenious theory for a source for John at this point (though he does not tie it to the Signs Source or to any other early gospel source). After noting the Elijah-like traits in the portrait of Jesus in John's Gospel, he asks whether an identification of Jesus as Elijah-who-is-to-come might have been present in the source, though now partially expunged by John. Martyn detects a residual structure of this source in the three denials of the Baptist, counterbalanced by three messianic affirmations stated about Jesus at the end of the chapter (the second of which is restored by Martyn's hypothesis):

Three denials	*Three messianic affirmations*
20 I am not the Christ.	41 We have found the Messiah.
21 I am not Elijah.	(43 We have found Elijah.)
21 I am not the prophet.	45 We have found the (prophet) of whom Moses wrote

Martyn's suggestion is intriguing, and points to an identification of Jesus with Elijah in the sources of John. He, along with Brown and others, points out, for example, that the two numbered signs in John, the changing of the water into wine (2: 1–11) and the healing of the nobleman's son (4: 46–54), may allude to Elijah's two miracles for the widow of Zarephath (1 Kgs 17: 8–16, 17–24). The collocation of the prophet Elijah and the one of whom Moses wrote (the "prophet like Moses" of Deut 18: 15) indicates the possibility of a strong prophetic interest in John's source, perhaps associated with Elijah in particular, perhaps with Moses, perhaps with the hope of an eschatological prophet in general. Although Mark's Gospel suggests an identification of the Baptist with Elijah (1: 6), it does not go as far as the Gospel of John at this point. One must wonder, however, whether other Elijah traditions were present in Mark's source, and if so, why Mark has deleted or moved them.[13]

MARK 1: 7–11/JOHN 1: 25–34, 51

Mark 1: 7–11	**John 1: 25–34, 51**
	[25]And they asked him and said to him, "Why then do you baptize if

7He proclaimed, saying "One stronger than I is coming after me; I am not worthy to stoop down and loosen the thong of his sandals. 8I baptized you with water, but he will baptize you with the holy spirit."

9And it happened in those days that Jesus came from Nazareth of Galilee and was baptized in the Jordan by John.

10And immediately getting up out of the water, he saw the heavens split open and the spirit descending like a dove upon him.
11And a voice came out of the heavens:

"You are my beloved son, in whom I am pleased."

(compare Mark 1: 10 above)

you are not the Christ nor Elijah nor the prophet?" 26John answered them and said, "I baptize with water. In your midst stands one whom you do not know, 27the one coming after me; I am not worthy to loosen the thong of his sandal."

28These things occurred in Bethany beyond the Jordan, where John was baptizing.

29On the next day he saw Jesus coming toward him and said, "Behold the lamb of God who takes away the sin of the world. 30This is the one concerning whom I said, 'After me comes a man who came to be before me, because he was prior to me. 31I did not know him, but in order that he be manifested to Israel, on account of this I came baptizing with water.'" 32John testified and said, "I saw the spirit descending like a dove from heaven, and it remained upon him. 33I did not know him, but the one who sent me to baptize with water said to me, 'Upon whomever you see the spirit descending and remaining, that one is the one baptizing with the holy spirit.' 34I have seen and testified that he is the chosen one of God."

51He said to him, "Truly, truly, I say to you, you will see heaven open and the angels of God ascending and descending upon the son of humanity."

Commentary on Mark 1: 7–11/John 1: 25–34, 51

The tradition which Mark renders in a very succinct form in verses 7–8 is also found in Matt 3: 11–12 and Luke 3: 16 in a slightly different form, and a comparison with those two gospels will be necessary here also. Mark differs from Matthew and Luke in certain details, and in the order of the crucial phrases. Since Matthew and Luke agree closely against Mark, most scholars assume that the former two gospels reflect the Q version of this saying, rather than Mark's:[14]

Matt 3: 11–12	Luke 3: 16	Mark 1: 7–8
I baptize you with water.	I baptize you with water.	
One coming is stronger, whose sandals I am not worthy to bear.	One coming is stronger, whose thong I am not worthy to untie.	One coming is stronger, whose thong I am not worthy to untie. I baptize you with water.
He will baptize with the holy spirit and fire.	He will baptize with the holy spirit and fire.	He will baptize with the holy spirit.

It is this difference that has suggested to scholars that the saying appeared in two slightly different forms in Mark and Q. The context of the Q saying also reveals a different emphasis from Mark's. In Q, John the Baptist is delivering a blistering prophetic condemnation, and the "baptism with the holy spirit and with fire" is eschatological judgment. Holy spirit may have even been added to an image of eschatological fire.[15] In Mark, the judgment aspect is lost, and we find instead a mere contrast of the two roles of Baptist and Messiah.

The order of John's source cannot be reconstructed with certainty, since the relevant phrases are broken up and found in several verses. Verses 26a and 27 stand as the clearest parallel to this tradition, although they are incomplete by themselves. Verses 30–31 repeat the same motifs, and reflect a thoroughgoing Johannine redaction (Fortna, *Gospel*, pp. 175–76); thus they probably do not reflect the source. It is likely that verse 33d is the conclusion to the sayings complex which was begun in verses 26a and 27. We arrive, then, at this suggested reconstruction (arranged in stanzas as above):

> I baptize with water.
> One is coming after me
> whose thong I am not
>   worthy to untie.
> He is the one who baptizes
>   with the holy spirit.

If that is so, then John reflects the same order as Q, not the order found in

Mark.[16] Although the Johannine order is hypothetical, it is still much closer to Q's order than to Mark's. To be sure, John does agree with Mark in omitting reference to fire, but this need not derive from Markan redaction. John is not likely dependent upon Mark; it is more plausible that John reflects an independent tradition, also reflected in Q. Mark has altered the order of the sayings to bring baptism with water and baptism with the holy spirit together to form a clearer contrast of the two roles and the two periods of activity.

Mark's Gospel describes the baptism of Jesus by John the Baptist in very few words. Although the significance is not being minimized – the heavens still open – there is a compression of the "period of the Baptist" into a very small space.[17] Traditional material can probably be detected in Mark: "And it happened in those days" (verse 9) is a Septuagintal Greek idiom which Mark rarely uses, and "Jesus from Nazareth of Galilee" is also unique in Mark. However, verse 10 begins with *kai euthus*, a very common Markan conjunctive phrase, and the "splitting open" of the heavens forms an *inclusio* with the "splitting open" of the temple curtain in Mark 15: 38; it is likely Markan.[18] John, on the other hand, like Matthew and Luke, treats the Baptist as a stronger and more vocal figure, though his glory is subordinated to Jesus'; nevertheless, John still omits the actual baptism. For the Gospel of John, the "beginning" for Jesus was in primordial time, not at baptism, and the adoptionist christology inherent in Mark's baptism scene, and perhaps in the earlier tradition as well, was corrected accordingly.[19] The baptism scene, rather than being the moment of Jesus' elevation, is one of the Baptist's recognition and witnessing (verses 32–34). Some of the sayings likely associated with the baptism in the source remain in John, and in particular, we note that John may retain vestiges of the original eschatological message: the angels of God and the Son of Humanity in John 1: 51 are paralleled in preaching now found in Mark 8: 38–9: 1 (Brown, *John*, pp. 1.88–91). Also, what a voice from heaven says in Mark at the moment of baptism is found in the mouth of the Baptist in John 1: 34: "And I have seen and witnessed that he is the chosen one [variant reading: son] of God."

Most scholars find echoes of both Ps 2: 7 and Isa 42: 1 woven together in Mark's pronouncement from heaven at 1: 11:[20]

Ps 2:7	*Mark 1: 11*	*Isa 42: 1*
You are my son;	You are my beloved son	Behold my servant whom I have chosen, my beloved,
	with you I am well pleased.	with whom my soul is well pleased.
today I have begotten you.		

Some scholars stress the distinction between the royal-messianic son tradition of Ps 2: 7 and the prophet/servant tradition of Isa 42: 1.[21] The two traditions have evidently been brought together by Mark's redaction, while John's shorter utterance is most likely an allusion to Isa 42: 1 alone.[22] If this is correct, then it stands as evidence against the view that John read Mark, since it is difficult to believe that John decided to separate the biblical allusions at this point, retaining one while discarding the other. Even if a redactional motive could be suggested for such a move, the simpler solution presents itself: John attests an early messianic exegesis of Isa 42: 1 which is reflected in Mark in a more developed form, that is, combined with Ps 2: 7, a biblical passage treated as messianic elsewhere in early Christian texts.[23]

When all these considerations are brought to bear, we may conclude that the tradition common to Mark and John for this section reads something like the following (avoiding, of course, any suggestion of a precise reconstruction):

There appeared a man, sent from God, whose name was John. He came as a witness so that all people might believe through him. All the Judean countryside and all the Jerusalemites came out to him, and they were baptized by him. He proclaimed and said, "I am a voice of one crying in the desert: Make straight the way of the Lord,' as Isaiah the prophet says. I baptize in water; one stronger than I is coming after me, the thong of whose sandal I am not worthy to untie. He will baptize you with the holy spirit [or perhaps, with fire]." And it also happened in those days that Jesus came from Nazareth of Galilee and was baptized by John. John saw the heavens open and the spirit descending as a dove from heaven on Jesus, and a voice came from heaven: "This man is the chosen one of God."

MARK 1: 14–20/JOHN 1: 35–50

Mark 1: 14–20

14After John was handed over, Jesus came into Galilee preaching the good news of God and saying, 15"The time has been fulfilled and the kingdom of God is near; repent and believe in the good news." 16Passing by the Sea of Galilee, Jesus saw Simon and Andrew the brother of Simon casting nets in the sea; for they were fishermen. 17Jesus said to them,

John 1: 35–50

(compare John 3: 24, displayed above)

35On the next day John was again standing with two of his disciples, 36and he looked at Jesus walking about and said, "Behold the lamb of God." 37And the two disciples

"Come, follow me, and I shall make you fishers of people." ¹⁸Immediately they left their nets and followed him. ¹⁹And going on a bit further, he saw James the son of Zebedee and John his brother; they were in the boat mending their nets. ²⁰Immediately he called them. Leaving their father Zebedee in the boat with the hired workers, they followed after him.

(compare Mark 1: 17 above)

heard him speaking and followed Jesus. ³⁸Jesus turned and saw them following and said to them, "What do you seek?" They said to him, "Rabbi (which translated means 'teacher'), where are you staying?" ³⁹He said to them, "Come and see." They then went and saw where he was staying and remained with him that day. The hour was about the tenth. ⁴⁰Andrew the brother of Simon Peter was one of the two who heard John and followed him. ⁴¹He first found his own brother Simon and said to him, "We have found the Messiah (which translated means 'Christ')." ⁴²He led him to Jesus. Jesus looked at him and said, "You are Simon the son of John; you shall be called Cephas" (which translated means "Peter").

⁴³On the next day he wanted to go to Galilee, and he found Philip. Jesus said to him, "Follow me." ⁴⁴Philip was from Bethsaida, from the city of Andrew and Peter. ⁴⁵Philip found Nathaniel and said to him, "We have found the one Moses wrote about in the law and the prophets, Jesus son of Joseph from Nazareth." ⁴⁶Nathaniel said to him, "Can anything good come out of Nazareth?" Philip said to him, "Come and see." ⁴⁷Jesus saw Nathaniel coming toward him and said concerning him, "Behold an Israelite in whom there is no guile." ⁴⁸Nathaniel said to him, "From where do you know me?" Jesus answered and said to him, "Before Philip called you, while you were under the fig tree, I saw

you." [49]Nathaniel answered him, "Rabbi, you are the son of God! You are the king of Israel!" [50]Jesus answered and said to him, "Because I said to you that I saw you under the fig tree, you believe? You shall see greater things than these!"

Commentary on Mark 1: 14–20/John 1: 35–50

Although Mark and John both move immediately from the baptism of Jesus by John the Baptist to the introduction of the first disciples, they describe this latter event quite differently. In Mark the disciples, before being called, are independent of any religious group, and are identified with their fishing trade. Jesus finds them, calls them, and they follow. These succinct and formulaic narratives are grouped by Bultmann (*History*, p. 28) as "biographical apoph-thegms," and as he notes, they do not "involve any psychological interest in those who are called." In John, however, the disciples begin the narrative as followers of John the Baptist; they hear the Baptist's witness to Jesus, and they find Jesus, rather than Jesus finding them. They are only identified as fisher-men in chapter 21, which was likely added to the gospel. The psychological interest is now also squarely on the disciples, as they respond to the sudden and unexpected presence of the Messiah.

Mark's Gospel clearly places Peter first among the disciples called, and the importance of James and John, the sons of Zebedee, is also emphasized (compare Mark 9: 2; 14: 33), both in contrast to John's Gospel. In John, Andrew is introduced first, who then fetches his brother Peter; Philip and Nathanael are similarly introduced.[24] Although John has placed Peter second in the order of disciples who discover Jesus, this does not necessarily reveal an attempt to sub-ordinate Peter, as happens, for instance, in the late additions of 20: 2–10 and 21: 20–22. As Brown notes (*John*, pp. 1.77–78, 84–85), it is more likely that we find here a pattern of Andrew: confession/Peter: higher confession//Philip: confession/Nathanael: higher confession. At any rate, the renaming of Simon to Cephas/Peter would have been a tradition too strongly established for John to change or suppress (see also below re Mark 8: 27–33/John 6: 60–71).

Verses 14–15 on Mark's side are usually considered to be redactional. They are typical of Mark's other summaries and use Markan vocabulary (especially *euangelion*). Still, these Markan elements may have been grafted onto an ear-lier tradition, as the parallel in John 3: 24 concerning John's imprisonment indicates: the manner in which John the Baptist is presented as both forerun-ner *and* contemporary is different in the two gospels, and John does not appear to be dependent upon Mark's redactional timeframe.[25] What the gospels have in common is the motif, located early in the narrative, of the call of the first disciples. John has evidently introduced more significant changes than Mark, although we shall consider below the possibility that John's location of the renaming of Peter is older than Mark's in chapter 8.

In this section we also find three occasions where Semitic words are translated for the reader: rabbi (verse 38), Messiah (verse 41), and Cephas (verse 42), all with the same translation formula ("which translated means"). One may wonder whether the use of Semitic terms reflects an early layer of tradition. Mark also uses Aramaic terms at certain points (cf. below re Mark 15: 22), but the list of such terms does not overlap with John's.

MARK 1: 21–28/ JOHN 7: 14–18

Mark 1: 21–28

21They proceeded to Capernaum. Immediately on the Sabbath he entered the synagogue and taught. 22They were astounded at his teaching, for he was teaching as one who had authority, and not as the scribes.

23And immediately in their synagogue there was a man with an unclean spirit, who cried out and said, 24"What do you have to do with us, Jesus of Nazareth? Have you come to destroy us? I know who you are, the holy one of God." 25Jesus rebuked him and

John 7: 14–18

14When it was already the middle of the festival, Jesus went up into the temple and began to teach. 15The Judeans were amazed and said, "How does he know letters when he has not been taught?"
16Then Jesus answered them and said, "My teaching is not mine, but is from the one who sent me. 17If someone wants to do his will, that person will know concerning the teaching whether it is from God or whether I speak from my own authority. 18The one who speaks from his own authority seeks his own glory. The one who seeks the glory of the one who sent him is true and there is no unrighteousness in him.

said, "Be silent and come out of him!" 26The unclean spirit convulsed him, and calling out with a loud voice, came out of him. 27And they were all amazed, so that they debated with each other, saying, "What is this? A new teaching with authority. He commands even the unclean spirits, and they obey him." 28Immediately, the report about him was everywhere, throughout the entire region of Galilee.

Commentary on Mark 1: 21–28/ John 7: 14–18

In this section we encounter passages in Mark and John that are parallel, but not found in the same order in the narrative. The same is true for several of the following sections. This constitutes a challenge to the hypothesis of a common source, but a full response to this problem must be postponed until chapter 4.

Bultmann (*History*, pp. 205–6) analyzed the first passage in Mark by isolating an older healing miracle in verses 23–27a, somewhat awkwardly introduced by verses 21–22. Jesus is teaching in the synagogue when an opportunity arises for him to perform a miracle, and the crowd, presented with the result, marvels instead at "a new teaching with authority," seemingly confusing the healing motif with the teaching. It is possible to see in Mark's redaction an attempt to show that Jesus' new teaching consists in his new authority over unclean spirits. "Authority" occurs in both parts, and Mark has combined them in a very characteristic way, since the teaching provokes a profound, even eschatological, reaction (compare Mark 11: 18 below). Certainly Mark the redactor is interested in the teaching theme, and especially in connecting this theme with "authority," but some aspects of verses 21–22, and the importance of teaching itself, may have already been present in the tradition.[26]

The parallels with John are very close, despite the fact that John reflects the typical process of opening up a limited exchange into a larger, more evocative discourse:

Mark	John
Jesus proceeds to Capernaum	Jesus proceeds to Jerusalem
in synagogue	in temple
teaches (*edidasken*)	teaches (*edidasken*)
people astounded (*exeplessonto*):	Judeans astounded (*ethaumazon*):
"he is one having authority, not like scribes (*grammateis*)"	"he knows letters (*grammata*); how?"

65

Other than the change of location from synagogue to temple, the first two verses of John's account are almost identical to Mark's. We can probably attribute some choices of words to John. "The Judeans," rather than scribes or Pharisees, is a favorite Johannine expression, just as on Mark's side, "immediately" is a characteristic term – but the two most important verbs in John 7: 14–15, *edidasken* and *ethaumazon*, are very close to Mark.[27] What is especially noteworthy, however, is that at the exact same point where Mark's redaction begins – the insertion of the miracle – so does John's: John 7: 16–18 is typical Johannine discourse. Both redactors evidently felt that the reference to the teaching was an appropriate point of departure for the inclusion of other material.

Mark had probably received something very similar to verses 21–22a as a source, and has inserted the notion of "authority" and shifted the idea of teaching to a more messianic conception of eschatological authority, authority even over the unclean spirits. Placing the miracle with the public acclamation over Jesus' teaching is thus Mark's redaction, a connection which John does not make.[28] In John, on the other hand, the narrative simply becomes another opportunity to launch a Johannine discourse. It is probable, therefore, that in the tradition there was a passage of Jesus' teaching which ended in the amazement of the audience, not unlike a passage at *Life of Aesop* 37: "This worthless creature has learning ["knows letters," *grammata oiden*]?" This has been altered in characteristic ways by both Mark and John.

In Mark it is the teaching that will later be seen as a major reason for Jesus to be crucified (compare Mark 11: 18), even though Mark the redactor has also associated the plot against Jesus with his healing on the Sabbath. John too associates Jesus' open teaching and the surprised acclamation of it (7: 15) with the attempt to kill him, and also the controversy over healing on the Sabbath (7: 21–30). Yet this connection between the provocative teaching of a philosopher, judgments against the philosopher's own people about ritual beliefs, and the resultant attempt to kill him was not invented by Mark or John; it is an integral part of the hero paradigm described in chapters 1 and 2, and is especially to be noted in the *Life of Aesop*.

MARK 2: 1–12/JOHN 5: 1–16, 7: 19–23

Mark 2: 1–12

1When he entered Capernaum again after a few days, it was heard that he was at home. 2So many were gathered there that there was no longer any room at the door, and he preached to them. 3Some

John 5: 1–16; 7: 19–23

1After this it was the festival of the Judeans, and Jesus went up into Jerusalem. 2There was in Jerusalem at the Sheep Gate a pool, which is called in Hebrew Bethzatha, and has five porticos.

people came to him with a paralytic, borne by four of them. 4Since they were unable to approach him on account of the crowd, they took tiles off the roof where he was, dug a hole, and lowered the mat on which the paralytic was lying. 5When Jesus saw their faith, he said to the paralytic, "Child, your sins are forgiven."

6Now some of the scribes were sitting there debating in their hearts, 7"What is he saying? He is blaspheming! Who can forgive sins except the one God?" 8And Jesus immediately knew in his spirit that they were debating among themselves and said to them, "Why do you debate these things in your hearts? 9Which is easier, to say to a paralytic, 'Your sins are forgiven,' or to say, 'Rise, pick up your mat and walk'? 10But in order that you know that the Son of Humanity has authority to forgive sins on earth" – he said to the paralytic, 11"I say to you, rise, pick up your mat and go to your home." 12He got up and immediately picked up his mat and went away before everyone, so that all were amazed and glorified God saying, "We have never seen anything like this!"

3Within them sat a throng of the sick, blind, lame, and withered. 5There was a certain man there who had been sick for thirty-eight years. 6Jesus saw him lying there, and since he knew that he had been sick for a long time, said to him, "Do you want to become well?" 7The sick man answered him, "Sir, I do not have anyone to put me into the pool when it is disturbed, and while I am coming, another goes in before me."

(cf. John 5: 8 below)

8Jesus said to him, "Rise, pick up your mat and walk." 9And immediately the man became well and picked up his mat and walked.

And it was the Sabbath on that day. 10The Judeans then said to the one who had been healed, "It is the Sabbath, and you are not permitted to pick up your mat." 11But he answered them, "The one who made me well, he said to

67

me, 'Pick up your mat and walk.'"
[12]They asked him, "Who is the one who said to you, 'Pick up your mat and walk'?" [13]But the man who had been healed did not know who it was, for Jesus had slipped away, since there was a crowd in that place. [14]Later, Jesus found him in the temple and said to him, "Behold, you have become well; sin no more, lest something worse happen to you." [15]The man went away and announced to the Judeans that Jesus was the one who had made him well. [16]On account of this, the Judeans persecuted Jesus, because he did these things on the Sabbath.

7: 19–23

[19]"Did not Moses give you the law? Yet none of you keeps the law. Why do you seek to kill me?" [20]The crowd answered, "You are possessed by a demon! Who is trying to kill you?" [21]Jesus answered and said to them, "I have done one deed and you are all amazed. [22]For this reason Moses gave you circumcision – not that it is from Moses but from the fathers – and on the Sabbath you circumcise someone. [23]If someone receives circumcision on the Sabbath so that the law of Moses not be violated, why are you angry with me because I heal on the Sabbath?

Commentary on Mark 2: 1–12/John 5: 1–16; 7: 19–23

These miracle stories in Mark and John have similar motifs, but it is not clear that there is any close relationship between them.[29] For the present study, however, their relationship should at least be considered; if they are not related in narrative structure, they are often still parallel in their development and function within the larger narrative.

Despite the fact that Mark 2 and John 5 both concern the healing of a paralytic, they are characterized by pictorial, even cinematic, effects which are quite different. In Mark, Jesus' address in a crowded room is interrupted by four devoted friends of a paralytic who strip away the roof to lower him down, while in John Jesus initiates a conversation with a paralytic who is seated helplessly at the edge of the healing waters. A different structuring of the dramatic conflict is found in the two stories also, since in Mark the dispute is joined *before* Jesus heals, while in John the healing is private and the dispute occurs *afterward.* However, these narratives both betray signs of a kind of literary development that indicates a similar function in Mark and John.

The pronouncement story in Mark 2: 1–12 falls apart in the reader's hands into a simple miracle story – verses 1–5a and 10b–12 – and a controversy with Jewish scribes which has evidently been inserted into the middle – verses 5b–10a.[30] When the controversy is removed, the original miracle can be read smoothly as an account of the miracle worker's powers. In addition, the faith of the four friends of the paralytic, central to the frame miracle story (compare verse 5a), disappears completely in the central controversy section, while the controversy over Jesus' authority to forgive sins is not mentioned again in the frame miracle story. Form critics have focused a great deal of attention on this process, common in the gospel tradition, of straightforward miracle stories being altered into conflicts with Jewish representatives. The process of opening up a narrative to sandwich other material in between can also be seen often in Mark.[31]

Turning to John 5: 1–16, we note that verses 2–9a contain a miracle story with no hint of a conflict. In 9b, we are told for the first time that this healing occurred on the Sabbath, and the healed man is then interrogated, not by Jesus, but by "the Judeans." The dialogues which follow in 5: 10–15 reflect Johannine themes and methods. Opposition to Jesus' *healing* on the Sabbath, the usual charge leveled against him, is replaced in John by the charge that a man who has already been healed has merely *carried* something on the Sabbath. This reaction of the Judeans is depicted as an ironic but offensive pettiness. It is a typical Johannine technique to create an ironic contrast between the obtuseness of the opponents and the reality of Jesus' divine presence. The satirical tone is unmistakable, and is not unlike the irony of Plato's dialogues: the true sage is condemned by a narrow interpretation of the letter of the law over the spirit of the law (see further below regarding the trial of Jesus before Pilate). In addition, other typical Johannine elements present include the initial lack of recognition on the healed man's part of who Jesus really is (compare 4: 9), and the secret departure of Jesus (compare 7: 10).

Fortna (*Gospel,* pp. 48–54) suggests that John 5: 1–9a originally stood alone as a miracle story, with no reference to the Sabbath at all. The Sabbath issue is nowhere to be found in the miracle story itself, but only arises as an afterthought in verse 9b. The original ending of the miracle would in that case have been 14b: "Sin no more, lest something worse happen to you." Harold Attridge, however, suggests that the Sabbath issue is already present in John's source; John 7: 19–23 evidently continues the controversy that was broken off in 5: 16 in order to insert discourse material. This is indicated by the fact that 7: 19–23 does not fit well in its present location in chapter 7, and the healing Jesus refers to in 7: 23 must be that of the paralytic in chapter 5. Attridge notes that in John 9: 14 as well, the Sabbath issue is only encountered after the miracle is over, and here too John has evidently interpolated long discourses.[32]

As we look more closely at 7: 19–23, we discern layers of editing there, as we did in 5: 1–16. To begin with, verse 19 and verse 22 are very similar – the former says that Moses gave the law, while the second says that Moses gave circumcision – and they appear to represent two seams, between which we might expect to find redactional material interpolated, and we apparently do. Between the two seams is the more sweeping condemnation that none of the Judeans keeps the law. This is to be contrasted with the limited argument that follows the second part of the seam, which is that if circumcision is permitted on the Sabbath, then healing should be as well. This latter argument probably reflects an earlier moment in the Christian interpretation of Judaism.[33] If verses 19–21 are deleted, and also verse 22b as an obvious attempt to make Jesus' limited abrogation apply to all Mosaic law, then we are left with a much more coherent exchange, which can be formulated as a *chreia* response (although the exact wording is not recoverable):

(Challenge: Why do you heal on the Sabbath?)
Response: If someone receives circumcision on the Sabbath, in order that the law of Moses not be broken, are you upset at me because on the Sabbath I made a whole man well?

If this reconstructed interchange is then added to 5: 1–16, introduced by something like "Jesus answered and said" (compare verse 21a), we can postulate a coherent line of argument. The response represents an older and more limited definition of the conflict than is the case in John, and in the redactional layer the condemnation has been broadened to inlcude the total abrogation of Jewish law.[34]

Both Mark and John, then, contain miracle stories in which the controversy element is either added entirely or heavily redacted. They also both involve a paralytic who needs to be carried to be healed, although in one case he does have friends to carry him, and in the other he does not. In addition, the exact same words of healing are used in both cases (even the unusual word *krabattos*, "mat"): "Rise, pick up your mat and walk!"[35] In popular tradition, where textual fixity is not imposed, there is sometimes still a stubborn motif, a memorable association often irrelevant to the narrative movement of the story, and this motif is sometimes more durable than the structure of the story itself. This is the memorable and evocative tag-line that may remain in the oral transmission of the story, even as the surrounding elements change. Thus, although many of the motifs of the story are different in Mark and John, the almost identical words of healing may indicate that a common story tradition is present here, altered and expanded to function in similar ways in the two gospels.

Anitra Bingham Kolenkow also argues that Mark 3: 1–6 should be included in the comparison with Mark 2: 1–12 and John 5: 1–16.[36] It is a healing controversy which, like John 5: 1–16 (but unlike Mark 2: 1–12) presents as the point of contention Jesus' authority to heal on the Sabbath. Like John 7: 19–23, Jesus' response is in the form of a *chreia* (Mack, *Myth*, pp. 183, 194), although it runs differently:

(Challenge: Why do you heal on the Sabbath?)
Response: Is it permitted to do good on the Sabbath or do ill,
to save life or to kill?

As Kolenkow notes, here and in John 5: 1–16 the controversy results in a plot of the Jewish opponents to kill Jesus. The same elements thus appear in Mark 2: 1–12 and 3: 1–6 on the one hand and John 5: 1–16 and 7: 19–23 on the other: healing controversy/*chreia* response/plot to kill Jesus. This combination of motifs has been spread across two miracle stories in Mark, and broken up in John to allow for the exploration of long Johannine discourses. More important for the issues at hand, she asserts that Mark and John both used a source that contained this combination, and that it was connected to a passion account that had been rewritten to depict the ultimate resolution of this tension. However, Mark works to break the connection between healing and death as the punishment, and looks to other causes for the persecution of Jesus, while John merely extends the connection between healing and persecution. Therefore, "[w]hen the critic observes how John keeps (although adding to) the healing-controversy pattern and how Mark breaks the pattern, it is difficult to argue that John used Mark. . . . It is [hard] to argue that John would find a basis for his healing-caused-death gospel in a work like Mark which not only said that Jesus was not legally guilty but also separated healings from death by so many other controversies."

MARK 2: 18–22; 7: 1–2, 5, 14–15/JOHN 3: 25–30

Mark 2: 18–22; 7: 1–2, 5, 14–15	John 3: 25–30
18The disciples of John and the Pharisees were fasting, and people	25Then there occurred a dispute between the disciples of John and

came to him and said, "Why do the disciples of John and the disciples of the Pharisees fast, but your disciples do not fast?"

a Judean concerning cleansing.

26They came to John and said to him, "Rabbi, the one who was with you beyond the Jordan, concerning whom you have testified, behold he is baptizing and everyone is coming to him." 27John answered and said, "No one is able to receive anything unless it is given to him from heaven. 28You yourselves testify concerning me that I said, 'I am not the Christ, but I was sent before him.' 29The one who has the bride is the groom. The friend of the groom, the one who stands and hears him, rejoices greatly at the groom's voice. This joy of mine has been fulfilled. 30It is necessary for him to increase, but me to decrease."

19Jesus said to them, "Can the wedding guests fast while the groom is with them? As long as they have the groom with them they cannot fast. 20The days will come when the groom will be taken away from them; then they will fast on that day.
21No one sews a piece of unshrunk cloth on an old coat; otherwise, the new patch will tear from the old and a worse hole will apear. 22And no one puts new wine into old wineskins; otherwise, the wine will break the wineskins and both the wine and the skins will be lost. No, new wine goes into new wineskins.

7: 1–2, 5, 14–15

1The Pharisees and some of the scribes who had come from Jerusalem gathered around him, 2and when they saw that some of his disciples ate bread with defiled- that is, unwashed – hands . . . 5the Pharisees and scribes asked him, "Why do your disciples not

(compare John 3: 25 above)

observe the tradition of the elders, but eat with defiled hands?" [14]Addressing the crowd again he said to them, "All of you, hear me and understand. [15]There is nothing outside a person that can enter and defile the body, but it is the things that come out of a person that defile.

Commentary on Mark 2: 18–22; 7: 1–2, 5, 14–15/John 3: 25–30

A close comparison of these two passages reveals that they have much more in common than simply the motif of the bridegroom. In Mark the disciples of John the Baptist and the Pharisees are introduced, but their common practice of fasting gives rise to a controversy concerning Jesus' disciples' failure to fast. In John, a dispute between the disciples of John and "a Judean" is introduced, but it concerns cleansing, and it does not give rise to a controversy concerning the disciples of Jesus, but to one concerning the Baptist's relation to Jesus. The saying of the bridegroom enters in both gospels as a pithy response to the interlocutors, but is put to quite different uses.

Mack notes that Mark's version in verses 18b–19a can be analyzed as a *chreia* response:[37]

Challenge: Why do your disciples not fast?
Response: Can the friends of the groom fast while the groom is with them?

Verses 19b–20 were probaby added later, since they violate the style of the *chreia* and reflect the need of the later church to emphasize that fasting was acceptable once the groom had gone, that is, at the time of the writing. The sayings of verses 21–22 have also been attracted to this complex, adapted somewhat enigmatically to this application.

Bultmann (*John*, pp. 168–69) notes the difficulties in John 3: 25, which he attributes to its derivation from a source. A dispute between the disciples of John and a Judean concerning cleansing rituals goes nowhere, and does not relate well to the rest of the pericope. The question quickly turns to the relationship of John the Baptist to Jesus, with the exchange exhibiting the same pattern of challenge-and-response as found in Mark, although here the response does not come from the sage directly, but from his supporter John the Baptist on his behalf:[38]

Challenge: The one who was with you is baptizing and all are coming to him.
Response: The one who has the bride is the bridegroom. The best man rejoices at the sound of the groom's voice.

The point here seems to be that while Jesus is the groom, John the Baptist is his best man, and that the wedding celebration must focus on Jesus. This particular application of the bridegroom image is likely Johannine, since it serves to subordinate John the Baptist, but the use of the image in a challenge-and-response format is very close to the core of Mark's passage. Once again, everything that could reasonably pass for Markan redaction is lacking in John. Mark more than likely preserves the original form of the pericope more exactly, since there the *chreia* response bears some relationship with the introduction. In John, the *chreia* response has been altered to such a degree that the introduction (verse 25) no longer has any bearing on the dialogue; it may derive, however, from a separate, similar *chreia* response in John's source that is parallel to Mark 7: 1–5, 14–15 (Mack, *Myth*, pp. 189–92, 381); John has conflated two similar response-scenes that are preserved separately in Mark.

The similar use of the *chreia* response pattern in both Mark and John here and in other sections indicates that it may have been a staple in the earlier gospel tradition, specifically to depict the small disputes that would lead to the one great dispute. The *Life of Aesop* is similar in developing the theme that the sharp words of the sage will eventually escalate and give rise to the expiatory death and subsequent cult of the hero.

MARK 3: 20–30/JOHN 7: 19–20; 8: 48–52; 10: 19–21

Mark 3: 20–30

John 7: 19–20; 8: 48–52; 10: 19–21

20He went home and the crowd gathered again, so that they were not able to eat any bread. 21When his family heard this they went out to seize him, for they said he was insane.

19"Did not Moses give you the law? Yet none of you keeps the law. Why do you seek to kill me?" 20The crowd answered, "You are possessed by a demon! Who is trying to kill you?"

8: 48–52

22The scribes who had come down from Jerusalem said, "He is possessed by Beelzebul, and it is by the ruler of demons that he casts out demons." 23Addressing them in parables he said to them, "How can Satan cast out Satan? 24If a kingdom is divided against itself, that kingdom cannot stand.

48The Judeans answered and said to him, "Are we not right in saying that you are a Samaritan and are possessed by a demon?" 49Jesus answered, "I am not possessed by a demon, but I honor my father, while you dishonor me. 50I do not seek my own glory; the one who seeks it is also the one who judges.

25And if a house is divided against itself, that house will not stand. 26If Satan rises up against himself and is divided, he is not able to stand but comes to an end. 27No one can enter a strong man's house to steal his possessions without first binding the strong man; then he can rob his house. 28Truly, I say to you that all sins will be forgiven people, and all the blasphemies they utter, 29but whoever blasphemes against the holy spirit will never have forgiveness, but will be guilty of an eternal sin." 30For they had said, "He is possessed by an unclean spirit."

51Truly, truly, I say to you, whoever keeps my word will never see death." 52The Judeans then said to him, "Now we know that you are possessed by a demon! Abraham and the prophets died, yet you say, 'If anyone keeps my word, that person will never taste death.'"

10: 19–21

19A division then arose among the Judeans concerning these words. 20For many of them said, "He is possessed by a demon and is mad. Why do you listen to him?" 21But others said, "These are not the words of one possessed by a demon. Could a demon open the eyes of the blind?"

Commentary on Mark 3: 20–30/
John 7: 19–20; 8: 48–52; 10: 19–21

Bultmann (*History*, p. 13) held that two accusations are contained in this Markan pericope: in verse 22a the scribes assert that Jesus "has Beelzebul," that is, he is possessed by Beelzebul, and in verse 22b they say that "by the ruler of the demons he casts out demons." In the former Jesus is not controlling Satan but is controlled by him, while in the latter, Jesus as a magician has learned to manipulate the demonic powers. Everything between verses 22 and 30 reflects this second understanding, which is also the charge that is found in the Q version of these sayings (Matt 12: 22–37/Luke 11: 14–23). At verse 30, however, we find added, somewhat woodenly, "for they had said, 'he is possessed by an unclean spirit.'" The original charge was probably that Jesus seemed mad, possessed by Beelzebul; verses 22a and 30 likely constitute a seam, between which new material has been added concerning Jesus invoking the power of Beelzebul, the same charge that is in Q.

Now we turn to what is in John. Four times John reflects the charge that Jesus "has a demon," but without much of a context or narrative. John never mentions the charge that Jesus heals by the power of Satan/Beelzebul. We can now compare the various conceptions of the charges against Jesus in this way:

Mark 3: 20–22a, 30	Mark 3: 22b–29	Q	John
possessed by Beelzebul	heals by power of Beelzebul	heals by power of Satan	possessed by demon

John's conception corresponds exactly with what has been postulated for the *source* level of Mark (3: 20–22a, 30), and in this level of Mark, just as in John, there is little narrative context. It is also striking that in both Mark and John the demon-possession charge is connected with the accusation that Jesus was insane (Mark 3: 21, John 10: 20, and by implication 7: 20 and perhaps 8: 52). In these texts the charge is also more connected with Jesus' words than with his healing. Thus Mark's likely source, but not Mark's redaction, is paralleled in John.

Part Two   Mark 5: 21–10: 52/John 4: 46–11: 57

With this section we proceed to a crucial test of our working hypothesis. Whereas the parallels in the first major section above at times reflected a different order, here the parallels are closer, and for the most part follow the same order. This is important for establishing both that the parallels are not simply independently circulating narratives and also that the similar order does not begin with the passion narrative. It is present to some extent at the beginning of the two gospels, grows more striking by Mark 5/John 4, and continues all the way to the end. As noted in chapter 1, Morton Smith argued in 1978 that the middle and end of Mark and John were parallel and reflected their use of a common narrative tradition.[39] Here I am carrying forward his suggestion, and shall try to argue his case more convincingly.

As we turn to this central section, an alternative theory for Mark's ordering that has won wide acceptance must also be considered. Paul Achtemeier, taking up the older observation that many of Mark's miracles are in doublets – two miraculous feedings, two women healed, two miracles on the sea – hypothesized that what the gospel author had at hand were two catenae or chains of miracle stories, which Mark incorporated into a connected narrative and rearranged slightly:[40]

Catena I	Catena II
Stilling of the storm (4: 35–41)	Jesus walks on the sea (6: 45–51)
Gerasene demoniac (5: 1–20)	Blind man of Bethsaida (8: 22–26)
Woman with a hemorrhage (5: 25–34)	Syrophoenician woman (7: 24b–30)
	Deaf man (7: 32–37)
Jairus' daughter (5: 21–23, 35–43)	Feeding of the 4,000 (8: 1–10)
Feeding of the 5,000 (6: 34–44, 53)	

Although Achtemeier was forced to rearrange the order of the blind man of

Bethsaida in Catena II, a possible reason for Mark's alteration lay at hand: Mark wanted to begin and end the crucial central section of chapters 8–10 with a healing of a blind man, a metaphor for the blindness of the disciples. The plausibility of Achtemeier's suggestion of two parallel catenae of miracles is so appealing that the theory quickly became an operating assumption of other scholars.[41] Each of the catenae begins with a miracle of Jesus on the sea, followed by three healing miracles, and then a miraculous feeding of a multitude. The miraculous sea crossings and miracles of abundant feeding which began and concluded each catena might have evoked the Exodus story, and the three central healings are parallel to the Elijah and Elisha cycles in 1 and 2 Kings. The thesis is extremely attractive, since it accounts for the doublets, accounts for the order which is almost the same, and provides a possible insight into how and why miracle stories were first collected before they were incorporated into the longer narratives of the gospels. Achtemeier himself notes the allusions to the eucharist in the culminating feeding miracles, and suggests that the miracle catenae functioned as narrative readings for a eucharistic mystery.

Since these miracles occupy a substantial portion of the Gospel of Mark, it would be very helpful for my present thesis that Mark and John used a common source if these central miracles were present in John in roughly the same order. We note that in John 6 there is a miraculous feeding of 5,000 followed by Jesus walking on the water, as above (which overlaps the ending of Catena I and the beginning of Catena II), and that a gentile's child is healed in both the story of the Syrophoenician woman's daughter in Mark 7: 24–30 and the official's son in John 4: 46–54. The possibility of a relation between the miracle catenae of Mark and the signs of John certainly suggests itself, but if the catenae circulated independently, it is significant that neither of them overlaps with John's miracles to any significant extent.[42] Achtemeier's attractive hypothesis, therefore, does not corroborate my thesis, and we are left with very little that can be called a common group of miracle stories between Mark and John.

However, if the miracles of the two catenae are lined up end to end – that is, in their actual order in Mark – and compared with the order of the miracles in John, other, more compelling similarities become apparent:

Mark	John
Stilling of the storm	
Gerasene demoniac	
Woman with a hemorrhage	Woman at well
Jairus' daughter	Official's son
	Healing at Bethzatha
Feeding of the 5,000	Feeding of the 5,000
Walking on water	Walking on water
Syrophoenician woman	

Deaf-mute
Feeding of the 4,000
Blind man of Bethsaida   Crippled man at Bethzatha

Note that the blind man of Bethsaida, which Achtemeier suggested had been moved by Mark from its earlier ordering, has been returned here to its original position. The Healing at Bethzatha in John, however, has been moved on the assumption that chapter 5 and 6 have been transposed (see below).

It might be objected that miracle stories listed as "parallel" here have little in common; for instance, the woman with a hemorrhage in Mark and the woman at the well in John are only alike in depicting a female interlocutor. However, this is also true in Achtemeier's parallel arrangement, specifically in regard to the woman with a hemorrhage and the Syrophoenician woman, and indeed to the other healing miracles as well. It might also be objected that to achieve this parallel arrangement one must introduce an external argument to justify reversing John 5 and 6. But the same thing is true for Achtemeier's hypothesis concerning the reordering of the blind man of Bethsaida. Following upon this attempt to unsettle Achtemeier, let us consider Smith's theory of the parallel structure of Mark and John, which is presented here slightly modified:

Mark		*John*	
5: 21–43	Healing Jairus' daughter	4: 46–54	Healing official's son
6: 1–6	Prophet without honor	4: 43–45	Prophet without honor

Non-parallel material:
  Mission of the twelve
  Death of John the Baptist

6: 30–44	Feeding of the 5,000	6: 1–15	Feeding of the 5,000
6: 45	And immediately he made his disciples get into the boat and go ahead of him to the other side to Bethsaida.	6: 16–17	When evening came, his disciples went down to the sea, and getting into a boat they proceeded across toward Capernaum.
6: 46	And taking his leave of them, he went up on the mountain to pray.	6: 15	Jesus then, knowing that they were about to come and seize him in order to make him king, went up on the mountain again by himself.
6: 47–52	Walking on the sea	6: 16–21	Walking on the sea
6: 54–55	And when Jesus and the disciples got out of the boat, immediately the people recognized him.	6: 24–25	When the crowd saw that Jesus was not there, or his disciples, they themselves got into the boats and went to Capernaum seeking Jesus.

Non-parallel material:
  Dispute on handwashing
  Syrophoenician woman
  Deaf man
  Feeding of the 4,000

8: 11 Demand for a sign	6: 30 Demand for a sign
8: 14–21 Discussion: Jesus suffices for bread	6: 31–59 Discussion: Jesus is the bread of life
8: 22–26 Blind man of Bethsaida	5: 2–47 Crippled man at Bethzatha (reordered)
8: 27–30 Peter's confession: Peter is Satan	6: 66–69 Peter's confession: Judas is a devil

Non-parallel material:
  Sayings on self-sacrifice
  Transfiguration
  Demoniac boy

9: 30–31 Leaving there, they proceeded through Galilee, but he did not want anyone to know; for he was teaching his disciples, saying to them that the Son of Humanity will be betrayed into human hands and they will kill him.	7: 1 After this Jesus was walking about in Galilee; for he did not want to walk about in Judea, because the Jews sought to kill him.
	Non-parallel material: Jesus' brothers taunt him.

Non-parallel material:
  Dispute on precedence
  Stranger who exorcised
  Sayings on scandals

10: 1a He arose from there and went into the region of Judea . . .	7: 10 When his brothers went up to the festival, he also went up.
	Non-parallel material: Disputes in Jerusalem Man born blind Sayings on door to sheep Appeal to witness of works
10: 1b . . . beyond the Jordan, and again crowds gathered around him, and again as was his custom,	10: 40–41a And again he went beyond the Jordan into the region where John was first baptizing,

79

he began to teach them.

and he remained there, and many came to him.

Non-parallel material:
   Question on divorce
   Blessing of children
   Rich young ruler
   Sayings on scandals

10: 32   They were on their way going up to Jerusalem, and Jesus was proceeding ahead of them, and they were amazed, and those who followed were afraid.

11: 7–8   After this he said to the disciples, "Let us go again into Judea." His disciples said to him, "Rabbi, just now the Judeans were seeking to kill you, and you are going back there?"

10: 32–34   Jesus prophesies his own passion and resurrection.

Secret Mark: Jesus raises dead man in Bethany

10: 35–45   Ransom for many

11: 11–16   Jesus prophesies Lazarus' resurrection.

11: 17–44   Jesus raises Lazarus in Bethany.

11: 45–53   It is better that one man die for the people.

Non-parallel material:
   Healing of blind Bartimaeus

Passion narrative begins.

Passion narrative begins.

Two important consequences of this chart demand our attention: (1) it is not just the episodes themselves that are parallel, but in many cases the transitions between episodes as well; and (2) the material in each gospel that is not paralleled in the other almost always appears in blocks, rather than isolated episodes, suggesting that an older narrative structure existed, into which each redactor, at certain points, has inserted a considerable amount of new material. These two points argue strongly against the position of those scholars, such as Helmut Koester and James Robinson, who attribute the parallel order of material to the independent use of a biographical literary model.

Now we proceed to this middle group of texts, keeping the closer parallel order in mind.

MARK 5: 21–24, 35–43/JOHN 4: 46–54

Mark 5: 21–24, 35–43

21When Jesus had crossed again in the boat to the other side, a great crowd gathered around him; he was beside the sea.

22And one of the leaders of the synagogue by the name of Jairus came to him, and when he saw him, he fell at his feet 23and implored him repeatedly, "My daughter is about to die. Come and lay your hands on her so that she will be made well and live." 24So Jesus departed with him.

35While he was talking, they came from the house of the leader of the synagogue and said, "Your daughter is dead. Why do you still trouble the teacher?" 36Jesus overheard what was said and said to the leader of the synagogue, "Do not fear, only believe."

(cf. Mark 5: 35 above)

John 4: 46–54

46He came again to Cana of Galilee, where he had turned water into wine.
And a certain official was there whose son was ill in Capernaum. 47When he heard that Jesus had come from Judea to Galilee, he went to him and asked him to come down and heal his son, for he was about to die.

48Jesus then said to him, "Unless you people see signs and wonders, you do not believe." 49The official said to him, "Lord, come down before my son dies." 50Jesus said to him, "Proceed. Your son is alive."

(cf. John 4: 51 below)

The man believed what Jesus said to him and proceeded.
51But as he was going, his servants met him and told him that his son was alive. 52He asked them when he began to recover, and they told him, "Yesterday at about the seventh hour the fever left him." 53The father realized that it was at that hour that Jesus said to him, "Your son is alive," so he and his

whole household believed.
54This was the second sign Jesus performed after he came out of Judea into Galilee.

37And he did not permit anyone to follow him except Peter, James and John the brother of James. 38They entered into the house of the head of the synagogue, and he saw a commotion and people weeping and wailing loudly, 39and he entered and said to them, "Why are you making a commotion and weeping? The child is not dead, but sleeping." 40But they laughed at him. He put all of them outside, and took the father and mother of the girl and those who were with him and entered into where the girl was. 41He took the girl by the hand and said, "Talitha koum," which translated means, "Little girl, I say to you, get up." 42And immediately the girl got up and walked about, for she was twelve years old. They were overcome with amazement. 43He strictly instructed them that no one was to know about this, and ordered them to give her something to eat.

Commentary on Mark 5: 21–24, 3–43/John 4: 46–54

Although John's miracle here of the healing of an official's son is more often compared with the healing of the centurion's servant in Q (Matt 8: 5–13/Luke 7: 1–10), this relationship is not important for our purposes; it merely indicates the existence of multiple versions of many of the miracle stories, one of which is now found in Q.43 Although the similarities of this passage in John to Mark's healing of Jairus' daughter are not as obvious at first and are rarely commented on, there are interesting formal similarities just beneath the surface of the two, and it becomes particularly interesting when we consider their parallel position in the series of episodes in this central section.

Mark	*John*
Jairus, leader of synagogue	royal official
beseeches Jesus	beseeches Jesus
concerning daughter near death	concerning son near death
	Jesus: "Your son lives"
	man believes
Jesus goes to daughter	Jesus goes to son
as they are walking, people come	as they are walking, servants come
saying that she has died	saying that he has recovered.
Jesus: "Do not fear; only believe."	

From this point, the two miracles proceed differently: in Mark, when Jesus arrives at the house, he commands the mourners to leave, and proceeds, with some fanfare, to heal the girl. The command to the girl is retained in Aramaic. In John, on the other hand, the report that comes is that the boy has been healed; the official then inquires the time, and finds that it is the very time when Jesus had said his son would live. The stories thus begin very similarly, and both contain the striking motif of the people met along the way. The different endings then follow necessarily upon the opposite reports: in one the child has died, and in the other, he has recovered. The motif of believing, which occurs in some but by no means all gospel miracle accounts, is also similar. If one excises the clearly Johannine addition in verse 48,[44] the motif of believing is much closer; it is simply found in a slightly different location.

Redactional features can be seen in Mark which, if eliminated, reduce the differences even further. Mark 5: 21 is the sort of geographical notice that is ubiquitous in the first few chapters of that gospel. Verse 37 also interrupts the flow of the narrative to focus on Mark's favorite disciples, and to cement their role in the account, a common Markan motif. The command to secrecy at the end is also Markan. As for John, other than verses 48–49, there is little that clearly derives from the pen of John. The introduction may be redactional, calling to mind the first "sign" in chapter 2, but along with the ending, it may also derive from the designations of the miracles in the tradition.

As noted, the similar position of Mark's and John's miracles in the gospel framework is important. These two miracles precede the feeding of the 5,000 and the walking on the water. Further, if, as many scholars aver, John 5 and 6 have been transposed, then the sequence issue becomes even more compelling: the two miracles are closely juxtaposed to the "prophet without honor" saying, with only a minor inversion of order (see below).

Mark 6: 1–6	John 4: 43–45
[1]Jesus left there and went to his hometown, followed by his disciples. [2]When the Sabbath came, he began to teach in the synagogue. Many who heard were astounded, saying, "Where does he get all this? What is this wisdom that has been given to him? How does he perform such miracles? [3]Is this not the carpenter, the son of Mary and brother of James, Joses, Judas, and Simon? And aren't his sisters here with us?" And they were offended by him. [4]Jesus said to them, "A prophet is not without honor except in his own country and among his own kin and in his own house." [5]And he was not able to perform any miracle there, aside from laying his hands on a few sick people and healing them. [6]He was amazed at their lack of faith.	[43]After two days, Jesus left there and went to Galilee, [44]for he himself had testified that a prophet receives no honor in his own country. [45]When he came to Galilee, the Galileans received him, because they had seen all the things he had done at the festival in Jerusalem, since they had been at the festival themselves.

Commentary on Mark 6: 1–6/John 4: 43–45

The saying of the prophet without honor is associated with the same episodes in Mark and John, but the order is somewhat different. This does not argue against the overall similarity of the order at this point, however; it simply indicates that there was some editorial rearrangement of scenes, just as we find in the minor inversions of material in Matthew's and Luke's appropriation of Mark and Q.

Mark 6: 1–6 is similar to Mark 1: 21–28, where Jesus' teaching in a synagogue also elicits a surprised reaction. Here, however, it turns negative: if Jesus is known to the people of his home territory, he must not be a true prophet.[45] Mark 6 situates the saying quite clearly: Jesus goes to his hometown and is rejected; in fact, the townspeople are scandalized because the greatness of his teachings and miracles cannot be reconciled with his local origins; he is only a carpenter, only the boy whom they know, only the brother of people they know. The exact nature of their objection is unclear. The underlying problem could be that Jesus was considered to have been born in the wrong city (Nazareth, where the story takes place, rather than Bethlehem, David's city and the expected birthplace of the Messiah), but this is not stated in Mark. It is not clear whether the negative reaction is from the townspeople who know Jesus' relatives, or from the relatives as well (verse 4). The story may reflect an attempt to explain Jesus' lack of popularity among his kin and friends in Nazareth, in a region where it was perhaps known that there were few converts.

The focus on the members of his family can be interpreted from two different perspectives. As Gerd Theissen asserts, Jesus' rebuke of his mother, brothers, and sisters in Mark can be seen as a justification for later wandering Christian prophets, who were forced to break their family ties.[46] From another point of view, however, the conflict between the immediate family members and the disciples reflects a tension which might have developed between those, on the one hand, who follow the family members' traditions, i.e., the traditions associated with Mary or those with James the brother of Jesus, and those, on the other hand, who follow the traditions of the disciples. According to Werner Kelber, in the early church the traditions which were in the name of the family members were still transmitted orally, while the apostolic tradition – especially the tradition about Peter – was in the process of becoming a written tradition, that is, a gospel.[47] In this view, Jesus here comes out strongly on the side of the disciples and the written gospel.

Both Mark and John contain odd contradictions that reflect their separate redactional concerns. Mark adds to Jesus' lack of honor his inability to perform miracles there, *although he healed some* (Mark 6: 5–6). Although it is difficult to reconcile these verses, Vernon Robbins argues persuasively that Mark intentionally suppresses the word *semeion* for miracle, usually associated with the eschatological prophet, and uses *dunamis* instead (as here).[48] The hand of Mark is therefore visible here, even if it is not clear what the redactor intends. At John 4: 43–45 as well, the saying about the lack of honor in Jesus' home area is preserved, but contradicted: a prophet has no honor in his own country, but Jesus is welcomed nevertheless, and the Galileans apparently believe because of his signs. In John's redaction, however, Jesus' "own country" could refer to Judea and not Galilee, in the sense that Jesus is a Jew and would consider Judea and Jerusalem his spiritual home.[49] Brown notes all this (*John*, p. 1.187), but insists that Judea is not Jesus' "country." This is much too limited a reading, however, tantamount to saying that the president of the United States does not count Washington, D.C. the capital of his country because it does not lie in his home state. Jesus' "nation" is Judea as the center of Judaism, Jerusalem being its "capital," or more precisely, its temple-city. The fact that Jesus' native region is Galilee does not contradict that. For John, the area of Galilee and its inhabitants, including Samaritans, are positive, and the stark contrast with Judeans (or Jews) is often brought up.[50] John's positive stance toward Galileans here takes precedence over the traditional saying about the prophet in his own country, which has now become merely vestigial (see chapter 4).

In the earlier gospel narrative tradition, Jesus was probably depicted as being rejected by both native Galileans and Judeans in turn. This episode, however, is the *locus classicus* of the rejection by Galileans.

MARK 6: 32–44/JOHN 6: 1–15

Mark 6: 32–44

32They went away in the boat to a deserted place by themselves, 33but many people saw them leaving and recognized them, and hurried there on foot from all the cities and arrived there ahead of them.

34And when he went ashore, he saw a great crowd and had pity on them, because they were "like sheep without a shepherd," and he began to teach them many things. 35It was already late, and his disciples came to him and said, "It is a deserted place and it is late. 36Send them away, so that they may go to the surrounding farms and villages and buy something to eat." 37He answered them, "Give them something to eat." And they said to him, "Are we able to go out and buy them two hundred denarii worth of bread and give them something to eat?"

John 6: 1–15

1After this, Jesus went away across the sea of Galilee, called Tiberias. 2A great crowd followed him, because they saw the signs that he had done upon the sick.

3Jesus went up on the mountain and sat there with his disciples. 4It was near Passover, the festival of the Judeans. 5Jesus lifted his eyes and saw that a great crowd had come to him.

He said to Philip, "Where are we to buy enough bread to feed them?" 6He said this to test him, for he knew what he was about to do. 7Philip answered, "Two hundred denarii worth of bread are not enough to give each of them a

38But he said to them, "How many loaves do you have? Go find out." And when they found out, they said, "Five, and two fish." 39So Jesus commanded them all to sit in groups on the green grass, 40and they sat in groups of hundreds and fifties.

41He took the five loaves and two fish, and looking up to heaven, he blessed it, broke the bread and gave it to the disciples for them to distribute, and the two fish he gave to them all.

42Everyone ate and was satisfied, 43and they collected twelve baskets full of pieces of bread and fish. 44The number of those who ate the bread was about 5,000 men.

little piece." 8One of his disciples, Andrew, brother of Simon Peter, said to him, 9"There is a child here who has five barley loaves and two fish, but what are they for so many?" 10Jesus said, "Have the people sit down," for there was much grass there, and the men sat down, their number being about 5,000.

11Jesus then took the bread, and after he gave thanks, distributed it to those who were sitting; he did the same with the fish, as much as they wanted.

12When they were filled, he said to the disciples, "Gather up the remaining pieces, so that nothing is lost." 13They then gathered them up and filled twelve baskets with pieces from the five loaves that they had left over after the people had eaten.

14When the people saw the sign which he did, they said, "This is truly the prophet who is coming into the world." 15Since Jesus knew that they were about to come and seize him to make him king, he went away again to the mountain by himself.

Commentary on Mark 6: 32–44/John 6: 1–15

One of the interesting aspects of the parallels between Mark and John is the fact that they often reveal a similarity in sense, structure, and motif, but not in the use of the same Greek words.[51] Here, for instance, in both Mark and John, a transition is effected by Jesus withdrawing with his disciples to a more deserted place. Yet, although Smith emphasizes the words in common, these are actually very few: in the first few verses, only "went away," "buy something to eat," and "two hundred denarii." Some of these differences can be immediately attributed to the redaction of the two gospel authors: the Markan phrase "began to teach," and the biblical quotation (verse 34), and John's brief reference to "signs" and Passover. John's singling out of Philip to ask a question is probably redactional; it is similar to the exchange at 12: 21–22. Further, Andrew is often favored in John's account, and here he suggests a solution: a child has five loaves and two fish.

The relation of the feeding narratives to the developing eucharistic traditions has long been recognized. Some of the words common to the two accounts would have been associated with the eucharist, which the Christian audience would have recognized: "he took the loaves . . . blessed/gave thanks . . . and gave . . ." Other words could early on have become fixed elements in the story: "fish," "they were filled," "pieces," "twelve baskets," "5,000 men." Both feeding stories, then, have eucharistic elements, although Mark's perhaps more than John's (Brown, *John*, p. 1.239). John also reflects possible influences of two other narrative traditions: the Elisha miracle at 2 Kgs 4: 42–44, and the early Christian eucharist tradition in *Didache* 9–10 (Brown, *John*, pp. 1.246, 248). In the latter, there is an emphasis on the mountain setting and the eschatological gathering of the people. It is likely, then, that John is not dependent on Mark at this point, but on an earlier gospel narrative that presented a "narrativized" version of the eucharist, and a eucharist tradition perhaps at some remove from Mark's and Paul's, but parallel to the *Didache*.

John's conclusion here, 6: 14–15, is confusing, but very intriguing in terms of early traditions. On the basis of the signs Jesus has performed, he is greeted as the eschatological prophet, and like Elijah who is to come, has multiplied loaves (Brown, *John*, pp. 1.234–35). Moreover, the people try to make him king, but he evades them, which implies a rejection of the royal messianic typology. Do these verses reflect a concern of the earlier gospel tradition about Jesus as a prophet or as the eschatological prophet? It is difficult to draw any conclusions, especially since Mark lacks any such reference here, but this question will be raised again in chapter 4.

MARK 6: 45–52/JOHN 6: 16–21

Mark 6: 45–52	John 6: 16–21
45Then Jesus commanded his disciples to board the boat and go ahead of him to Bethsaida on the other side, while he dismissed the crowd. 46He took his leave of them and went away to the mountain to pray.	16When evening came, his disciples went down to the sea, 17got on board a boat, and went across the sea to Capernaum.
47When evening came, the boat	Darkness had already fallen, but

was in the middle of the sea, and he was alone on the land. [48]He saw them struggling as they went, for the wind was against them. About the fourth watch of the night he came to them, walking on the sea, and passed beside them. [49]When they saw him walking on the sea, they thought he was a ghost, and cried out. [50]They all saw him and were terrified, but he spoke to them and said, "Have courage, it is I. Do not be afraid." [51]Jesus got into the boat with them and the wind subsided, and they were completely astounded, [52]for they did not understand about the bread, but their hearts were hardened.

Jesus had not yet come to them. [18]The sea was churning, for the wind was blowing.

[19]When they had proceeded about three or four miles from shore, they saw Jesus walking upon the sea, approaching the boat, and they were afraid,

[20]but he said to them, "It is I. Do not be afraid." [21]They wanted to take him into the boat, but immediately the boat came to the shore where they were heading.

Commentary on Mark 6: 45–52/John 6: 16–21

These two accounts of the walking on the water have many similarities. In both cases, the disciples embark in a boat across the Sea of Galilee (with different destinations in the two gospels), while Jesus stays behind and goes away by himself to a mountain. When evening comes, the boat experiences difficulties because of rough or contrary winds.[52] In each gospel, when Jesus appears walking on the water, the disciples are frightened. Jesus' response is nearly identical in the two narratives: "(Have courage,) it is I; do not be afraid." Mark and John in this passage reflect typical theophany scenes – the fear and confusion of the people, the reassurance of the one appearing – but as above, they often use different words to describe it. "It is I; do not be afraid" is one of the few phrases in common between the two versions, and was likely a stable line in the oral narrative tradition.[53]

There are also several minor differences in the two narratives. Although both Mark and John describe the embarking of the disciples onto a boat without Jesus, the action occurs somewhat differently in each gospel. Mark is more natural: Jesus commands the disciples to go ahead of him across the sea while he goes up the mountain to pray, while in John, Jesus' absence is unexplained. In both narratives the people descend upon Jesus once the boat makes shore, but for different reasons. In Mark, the crowds bring people to be healed; in John, there is an awkward digression in order to draw out the import of the walking on the water. But it is in the conclusions of the story that we find the most significant difference: in Mark, the obtuseness of the disciples is emphasized – a favorite Markan theme – while in John the miracle of walking on the sea is followed by what may be an accompanying miracle, the instantaneous transportation of the boat to land (verse 21). Thus it is easy to envision here a common miracle story that has been developed in a characteristic way in Mark and somewhat obscured in John. However, the distinctively Markan redaction does not appear in John.

MARK 8: 11–21/JOHN 6: 26–34

Mark 8: 11–21	John 6: 26–34
	26Jesus answered and said to them, "Truly, truly, I say to you, you seek me not because you saw signs, but because you ate your fill of the loaves. 27Do not work for the food that perishes, but for the food that remains for eternal life, which the Son of Humanity will give you. God the Father has placed his seal on him." 28They then said to him, "What must we do to work the works of God?" 29Jesus answered and said to them, "This is the work of God, that you believe in the one he has sent." 30They then said to him, "What sign are you doing for us to see and believe in you? What work are you doing?
(cf. Mark 8: 15–20 below)	
11The Pharisees came and began to debate with him, testing him by seeking from him a sign from heaven. 12He groaned in his spirit and said, "Why does this generation seek a sign? Truly, I say to you, no sign will be given to this generation." 13He departed from them and again got into a boat and went across to the other side. 14They, however, had forgotten to bring bread, and did not have any in the boat with them except for one loaf. 15Jesus instructed them and said, "Take heed, and beware the leaven of the Pharisees and the leaven of Herod." 16They said to	(cf. John 6: 26 above)

each other, "It is because we have no bread." [17]Jesus knew this and said to them, "Why are you discussing the fact that you have no bread? Do you not yet perceive or understand? Have your hearts become hardened? [18]'Having eyes, do you not see, and ears, do you not hear?' And do you not recall, [19]when I broke the five loaves for the 5,000, how many baskets full of pieces you collected?" They said to him, "Twelve." [20]"And when I broke the seven loaves for the 4,000, how many baskets did you collect?" They said to him, "Seven." [21]He said to them, "Do you not yet understand?"

[31]Our fathers ate manna in the desert, as it is written, 'He gave them bread from heaven to eat.'" [32]Jesus said to them, "Truly, truly, I say to you, Moses did not give you the bread from heaven, but my father gives you the true bread from heaven. [33]For the bread of God is the one who comes down from heaven and gives life to the world." [34]They then said to him, "Lord, gives us this bread always."

Commentary on Mark 8: 11–21/John 6: 26–34

Mark and John both have at the center of these two dialogues the request for a sign, *semeion*; in Mark it comes from the Pharisees, in John from the people gathered to hear him (6: 22). The Pharisees in Mark reveal a clearly hostile intent, coming as they do in order to test him. In John the hostile intent is only gradually revealed, in typical Johannine fashion (compare 7: 31–59), as the interlocutors come to be identified as "the Judeans" (6: 41).

Mark has likely inserted at 8: 12 a saying of Jesus (similar to the Q passage Luke 11: 29–30/Matt 12: 39–40) that is totally lacking in John, and yet the discourse in Mark that follows is almost "Johannine": a lofty and metaphorical statement by Jesus (verse 15) is met with an ironic misunderstanding on the mundane level (verse 16), which opens up into a theological discourse by Jesus (verses 17–21; compare John 3: 3–21; 4: 10–15). Still, there are several elements that appear to be Markan: the inclusion of Herod, the hardening of the disciples' hearts (compare 6: 52), and the reference to *two* feeding miracles (there is only one in John).

The two discourses are both concerned with the "true" meaning of "bread," following the miraculous multiplication of loaves. Mark contrasts the leaven of the Pharisees and of Herod with the multiplication of loaves that Jesus has accomplished. John provides a somewhat analogous argument: the manna that Moses provided in the desert is now superseded by the one who comes down from heaven (Brown, *John*, pp. 1.201–2). The two gospels have also, however, taken somewhat different turns: Mark's has attracted the saying in verse 12 that is paralleled in Q, while in John we find the "vertical" christology of the descending and ascending redeemer (Meeks, "The Man from Heaven").

MARK 8: 27–38/JOHN 6: 66–71, 12: 23–34

Mark 8: 27–38

27Jesus and his disciples went into the villages of Caesarea Philippi, and along the way he asked the disciples, "Who do people say that I am?" 28They said to him, "Some say John the Baptist, others Elijah, others one of the prophets." 29But he asked them, "Who do you say that I am?" Peter responded, "You are the Christ."

30Jesus commanded them not to tell anyone about him.

31He began to teach them that the Son of Humanity must suffer many things, and be rejected by the elders, chief priests and scribes, and be killed, and after three days, to rise. 32He said these things plainly. Peter took him aside and began to rebuke him, 33but he turned, and seeing the disciples, rebuked Peter and said, "Get behind me, Satan, because you are not devoted to the things of God, but to human things."

34Turning to the crowd and to his disciples, he said to them, "Let those who want to follow me deny themselves, take up their cross,

John 6: 66–71, 12: 23–34

66As a result of this, many of his disciples turned back, and would no longer accompany him. 67Jesus said to the twelve, "Do you also want to go away?" 68Simon Peter answered him, "Lord, to whom shall we go? You have the words of eternal life, 69and we believe and know that you are the holy one of God.

70Jesus answered them, "Did I not choose twelve? Yet one of you is a devil." 71He was speaking of Judas, son of Simon Iscariot, one of the twelve, for he was about to betray him.

12: 23–34

23Jesus answered them and said, "The hour has come for the Son of Humanity to be glorified. 24Truly, truly, I say to you, unless a grain of wheat falls to the ground and dies, it alone remains; but if it dies, a great harvest is produced. 25Those who love their life lose it, and those who hate their life in this and follow me. 35For those who would save their life will lose it, and those who would lose their life for my sake and for the sake of the gospel will save it. 36What advantage is it if people gain the whole world, yet lose their life? 37Indeed, what can they give in exchange for their life?

38And whoever is ashamed of me and my words in this adulterous and sinful generation, of that person will the Son of Humanity be ashamed when he comes in the glory of the Father, accompanied by the holy angels.

world preserve it for eternal life. 26If someone wants to serve me, let that person follow me, and wherever I am, there also will be my servant. Anyone who serves me will be honored by the Father. 27Now 'my soul is troubled,' but what shall I say – 'Father, save me from this hour'? But this was why I came to this hour. 28Father, glorify your name. A voice came from heaven, "I have glorified it, and I shall glorify it again." 29The crowd standing there who heard it said that there was a clap of thunder, but others said, "An angel spoke to him." 30Jesus answered and said, "This voice came not for my sake, but for yours. 31Now there is a judgment upon the world, now the ruler of this world has been cast out. 32I shall be lifted up from the earth, and draw all people to myself." 33He said this to indicate by what sort of death he was about to die. 34The crowd then answered him, "We have heard from the law that the Messiah remains forever, so why do you say that the Son of Humanity must be lifted up? Who is the Son of Humanity?"

Commentary on Mark 8: 27–38/John 6: 66–71; 12: 23–34

At the center of Mark there are three predictions of the death of the Son of Humanity (8: 31; 9: 31; and 10: 33–34); these have figured heavily in assessments of Mark's "theology of the cross" and "theology of the way."[54] Mark's three predictions can be summarized thus:

8: 31	*9: 31*	*10: 33–34*
Jesus teaches that Son of Humanity must suffer and	Jesus teaches that Son of Humanity will be betrayed into	Jesus tells disciples that Son of Humanity will be handed over to

be rejected by elders, chief priests, and scribes	human hands	chief priests and scribes
		who will condemn him, hand him over to Gentiles to mock him
to be killed; after three days he will rise	to be killed; after three days he will rise	and kill him; after three days he will rise

These detailed formulations are very similar to the early creedal statements such as 1 Cor 15: 1–3.

There are also three sayings in John concerning the "lifting up" of the Son of Humanity (3: 14–15, 8: 28, 12: 23–34), but they are not placed centrally, and also lack many of Mark's important motifs. John's predictions also bear no relation to the creedal formulas. Nevertheless, because there are three of them, and because they concern the fate of the Son of Humanity, they are often likened to Mark's three passion predictions. The Johannine predictions, pulled from their context in discourses, are:

3: 14–15	*8: 28*	*12: 23, 32–34*
Ascending Son of Humanity; glorified; as Moses lifted serpent		Son of Humanity
so will Son of Humanity be lifted	You will lift the Son of Humanity	when I am lifted;
	and know I am he;	who is Son of Humanity?
that believers may have eternal life	many believed	believe in light

John's predictions emphasize the vertical ascent of the Son of Humanity, the identity of Jesus as the Son of Humanity who ascends to the Father, and the relation of this to believing. This is likely Johannine redaction, even if it is a development of earlier traditions. The predictions in John are also made to outsiders, while Mark's are esoteric instruction to the disciples (Bultman, *History*, p. 331). The two gospels thus differ in the stereotyped pattern created for these prediction passages, as well as in the location of the sayings within the narrative. Although the temptation to compare these three Son of Humanity sayings in the two gospels is strong, their relation is not clear, and an alternative comparison will be offered below for the second and third of Mark's sayings.

Mark's presentation of the three passion predictions clearly includes redactional motifs that are not found in John, but is there some older tradition that both gospels use? Let us compare some of the motifs of Mark's and John's passages presented in this section. Mark here combines motifs that are found separated in John. Though perhaps originally from separate traditions, they now appear to have been gathered by Mark into an original and very dramatic scene.[55] Mark's passage appears to be a composite of at least three traditions: (1) the questions and answers concerning Jesus' identity and the confession and renaming of Peter; (2) the predictions concerning the fate of the Son of Humanity, and (3) originally independent sayings concerning discipleship.[56] Was Mark responsible for combining these three? This is probably true for the confession of Peter and the passion prediction; it would comport with Mark's redactional motif of the obtuseness of the disciples, and they are not found together as such in John. As for the joining of the prediction concerning the Son of Humanity with the sayings concerning discipleship, however, this combination also appears in John 12: 23–34, and may be traditional.[57] Was Mark also responsible for placing the three predictions in the same section of the gospel, chapters 8–10? This is surely possible, as Mark has evidently composed this section to begin and end with a healing of a blind man – a metaphor for the disciples' lack of insight – which is in turn a powerful transition to the passion story itself.[58] However, the synopsis below will be utilized to argue that sayings similar to Mark's were already present in the gospel tradition in approximately the same position. Mark's role may then have been to place a characteristic theological stamp upon them.

A powerful example of this may be seen in the startling rebuke of Peter as "Satan" at Mark 8: 33. It is assumed by Bultmann (*History*, pp. 258–59) that Mark has introduced this as yet another means of undermining the growing authority of Peter in the early church. John does not include this, but does depict Jesus referring to Judas as "devil," retaining what is perhaps an earlier, less ironic tradition.[59] Therefore, the discrepancies between Mark's and John's placement of the three predictions concerning the Son of Humanity may result from Mark's reshaping of the material, as does the shift of the "demonic" character from Judas to Peter. The other two passion predictions in Mark do not have as many parallels to John, and have evidently been reformulated for their present role in Mark's narrative (note the relation of Mark 10: 32–34 to the passion).

To turn now to the sayings on discipleship, we see that Mark's sayings are paralleled at John 12: 25–26, albeit in reverse order.[60] The sayings in Mark and John have many words in common: following, destroying (or losing) one's soul, world, father. Further, the sense of the sayings is similar:

Mark 8: 34	*John 12: 26*
If someone wants to follow me, let him deny himself,	If someone serves me, let him follow me,

95

take up his cross, and follow me.

and where I am,
there also the servant will be.

Also:

Mark 8: 35
Whoever wishes to save his soul
will lose it;
whoever will destroy his soul
for my sake
and for the sake of the gospel
will save it.

John 12: 25
The one who loves his soul
destroys it;
the one who hates his soul in this
 world

will preserve it for eternal life.

The connection of these sayings with each other and with the prediction concerning the Son of Humanity indicates that they were already joined in the tradition when Mark and John received them.[61] Some redactional features are readily detected on each side, but it is significant that the important Markan elements, "cross" and "for the sake of the gospel," are not present in John.

Thus it appears that Mark and John both found in the tradition before them three predictions concerning the fate of the Son of Humanity, and that this prediction may have been tied to sayings concerning discipleship. It was Mark, however, who tied this to the tradition of questions and answers concerning Jesus' identity and the confession of Peter. Further, Mark may have altered a reference to Judas as the devil to Peter as Satan. Mark has evidently sharpened the christological power of these traditions considerably by grouping independent traditions together in the central section of the gospel and by interpreting them in the direction of a theology of the cross and a theology of the way. John indeed might have had a motive to eliminate all evidence of this theology of the cross, but it is equally, if not more likely, that John was unaware of this Markan development.

MARK 9: 30–31; 10: 1, 32–34/
JOHN 7: 1, 10; 10: 40–41; 11: 7–8, 11–16

Mark 9: 30–31; 10: 1, 32–34

John 7: 1, 10; 10: 40–41; 11: 7–8, 11–16

9: 30–31

7: 1

30Departing from there, they proceeded through Galilee, but he did not want anyone to know, 31for he was teaching his disciples and saying to them, "The Son of

1After this, Jesus traveled about in Galilee; he did not want to travel in Judea, because the Judeans were seeking to kill him.

Humanity is being handed over to human hands, and they will kill him, and after he has been dead three days, he will rise up."

10: 1

¹Rising up from there, he went into the region of Judea

7: 10

¹⁰When his brothers went up to Jerusalem for the festival, he also went up – not openly, but in secret.

10: 40–41

and beyond the Jordan, and again crowds came to where he was, and as was his custom, again he taught them.

⁴⁰He went away again beyond the Jordan to the place where John the Baptist had been baptizing before, and he remained there. ⁴¹Many came to him and said, "John performed no sign, but whatever John said concerning him was true."

10: 32–34

³²They were proceeding along the way up to Jerusalem, and Jesus went ahead of them. They were amazed, and those who followed him were afraid.

11: 7–8

⁷After that, he said to the disciples, "Let us go up again to Judea." ⁸The disciples said to him, "Rabbi, just now the Judeans were trying to stone you, and you want to go there?

11: 11–16

Taking aside the twelve, again he began to tell them what was about to happen to him: ³³"We are going up to Jerusalem, where the Son of Humanity will be handed over to the chief priests and scribes. They will condemn him to death and hand him over to the Gentiles, ³⁴who will jeer at him, spit on him, whip him, and kill

¹¹He said to them, "Lazarus our friend is sleeping, but I shall go in order to awaken him." ¹²The disciples said to him, "Lord, if he is asleep he will recover." ¹³But Jesus was speaking about his death, while they thought he was speaking about sleep. ¹⁴Then Jesus said to them clearly, "Lazarus is dead, ¹⁵and I am happy for your sake, so that you may believe, since I

him, and after three days he will rise again."

was not there. Let us go to him now." [16]Thomas, called the twin, then said to his fellow disciples, "Let us also go, so that we may die with him."

Commentary on Mark 9: 30–31; 10: 1, 32–34/ John 7: 1, 10; 10: 40–41; 11: 7–8, 11–16

In Morton Smith's comparison of the middle of Mark and John (see above), he includes at this point a series of minor resemblances between the gospels. They are not particularly significant from the point of view of narrative motifs, but the fact that they are *transitional*, and often *trivial*, leads one to conclude that the parallels cannot be explained as a similar ordering of originally independent episodes, as Helmut Koester and James Robinson would assert. The use of independent traditions by Mark and John would not result in similar usages in the transitional sentences, especially in connection with phrases that were not significant to the episodes. These sections might argue for the *literary* dependence of John on Mark, as some have held, but they argue *against* any view of the independent ordering of the traditions on a biographical model. Thus I combine in this section a number of passages in sequential order, albeit pulled from their context.

Mark 9: 30–31, the second passion prediction, may find a parallel in a John passage that concerns Jesus' death, but which does not mention the Son of Humanity. Mark's three passion predictions all contain references to Jesus teaching the disciples, and this redactional motif is lacking in John. John, on the other hand, is likely responsible for some of the phrasing, particularly the menacing aspect of "the Judeans," and the implication that Jesus moves back and forth between Galilee and Judea. After some non-parallel material, the Galilee/Judea issue is played on again in both gospels at Mark 10: 1a and John 7: 10.

Mark 10: 1b presents a problem. If the parallels listed here are significant, then it is odd that there would be so much added by John *between* the points corresponding to Mark 10: 1a and 10: 1b. In other words, if the parallels between Mark and John do represent the contours, and in some cases the phrasing, of the older narrative tradition, why would John appear to split a verse and insert almost four chapters of material? This is, however, a mistaken way of perceiving what has probably occurred. What John retains of the tradition behind Mark 10: 1 is two geographical references, "Judea" and "beyond the Jordan." After the first, John inserts both narratives and discourses, and returns at 10: 40–41a (equivalent to Mark 10: 1b) to move Jesus beyond the Jordan to where John had been baptizing. Retaining the parallels was never an intentional part of John's editing process, but adapting a narrative and geographical structural to a new schema.

At the end of these parallels we find Mark's third passion prediction, 10: 32–34, which is similar to Jesus' prediction of the resurrection of Lazarus in John 11: 11–16. The latter is neither a prediction of the passion of Jesus nor a Son of Humanity saying, so it is not usually likened to the three passion predictions in Mark. The synopsis, however, suggests that it is similar nevertheless. Although the three "lifting up of the Son of Humanity" passages in John are often likened to Mark's three predictions of the death of the Son of Humanity, this may be a misleading comparison. The present Johannine parallel may more closely reflect a tradition common to Mark and John. However, it is still not clear precisely what the earlier tradition may have contained at this point. Mark, as noted above, likely altered the traditional material to create three pointed predictions of the passion and death of the Son of Humanity. Likewise, John highlights the death and resurrection of Lazarus, and may have restructured this section of the narrative significantly to achieve this end.

SECRET MARK (AFTER MARK 10: 34)/ JOHN 11: 1–3, 20–22, 32–41, 43–46

Secret Mark 1: 1–13	John 11: 1–3, 20–22, 32–41, 43–46
¹They came to Bethany, where there was a woman whose brother had died.	¹There was a certain man who was ill, Lazarus of Bethany, from the same village as Mary and her sister Martha. ²Mary was the one who had anointed the Lord with ointment and wiped his feet with her hair; Lazarus, the man who was ill, was her brother. ³The sisters sent word to Jesus and said, "Lord, behold, the one whom you love is ill."
	²⁰But when Martha heard that Jesus was coming, she went to meet him, while Mary remained in the house. ²¹Martha said to
²She came and knelt before Jesus and said to him, "Son of David, have mercy on me!" ³But the disciples rebuked her.	Jesus, "Lord, if you had been here, my brother would not have died. ²²But even now I know that whatever you ask of God, it will be granted."

99

32When Mary came to where Jesus was, she saw him and fell at his feet and said, "Lord, if you had been here, my brother would not have died." 33When Jesus saw her crying, along with the Judeans who had accompanied her, he became troubled [or angry, *embrimaomai*] in his spirit, and was greatly disturbed. 34He said, "Where have you laid him?" They said to him, "Lord, come and see." 35Jesus wept. 36The Judeans then said, "Behold how he loved him!" 37But some of them said, "Could not this man, who opened the eyes of the blind, have kept this man from dying?" 38Jesus, again troubled [or angry, *embrimaomai*] in his heart, came to the tomb. It was a cave with a stone resting over the entrance. 39Jesus said, "Remove the stone." Martha, the sister of the one who died, said to him, "Lord, there is already a stench, for he has been dead for four days." 40Jesus said to her, "Did I not say that if you believe, you will see the glory of God?" 41They removed the stone.

4Jesus became angry (*orgizomai*), and went with her to the garden where the tomb was. 5Immediately a loud voice (*phone megale*) was heard from within the tomb. 6Jesus approached the tomb and rolled the stone away from the entrance. 7Immediately, he entered into where the young man was, reached out his hand, took the young man's hand and raised him. 8The young man looked at Jesus and loved him, and began begging him to be with him.

43Jesus cried out with a loud voice (*phone megale*), "Lazarus, come out!" 44The one who had died came out, his hands and feet bound with cloth, and his face wrapped with a kerchief. Jesus said to them, "Unbind him and let him go." 45Many of the Judeans who came with Mary and saw the things Jesus did believed in him, 46but some of them went to the Pharisees and told them what Jesus had done.

9They left the tomb and went to the young man's house, for he was rich. 10After six days, Jesus instructed him, 11and when evening came, the young man came to him, clothed only with a linen cloth. 12He remained with him that night, and Jesus taught him the mystery of the kingdom of God. 13He left there and returned to the other side of the Jordan.

Commentary on Secret Mark *(after Mark 10: 34)/John 11: 1–3, 20–22, 32–41, 43–46*

The fragment of Mark known as *Secret Mark* is found in a letter of Clement of Alexandria, published in 1973 by Morton Smith.[62] The text of *Secret Mark* quoted by Clement of Alexandria contains a miracle story parallel to the raising of Lazarus in John 11. Since Clement gives the location of this miracle in the text of Mark (after 10: 34), we know that it corresponds in position to John 11. It is also clear that both narratives are variants of the same miracle story. The location (Bethel), the characters (brother and sister), the raising from a tomb, the love between healer and healed – all indicate a close connection between the two. It is also significant that in *Secret Mark* 10, Jesus stays for six days, for John 12: 1 states, amid a flurry of confusing and probably interpolated movements, that six days before Passover Jesus came again to Bethel. These time designations occur nowhere else in Mark or John. Although the fragment probably did not appear in the texts of Mark that Matthew and Luke used, it is Markan in style and not dependent on the parallel story in John 11, since it lacks any of the signs of Johannine redaction found there.[63] The close relationship of *Secret Mark* to Mark is also indicated by the reference later in the text of *Secret Mark* to the healed man being naked, covered only with a linen cloth. This gives some background to the otherwise inscrutable reference at Mark 14: 51–52 to a naked man, who flees covered with a linen cloth.[64]

Secret Mark tells the story quite simply, while John's text is now rather muddled. There are two women in John who come out separately to meet him, each saying the same thing (11: 21, 32). Further, Martha is introduced at verse 39 as if for the first time. Verses 6–10 contain a separate subplot of the growing antipathy toward Jesus. Verse 38 is similar to verse 33, and a redactional digression is found in between. The issue of "sleeping" is interpreted in a Johannine fashion (11: 11–16).[65] In addition, Lazarus clearly comes in for favored treatment in John. He is loved by Jesus (11: 3, 5),[66] and it is on account of his resuscitation that plans are set in motion to kill Jesus (11: 46; compare 12: 10–11), but these are likely Johannine ideas introduced into the story; the reader was probably more familiar with Mary and Martha, with reference to whom Lazarus is introduced (Brown, *John*, p. 1.422–23). The fact that the brother is unnamed in *Secret Mark* comports well with the suggestion that Lazarus was introduced secondarily into the story.

On each side we can therefore detect the same miracle-story tradition, told in part very simply, though the story has likely been altered in each case. However, neither narrative reflects the redactional changes of the other. And it is also significant that, regardless of when *Secret Mark* was written, its location *at this point* in the gospel narrative seems assured, and its independence of John 11 indicates that it is a separate witness to the order and structure of the early gospel narrative.

MARK 10: 35–47/JOHN 11: 45–53

Mark 10: 35–45

John 11: 47–53

47The chief priests and Pharisees called a meeting of the Sanhedrin and said, "What should we do, since this man performs so many signs?"

35James and John, the sons of Zebedee, came to him and said, "Teacher, we want you to grant our request." 36He said to them, "Whatever you want me to do, I shall do for you." 37They said to him, "Grant that at the time of your glorification, one of us may sit on your right and one of us on your left." 38Jesus said to them, "You do not know what you are asking. Are you able to drink the cup that I drink or receive the baptism that I receive?" 39They said to him, "We are able." Jesus said to them, "You will drink the cup that I drink and receive the baptism that I receive, 40but to sit at my right or my left is not mine to give, but it is for those for whom it has been prepared."

41When the twelve heard this, they became upset at James and John. 42Jesus turned to them and said, "You know that among the Gentiles those whom they recognize as their rulers lord it over them, and their leading citizens oppress them. 43It should not be this way among you, but whoever would be great among you should become your servant, 44and whoever would be first among you should become the slave of all. 45For indeed the Son of Humanity did not come to be served, but to serve, and to give his life as a ransom for many."

48If we permit him to continue in this way, everyone will believe in him, and the Romans will come and destroy both our temple and our nation."

49But one of them, Caiaphas, who was high priest that year, said to them, "You know nothing, 50nor do you realize that it is far better for you if one man dies for the people, so that the whole nation not be destroyed." 51He did not say this through his own insight, but because he was high priest that year, he was prophesying that Jesus was about to die for the nation, 52and not for this nation alone, but also to gather into one all the children of God scattered abroad. 53From this day on, then, they conspired to kill Jesus.

Commentary on Mark 10: 35–45/John 11: 47–53

The parallelism here does not appear great at first, but several important similarities indicate that the parallel location of these passages in the gospel narrative is not coincidental.[67] In Mark we note first of all that the petulant request of James and John is followed by two responses, verses 38–40 and 41–45. It was argued by Martin Dibelius that verses 38–40 were inserted, and that the original response by Jesus came in verses 41–45.[68] Here Dibelius is probably correct. Verses 38–40, which contain a typically Markan emphasis on the suffering of the cross, shifts the emphasis that is found in verses 41–45. The latter is more directly political in tone: "Among the Gentiles those whom they recognize as their rulers lord it over them, and their leading citizens oppress them." It is likely that this second response is original to the story, and pre-Markan.[69] A contrast follows: "The Son of Humanity did not come to be served, but to serve, and to give his life as a ransom for many." Although the derivation of the notion of humility and service from the Son of Humanity may be Markan – a corollary of Mark's theology of the cross – the giving of life as a ransom for many may not be. It probably derives from the early Christian cult of Jesus as the dead hero, as described in chapter 2 above.

Here I have posited two motifs in Mark's passage that are pre-Markan – the oppression by Gentile rulers and the death of Jesus as a ransom for many – and it is precisely these two motifs that are visible in the quizzical passage of John 11: 45–53. In chapter 2 I argued, following C. H. Dodd, that behind the John passage lies a pre-Johannine tradition in which the death of the hero on behalf of his people is predicted through the unconscious prophecy of the high priest Caiaphas.[70] The sacrificial aspect is similar to Mark's "ransom": "You do not realize that it is far better for you if one man dies for the people, so that the whole nation not be destroyed." This similarity is often recognized, but it is also interesting that the political language, in positing an oppression by Gentiles, is similar as well: "The Romans will come and destroy both our temple and our nation." Both Mark and John evidently reflect an early Christian view that the context of Jewish–Christian conflict is the oppression by Gentile powers, and that Jesus had died as a sacrificial victim. John further contains themes of an eschatological in-gathering, paralleled in *Didache* 9–10 (verse 52), that reflect a concern for the whole people of Israel that is pre-Johannine.[71]

Part Three   Mark 11: 1–16: 20/John 12: 12–20: 23

Martin Kähler's oft-quoted characterization of Mark as a passion story with a long introduction has found much less support today than it once did, especially among those who would attribute to Mark a greater role in the creation of the gospel genre. The tendency to see the Gospel of Mark as an integrated whole is certainly correct, although I would hold that a good deal of the integrated structure of Mark's Gospel goes back to the earlier gospel narrative, and not to Mark's creation of a genre out of whole cloth. Many source-critical theories have focused on the passion narrative alone, presuming that it circulated as an independent narrative, or even on the crucifixion alone. These theories will be mentioned below. A cornerstone of these arguments is that the parallels between Mark and John are much closer in the passion narrative than in the previous chapters. I tried to show above, however, that the parallels in the central section of the gospels are almost as close as in the passion, taking away a fundamental plank of the passion-source theories. It is still quite possible that a separate passion narrative did exist early on, only to be incorporated into a longer gospel, but that hypothesis will be investigated here only in passing. It is the thesis of this study that if there was a separate passion narrative, it was already incorporated into a longer connected narrative before Mark and John used it. The present division of the gospel narrative, which separates out the passion narrative, has thus been adopted for the purposes of discussion only, not in order to argue that an independent passion narrative was used by Mark and John.

104

As the gospels now stand, the order of most of the events in the passion accounts of Mark and John are the same:

Mark	*John*
triumphal entry 11: 1–11	(see below)
prophecy in temple 11: 15–19	(moved to John 2)
Jesus' authority 11: 27–33	(moved to John 2)
teachings chs 12–13	
plot to kill Jesus 14: 1–2	plot to kill Jesus 11: 45–57
anointing at Bethany 14: 3–9	anointing at Bethany 12: 1–8
(see above)	triumphal entry 12: 12–19
Judas' plot 14: 10–11	Judas' plot 13: 1–2a
Passover with disciples 14: 12–16	Supper before Passover 13: 2b–20
prediction of betrayal 14: 17–20	prediction of betrayal 13: 21–30
Son of Humanity 14: 21	Son of Humanity 13: 31–32
Lord's Supper 14: 22–25	(compare footwashing, above 13: 2b–20)
Peter's denial 14: 26–31	Peter's denial 13: 36–38
Gethsemane prayer 14: 32–41	prayer fragment 12: 27–28a
"Arise, let us be going" 14: 42	"Arise, let us be going" 14: 31b
	Jesus' discourse and prayer 15–17
betrayal and arrest 14: 43–15: 52	betrayal and arrest 18: 1–19: 11
trial 14: 53–15: 5	trial 18: 12–19: 16
crucifixion, death, and burial 15: 6–47	crucifixion, death, and burial 19: 17–42
empty tomb 16: 1–8	empty tomb 20: 1–10
	resurrection appearances 20: 11–21: 25

In addition to these episodes, there are others in both gospels that are not parallel, but in almost every case they clearly serve a redactional function. On the Markan side, for example, are Jesus' two-part cursing of the fig tree, the controversies of chapter 12, and the apocalypse of chapter 13.

In Mark's present construction of the gospel, 14: 1 looks like the beginning of a major new section, and John's closer agreements from this point on have only served to confirm this judgment for most scholars. Lightfoot, however, suggested that the passion account which Mark used may have actually begun instead with Jesus' triumphal entry into Jerusalem in Mark 11.[72] A festal procession such as the triumphal entry would likely have ended at the temple, and the temple pronouncement of Jesus may have originally followed more closely. Lightfoot notes that Mark 11: 18, which tells of the plan of the chief priests and scribes to kill Jesus, is essentially repeated in 14: 1, creating a seam. Mark has evidently separated the entry from the passion by inserting a number of episodes, including a good deal of teaching material, culminating in the

"Markan apocalypse," chapter 13. The insertion of the teaching material can be explained as a Markan redactional alteration, since teaching is now more closely tied to the cause of the crucifixion: at Mark 11: 18, the crowd is astounded at his teaching.[73] In the present analysis, however, the distinction between the short account and the long account makes very little difference; if either existed separately, it was probably taken up very early on into a connected account that corresponds in overall scope to Mark and John.

MARK 11: 1–11/JOHN 12: 12–19

Mark 11: 1–11

[1]When they approached Jerusalem and came to Bethphage and Bethany, near the Mount of Olives, he sent out two of his disciples [2]and said to them, "Go into the village ahead of you, and when you enter it you will immediately find a colt tied up on which no one has ever sat. Untie it and bring it here. [3]If anyone says to you, 'Why are you doing this?' say, 'The Lord needs it, and will immediately send it back here.'" [4]They then went and found a colt tied in the street near a door, and they untied it. [5]Some of those standing there said to them, "What are you doing untying this colt?" [6]They responded to them as Jesus had instructed, and they permitted them to take it. [7]They brought the colt to Jesus, laid their cloaks on it, and he sat upon it.

[8]Many of them also spread their cloaks on the road, and others spread out branches that they had cut from the fields. [9]Both the ones running ahead and those follow-

John 12: 12–19

[12]On the next day, the large crowd that came to the festival heard that Jesus was coming to Jerusalem.

[13]They took palm branches and went out to meet him,

106

ing behind shouted, "Hosanna! Blessed is the one who comes in the name of the Lord! 10Blessed is the coming kingdom of our ancestor David! Hosanna in the highest!"

and cried out, "Hosanna! Blessed is the one who comes in the name of the Lord, the king of Israel!" 14Jesus found a donkey and sat upon it, as it is written, 15"Do not fear, daughter of Zion! Behold, your king is coming, sitting on the colt of an ass!" 16The disciples did not understand these things at first, but when Jesus was glorified, they remembered that these things were written about him and they had done these things for him. 17The crowd that was with him when he called Lazarus out from the tomb and raised him from the dead therefore testified. 18For this reason, the crowd met him, because they had heard that he had done this sign. 19Therefore the Pharisees said to themselves, "Just look! Nothing will avail us. Indeed, the world has gone after him!"

(compare Mark 11: 18 below)

11He entered Jerusalem and went up into the temple. When he had looked around at everything, since the hour was late, he went out to Bethany with the twelve.

Commentary on Mark 11: 1–11/John 12: 12–19

Although John has several movements into Jerusalem, Mark follows a more dramatic itinerary in which there is one fateful pilgrimage to Jerusalem, one "way of the cross," placed after Jesus' three passion predictions to his disciples. Thus, Mark's Passion Week has a more clearly demarcated beginning, at Jesus' triumphal entry seated on an ass.

Mark places the events preparatory to the triumphal entry in Bethphage and Bethany. Although the anointing of Jesus is placed later in Mark, it too takes place in Bethany. Many scholars have noted its awkward placement;[74] it is likely that Mark has moved the anointing scene later in the gospel. If these two events in Bethany are placed together, they correspond closely to the events in John 12: 1–11 and 12: 12–19. John, therefore, does not reflect

Mark's order, but more likely the order of the earlier gospel tradition. The anointment thus placed before the triumphal entry (as in John) would emphasize the theme of the installation of the king – even if it is played out ironically – for which anointment precedes the procession.

The account in Mark 11: 1–7 of Jesus sending disciples to fetch a donkey on which to ride is lacking in John. John relates the acclamation of the crowd and the prophecy/fulfillment citation very simply, while in form-critical terms, Mark includes an elaborate legend of supernatural finding, which Bultmann refers to as a fairytale.[75] This legend is balanced later in Mark with a similar one in which Jesus sends disciples to prepare the upper room for the Last Supper, also lacking in John. What Mark and John do share is "messianic exegesis" of Ps 118: 25–26. The laying of garments and branches on Jesus' path indicates a joyous celebration of victory (compare 1 Macc 13: 51; 2 Macc 10: 7) and the installation of a new king (compare 2 Kgs 9: 13). In both cases this psalm, a common part of the Jewish liturgy at festivals, is sung by the crowds at Jesus' triumphal entry into Jerusalem. Although Mark and John differ at this point in details (for example, cloaks and leafy branches in Mark, palm branches in John), what concerns us here is their methods of exegesis. First, the quotation of Psalm 118 is the only one in John not preceded by a formula of quotation, such as "as it is written." It is also one of the few scriptural quotations which Mark and John have in common. It was likely present in the traditional narrative framework in this way, with no introduction, a practice which John the redactor amended with other quotations.

John also includes, in addition to the Hosanna from Psalm 118, a quotation from Zech 9: 9, after which it is emphasized that it was only later, after Jesus had been crucified and raised from the dead, that the disciples understood the fulfillment of scripture in the events of Jesus' life. This same motif of "apostolic remembering" is found twice in John 2 (see below regarding Mark 11: 15–18 and John 2: 13–22). Mark, however, does not *quote* Zech 9: 9, which "predicts" that the Messiah will arrive on the unridden colt of an ass, but merely *presumes* this biblical passage by placing a special emphasis on the colt that Jesus rides. In Mark, therefore, the Hebrew Bible text is fulfilled in the narrative by being interwoven into it. Mark likewise interweaves other texts without quoting them. The location on the Mount of Olives may also recall Zech 14: 4, where, it is predicted, God's triumphant battle will occur.

A remarkable feature of Mark's version is to "suppress" the identity of Jesus as the Messiah. The Zechariah passages are hidden in the narrative, the Hosanna is for the "coming kingdom of our father David," and though the throngs treat Jesus as the arriving king, their acclamation is not explicit. Nineham argues that this is one more example of Mark's doctrine of the "hidden messiah."[76] This distinctively Markan redactional trait, however, is lacking here in John; in the latter we see what is likely a more primitive messianic exegesis from the early church (verses 13b–15), combined with John's theme of apostolic remembrance (verse 16).[77] Last, we should also note that in John the entry is triumphal not only because of Jesus' symbolic enthronement, but also because of the witness of the people to the great deed done through the raising of Lazarus in the previous chapter (Brown, *John*, pp. 1.461–4). This is John's redactional addition.

Mark's last verse is awkward and anticlimactic; in the tradition the triumphal entry likely connected directly with Jesus' prophecy at the temple (which John has probably moved; see below). A common Markan technique is to divide episodes in two and sandwich material in between. Here Mark likely pauses at the triumphal entry, inserts the first part of the withered fig account (11: 12–14), continues with the prophecy against the temple (11: 15–19), and then resumes with the conclusion of the withered fig story (11: 20–25). Other awkward transitional sentences are inserted between these passages to move the characters in and out of Jerusalem (11: 19, 27).

MARK 11: 15–18, 27–30/JOHN 2: 13–22

Mark 11: 15–18, 27–30

15They came to Jerusalem, and he entered the temple and began to drive out those selling and buying there. He overturned the tables of the moneychangers and the chairs of those who sold doves, 16and would not allow anyone to carry anything through the temple. 17He taught them, saying, "Is it not written, 'My house shall be called a house of prayer for all nations'? But you have turned it into a den of thieves." 18When the chief priests and scribes heard this, they sought a way to kill him. They feared him, since the whole crowd was spellbound by his teaching.

27They came again into Jerusalem, and as he was walking about in the temple, the chief priests, scribes, and elders came to him 28and said, "By what authority are you doing these things?

John 2: 13–22

13It was near the Passover of the Jews, and Jesus went up to Jerusalem. 14In the temple he found those selling cattle, sheep, and doves, and the moneychangers sitting there. 15He made a whip of cords and drove everyone out of the temple, along with the sheep and cattle, and he poured out the money of the moneychangers and overturned the tables. 16He said to those selling doves, "Get these out of here! Do not turn my father's house into a marketplace!" 17His disciples remembered that it had been written, "The zeal for your house will consume me."

(compare John 12: 19 above)

18Then the Judeans said to him, "What sign are you showing us by doing these things?" 19Jesus answered and said to them, "Destroy this temple and in three days I shall raise it up." 20The

Who has given you the authority to do this?"

29Jesus said to them, "I shall ask you one question, and if you answer me, I shall tell you by what authority I do these things: 30Did the baptism of John come from God, or was it of human authority only? Answer me."

Judeans then said to him, "This temple took forty-six years to build; are you going to raise it in three days?" 21But Jesus was speaking about the temple of his body. 22Therefore, when he was raised from the dead, his disciples remembered that he had said this, and believed in the scripture and the word that Jesus had spoken.

Commentary on Mark 11: 15–18, 27–30/John 2: 13–22

Jesus' action in the temple and the resulting questions of the Jewish representatives have many similar elements in Mark and John:

Mark	John
arrival in Jerusalem	arrival in Jerusalem
Jesus enters temple	Jesus enters temple
provocative action	provocative action
scripture quotation	
negative metaphor: den of thieves	negative metaphor: market
	scripture quotation
officials challenge: "By what authority?"	Judeans challenge: "What sign?"
saying re John the Baptist	saying re temple

In Mark the temple pronouncement and question of authority are found late in the gospel, as one of the first events of the passion, while John places them early, in chapter 2. Brown, Bultmann, and many others prefer Mark's placement as the more original; John evidently did not want these acts seen as the immediate provocation for the passion, and has separated them from the culminating events.[78] In their place John has raised the significance of the healing of Lazarus to the level of the *semeion* which precipitates a reaction (see above re Secret Mark/John 11). Traces of this move can still perhaps be seen in the introduction of John's telling of the story in 2: 13: "the Passover of the Judeans was near . . ." This was probably originally part of the passion narrative, but when placed earlier, gave rise to a separate Passover in John's timetable.[79]

Mark and John introduce different scriptural quotations in the course of their narratives. Mark quotes Isa 56: 7 and Jer 7: 11, which emphasize not so much the profanation by trading as the new universal focus of the temple. Perhaps more significantly, Mark places these quotations in the mouth of Jesus as teaching. John 2: 17 quotes Ps 69: 10, but not as the words of Jesus; it is the remembrance of the disciples after the resurrection. This quotation only attests to the intensity of Jesus' emotions, and not to a particular theological stance. Upon close inspection, it is surprising that neither Mark nor John betrays any close connection between the narrative and the scripture quotation; in both cases the quotation may be secondary to a narrative which had a slightly different center: the saying of Jesus at John 2: 16, "Do not turn my father's house into an emporium!" (Bultmann, *History*, p. 20). This alludes to Zech 14: 21, but again, the exact reasoning behind the expulsion is not clear, since the sale of sacrificial animals in the temple was an ancient and venerable custom in Judaism, sanctioned and even required by Jewish law. Bruce Chilton has proposed that Jesus was actually opposed to the *way* that sacrifices were being conducted in the temple,[80] but this conclusion is hardly necessary. What seems more likely is that Jesus is remembered as condemning the "vice" of the temple at the Endtime, and he envisions an eschatological purification similar to Zechariah's (Sanders, *Jesus and Judaism*). John's interpretation of the scene is thus a very plausible theme of the earlier gospel tradition, while Mark reflects here one of the redactional themes of that gospel: universalism.[81] Mark's Gospel thus retains the original *location* of this episode, but John the original *theme*. And once again we see that Mark's redactional changes are lacking in John.

The ending of the temple pronouncement scene in Mark also contains redactional motifs. Not only are the scribes likely added at 11: 18 (a favorite Markan designation, not found in John), but the fact that the crowd is "astonished at his teaching" is probably redactional (compare Mark 1: 22). Further, just as John has raised the healing of Lazarus to the level of provocation for the passion, Mark has raised up the teaching of Jesus as the cause of the irresoluble break with the Jewish authorities. The teaching is not, of course, simply a set of new moral commands, but represents the cosmological advent of the redeemer, analogous to the advent hymn at Ignatius of Antioch's *Ephesians* 19.

In both Mark and John the temple protest is followed by a reaction from the Jewish authorities, although as noted above, Mark has inserted the conclusion of the withered fig narrative in between. The temple protest and reaction were thus almost assuredly connected in the tradition.[82] The question posed by the Jewish authorities is similar in the two cases, although the direction in which each author pushes the question is interesting. Mark's "by what authority" in verse 28 is reminiscent of Jesus' "new teaching with authority" in Mark 1: 27, and is likely redactional. John, on the other hand, interprets the scenario in terms of "signs" (verse 18), which derives from an older tradition concerning *semeia* that Mark has probably suppressed.[83] We also see that John

111

has associated this scene with the prediction of the destruction of the temple, a saying that may in fact reflect an early and historically accurate tradition about the charge against Jesus which was well known about him.[84] It is represented as such in the trial scenes in Mark, Matthew, and Luke, but it is treated as an embarrassment in every case, and therefore was probably not invented. Mark has perhaps intentionally dissociated it from the prophetic action in the temple, and sequestered it in the trial scene, where it is refuted and defused as far as Christians are concerned. Mark has removed the prediction of destruction from this public discourse, and retained it as a saying of Jesus only in the apocalyptic discourse at 13: 1–2, and then only to disciples. Otherwise, in Mark it is reported only by "false witnesses" in the trial scene at Mark 14: 56–58. John likely contains the original connection of this saying with the expulsion from the temple.

Mark introduces the plot against Jesus' life here, at the end of the temple expulsion scene.[85] It is not clear in Mark's telling whether the temple authorities conspire to kill him because he expelled the sellers from the temple, or because the people "were astonished at his teaching." The latter appears more likely to be Mark's redactional alteration.

MARK 13: 3–13/JOHN 15: 18–16: 4A

Mark 13: 3–13

[3]He sat down on the Mount of Olives opposite the temple, and Peter, James, John, and Andrew asked him privately, [4]"Tell us, when will these things happen, and what is the sign that they are about to take place?" [5]Jesus then began to say to them, "Be careful that no one leads you astray. [6]Many will come in my name, saying, 'I am he,' and they will lead many astray. [7]Whenever you hear of wars and reports of wars, do not be alarmed; it is necessary for all this to happen, but it will still not be the end. [8]Nation will rise up against nation, and kingdom against kingdom. There will be earthquakes in some places, and famines. These things are the beginning of the birth pangs.

John 15: 18–16: 4a

[18]"If the world hates you, know that it first hated me. [19]If you had been from the world, the world would have loved its own. But you are not from the world; I have chosen you out of the world, and on account of this the world hates you. [20]Remember the word that I spoke to you: no slave is greater than the master. If they have persecuted me, they will also persecute you. If they kept my word, they will keep yours also. [21]But they will do all these things to you on account of my name, since they do not know the one who sent me. [22]If I had not come and spoken to them, they would not have sin. But now they have no excuse for their sin. [23]The one who hates me hates my father also.

9Watch out for yourselves. They will hand you over to councils, you will be beaten in synagogues, you will be brought before governors and kings as a witness because of me. 10But it is first necessary that the good news be proclaimed to all the nations. 11When they take you into custody to hand you over, do not be concerned ahead of time about what you will say, but whatever is given you in that hour, that you will say. For it is not you who is speaking, but the holy spirit. 12Brother will hand over brother to death, and a father his child, and children will rise up against their parents in order to have them put to death. 13You will be hated by everyone on account of my name. But the one who endures until the end will be saved.

24If I had not performed deeds among them that no one else had done, they would not have sin. Now, however, they have seen and have hated both me and my father. 25But it was to fulfill the word that is written in their law, 'They have hated me without cause.' 26But when the Advocate comes whom I shall send to you from the Father – the spirit of truth that proceeds from the Father – he will testify on my behalf. 27And you are testifying, because you have been with me from the beginning. 16:1I have said these things to you so that you will not stumble. 2They will throw you out of the synagogues. But the hour is coming when all who kill you will believe they are bringing an offering to God. 3They will do these things because they have known neither the Father nor me. 4But I have spoken these things to you so that when their hour comes, you will remember that I told you about them."

Commentary on Mark 13: 3–13/John 15: 18–16: 4a

Mark 13 is the longest discourse in that gospel, and although it partakes of both the "apocalypse" and "farewell discourse" genres, it does not correspond closely to either (Nineham, *Saint Mark*, pp. 339–43). John 15: 18–27 is likewise associated with Jesus' elongated farewell discourses of John 13–17. The two passages quoted here are thus in the same position in their respective gospels – although a farewell discourse could hardly be anywhere else. Mark places the discourse at the Mount of Olives, the location of Jesus' private instruction elsewhere in Mark (11: 1, 14: 26). This location may be inspired by Zech 14: 4, where it is stated that the Lord will fight the eschatological battle from this mount.[86]

The early church's difficulty in accommodating Jesus' prediction of the destruction of the temple was alluded to above at Mark 11: 15–17 (see also below at Mark 14: 57–59). Here the prediction is introduced in Mark 13:

1–2, but the discourse that follows seems to minimize it, suggesting that the destruction of the temple is not the looked-for sign (*semeion*, verse 4). Mark's discourse also does not cohere well, and is generally divided into several sections that are probably attributable to different sources: (1) verses 1–4: introduction; (2) verses 5–8: sufferings before the last days; and (3) verses 9–13: sayings of Jesus on the sufferings. The discourse goes on to include (not displayed above): (4) verses 14–23: the last days (not from same source as (2); (5) verses 24–27: the end (originally a continuation of verses 5–8?) (6) verses 28–37: conclusion based on sayings of Jesus.

The parallels between Mark and John here are vague, yet eschatological sayings of Jesus may lie behind the two farewell discourses. A significant parallel occurs in Mark 13: 13. There Jesus warns that the disciples will be "hated by everyone on account of my name," a motif that is found in John divided between two verses: "If the world hates you, know that it first hated me" (verse 18), and "They will do all these things to you on account of my name" (verse 21). Further, the help that will come in those days is from above: "It is not you who is speaking, but the holy spirit" (Mark 13: 11), and "When the Advocate (*parakletos*) comes whom I shall send to you from the Father – the spirit of truth that proceeds from the Father – he will testify on my behalf" (John 15: 26). Behind Mark 13: 9 (the prediction of the beatings in the synagogue) there may also be seen a parallel to the Johannine theme of Christians being expelled from the synagogues (9: 22, 12: 42, 16: 2).

Mark's arrangement of this scene betrays a number of redactional traits, even if older traditions are used as building blocks. The urgent question of verse 4 reflects the prophetic-eschatological function of sign (*semeion*), which Mark wants to undermine.[87] Mark is also negative about the clause "I am he" (*ego eimi*) in verse 6. This phrase reflects the same background of messianic pronouncements that John knows, but develops in a positive direction as part of a revelation discourse (compare 8: 24, 28, 58; 13: 19).

MARK 14: 1–2/JOHN 11: 55–57

Mark 14: 1–2	John 11: 55–57
[1]It was two days before Passover, the feast of unleavened bread,	[55]It was near the Passover of the Jews, and many from the countryside were going up to Jerusalem before Passover in order to purify themselves. [56]They were seeking Jesus, and as they were standing about in the temple, they said to each other, "What do you think? Surely he will not come to the
(compare Mark 14: 2 below)	

114

and the chief priests and scribes were looking for a way to arrest Jesus by deceit and kill him, 2but they said, "Not during the festival, lest there be a public disturbance."

festival, will he?" 57The chief priests and Pharisees gave orders that they should be informed if anyone knew where Jesus was so that they could seize him. (compare John 11: 56 above)

Commentary on Mark 14: 1–2/John 11: 55–57

With Mark 14 we enter into the central section of the passion narrative, what Jeremias calls the "shorter passion." Mark has set this section off from the previous narrative more than John has, and probably more than was the case in the earlier gospel tradition.[88] Although the relation of Mark and John in the first verses is vague at best, in the last verses of this section it is close. A number of parallels between the two passages can be seen here, although the order of events in John has been changed for this comparison:

Mark	John
two days before Passover	near Passover
chief priests and scribes	chief priests and Pharisees
	conspired to kill him
were seeking (*zeteo*) a way	many were seeking (*zeteo*) Jesus;
to capture Jesus and kill him	Pharisees trying to capture him
but they said "not in the festival."	"Surely he will not come to the festival."

The language of the two accounts is different in almost every line, but the intent is often very close, even to the extent that a direct quotation is used in both cases (though by different groups) to communicate the belief that the capture of Jesus would not occur during the festival. As noted before, where opponents not only challenge Jesus but also threaten to kill him, especially in passages found in both Mark and John, they are designated as chief priests plus some other group. This short passage is very important in providing the transition from debate to persecution. (Compare chapter 2 on this transition in *Life of Aesop*.)

MARK 14: 3–9/JOHN 12: 1–11

Mark 14: 3–9

John 12: 1–11

3While he was in Bethany reclining at table, in the house of Simon the leper,

1Six days before Passover, Jesus came to Bethany, the home of Lazarus, whom he had raised from the dead. 2They made a dinner for him there. Martha served, and a woman came to him with an alabaster jar filled with very expensive perfume of nard. She broke open the jar and poured out the ointment upon his head. 4But some were upset at this, and said to each other, "Why was this perfume wasted? 5It could have been sold for over three hundred denarii and given to the poor." They then became angry with her.

6But Jesus said, "Let her do this. Why do you trouble her? It is a beautiful thing she has done for me. 7The poor you will always have with you, and whenever you want you can show kindness to them, but you will not always have me with you. 8She has done what she could; she has anointed my body for burial ahead of time. 9Truly, I say to you, wherever the good news is proclaimed throughout the world, what she has done will be told in memory of her."

Lazarus was one of those reclining at table with him. 3Mary then took a pound of very expensive perfume of nard and anointed Jesus' feet and wiped them with her hair. The house was filled with the fragrance of the perfume. 4Judas Iscariot, one of his disciples (who was soon to betray him), said, 5"Why was this perfume not sold for three hundred denarii and given to the poor?" 6He said this not because he was concerned for the poor, but because he was a thief and stole money from the common money pouch which he carried. 7Then Jesus said, "Let her do this, for she has saved this for the day of my burial. 8The poor you will always have with you, but you will not always have me with you."

9The great crowd of the Jews then knew that he was there, and came not on account of Jesus alone, but also to see Lazarus, whom he had raised from the dead. 10So the chief priests plotted to kill Lazarus as well, 11since it was because of him that many of the Judeans were leaving and believing in Jesus.

Commentary on Mark 14: 3–9/John 12: 1–11

In Mark the anointing scene is placed within the shorter account of the passion (i.e., chs 14–15), but in John the anointing with costly nard takes place six days before the Passover, and is also placed before the long discourses of chapters 13–17; this separates it from the main body of the passion narrative. In both gospels it is explicitly presented as a preparation for burial. Mark's pericope is well constructed, placing a scene of withdrawal and calm – calm to the point of death, in fact, since the act is related to Jesus' burial – between two accounts of threatening narrative action. John does not draw this contrast quite as provocatively, but it is present nevertheless. It has been suggested that this scene of a woman anointing Jesus was risqué, and Luke's parallel account, Luke 7: 36–38, 50, may imply this by saying that she is a "sinner."[89]

Many scholars argue that the anointing is a late addition to Mark's passion account, or moved from some other location. It certainly helps to define the passion narrative in Mark, constituting an anticipation of the death and resurrection of Jesus.[90] The women arriving at the end of the gospel to prepare his body for funeral cannot find it, but at this earlier point in the narrative the task of anointing for burial is completed while it is still possible. Elisabeth Schüssler Fiorenza argues that women are depicted as alternative disciples in Mark's passion.[91] The fact that the woman here is unnamed, therefore, does not diminish her role as the ironic counterpart to the disciples, who in Mark are never quite comprehending. It could be argued that the disciples' reaction to the woman is introduced by Mark, and that John has copied this, since the disciples' peculiar obtuseness in Mark is rightly considered a Markan redactional trait. In fact, however, it is only Judas who reacts negatively in John; the scene in John sets *him* off from the woman, not the disciples, and we may wonder whether John reflects here the earlier tradition, which Mark has altered in a characteristic way (compare also Mark 8: 33/John 6: 70–71).

Parallel in the two accounts are the hyperbolic indulgence in a luxury item (expressed in an almost identical way, "alabaster jar/pound of very expensive perfume of nard"), the reproach that it should have been sold for 300 denarii and given to the poor, and Jesus' response (also expressed in an almost identical way). The saying about "the poor always with you" and the other motifs in common, using many of the same words, are precisely those memorable elements that are necessary to the transmission of the story. They by no means imply a literary dependence. By contrast, some of the elements unique to Mark are probably not original to the story, but part of Mark's redaction: "some were angry" (*aganakteo*) in relation to the disciples, and "truly, I say to you" are found together in a very similar story at Mark 10: 13–16 (compare 10: 41). They contribute to a depiction of the disciples as obtuse.[92]

Mark 14: 10–21	John 13: 1–11, 18–31
	[1]Before the Passover feast, Jesus knew that his hour had come when he would leave this world to go to the Father, and he loved his own who were in the world to the very end. [2]Since the devil had already entered into the heart of Judas, son of Simon Iscariot, to hand Jesus over,
[10]Judas Iscariot, one of the twelve, went to the chief priests in order to hand Jesus over to them, [11]and when they heard this, they were overjoyed, and promised to give him money. He then sought a good opportunity to hand him over. [12]On the first day of the feast of unleavened bread, when the Passover lamb was being slaughtered, his disciples said to him, "Where should we go to prepare to eat the Passover meal?" [13]So he sent two of his disciples, saying, "Go into the city, and a man will meet you carrying a jar of water. Follow him. [14]Whatever house he enters, say to the owner of the house, 'The teacher says, "Where is the guest room where I may eat the Passover meal with my disciples?"' [15]He will show you a large upper room already arranged. Prepare for us there." [16]The disciples left and went into the city and found everything as he had told them, and prepared the Passover feast.	
	[3]Jesus knew that the Father had given all things into his hands, and that he had gone forth from God and would return to God. So

when dinner came, [4]Jesus got up, took off his garments, and wrapped a towel around his waist. [5]He then poured water into a bowl, and began to wash the feet of the disciples and wipe them with the towel around his waist. [6]When he came to Simon Peter, Peter said, "Lord, should you wash my feet?" [7]Jesus answered and said, "You do not yet understand what I am doing, but later you will." [8]Peter said, "Surely you will never wash my feet!" Jesus answered him, "Unless I wash you, you have no share with me." [9]Simon Peter said to him, "Lord, not my feet only, but also my hands and my head." [10]Jesus said to him, "The one who is cleansed has no need to wash, except for his feet, but is thoroughly clean. You here are clean, but not all of you." [11]For he knew the one who was going to hand him over. Thus he said, "You are not all clean."

[18]"I am not speaking of all of you. I know whom I have chosen. But it is to fulfill the scripture, 'The one who ate my bread lifted his heel against me.' [19]Now I am telling you this before it happens, so that when it takes place you may believe that I am he. [20]Truly, truly, I say to you, the one who receives whomever I send receives me, and the one who receives me receives him who sent me." [21]When Jesus said these things, he became troubled in spirit, and

[17]Evening was falling, and Jesus came with the twelve. [18]As they were reclining and eating he said, "Truly, I say to you that one of you will betray me, one who is eating

with me." ¹⁹They began to be distressed and said to each other, "Surely it is not I?"

testified, saying, "Truly, truly, I say to you that one of you will betray me."

²²The disciples looked at each other, wondering to whom he was referring. ²³One of the disciples was reclining on Jesus' bosom, the disciple whom Jesus loved. ²⁴Simon Peter nodded to him to find out to whom he could be referring. ²⁵So that disciple, lying at Jesus' side, said to him, "Lord, who is it?" ²⁶Jesus answered, "It is the one to whom I shall give my bread when I have dipped it." And dipping his bread, he took it and gave it to Judas son of Simon Iscariot. ²⁷After Jesus gave him the bread, Satan entered into him. Jesus said to him, "What you are going to do, do quickly." ²⁸None of those reclining there knew why he said this to him, ²⁹though some supposed that since Judas kept the money pouch, Jesus had said to him, "Buy what we need for the festival," or that he should give something to the poor. ³⁰After Judas took the bread, he immediately left. It was now night time.

²⁰He said to them, "It is one of the twelve, the one dipping into the bowl with me.

²¹For the Son of Humanity goes as it is written concerning him, but woe to that person by whom the Son of Humanity is betrayed. It would be better if that person had never been born."

³¹When he had gone out, Jesus said, "Now the Son of Humanity has been glorified, and God has been glorified in him."

Commentary on Mark 14: 10–21/John 13: 1–11, 18–31

Both gospels recount here the last meal that Jesus takes with the disciples and the announcement of the betrayal by Judas, but with many differences. Judas' treachery in Mark is set off from the surrounding narrative, but more integrated in John. Mark's explanation of events is very realistic, while John's involves the cosmic drama of Satan entering into Judas. In both Mark and John there is a transition to a meal: in Mark a Passover meal, and in John a meal before Passover. This difference has important implications for the timing of the crucifixion. In Mark the Last Supper coincides with the time of the Passover, while in John Jesus is crucified on the day before Passover, at the time of the sacrifice of the Passover lamb. Most scholars agree that John reflects the earlier tradition at this point.[93] It is also noteworthy that John introduces a footwashing scene here, and has no institution of the eucharist as Mark does. The beginning of Mark's supper scene is also dominated by the finding of the upper room. Bultmann (*History*, pp. 261–64) considers it a fairytale-like account, parallel to Mark 11: 1–7 (see above), added secondarily to the passion account. In inserting this story, Mark employs a favorite technique, which is to sandwich episodes, thus interweaving the narrative into a more unified whole.

Despite the numerous differences, many similarities can be seen between the two gospels here. The central prediction in the two accounts here is nearly identical: "Amen (amen), I say to you: one of you will betray me." Mark adds to this, somewhat abruptly, "one who is eating with me." This is an allusion to Ps 41: 9, which John has explicitly quoted in verse 18. Mark often incorporates biblical allusions in the narrative, while John quotes the text explicitly. Nineham notes (*Saint Mark*, pp. 378–79) that this saying does not name Judas, and this may have been true of the earlier tradition. The lack of a named betrayer naturally calls for a resolution, but the two gospels handle it differently: "they began to be distressed . . ." is a typical Markan construction (*archomai* plus infinitive), and John introduces the beloved disciple, unique to that gospel. Both gospels do, however, also connect the saying above with Ps 41: 9; it is likely that the tradition that lies behind Mark and John connects the messianic exegesis of Ps 41: 9 with this saying about a betrayer from among the group of disciples. Further, Jesus' prediction that one of the group would betray him provokes a similar searching response on each side, again using different words (Mark 14: 19; John 13: 22). Although the Son of Humanity sayings here are quite different, it is possible that some such saying was present at this point in the traditional narrative. Mark's version is better integrated into the narrative, while John's reflects the typical style and themes of the Johannine discourses. Still, the content of Mark's Son of Humanity saying is similar to John 13: 3, and both use the same word for "goes" (*hypagei*).

Mark turns in the next verses to the institution of the eucharist, which John

121

lacks. Did John know of a eucharist at this point in the narrative and suppress it, or was it not a part of the pre-Johannine tradition? Certainly, other eucharistic traditions did exist in early Christianity, such as that found in *Didache* 9–10. Indeed, this tradition, rather than the one in Mark, may be reflected at John 11: 52 (see above), and John may also have substituted the footwashing for a meal ritual. However that may be, it appears that Mark's institution of the eucharist is not well integrated into the narrative, and may not have been part of the pre-Markan tradition (Nineham, *Saint Mark*, pp. 378–81). Its beginning, verse 22, repeats verse 18, and there is no indication in the eucharistic passages themselves of an association with Passover. This should not surprise us if the passage was introduced into pre-Markan tradition; there is also no allusion to Passover in the eucharistic passage at 1 Cor 11: 23. The Lord's Supper was instead thought of as a "messianic banquet," or fellowship meal with the risen deity. Although there were early interpretations of the death of Jesus as Passover lamb or sacrifice (see chapter 2), they were probably not present in the original Lord's Supper, but added secondarily in early Christianity.[94] Mark has included in the eucharist the motif of vicarious atonement, "which is poured out for many" (verse 24b), not present in 1 Corinthians. This is perhaps a theme of the pre-Markan gospel tradition, as indicated above in chapter 2, but it cannot be argued here by reference to John.

In Mark, Judas connives with the chief priests; no other Jewish figures are mentioned. This corresponds to what we find throughout: where Mark and John are parallel in describing a plot to kill Jesus, the Jewish opponents mentioned are the chief priests, often accompanied by others; where the conflict does not mention a plot to kill Jesus, the Jewish group is usually the Pharisees, sometimes accompanied by others.[95] This observation will be taken up again in chapter 4.

MARK 14: 26–31/JOHN 13: 36–38

Mark 14: 26–31	John 13: 36–38
26When they had sung a hymn, they went out to the Mount of Olives. 27Jesus said to them, "All of you will take offense at me, for it is written, 'I shall strike the shepherd and the sheep will be scattered.' 28But after I am raised I shall go before you to Galilee." 29Peter, however, said to him, "Even if everyone else takes offense	36Simon Peter said to him, "Lord, where are you going?" Jesus answered him, "Where I am going you cannot now follow, but you will follow later. 37But Peter said to him, "Lord, why can I not follow you now? I shall give my

at you, I will not!" 30And Jesus said to him, "Truly, I say to you that this very night, before the cock crows twice, you will deny me three times." 31But Peter said vehemently, "Even if you ask me to die with you, I will not deny you!" And the others all said the same thing.

life for yours." 38Jesus answered, "You will give your life for me? Truly, truly, I say to you, the cock will not crow until you have denied me three times."

Commentary on Mark 14: 26–31/John 13: 36–38

Here again, although the accounts in Mark and John are very similar in terms of content, there are almost no words used in common. Some of the differences are characteristic of the redaction of the two gospels. Markan redaction may include the placement of the scene at the Mount of Olives (compare 13: 3), "offended" (used more often in Mark than in John), and the prediction of the resurrection appearance in Galilee. Likewise the question and answer of Jesus and Peter in John is written in a way typical of the discourses in that gospel. One might have speculated that the actual words of the prediction of Peter's denial, which are very similar, circulated independently, but they require a narrative setting. The similarity is more likely to be attributed to the resiliency of the memorable elements of traditional narrative. One also wonders whether there is some common tradition behind "I shall go before you" in Mark and "You will follow me later" in John.

MARK 14: 32–41/JOHN 18: 1; 12: 27–28

Mark 14: 32–41

John 18: 1; 12: 27–28

18: 1

1After Jesus said these things, he went out with his disciples across the Kidron Valley to a place where there was a garden, which he and his disciples entered.

32They came to a place named Gethsemane, and he said to the disciples, "Sit here while I pray." 33He took aside Peter, James, and John, and became troubled and agitated. 34He said to them, "'My soul is grieved' to the point of death. Remain here and keep

12: 27–28

27"Now 'my soul is troubled,'

watch." [35]And proceeding on a bit further, he fell upon the ground and prayed that, if possible, his hour should pass from him. [36]He said, "Dear Father, all things are possible for you. Take this cup from me. But not what I want – what you want."

but what shall I say? 'Father, save me from this hour'? But this was why I came to this hour. [28]Father, glorify your name."

A voice came from heaven, "I have glorified it and I shall glorify it again."

[37]He returned and found them sleeping, and said to Peter, "Simon, were you sleeping? Were you not able to stay awake for just one hour? [38]Be vigilant and pray, lest you fall into temptation. The spirit is willing but the flesh is weak." [39]Again he went away and prayed the same prayer, [40]and again, when he returned, he found them sleeping, for their eyes were heavy, and they did not know what to say to him. [41]When he came a third time he said to them, "Are you sleeping again and taking your rest? Enough! The hour has come; behold, the Son of Humanity has been handed over into the hands of sinners."

Commentary on Mark 14: 32–41/John 18: 1; 12: 27–28

The parallelism between Mark and John at first sight appears to break down here, as it is not clear whether John has any scene exactly equivalent to the prayer scene in Gethsemane. John 18: 1 depicts a movement of Jesus and his disciples into a garden, but there is no prayer scene immediately following, and 18: 1 is disruptive to the narrative flow. (As we shall see below, John 14: 31 probably connected at one time directly to 18: 2.) However, there is much prayer language in John 12–17, and the content of Mark's Gethsemane scene finds parallels especially in John 12: 27–28. The prayer in John 12: 27–28 is uncharacteristically short, but verse 27 touches on the same theme as Mark's Gethsemane prayer (Mark 14: 35–36). Mark and John also both include a quotation of scripture that is not only similar, making use of the word "soul," but may in fact be derived from the same text, Ps 42: 5.[96] They both also contain or are in close proximity to a Son of Humanity saying (Mark 14: 41 and John 12: 23) that refers to Jesus' end as his "hour," and comment upon Jesus' praying to the "Father" to be saved from his destiny. At the center of this group of texts on both sides is a scene in which Jesus withdraws to the garden, where Judas finds him and betrays him to the Jewish leaders. But there are some very important differences as well. Unlike Mark, John does not report the name of the garden as Gethsemane, nor is there any elaborated "Gethsemane scene." Either this evangelist does not know this tradition, which would imply that John is not dependent on Mark, or he has chosen to omit this intimate portrait of Jesus' suffering for theological purposes.

Some redactional changes on both sides are clear. John treats Jesus' petition to be saved rhetorically, introduced as a possibility only, which Jesus rejects: "What shall I say? 'Father, save me?'" This distances the Johannine Jesus from any real suffering or hesitation about his role: "But this was why I came to this hour."[97] The majesty of the redeemer in John would be compromised by a petition of deliverance, although Mark emphasizes it all the more. Mark quotes Jesus' prayer and allows this to introduce a favorite Markan theme: the obtuseness of the disciples. It is quite likely that Mark has inserted Jesus' discovery of the sleeping disciples immediately after the mentioning of the hour here.

Mark contains an account that at first sight appears more coherent; however, many scholars have advanced source-critical theories to explain certain anomalies. The prayer is reported first in indirect discourse, then in direct (verses 35, 36). Immediately thereafter, the focus of the story shifts from the prayer to the fact that the disciples are sleeping; Mark's dramatic interest in the account appears to be found here rather than in the prayer. Also, although Judas is mentioned in verse 42, he is introduced in verse 43 as though for the first time. Kelber has countered that the difficulties present in this text do not indicate separate sources, but result from Mark's careful composition.[98] There are many Markan redactional elements here. Kelber points out several that are also clustered at the end of the Markan apocalypse in chapter 13: watching, coming, finding, and sleeping. We might also note that Peter, James, and John are elevated to a position of primacy in the Gethsemane scene, just as at the beginning of Mark, and that this scene's emphasis on the disciples' lack of understanding is distinctly Markan. In addition, the use of *archomai* plus infinitive (verse 33) is common in Mark. Yet none of this is found in John's scene. Although Kelber is successful in proving that the Gethsemane scene is not created by interweaving two pre-existing sources, I would aver that there is still a source behind this passage: Mark's source is paralleled in John's Gospel, but the redaction is not.

Is it possible that John has removed these themes on the grounds that they are objectionable to a triumphalist christology? It is more likely that Mark and John have redacted a common source. Visible beneath the redactional tendencies of the two evangelists are the same events, perhaps in the same order:

a private interchange between Jesus and the disciples, then "Rise, let us go" (see next section), which leads directly into the arrest scene.

MARK 14: 42–50/JOHN 14: 30-31; 18: 2–11

Mark 14: 42–50	John 14: 30–31; 18: 2–11

14: 30–31

30"No longer shall I be telling you many things, for the ruler of the world is coming. He has no power over me, 31but so that the world may know that I love the Father, I do as the Father commanded me. Rise, let us be going from here.

42"Rise, let us be going. Behold, the one who is betraying me is coming."

18: 2–11

43But while he was still speaking, Judas, one of the twelve, came with a crowd bearing swords and clubs, sent from the chief priests, scribes, and elders. 44Now the one who betrayed him arranged with them a sign, saying, "The one whom I kiss is he. Arrest him and lead him away under guard." 45And when he arrived he went up to Jesus and said, "Rabbi," and kissed him. 46The others then seized Jesus and placed him under arrest.

2Judas, the one who was betraying him, knew this place, because Jesus often gathered there with his disciples. 3Judas took a detachment of soldiers and officers from the chief priests and Pharisees, and came there with lamps, torches, and weapons. 4Since Jesus knew everything that was going to happen to him, he went out and said to them, "Whom do you seek?" 5They answered him, "Jesus the Nazorean." He said to them, "I am he." And Judas, who had betrayed him, stood with them. 6When he said to them, "I am he," they stepped back and fell to the ground. 7Again he asked them, "Whom do you seek?" And they said, "Jesus the Nazorean." 8Jesus answered, "I told you that I am he. If you seek me, let these people go." 9He said this to fulfill what he had said earlier, "I have

47But one of those standing there drew his sword and struck the servant of the high priest, cutting off his ear. 48Jesus answered and said to them, "Have you come out to catch me with swords and clubs, as if I were a bandit? 49Every day I was with you, teaching in the temple, and you did not arrest me. But all of this happened so that the scriptures would be fulfilled." 50And the disciples all fled away, leaving him behind.

not lost one of those you have given me."
10Then Simon Peter, who had a sword, drew it and struck the servant of the high priest, cutting off his right ear. The name of the servant was Malchus. 11Jesus then said to Peter, "Put your sword back into its sheath. Am I not to drink the cup that my father has given me?"

Commentary on Mark 14: 42–50/John 14: 30–31; 18: 2–11

Mark's effective transition stands between Jesus' prayer in Gethsemane and the betrayal and arrest of Jesus. At the same time that it signals a rising from prayer and a physical movement, it also suggests the dramatic movement – which Jesus wilfully engages – toward the betrayal, arrest, and crucifixion. Mark and John both continue motifs from above: Mark's betrayer is realistic, as in Mark 14: 10–21, but John's is cosmic as well in 14: 30 (compare John 13: 2, 27).

At least some part of John 14 must have stood originally as the conclusion of the farewell discourses in John, leading directly to the passion narrative, as Bultmann argued (*John*, pp. 459, 595). The last verse of John 14, "Arise, let us go," does not lead coherently into chapter 15, but would be appropriate as the transition to the arrest and passion, and this is precisely where the same phrase is found in Mark. For whatever reason, the text of John here must have become displaced either in redaction or transmission. Displacement theories in John must always remain hypothetical, but at this point it seems a compelling suggestion.

In both Mark and John, Judas, referred to as "the one who betrayed him," arrives with an armed crowd from the chief priests and other Jewish groups. Once again, the chief priests remain constant in parallel scenes where Jesus is threatened with death, but the other groups vary: scribes and elders in Mark, Pharisees in John. Both gospels create scenes of dramatic irony, but it is different in the two cases. In Mark, Judas has arranged to betray Jesus with a kiss, and calls him "Rabbi" as the mob apprehends him. In John, Jesus initiates a short but quite typical dialogue with his interlocutors, except that in this case his statement "I am he" – or "I am," the formula of God's self-revelation – provokes them to fall down before him. Jesus' reference to his impending death as his "cup" in John 18: 11, though not paralleled here in Mark, is found above at Mark 14: 36.

Both narratives include the attack on the high priest's slave by a disciple (an unnamed disciple in Mark, Simon Peter in John). Only here are there any words used in common between the two gospels. Both passages also indicate that the events involve a fulfillment of divine intention. In Mark Jesus says that he should proceed with the crowd so that the scriptures may be fulfilled – presumably a reference to Zech 13: 7 ("I shall strike the shepherd and the sheep will be scattered," quoted above at Mark 14: 27). The next verse, Mark 14: 50, seems to confirm this. John presents a quite different form of "exegesis": these events fulfill Jesus' own words from earlier in the discourses. The former is probably closer to the earlier tradition, since Zechariah is quoted or alluded to often in Mark and John.

These two passages thus contain many of the same motifs, though generally expressed differently. The only identical Greek words are found in the memorable phrases: "Arise, let us be going," "the one who betrayed him," and "struck the servant of the high priest." Although John contains several redactional expansions, there is little, if any, evidence of redaction in Mark.[99] Even verse 49, "teaching in the temple," sounds more Johannine, since the teaching occurs in the temple (compare John 7: 14, 28; 18: 20).

MARK 14: 53–65/JOHN 18: 12–14, 19–24

Mark 14: 53–65

John 18: 12–14, 19–24

[12]Then the detachment of soldiers, the commanding officer, and the officers of the Jews took Jesus into custody and bound him. [13]They led him first to Annas, who was the father-in-law of Caiaphas, the high priest that year. [14]It was Caiaphas who had counseled the Judeans that it was better for one man to die for the people.

[53]They led Jesus away to the high priest, and the chief priests, elders, and scribes were assembled.

[54]Peter followed from a distance until Jesus was inside the courtyard of the high priest. He sat with the officers, warming himself at the fire.
[55]The chief priests and the whole Sanhedrin sought testimony against Jesus in order to put him to death, but could not find any.

56Many gave false testimony against him, but their accounts did not agree. 57Still others came forward to give false testimony against him and said, 58"We heard him say, 'I shall destroy this temple made with hands, and after three days build another not made with hands.'" 59But their testimony also did not agree.

60The high priest stood before them and interrogated Jesus, saying, "Do you have anything to say? What is it that they testify against you?" 61But he was silent and did not answer. Again the high priest interrogated him, and said, "Are you the Messiah, the son of the Blessed One?" 62Jesus said, "I am, and 'you shall see the Son of Humanity sitting on the right hand of the Power,' 'coming with the clouds of heaven.'" 63The high priest tore his clothes and said, "What further need do we have of witnesses? 64You have heard the blasphemy. What is your decision?" All of them condemned him to death. 65Some then began to spit on him, blindfold him, and beat him, saying, "Prophesy!" The guards then took him and beat him as well.

19The high priest interrogated Jesus concerning his disciples and his teaching. 20Jesus responded, "I have been speaking openly to the world, and I have taught constantly in the synagogues and in the temple, where all Judeans come together; I have said nothing in secret. 21Why do you interrogate me? Interrogate those who have heard what I was speaking to them. Indeed, they knew what I was saying."

22As he was saying this, one of the guards standing nearby struck Jesus and said, "Thus you would answer the high priest?" 23Jesus answered him, "If I have spoken wrongly, testify against the crime; but if well, why then do you beat me?" 24Annas then sent him bound to Caiaphas the high priest.

Commentary on Mark 14: 53–65/John 18: 12–14, 19–24

As a result of certain difficulties in Mark's text, many source-critical theories have been proposed for this section that posit either the interweaving of two separate source texts, or alternatively, the interweaving of one source text and redaction. However, partly because the theories vary so widely, no consensus has been reached. First, we must describe some of the difficulties in the text of Mark that have provoked source-critical analyses:[100] (1) at times it appears that there is one high priest who is interrogating Jesus, at other times a group (one: 14: 53a, 60, 61, 63; group: 14: 53b, 55); (2) this episode seems to have at least two separate introductions, 14: 53a and 55; (3) while the charge against Jesus, that he threatened to destroy the temple, is referred to in verses 58 and 60, the issue abruptly shifts in verses 61b–64 to one of blasphemy; (4) the charge that he threatened to destroy the temple (verses 57–58) appears to be inserted, since the same line is found before and after it, indicating a seam; (5) the summary statement in 14: 56 does not cohere well with the further testimony of verses 57–58; (6) verse 59 does not prepare for the clear charges presupposed by the high priest in verse 60; (6) at verse 61a Jesus' response to the charges is silence, yet in verses 61b–62 he responds without hesitation. These sorts of observations naturally gave rise to the idea that two versions of events were interwoven here, although reconstructing them has proved difficult.

Despite the lack of a consensus on the source division of Mark's trial narrative, one aspect of these passages should not be overlooked. If we return to the first inconsistency in Mark, one high priest versus a group, and compare that to the parallel scene in John, we note that in the latter case there is only one high priest interrogating Jesus. For the modern reader who suspects that John has not read Mark, but has instead used a common source, this provides a possible explanation for the difficulties in Mark: the scene in John likely reflects only Mark's one-priest tradition. But where, then, do we find a tradition involving a group of interrogators? It is possible that the group effort to find testimony condemning Jesus results from Mark's redaction, especially as Mark tries to provide an explanation for why there was a tradition that Jesus had threatened to destroy the temple (Mark 14: 57–58).[101] One might also examine, however, another pericope in John, 11: 47–53, which is referred to in John 18: 14 (analyzed also above at Mark 10: 35–45/John 11: 47–53). This is not an interrogation scene as it stands, but contains many motifs parallel to Mark 14: 53–64. The group that is assembled in Mark 14: 55, "the chief priests and the Sanhedrin," is almost identical to "the chief priests and the Pharisees (who called a meeting) of the Sanhedrin" in John 11: 47. Also, it is stated in Mark 14: 55 that it is the group, not the single high priest, who "sought testimony in order to put him to death." Likewise, in John 11: 53 it is the group who "devised a plan in order to kill him." We also see that the charge regarding the destruction of the temple in Mark 14: 57–58, which betrays signs of having been inserted (Bultmann, *History*, p. 270), is an issue which comes up – albeit in a different form – in John 11: 48. As we might expect from the present hypothesis, such a charge does not appear in John's single-high-priest narrative, where the issue is rather blasphemy. It is possible that in the earlier gospel narrative tradition there were two separate deliberations, one involving a gathering such as the Sanhedrin – whether Jesus was present for interrogation is not clear – and another involving an interrogation before the high priest.[102] These two scenes have perhaps been conflated in Mark.

Neither of these two scenarios indicates that John has been influenced by the redactional elements in Mark; in fact, John can more readily be divided into a short traditional narrative of the interrogation by the high priest and the beating by the guards (John 18: 19, 22, parallel to Mark's single-high-priest verses), expanded by the addition of dialogue (John 18: 20–21, 23).

MARK 14: 66–72/JOHN 18: 15–18, 25–27

Mark 14: 66–72

John 18: 15–18, 25–27

[15]Simon Peter followed Jesus, along with another disciple who was known to the high priest. The latter entered with Jesus into the courtyard of the high priest [16]while Peter remained outside by the gate. The other disciple, who was known to the high priest, went out, spoke to the gatekeeper, and led Peter in. [17]The woman who kept the gate said to Peter, "Aren't you one of the disciples of this man?" But he replied, "I am not." [18]Since it was cool, the slaves and officers had made a coal fire and were standing around it warming themselves. Peter was also standing with them, warming himself. [25]Simon Peter was standing and warming himself, and they said to him, "Aren't you one of his disciples?" But he denied it and said, "I am not." [26]One of the servants of the high priest, a relative of the man whose ear Peter had cut off, asked, "Didn't I see you in

[66]While Peter was below in the courtyard, one of the maids of the high priest came by, [67]and when she saw Peter warming his hands she stared at him and said, "You were also with Jesus the Nazorean." [68]But he denied it and said, "I don't know what you're talking about!" He went outside into the outer court, and the cock crowed. [69]When the maid saw him again she started saying to those standing there, "He is one of them," [70]but again he denied it. And a bit later, those standing there said to Peter, "Indeed, you are one of them, for you are a Galilean."

71Peter then began to curse and swore, "I do not know this man you are talking about." 72Immediately, a cock crowed a second time, and Peter remembered what Jesus had said to him, "Before a cock crows twice you will deny me three times." Peter broke down and wept.

the garden with him?" 27But again Peter denied it, and immediately the cock crowed.

Commentary on Mark 14: 66–72/John 18: 15–18, 25–27

Although the words that are similar between the two gospels at this point are few (limited to the memorable conclusion "And immediately the cock crowed"[103]), the scenes displayed here share an important literary technique. The depiction of Peter first accompanying Jesus, and then denying that he ever knew him, is divided into two parts which frame the interrogation scene. This sandwiching technique or *inclusio* is used a number of times in Mark, and often presented as one of the redactional characteristics of that gospel. Norman Perrin thus argued that the presence of this literary technique in John at this point as well as in Mark indicated that John must have borrowed it from Mark, and Donahue expanded upon this observation in his study of the trial scene.[104] This is one of the strongest pieces of evidence yet mustered that John is directly indebted to Mark. But is this sort of framing technique so uncommon in ancient literature as to be considered peculiarly "Markan"? Fortna mounted a rebuttal to Donahue on the grounds that *inclusio* was a common literary technique, and therefore Mark could claim no copyright on its use. Donahue himself states (p. 59): "It may well be that Mark found this technique as part of the tradition available to him, and modified it for his own purposes. It is in accord with the technique of *inclusio* which is frequent in both classical and biblical literature." Though Fortna's and Donahue's discussion focused on *inclusio* in genres other than prose narrative, such as epic poetry (which perhaps should have been ruled out of consideration), framing techniques occur also in prose narratives. Acts 8: 4-40, for example, places the interchange between Peter and Simon Magus between the two halves of the account of Philip's Samaritan mission. Luke, the astute author, could have learned this technique from Mark, but it also occurs in *Life of Aesop*, as noted in chapter 2 above. When Aesop is sent to the baths on an errand for his master, he encounters the governor on his way and has an exchange with him, and when this episode is concluded, proceeds to the baths and the events that will befall him there. This is evidently a novelistic narrative technique that is found in the new popular literature of the period.[105]

Donahue also emphasizes, however, that Mark's technique is not simply one of breaking apart the main narrative and sandwiching in a new subplot between the two halves. In Mark, the middle section of the narrative concerns Jesus and his destiny, and is raised by the framing structure into greater prominence. The frame sections consist of teaching regarding discipleship or the reaction of disciples. Where Mark does this, it is done for a truly profound literary end; the destiny of Jesus is framed by teachings or narrative about the meaning of discipleship: "He uses [the *inclusio* technique] to cast over the whole gospel the shadow of the cross, and all the intercalations contain some allusion to the suffering and death of Jesus" (p. 60). Here Fortna does not really grant Donahue his due, and his rebuttals are not sufficient in and of themselves to derail Donahue's line of reasoning. Mark's redactional use of this technique does seem quite remarkable, raising a christological understanding of suffering to prominence, and associating it with discipleship in the narrative frame.

But there are other problems with Donahue's theory. A minor point is that John does not divide the denials where Mark does. Mark introduces Peter before the trial scene, then concentrates all three of Peter's denials immediately after the trial scene, while John introduces Peter and places the first denial before the trial, the other two afterward. A further question, however, is whether John's examples of intercalation really indicate that Mark's distinctive characteristics are reflected in John as well, or whether John is utilizing a more common, less profound, and ultimately less Markan technique. There is a curious aspect of John's intercalation here that indicates that the latter alternative is the case. John's intercalation is rather primitive: it is stated in verse 18 that "Peter was also standing with them, warming himself," and at verse 25, where the frame narrative is taken up again, John uses nearly the same words as before: "Simon Peter was standing and warming himself." Although it is possible that John bungles Mark's charming novelistic technique in copying it, it is more likely that it is John's Gospel that reflects the earlier attempt at this new literary technique.[106] Mark perceived a greater potentiality for it, rewriting and improving the intercalation here (varying the language and moving all the denials to the point after the interrogation), and also utilized the technique quite ably elsewhere in the gospel.

Other aspects of the passages can readily be seen as redactional. Peter's pointed and repeated use of "I am not" in John is a deliberate reversal of Jesus' formula of self-revelation, "I am." John also includes the relations of some of the characters of the drama. Mark's depiction is much more dramatic in varying the dialogue and focusing it on what Erich Auerbach called the "pendulation" of Peter in his tragic situation.[107] And yet, the intercalation technique notwithstanding, there is no clearly Markan feature discernible in John.

Mark 15: 1–15

[1] Early the next morning, the chief priests held a meeting with the elders, scribes, and the whole Sanhedrin, and bound Jesus and led him away to turn him over to Pilate.

[2] Pilate asked him, "Are you the king of the Judeans?" And he answered, "You say so." [3] The chief priests then accused him of many things. [4] Pilate then interrogated him again, and said, "Do you offer any rebuttal? Just look what charges they are bringing against you!" [5] But Jesus said nothing further, and Pilate was amazed.

John 18: 28–40

[28] They then led Jesus from Caiaphas to the pretorium. It was early in the morning.

They themselves, however, did not enter into the pretorium, so that they would not be defiled and prevented from eating the Passover meal. [29] Pilate came outside to them and said, "What charges do you bring against this man?" [30] They answered and said to him, "If this man had not committed some crime, we would not have handed him over to you." [31] But Pilate responded to them, "Take him yourselves and judge him according to your own law." The Judeans then said to him, "We are not permitted to execute anyone," [32] so that the word of Jesus be fulfilled, that is, the word that he had said to signify by what death he was about to die. [33] Pilate entered the pretorium again and called Jesus and said to him, "Are you the king of the Judeans?" [34] Jesus responded, "Do you say this of your own accord, or have others spoken to you concerning me?" [35] Pilate answered, "Am I a Judean? Your own people and the chief priests have handed you over to me. What have you done?" [36] Jesus replied, "My kingdom is not of this world. If my kingdom were of this world, my servants would fight to keep me from being handed over to the Judeans. But my kingdom is not of this world." 37Pilate then said to him, "Are you then a king?" Jesus answered, "You have said that I am a king. I was born for this, and for this I have come into the world, to testify to the truth. Everyone who is of the truth hears my voice." 38Pilate said to him, "What is truth?"

After he said this, Pilate again went out to the Judeans and said to them, "I find no charge against him, 39but it is a practice that I release one prisoner for you during Passover.

6On each festival Pilate would release for them one prisoner, whomever they requested. 7There was a prisoner named Barabbas who was one of the rebels who had committed murder during the insurrection. 8The crowd gathered to ask Pilate to do as he was accustomed to do, 9and Pilate answered them, "Do you want me to release for you the king of the Judeans?" 10For he knew that the chief priests had turned him over because of their envy. 11The chief priests had stirred up the crowd to have Pilate release Barabbas for them, 12but Pilate again said, "What then shall I do with the one whom you call the king of the Judeans?" 13They cried out, "Crucify him!" 14Pilate said to them, "What crime has he committed?" But they cried out even more, "Crucify him!" 15So Pilate, in order to please the crowd, released Barabbas for them, and after he had Jesus whipped, he handed him over to be crucified.

Do you want me to release for you the king of the Judeans?"

40They cried out again and said, "Not him, but Barabbas!" Now Barabbas was a bandit.

135

Commentary on Mark 15: 1–15/John 18: 28–40

In both gospels the interrogation by Jewish authorities results in the handing over of Jesus to the Roman governor Pontius Pilate. The details
common to the two provide intriguing suggestions of what the earlier narrative tradition might have included. In both gospels Jesus is brought in
"early" (*proi*). The groups who "hand over" Jesus are the chief priests and
others (Mark 15: 1; John 18: 35), as is usually the case in Mark and John.
Although Pilate engages in a separate dialogue with the Jewish authorities in
John 18: 29–32, he resumes the interrogation with words identical to those
in Mark: "Are you the king of the Judeans?" Jesus' first response in John is
different from that in Mark 15: 3, but when Pilate presses his question again
(verse 37), he receives a response very similar to Mark's: "You say that I am
king."

The Barabbas episode is much larger in Mark, where there is a drama
played out over the choice of criminals to be released. Barabbas is depicted as
a more reprehensible criminal in Mark (verse 7), and the chief priests incite the
crowds to shout down Pilate's own inclination to release Jesus. Once again,
however, some of the memorable lines are almost identical:

Mark 15: 9:   "Do you want (*thelete*) me to release for you the king of the
              Judeans?"
John 18: 39: "Do you want (*boulesthe*) me to release for you the king of the
              Judeans?"

And:

Mark 15: 13: "They cried out, 'Crucify him!'"
John 18: 40: "Then they again cried out, 'Not him, but Barabbas!'"

Both gospels develop the dramatic irony of Pilate's interrogation, but in different ways. In Mark, the ironic "distance" between Jesus and Barabbas is
emphasized. The latter is a scurrilous enemy of Rome, whom Pilate would not
wish to see released, though the crowds, whipped into a frenzy by the chief
priests, refuse to allow Jesus to be released. They cry "Crucify him!," which
points the way, as it were, to the conclusion of the drama on the cross, a
favorite Markan theme. Jesus is then defended by the Roman governor, while
being condemned by his own people. Pilate, wishing to satisfy the crowd,
releases the insurrectionist Barabbas, and scourges Jesus in preparation for crucifixion.[108]

In John the irony is rich as well. Here the drama is carried out by a fascinating bit of stagecraft, as Pilate moves in and out of the pretorium.[109] The
Jewish leaders, called simply "the Judeans" in verse 36, refuse to enter the pretorium so that they may remain ritually pure for the celebration of Passover.
Thus their design, to kill a righteous man, stands in ironic contrast to their
scruples over a matter of ritual purity. Similar to this is John 19: 31: the

Jewish leaders ask that Jesus' legs be broken to hasten death, so that the bodies will not be allowed to pollute the sanctity of the coming holiday. John means to focus the reader's attention on the ritual scruples of the opponents at precisely the time when they are instigating the death of the Son of God. In Plato as well, we see that Socrates' accusers are characterized as overly concerned with their ritual purity. Socrates' execution is postponed during a period of ritual purity in Athens, while a ship bearing an offering travels to Delos and back again (*Phaedo* 58a–c). Both Socrates and Jesus were depicted as speaking the clear words of truth, while those around them were too obtuse to understand the import of these words. Plato and John used irony to help solve the same literary problem: how can one explain why the wisest and most righteous person who ever lived was executed? In both cases, the irony points the reader in the same direction. The world, which has the power over the wisest and most righteous person who ever lived, has no idea what he is saying. The creation of an ironic distance between the petty scrupulousness of the opponents and the larger moral issue at hand is not uncommon in literature contemporary to John; John may have been influenced in this regard by *Gospel of Peter* 5.15 (compare below re John 19: 31), and the later *Martyrdom of Polycarp* 12: 2–3 reflects it as well.

In the course of their gospels, Mark and John are both indebted to the Greco-Roman tradition of the defense of the true philosopher, but in different ways.[110] Mark has Jesus refuse to perform a miracle that would authenticate his mission (8: 11–13; compare Philostratus, *Apollonius of Tyana* 8.7), while in the dialogue with Pilate, John depicts Jesus engaging the representative of the state in a philosophical dialogue, and by this creating a solidarity between them over against the accusers. The accusers, in turn, reveal themselves to be flatterers, opposed to true philosophy. John's further irony, however, is this: while Jesus' message is that everyone who is of the truth hears his voice, Pilate remains in a lost middle ground, neither hearing nor opposing, and asks, "What is truth?" John therefore develops an irony in the Socratic tradition, but shows no sign of borrowing any of the irony that can be laid to Mark's own invention. It could be argued that even the basic irony of the weakness of a Roman governor before the Jewish authorities is Markan, but this irony is older than Mark. In Daniel 6 and Bel and the Dragon, for example, the king, against his will, is pressed by an angry mob to execute the righteous Daniel. There is much that is specifically Markan in the passage under analysis, but that need not include the central irony of the relationship of Pilate, the Jewish leaders, and Jesus.

Frank J. Matera has produced an excellent redaction-critical study of Mark 15[111] in which he shows convincingly that Mark has ordered and redacted the traditions at hand in very significant ways. His study is a model of redaction criticism, dividing the text of Mark into what are likely the received elements of tradition – "the silence of Jesus before his accusers, the release of Barabbas, a series of mockeries, the burial of Jesus" (p. 60) – and Mark's own additions and rearrangements – the hour designations, the arrangement and bracketing of the mocking scenes, the emphasis on "king," the drawing out of the Barabbas episode, and others. And yet, against his own conclusions that John knew Mark (pp. 21–22, 29), the force of Matera's study presses in the opposite direction: the traditional elements are found in John, but the redactional changes are not.[112] The results of Matera's work should be kept in mind throughout our discussion of Mark 15.

MARK 15: 16–20a/JOHN 19: 1–12

Mark 15: 16–20a	John 19: 2–12
16The soldiers then led Jesus into the courtyard, which is the pretorium, and called the entire cohort to arms. 17They clothed him in a purple robe, and weaving a crown of thorns, placed it on his head. 18They began to salute him, saying, "Hail, King of the Judeans!" 19They struck his head with a reed and spat on him, and knelt before him in homage. 20They mocked him, then took off his purple robe and put his own clothes back on him.	2The soldiers wove a crown of thorns and placed it on his head, and clothed him in a purple robe. 3They approached him and said, "Hail, King of the Judeans!" and gave him many blows.
(compare Mark 15: 13–14 above)	4Pilate then went outside again and said to them, "Behold, I am bringing him outside to you, so that you will know that I find no fault in him." 5Jesus went out, still wearing the crown of thorns and purple robe. Pilate said to them, "Behold the man!" 6When the chief priests and their officers saw him, they cried out, "Crucify him! Crucify him!" Pilate said to them, "You take him and crucify him. I do not find any fault with him." 7The Judeans responded, "We have a law, and according to this law, he must die, because he claimed to be the Son of God!" 8When Pilate heard this, he

(compare Mark 14: 61 above)

became even more frightened, [9]and went back in the pretorium and said to Jesus, "Where are you from?" But Jesus did not respond. [10]Pilate then said to him, "Are you not going to speak with me? Do you not know that I have the authority to crucify you?" [11]Jesus answered, "You do not have any authority over me except what has been given to you from above. For this reason, the one who handed me over to you has the greater sin." [12]From that point on, Pilate tried to release him, but the Judeans cried out and said, "If you release him, you are no friend of Caesar, for anyone who claims to be king is opposed to Caesar."

Commentary on Mark 15: 16–20a/John 19: 2–12

This scene portrays the scourging of the mock-king. Mark's depiction of the soldiers mocking Jesus is essentially a separate episode, a brief moment between the trial of Jesus and his crucifixion. In John, it is carefully interrelated with the other scenes of the trial and crucifixion. The Carabas tradition, noted in chapter 2, is more in evidence in Mark's version, but in both some of the motifs are derived from the exegesis of certain biblical passages (Isa 50: 6–7; 53: 3, 5; and Mic 5: 1).[113]

John has created a complex scenario regarding the three-way dialogue of Pilate, Jesus, and the Jewish accusers, and has likely moved traditional motifs from their original placement in the interrogation scene. Among them are: Pilate's declaration that he can find no fault in Jesus (verse 4), the cry of the crowd to crucify him (verse 6), the accusation that Jesus "claimed to be the Son of God" (verse 7), and the silence of Jesus (verse 9). John's staging of this dramatic scenario is not unlike that of Bel and the Dragon, although it is much more artfully structured.

The suffering of Jesus that we see here in Mark will be paralleled by the further insults when Jesus is on the cross, but John has continued the separation of dramatic locations begun earlier (inside/outside of the pretorium) to emphasize the relative innocence – or ambiguity – of Pilate and the guilt of "the Judeans." Here again scenes of very similar content are presented in each instance using different words. Still, the central memorable declaration, "Hail, King of the Judeans!," is almost identical.

Mark 15: 20b–27, 29–32	**John 19: 13–25a**
20bThey then led him away to crucify him.	13When Pilate heard these words, he led Jesus out and sat on the judge's bench at a place called the Stone Pavement, or in Hebrew, Gabbatha. 14It was the day of Preparation for the Passover, about the sixth hour. Pilate said to the Judeans, "Behold your king!" 15But they cried out, "Away with him! Crucify him!" Pilate said to them, "Shall I crucify your king?" And the chief priests answered, "We have no king but Caesar!" 16Pilate then handed Jesus over to them to be crucified, and they took him into custody.
21They forced a man who had just come in from the country to carry the cross, whose name was Simon of Cyrene, the father of Alexander and Rufus. 22They brought Jesus to a place called Golgotha, which translated means "Place of the Skull," 23and offered him wine mixed with myrrh to drink, but he would not take it. 24They crucified him and "divided his garments by casting lots for them" to see who would get them. 25It was the third hour when they crucified him. 26The inscription which stated the charge read, "The King of the Judeans." 27With him they also crucified two bandits, one on his right and one on his left.	17Carrying his own cross, he went out to a spot called Place of the Skull, or in Hebrew, Golgotha. 18There they crucified him, along with two others, one on either side, with Jesus in the middle. (compare John 19: 23–24 below) 19Pilate wrote this inscription and placed it on the cross, "Jesus the Nazorean, king of the Judeans." 20Many of the Judeans read this inscription, because the place where Jesus was crucified was near the city, and it was written in Hebrew, Latin, and Greek. 21But the chief priests of the Judeans then said to Pilate, "Do not write,

'The king of the Judeans,' but 'This man said, "I am the king of the Judeans."'" 22Pilate responded, "What I have written, I have written."

(compare Mark 15: 24 above)

23When the soldiers had crucified Jesus, they took his clothes and divided them into four parts, one part for each soldier. They also took the tunic, but it was seamless, woven from the top down of one piece. 24So they said to each other, "Let us not tear it, but let us cast lots for it to see who will get it." This occurred to fulfill the scripture that says, "They have divided my garments among themselves, but for my cloak they cast lots." 25aThat is what the soldiers did.

29The passersby blasphemed him, shaking their heads and saying, "Ha! You who would destroy the temple and rebuild it in three days, 30save yourself and come down off the cross!" 31In the same way, the chief priests, along with the scribes, mocked him among themselves, saying, "He saved others, but cannot save himself. 32Let the Messiah, the King of Israel, come down now from the cross, so that we may see and believe!" Even those who were crucified with him insulted him.

Commentary on Mark 15: 20b–27, 29–32/John 19: 13–25a

This central scene of the crucifixion requires special attention in any investigation of gospel origins for a number of reasons: (1) the crucifixion is the central historical fact of Jesus' biography. Whatever else may be attributed to legendary accretions of early Christian tradition, this datum is the closest we may come to historical certainty (Sanders, *Jesus and Judaism*); (2) this fact of the ignoble end of Jesus' mission had to be explained by early Christians and treated as God's holy plan; (3) a very high concentration of quotations or allusions to scripture appear in this section, so that almost every detail of Jesus' crucifixion is explained as a fulfillment of some passage of scripture, usually of Psalms 22 and 69 and Isaiah. Since the early creedal formula in 1 Cor 15: 3–5 states that Jesus' crucifixion came about "according to the scriptures," we can assume that the high number of formula quotations represents an apologetic intent to prove to Jews and Christians that the scriptures were indeed fulfilled in Jesus' death.[114]

The important biblical allusions and quotations in the last half of Mark and John are:

	Mark's gospel	*John's gospel*	*Scripture passage*
on colt of ass	Mk 11: 1–8	Jn 12: 15	Zech 9: 9
hosanna	Mk 11: 9–10	Jn 12: 13	Ps 118: 25–26
who has believed?		Jn 12: 38	Isa 53: 1
see and not understand		Jn 12: 40	Isa 6: 1
one will betray	Mk 14: 18	Jn 13: 18, 21	Ps 41: 9
strike the shepherd	Mk 14: 27		Zech 13: 7
my soul is troubled	Mk 14: 34	Jn 12: 27	Ps 6: 4–5; 42: 5, 6, 11; 43: 5
bearing false witness	Mk 14: 57–58		Ps 35: 11, 27: 12
Jesus silent	Mk 14: 61; 15: 5	Jn 19: 9	Isa 53: 7
Jesus struck	Mk 14: 65; 15: 19	Jn 18: 22–23; 19: 1, 3	Isa 50: 6
Jesus given wine	Mk 15: 23, 35–36	Jn 19: 28	Ps 69: 21
parting garments	Mk 15: 24	Jn 19: 24	Ps 22: 18
wagging heads	Mk 15: 29–30		Ps 22: 7–8; 109: 25
why have you forsaken me?	Mk 15: 34		Ps 22: 1
Jesus given vinegar	Mk 15: 36	Jn 19: 28–29	Ps 69: 21
no bone broken		Jn 19: 36	Ex 12: 10,46; Ps 34: 21
they will see one pierced		Jn 19: 37	Zech 12: 10

A glance at the table reveals that, in spite of the reliance on biblical quotations and allusions in both gospels, in these chapters Mark and John have fewer than half of them in common; that is, they generally quote or allude to different passages, and utilize them at different points in the narrative. The overlap, however, in their use of biblical citations is much greater in the interrogation scene (Mark 14: 53–65/John 18: 12–14, 19–24) and in the crucifixion scene proper. Even here, however, Mark and John relate the details to the biblical passages in different ways. John often specifies explicitly that a particular detail is to be taken as a fulfillment of scripture, using a fulfillment formula to express this. Mark, on the other hand, incorporates these same details into the narrative without stating explicitly that there is a correspondence with scripture. For instance, in 15: 24, a direct quotation from Ps 22: 19 has been incorporated into the text, and is now part of a longer sentence (indicated in italics): "They crucified him and *divided his garments by casting lots for them* to see who would get them." At Mark 15: 36 (see below), the offering of the sponge filled with vinegar is also included as part of a longer sentence. These differences correspond to their hermeneutical methods earlier in the gospels as well: at Mark 14: 18 the scriptural allusion is incorporated into the text, while at John 13: 18 it is quoted explicitly. The explicit reference to Zech 9: 9, where Jesus enters riding on an ass, is in Mark transformed into an entire novelistic digression of searching and finding the ass, with no explicit reference to scripture (Mark 11: 1–8).

Because of Mark's incorporation of biblical allusions into the narrative, rather than explicit quotation, some scholars have maintained that Mark has moved away from a strict prophecy/fulfillment schema.[115] Mark's redaction of the older prophecy/fulfillment passages looks to larger themes than the individual correspondences of a detail in the passion to a biblical text. At the same time that these details are incorporated and interwoven more thoroughly into the narrative of Mark, they are also ordered more rigorously according to a redactional theme. John records Psalms 69 and 22 as passages for prophecy and fulfillment only, without any apparent awareness of what the passages might have meant in their original contexts as laments, while Mark consciously organizes the scriptural passages around the redactional motif of the suffering righteous one. Thus at Mark 15: 34 (next section), Ps 22: 2 is placed in the mouth of Jesus in Aramaic with a Greek translation, but more to the point, the offering of vinegar in verse 36a has been reduced and sandwiched in between the descriptions of mocking in verses 35 and 36b, a typical Markan technique.[116] John's use of the formula quotations, then, is less developed in this direction, and remains typical of the method which arose in the church as an apologetic device to explain the crucifixion as a fulfillment of scripture in every detail. John's presentation of this evidence gives equal prominence to each of the fulfillment-events which are noted; they stand as arguments for a dogmatic understanding of Jesus' crucifixion as a fulfillment of scriptural prophecy.

If John was familiar with Mark, we would have to assume that the motifs of the suffering righteous one were eliminated – not impossible considering John's more triumphalist theology – but also that the text of Mark was unraveled, strand by strand, and that some strands were discarded and others were used to generate an entire prophecy/fulfillment scene, described quite simply and directly. This last step is also not impossible, but it requires a complicated reconstruction on John's part. The thesis that Mark and John reflect a common source, which John – in part, at any rate – reproduces more faithfully is the more likely scenario.

On a different note, both Mark and John include the Hebrew place name of the hill where Jesus is crucified, Golgotha, and both provide a Greek translation of its meaning: "Place of the Skull." What is pertinent for our investigation is that Mark interestingly uses the same translation formula that John uses three times in John 1, "which translated means." In reference to John 1, I argued that this formula may reflect the use of a relatively early tradition, where translation of Hebrew terms was necessary. Here (and in Mark 15: 34 below) it is Mark who preserves evidence of this same usage.[117]

MARK 15: 33–39/JOHN 19: 28–30

Mark 15: 33–39

33From about the sixth hour, a darkness began to cover all the earth, lasting until the ninth hour. 34On the ninth hour, Jesus cried out with a loud voice, "Eloi, Eloi, lema sabachthani?," which translated means, "My God, my God, why have you forsaken me?" 35When some of those standing there heard this, they said, "Listen! He is calling Elijah."

36A person standing there ran and got a sponge dipped in vinegar, placed it on a stick, and offered it to Jesus,

John 19: 28–30

28After this, Jesus knew that everything had now come to pass, and so he said, in order to fulfill the scriptures, "I am thirsty.' 29Lying at hand was a jar full of vinegar. They placed a sponge dipped in vinegar on a hyssop branch, and offered it to him to drink. 30When he had sipped the vinegar he said, "Now it is complete," and leaned his head and gave up his spirit.

saying, "Come, let us see whether
Elijah will come to take him
down." 37Jesus then uttered a
loud cry and breathed his last.
38The curtain of the temple was
torn in two from top to bottom.
39When the centurion who was
standing beside Jesus saw that he
had thus breathed his last, he said,
"Truly this man was the Son of
God!"

Commentary on Mark 15: 33–39/John 19: 28–30

The redactional theme of the suffering Messiah could be noted above in
Mark, but here the distinction between Mark and John becomes very dramatic. Mark emphasizes the abandonment of Jesus, quoting Ps 22: 1 and
alluding to Ps 69: 21 in Mark 15: 36. Jesus' "cry of dereliction" in Mark, "Eloi,
Eloi, lema sabachthani," a quotation in Aramaic of Ps 22: 1, is translated into
Greek using the same translation formula found just above (Mark 15: 22) and
in John 1. It was suggested above that the formula is an early part of the gospel
tradition that Mark retains here (just as John does in John 1). John does not
include this line, but one could easily imagine John wanting to omit it.
Nineham (*Saint Mark*, p. 428) notes that it is possible that Jesus' cry of dereliction in Mark is not a cry of despair, but the confident prayer of one who
expects deliverance (so the rest of Psalm 22 and ancient Jewish interpretations
of it). However, the context, especially verse 37, indicates that it was understood as the last cry of a suffering Messiah. Indeed, the irony that Jesus' cry of
"Eloi" is understood by the Jewish passersby as "Elijah" would tend to confirm
this (although this may be Mark's redaction), as would the parallel at the
Gospel of Peter 5.19. What Mark and John do share is the motif of Jesus being
given vinegar to drink. In John, this is explicitly related to "the scripture," in
this case, Ps 69: 21, while in Mark the scriptural association is once again written into the narrative without an explicit formula.

Mark has carefully noted the passage of time in the passion story, marked
off in three-hour units (15: 25, 33, 34; compare 15: 42). In Mark these designations seem to follow on Jesus' Gethsemane prayer that his "hour" might
pass from him. This cross of suffering is minimized in John (if it was ever there
to that extent in the pre-Johannine tradition), and the "hour" becomes in that
gospel a timeless moment of exaltation. Although it is conceivable that John
derived this notion of the hour from Mark, it is unlikely; it is now funda-
mentally different, and has been moved outside of the crucifixion scene to the
whole of the gospel (Brown, *John*, pp. 1.517–18).

Although narrative description in John often builds and develops, here
John is very economical in telling these crucial events of the crucifixion itself.

John's wordiness in many scenes evidently comes about as a result of opening up the narrative to develop Johannine dialogue and discourses. These verses of John are largely traditional, part of the exegetical tradition that Koester postulates for the development of the passion narrative (see section above).[118] It is interesting, but hardly conclusive for the questions at hand, that John lacks the quotation of Ps 22: 1, and the reference to Elijah. This could be explained by either theory of the relation of John to Mark. John's omission of the darkness, however, is somewhat more complicated. It is possible that Mark has introduced this into a gospel tradition that lacked it (so Lührmann, *Das Markusevangelium*, pp. 262–63; compare Mark 13: 24), but the *Gospel of Peter* 5.15 connects the darkening of the sky to the fear of the Jews that Jesus would remain on the cross after sunset, in violation of Jewish law. The latter motif, unconnected to a premature darkening of the sky, is found at John 19: 31. It is difficult to argue here for the priority of any of these traditions, but regarding other passages I argue below that the *Gospel of Peter* reflects the earliest tradition, and that may be true here as well.

MARK 15: 40–41/JOHN 19: 25–27

Mark 15: 40–41	John 19: 25–27
40Several women were standing there, watching from a distance. Among them were Mary Magdalene, Mary the mother of James the younger and of Joses, and Salome. 41They had all followed Jesus when he was in Galilee and served him. Others were also there who had come up with him to Jerusalem.	25Jesus' mother was standing at the cross, along with his mother's sister, Mary the wife of Clopas, and Mary Magdalene. 26When Jesus saw his mother and the disciple whom he loved, he said to his mother, "Woman, this is your son." 27Then he said to the disciple, "This is your mother." From that moment on, the disciple took her into his home.

Commentary on Mark 15: 40–41/John 19: 25–27

These short accounts identify, with some attempt at precision, women who were standing by as Jesus died on the cross. In Mark they have little role here, but return later at the discovery of the empty tomb. Their presence at the cross at the time of death establishes a continuity and an eyewitness perspective for the events that follow. Mark's emphasis on their role in Galilee may be redactional, although Galilee itself may also have been found in the tradition.

With all the characters named on both sides, several with the name of Mary, there is only one person in common between them: Mary Magdalene.

She is also the only woman to discover the empty tomb in John, in the longer ending of Mark, and in the *Gospel of Peter* (see below). Mary Magdalene was likely the only witness at this point in the earlier gospel tradition, although there was perhaps one other Mary, now variously identified.

John has likely added the mother of Jesus in order to establish a relationship between her and the "disciple whom Jesus loved." This unnamed disciple was evidently important for the Johannine community's identity, and the connection with Jesus' family was important. It was for this reason that John has moved this scene forward a few verses, in order to allow for Jesus' utterances just before his death.

MARK 15: 42–47/JOHN 19: 31, 38–42

Mark 15: 42–47

42When evening came, since it was the day of Preparation (which is the day before the Sabbath),

43Joseph of Arimathea, an honored member of the Sanhedrin, who was also awaiting the kingdom of God, boldly decided to enter in before Pilate and request permission to take down the body of Jesus. 44Pilate wondered if Jesus was already dead, and calling for the centurion, he asked him whether Jesus had been dead long. 45When he received word back from the centurion, he granted Joseph permission to take the corpse.

46Joseph procured a linen cloth,

John 19: 31, 38–42

31Since it was the day of Preparation for the Sabbath – and that Sabbath was a major holiday as well – the Jews did not want the bodies to remain on the cross overnight. They therefore asked Pilate to have the legs of those crucified broken, and the bodies removed.

38Joseph of Arimathea, who was a disciple of Jesus – but in secret, for fear of the Judeans – then asked Pilate for permission to take down the body of Jesus. Pilate agreed, and Joseph proceeded to take the body.

39Nicodemus, who had come to him at first by night, also arrived, bringing with him a mixture of myrrh and aloes that weighed about a hundred pounds. 40They

147

and took Jesus' body and rolled it up in it, and placed it in a tomb that was hewn out of rock. He then rolled a stone over the entrance of the tomb.

took the body of Jesus and wrapped it with the spices in linen cloths, in keeping with the burial custom of the Judeans. [41]Now there was a garden near where he was crucified, and in the garden was a new tomb in which no one had been buried. [42]Since it was the day of Preparation of the Judeans and the tomb was nearby, they laid him there.

[47]Mary Magdalene and Mary mother of Jesus saw where he was laid.

Commentary on Mark 15: 42–47/John 19: 31, 38–42

The request of Joseph of Arimathea to retrieve the body of Jesus is common to the two gospels, as is Jesus being wrapped for burial and placed in a nearby tomb. The social status of Joseph of Arimathea and Pilate's inquiry into the time of Jesus' death are both found only in Mark. Nineham (*Saint Mark*, p. 435) considers the latter a secondary insertion on other grounds as well. It is significant that this Markan redaction is lacking in John.

John, on the other hand, contains a motif that was developed also in *Gospel of Peter* 12.50, 52, 54: "but in secret, for fear of the Judeans," and continues also the ironic theme begun at 18: 28-40 (also found at *Gospel of Peter* 5.15), wherein the execution of the righteous man is delayed out of a concern for ritual purity. John also adds the report about Nicodemus, who displaces Joseph of Arimathea, and the hyperbolic amount of burial unguents.

MARK 16: 1–8; LONGER ENDING (MARK 16: 9–20)/ GOSPEL OF PETER 12.50–14.60; JOHN 20: 1–31

Mark 16: 1–8

[1]When the Sabbath was over, Mary Magdalene, Mary mother of James, and Salome bought spices to bring to anoint him. [2]Very early on the first day of the week, just past sun up, they came to the tomb.

Gospel of Peter 12.50–14: 60

[50]Out of fear of the Judeans – for they were inflamed with wrath – Mary Magdalene, a female disciple of the Lord, had not done the things women generally do for their loved ones who die. So early on the morning of the Lord's Day, [51]she took her friends and went to the tomb where he lay. [52]They

3But they asked each other, "Who will roll away the stone for us from the entrance of the tomb?"

4When they looked up, however, they saw that the stone, which was very large, had already been rolled away. 5When they entered the tomb, they saw a young man sitting on the right side, dressed in a white robe, and they were alarmed. 6But he said to them, "Do not be alarmed. You are seeking Jesus the Nazarene who has been crucified. He has been raised, and is not here. Here is the place where they laid him. 7Go now and say to his disciples and to Peter that he is going before you to Galilee. There you will see him, as he told you." 8Running out, they fled from the tomb, for they were gripped by fear and amazement. And they said nothing to anyone, for they were afraid.

were afraid that the Judeans would see them, but they said, "Although we were not able to weep and mourn on the day he was crucified, yet now let us do these things at the tomb. 53But who will roll away the stone that is placed at the entrance of the tomb, so that we may enter and perform the proper rites?" – 54for the stone was large – "and we are afraid that someone may see us. Even if we cannot perform them, we may still place what we bring at the entrance as a memorial for him, and weep and mourn until we go home again." 13.55But when they arrived, they found the tomb already open. They approached and stooped down, and saw inside a young man sitting in the center of the tomb, shining brightly and clothed with a gleaming robe. He said to them, 56"Why have you come? Whom do you seek? Surely not the man who was crucified? He has risen and gone away. If you do not believe it, bend down and look at the place where he lay, for he is not here. He has risen and gone away to the place from which he was sent." 57Frightened, the women ran away.

14.58On the last day of the festival of Unleavened Bread, many people left to return to their homes, since the festival had ended. 59But we, the twelve disciples of the Lord, wept and mourned, and each of us, still grieving at what had happened, went to his own home. [60]But I, Simon Peter, and Andrew my brother took our nets and went to the sea. With us was Levi son of Alphaeus, whom the Lord . . . (here the fragment of the *Gospel of Peter* ends)

Longer Ending (Mark 16: 9–20)	**John 20: 1–23**
[9]After he arose again early on the first day of the week, Jesus appeared first to Mary Magdalene, from whom he had cast out seven demons.	[1]On the first day of the week, while it was still dark, Mary Magdalene came to the tomb early, and saw that the stone had been rolled away from the entrance.
[10]She went to tell those who had been with him, as they were mourning and weeping, [11]but when they heard that he was alive and had been seen by her, they did not believe. [12]After this, he appeared in a different form to two of them as they were on their way out to a field.	(compare John 16: 15 below)
	[2]She ran to Simon Peter and the other disciple, whom Jesus loved, and said, "They have taken the Lord from the tomb, and we do not know where they have put him." [3]Peter and the other disciple then went to the tomb, [4]both running side by side. But the other disciple quickly ran ahead of Peter and arrived first at the tomb. [5]He bent over and looked in, and saw the linen wrappings lying there, but he did not go in. [6]Simon Peter then ran up from behind and entered the tomb, where he also saw the linen wrappings on the ground, along with the cloth that was on his head. The cloth was not lying with the wrappings, but was over to the side, neatly rolled up.

8Then the other disciple, who had arrived first, entered the tomb, saw everything, and believed. 9For they did not yet understand the scripture that says that it is necessary for Jesus to be raised from the dead. 10The disciples then returned to their homes.

13They returned and reported this to the others, but they did not believe them either.

11Mary stood and wept outside the tomb, and as she cried, she bent down to look inside the tomb, 12and saw two angels in white, sitting where the body of Jesus had lain, one at the head and one at the foot. 13They said to her, "Woman, why are you crying?" She replied, "They have taken away my lord, and I do not know where they have put him." 14When she had said this, she turned around and saw Jesus standing there, but she did not know it was Jesus. 15Jesus said to her, "Woman, why are you crying? Whom do you seek?" She supposed that he was the gardener, and said to him, "Sir, if you have carried him away, tell me where you have put him, and I will take him away." 16Jesus said to her, "Mary." She turned to him and said in Hebrew, "Rabbouni," which means Teacher. 17Jesus said to her, "Do not touch me, for I have not yet ascended to the Father. Go to my brothers and say to them, 'I am ascending to my Father and your Father, my God and your God.'" 18Mary Magdalene then returned to the disciples and announced, "I have seen the Lord," and told them that he had spoken these things to her.

(compare Mark 16: 10–11 above)

14Later, he appeared to the eleven

19Evening came on the first day

151

as they were eating, and rebuked them for their lack of faith and hardness of heart, because they had not believed those who saw him after he had been raised.

15He said to them, "Go out to the whole world and preach the good news to all creation.

16The one who believes and is baptized will be saved, but the one who does not believe will be condemned. 17And these signs will accompany those who believe: they will cast out demons in my name, they will speak in new tongues, 18they will take up snakes in their hands, and if they drink any poison it will not harm them; if they lay their hands upon the sick they will become well." 19When he had said these things to them, the Lord Jesus was taken up into heaven and sat down at the right hand of God. 20But they went out and preached everywhere, and the Lord worked with them, confirming the word through accompanying signs.

of the week, and although the doors of the room where the disciples met were locked out of fear of the Judeans, Jesus came and stood before them and said, "Peace be with you." 20When he said this, he showed them his hands and side, and they rejoiced when they saw him. 21Jesus then said to them again, "Peace be with you. As the Father sent me, so I am sending you." 22Then he breathed into them and said, "Receive the holy spirit. 23If you forgive the sins of any, they are forgiven; if you retain the sins of any, they are retained."

Commentary on Mark 16: 1–8; Longer Ending (Mark 16: 9–20)/Gospel of Peter 12.50–14.60; John 20: 1–23

By bringing the so-called Longer Ending of Mark (Mark 16: 9–20) and the *Gospel of Peter* into the discussion, I have greatly complicated the picture of the conclusion of the gospel narrative. The Longer Ending is missing from the best ancient manuscripts, and was clearly not present in the versions of Mark used by Matthew and Luke. Further, it is quite disconsonant with Mark 16: 1–8, since it repeats some of the same events. As a result, there is agreement among most scholars that it is a later addition to Mark, perhaps culled from the other gospels. Dodd and Brown, however, maintain that in part it may reflect a tradition independent of the synoptics, and more recently, Paul Mirecki has pressed this question even further, arguing that the Longer Ending is not dependent on the synoptic Gospels or John.[119] Although the Longer Ending could not possibly have originally come after the present ending of canonical Mark (16: 8), it might have been an *early* gospel ending, perhaps even an ending that Mark has intentionally displaced. Although it does not cohere easily with 16: 1–8, it could have followed quite readily after chapter 15. According to this theory, Mark has radically trimmed back the miraculous elements in the tradition, and this early gospel conclusion is supplanted by one in which there is no resurrection appearance and no clear miracle, or any note of proclamation of the gospel. The Longer Ending could be an early, even pre-Markan, witness to the gospel tradition. Although scholars are not in agreement as to (a) whether the Longer Ending of Mark contains early traditions and (b) which parts, if any, of the *Gospel of Peter* reflect early traditions, it is my view, along with other scholars, that these texts can be utilized to reconstruct the earliest traditions. (The same was also said for Secret Mark above.)

Mark 16: 1–8, printed in most New Testaments as the canonical ending of Mark, recounts the Easter morning experiences of the women who witnessed the crucifixion in 15: 40. Upon arrival at Jesus' tomb with spices to anoint him for burial, they find the heavy stone rolled away, and a young man in a white robe sitting in the tomb. Although his presence is in many ways typical of other appearances of angels at the empty tomb, the description is remarkably restrained. His robe is white, but he is in no way described as an angelic or supernatural figure.[120] The understated presentation of the angel, and the fact that he points the way to Galilee, are probably Markan. In addition, verse 8a is surely from the hand of that redactor; it breathes the same spirit as the messianic secret passages in the miracle stories. The expected triumphal proclamation to the people is expressed here not by Jesus' command, but by his presumed effect.[121] Still, Mark has probably not invented 16: 1–8 from whole cloth. The *Gospel of Peter*, which likely represents an early gospel tradition independent of the synoptic gospels,[122] is more similar to Mark at this point than anywhere else; several lines are closely parallel. If the *Gospel of Peter* is old and not derived from the canonical gospels, then this would have important implications for the reconstruction of the tradition behind Mark 16: 1–8. Some parts of Mark 16: 1–8 that have been considered redactional have parallels in the *Gospel of Peter*, and are thus pre-Markan.

It is also significant that the four gospel endings displayed here contain motifs that fall into two categories: the empty tomb motif (Mark 16: 1–8, *Gospel of Peter*) and the resurrection appearance (Mark 16: 9–20). John 20 appears to contain both. As Elias Bickerman has shown, the empty tomb is part of a widely attested legendary motif in the ancient world of the *rapture*, that is, the disappearance into heaven of the revered figure, rather than his *res-urrection from the dead* and reappearance on earth.[123] These two theological beliefs are not the same, and are not represented by the same kinds of narratives. Bickerman argues, contra Bultmann, that the empty tomb is not only totally separate in its origin and intention from the resurrection, but appears *earlier* in the Christian tradition. It is thus intriguing for our purposes to note the division of gospel endings into the "rapture" and "resurrection appearance" varieties.[124] Analogously, the conclusions of the gospels can be divided into those that contain resurrection appearances in Galilee (Mark 16: 1–8; John 21) and those that place the appearance in Jerusalem (Mark 16: 9–20; John 20). Although Galilee was likely an important geographical setting for much of the pre-Markan and pre-Johannine gospel narrative (as I shall argue in chapter 4), the earliest appearance tradition was likely set in Jerusalem.

To turn once again to the Longer Ending, it is interesting to note how much happens here in a few verses. After Mary Magdalene appears alone to anoint the body of Jesus,[125] three separate resurrection appearances are mentioned in succession (though not described as in John, Matthew, and Luke), along with the disbelieving reaction of the disciples. The resurrection appearances here do not serve to create a sense of wonder at the miraculous, but highlight instead the issue of belief and unbelief. This is also an important issue of John 20, but in the Longer Ending of Mark it is much more economically presented. When Jesus makes his third appearance and upbraids the disciples for their unbelief, he somewhat abruptly commissions them to proclaim the good news. Those who do not believe will be condemned, while miraculous signs will accompany those who believe.

Here I have omitted John 21 as secondary,[126] and focus instead on John 20 as the ending of the gospel. John 20 appears to be a composite scene, expanded at a number of points by Johannine redaction. It begins in the same way as the canonical and Longer Ending of Mark and the *Gospel of Peter* do, with the arrival of Mary Magdalene at the tomb. However, it has been argued that the race to the tomb between Peter and the Beloved Disciple, verses 2–10, is inserted into the narrative at this point.[127] Verse 11 betrays no knowledge of this interlude, and continues the story of verse 1. Here there is an empty tomb story, with two angels instead of one, but it quickly changes to a resurrection appearance of Jesus. One may wonder, with Brown (*John*, pp. 2.978, 1027–28), whether this has also been added.

Other parallels between the Longer Ending and John are discernible, though the tradition they share has been modified on both sides. In the Longer Ending the appearances are first to Mary, then to two of Jesus' followers, but when this is reported, the other followers do not believe. When Jesus appears to "the eleven," he censures them for their unbelief, then switches abruptly to the commission to preach. In John there is an appearance of the risen Jesus to Mary and then to the disciples, whereupon he gives them their commission to receive the holy spirit. Several parallels here are worthy of note: (1) The motif of general disbelief in the Longer Ending is found in John, but now focused upon "doubting Thomas"; (2) The correspondence of "believing" with "signs," characteristic of certain passages of John usually assigned to the Signs Source (2: 11; 4: 53; 6: 14; 12: 37 and especially John 20: 30–31), is also emphasized in the Longer Ending. In the Longer Ending, however, the signs are no longer associated with Jesus, but with the followers; and (3) The inclusion/exclusion formula in each commission is different in content, but arranged in a similar antithetical bicolon:

> Longer Ending: "The one who believes and is baptized will be saved, but the one who does not believe will be condemned."
> John 20: 23: "If you forgive the sins of any, they are forgiven; if you retain the sins of any, they are retained."

The two angels in John 20: 12–13 probably do not derive from the empty tomb tradition, but from a separate angelophany (compare *Gospel of Peter* 9.35–11.49). Interestingly, the single angel of the empty tomb tradition has become Jesus in John 20: 14–15, who says some of the same words ("Whom do you seek?"), as does the angel in Mark 16: 1–8 and the *Gospel of Peter*. An indication of John's motive for changing the angel to Jesus is quickly seen. Once Jesus is known to Mary, the motif of touching Jesus is introduced, which is amplified in the redactional section concerning Thomas in John 20: 24–28. The appearance of Jesus is probably originally foreign to the empty tomb tradition. John 20 is a combination of an empty tomb tradition (similar to but independent of Mark 16: 1–8 and *Gospel of Peter* 12–13) and a resurrection appearance tradition (similar to the Longer Ending of Mark 16: 9–20).

Thus, at the conclusion of the gospel narrative, we find a plurality of endings in the earliest gospel traditions, which can be divided into two basic types, the empty tomb (Mark 16: 1–8; *Gospel of Peter*) and the resurrection appearance (Mark 16: 9–20; John 20). Even here, I have simplified this complex situation by excluding Matthew, Luke, and John 21. Also, the *Gospel of Peter* breaks off before what may be a resurrection appearance in Galilee. Most scholars would, perhaps wisely, resist any temptation to reduce the plurality of endings to any single set of motifs. Thus, although I have postulated a core narrative tradition behind most of Mark and John, here the question of a single tradition must remain unresolved. It is certainly the case, however, that the ending of canonical Mark, Mark 16: 1–8, should not continue to determine our view of how the earliest form of the gospel should end. The Longer Ending, John 20, and the *Gospel of Peter* all provide provocative reasons for trying to look back behind Markan redaction to perceive other possible gospel endings.

4

CONCLUSION

By using the two gospels as lenses through which we can perceive the refracted image of the earlier gospel tradition, we can hypothetically reconstruct its outline and many of its motifs. Although some of the material found in one gospel, but not the other, could have been part of an earlier core, and material common to both might have circulated in smaller units, and been inserted by both authors independently, the process of determining the *likely* core by isolating the parallel material is a justifiable method. The process is analogous to the reconstruction of Q, although there we have not just Matthew and Luke, but a third comparison point as well to tell us what Q is not, that is, Mark. In addition, while Matthew and Luke have made use of a written source, keeping fairly close to it, Mark and John have evidently utilized a much more fluid tradition, perhaps one or more oral accounts of the gospel narrative. Nevertheless, the opportunity exists here to address the question of the earlier elements of the gospel narrative tradition through a comparison of Mark and John, with intriguing results. We find that what the two gospels share – and therefore what we can postulate as a core tradition that could explain each of their developments – constitutes an entire gospel. The conclusions of this study cannot be proven, but the case for any of the possible explanations for the relationship of Mark and John must be made on the basis of the theory's overall plausibility, in much the same way that the argument for the existence of Q ultimately convinces, or fails to convince, on the basis of its overall plausibility. The scholarly debate over whether John is dependent upon Mark has often focused on details of comparison between the two, but the most compelling arguments on both sides have tried to create a plausible theory of the whole. Just as in text criticism, where a reading is considered likely if it can explain other divergent readings, so here a hypothetical source is considered likely if it can explain two other texts.

What I have derived from the first two chapters of this study is the origin of the genre of Mark and John – aretalogical biography associated with cult – and what I have derived from the third chapter is the overall structure of the core narrative that Mark and John had in common. The proposed core is similar in many passages to the sources reconstructed by M.-E. Boismard, Robert

T. Fortna, or Howard M. Teeple,[1] although none of these are precisely the same in their particulars, and they are all argued on the basis of very different criteria. In this final chapter I shall assume the results of the foregoing discussion, and indicate some of the implications of this hypothesis. If the results of the preceding comparison reveal anything of the contours of the earlier gospel tradition, then we can suggest what themes were present and how they were treated. Here I shall treat separately some of the most important of these to indicate in what way the tradition likely developed.

A. PROPHET, "PROPHET LIKE MOSES," AND THE AUTHENTICATING SIGNS OF THE PROPHET

The hypothesis of the present study, as presented in chapters 1 and 2, is that the hero narrative depicts the death of the prophet at the hands of his own people. "Prophet," however, is an ambiguous word, and we must define its use more carefully. We need not engage in a full exploration of the use of this term in the first century, but a few of the parameters of its meaning must be sketched. To begin with, there was some disagreement in first-century Judaism as to whether prophecy had in fact already ceased in Israel. Josephus is careful to limit the word "prophet" to figures from the ancient past, although in his view seers or diviners are still forewarned by God of events to come.[2] More to the point, Josephus' limitation of prophecy to the past was evidently not shared by all Jews and Christians. The popular Jewish leaders whom Josephus describes negatively took on the mantle of prophecy enthusiastically, as did the author of Revelation (see especially Rev 1: 3; 19: 10; and 22: 10). Josephus indicates that the popular leader Theudas called himself a prophet, claiming that in his actions he would manifest parallels to the Exodus (*Antiquities* 20.5.1 §97).[3] According to Josephus, other "deceivers" arose who fomented rebellion, led followers into the desert, and promised "wonders and signs" (*terata kai semeia, Antiquities* 20.8.6 §§167–70). One in particular claimed that he was a prophet and led his followers to the Mount of Olives, presumably to await the advent of God at the Endtime (compare Zech 14: 4). The signs that these popular leaders claimed to perform were considered "signs of deliverance," probably calling to mind the deliverance of Exodus (*semeia eleutherias, Jewish War* 2.13.4 §259; *semeia soterias, Jewish War* 6.5.2 §285).

This apparent contradiction between the view that prophecy had ceased and the view that certain people were sent by God to lead the people as prophets has been partially resolved by Benjamin Sommer, who points out that wherever the term "prophet" is mentioned concerning a contemporary figure, it is as a "prophet of the Endtime," whether the title "prophet" is uttered by the person himself or by a critic, such as Josephus.[4] In other words, most Jews apparently believed that, although the generally recognized period of prophecy in Israel was confined to the past, the Endtime would be a time of renewed prophecy. Sommer's theory will sit well with those scholars who detect in some Jewish and early Christian documents a belief in the coming of an eschatological prophet, a "prophet like Moses," or the return of Elijah. Richard Horsley, however, has argued strongly against such notions.[5] He notes that the view that prophecy had ceased in ancient Judaism often goes hand in hand with the view that a prophet would arise in the eschatological age; in other words, one notion seems to require the other. Horsley sees problems with both propositions: Josephus and others did not represent the majority of Jews in asserting that the age of prophecy was over, and the expectations of an eschatological prophet, a "prophet like Moses," or the return of Elijah were not common in first-century Judaism. Horsley instead divides the first-century Jewish prophets into two groups: oracular prophets and leaders of popular movements. The former, by uttering oracles, communicate what God is going to bring about, much as prophets had for centuries in Israel. The leaders of popular movements, on the other hand, evidently called themselves prophets, but did not promulgate oracles; rather, they raised large followings to go out into the wilderness to await the deliverance of God. Although Horsley correctly cautions us that in first-century Judaism there is not a great deal of evidence for eschatological expectations of a prophet, there is some, both in the Christian gospels and elsewhere, as Horsley in fact grants.

But regardless of which scholar is correct here, the prophet role was certainly available to Jesus or to others. The words "prophet" and "to prophesy" are used in the first-century Christian writings without any hesitation or sense of historical incongruity. First Corinthians 12 and 14 contain an extended discussion of the practice of prophecy in the Pauline churches. It is clear from the gospels that the early followers of Jesus believed that the holy spirit had fallen upon them to prophesy (Matt 7: 22).[6] In Q we find both prophetic sayings and the motif of Jesus as the rejected prophet.[7] John 11: 51 states that Caiaphas, because he was high priest, could "prophesy" concerning Jesus.

One particular example of first-century prophecy, described by Josephus at *Jewish War* 6.5.3 §§300–9, is so interesting for a comparison with the gospels that I quote it in full:

> At the time of the pilgrimage festival known as Shabuot (Pentecost), the priests entered the inner court of the temple at night, as was their liturgical practice, and reported that they were aware, first of all, of a commotion and a disturbance, and then also of the sound of many voices sayings, "We are departing from here."
>
> But later, there occurred an even more alarming portent. Four years before the outbreak of war, when the city was enjoying a period of peace and prosperity, an uneducated peasant named Jesus son of Ananias came to Jerusalem during the feast in which it is the custom for all Jews to erect booths to God (Sukkot), and going into the temple he began to shout,

A voice from the east,
A voice from the west,
A voice from the four winds;
A voice against Jerusalem and the temple,
A voice against bridegrooms and brides,
A voice against the whole people!

Day and night he walked up and down the streets and alleyways, crying out in this way. Some of the leading citizens took offense at his evil-sounding words, seized him, and beat him severely. He, however, made no statement on his own behalf, nor said a word in private to those who beat him, but only continued crying out as before. Then the magistrates, supposing, as was indeed the case, that the man was driven by some power beyond himself, brought him before the Roman governor. He was beaten till the lashes cut to his very bones, but did not beg for mercy or shed a tear. Instead, in the most mournful voice imaginable, quivering with each stroke, he continued to call out, "Woe to Jerusalem!" When Albinus, the governor, asked him who he was and where he was from, and why he spoke in this manner, he gave him no reply, but continued without ceasing to cry out this lament for the city. Albinus declared that he was insane and released him.

During the entire time up to the outbreak of the war, he neither approached any of the citizens nor was seen talking to them, but each day, as if it were a carefully composed prayer, he intoned his lament, "Woe to Jerusalem!" He neither cursed any of those who occasionally beat him, nor bestowed a blessing on those who gave him food, but to all gave this same mournful prophecy as his only reply. It was especially at the times of the pilgrimage festivals that he wailed the loudest.

For seven years and five months his voice neither wavered nor ceased, until he witnessed his prophecy fulfilled in the siege of the city, and he found his rest. While walking about and shouting his piercing cry from the city wall, "Woe again to the city, the people, and the temple," he added a final pronouncement, "Woe also to me." A stone shot from a catapult struck him, killing him instantly, while he was uttering these last words.

Although our present goal is not the recovery of the actual practices of early Jewish and Christian prophecy, the information found here provides interesting parallels to the gospel depiction of Jesus. This Jesus is not called a prophet by Josephus, but as we saw above, Josephus had reservations about applying the term to his contemporaries. This figure is nevertheless described as someone through whom the will of God is made known. Among the parallels to the depiction of Jesus in Mark and John are the following:

• the prophet is from a rural area[8]

159

- he enters Jerusalem for a pilgrimage festival (here Sukkot, following an omen at Shabuot)
- he delivers an oracle against Jerusalem, the temple, and the people
- he is seized by the leading citizens
- he is beaten, later scourged
- he offers no answer to interrogators
- he is taken by them to the Roman procurator
- he is considered a madman (*exestekos*; compare Mark 3: 21, *exeste*, and also John 7: 20)
- he prophesies his own death
- he dies.

The similarities can be ascribed to the fact that these were probably all expected actions that would surround a prophet; the social role that Jesus was enacting was thus not unknown.

Although sociological studies of such figures as these have made much progress in describing the actual social roles of prophets and the social structure of prophetic movements in the first century, the study of the narrative role of prophets is often taken up strictly as a means of reconstructing these practices. There the interest ends. But we are here concerned with the depiction of the protagonist as "prophet" in the narrative prose of the period. The narrative role is central to Mark and John, but is also similar to pagan texts such as *The Life of Aesop*, Plato's *Apology*, and even Lucian's *Peregrinus*. The depiction need not, therefore, be considered exclusively Jewish or Christian. And just as Mark, John, and *Aesop* all present the "tragic" results of the narrative tension of the prophetic protagonist, we can also compare this with its mirror image, the "comic" results that occur in other narrative literature of antiquity. In the so-called *Tobiad Romance* from Josephus' *Antiquities*, in Philostratus' *Apollonius of Tyana*, and even earlier in a narrative concerning the wise Bias of Priene in Herodotus,[9] we find stories of the brash protagonist who is, like a prophet, set off over against the king. The hero in each case sets out to correct the king, and comes perilously close to angering him as a result. In each case, however, the king is so struck with the logic of the correction and its cleverness that he is "delighted" with the hero; in fact, the same root for "delighted," *hedomai*, is used in all three instances. Thus the narrative motif of the "tragic" prophetic protagonist has as its counterpart the motif of the "comic" protagonist. These two possibilities, the tragic and comic results of upbraiding the ruling authorities, are opposite sides of the same issue, *parresia*, freedom of speech or boldness of speech, and in all these texts boldness of speech is played out as a common novelistic motif concerning the activities of the righteous sage. We may even be so bold ourselves as to say that the narrative tension between sage and authorities is the motive force of many of the novelistic, aretalogical texts of the Greco-Roman period.

Turning to the gospel texts, we see that John takes up the terminology of the prophet (John 1: 21; 4: 19; 6: 14; 7: 40, 52; 9: 17), and includes associations with Elijah and Elisha and especially the "prophet like Moses" predicted in Deut 18: 15–18.[10] Regardless of how John the redactor may have elevated Jesus to the level of the incarnation of the cosmic, pre-existent *logos*, it is probable that Jesus-as-prophet was a fundamental part of the tradition that John received. The term *semeion*, though developed in a very particular way by John, more generally had a fundamental role in this prophetic tradition, referring to the deed of the prophet that authenticates his having been sent from God, or, as also in the case of some of the popular leaders mentioned in Josephus, the signs of the new Exodus.[11] In the Greek translation of the Hebrew Bible, the term *semeion* was generally used to translate *ot*, and was coupled in the plural with *terata* in the stock phrase "signs and wonders" to refer to Moses' deeds that authenticate his authority from God (Deut 4: 34; 6: 22; 7: 19; 11: 3). In the first century, the term would naturally conjure up images of a "prophet like Moses," and is also used in regard to popular prophetic leaders, where there is often an appeal to an Exodus/deliverance typology.

This same understanding of the *semeia* as authenticating the messenger of God is found in 2 Corinthians 12, where Paul, in competition with the "superlative apostles," claims that he has performed the "*semeia* of the apostle" (verse 12). Although here it is the *semeia* of the apostle at issue and not the *semeia* of the prophet *per se*, clearly the signs would mark the true messenger of God. The only use of *apostolos* in the Greek Old Testament is at 3 Kingdoms (1 Kgs) 14: 6, in regard to the prophet Ahijah. Paul also connects the *semeia* with *terata* and *dunameis* (miracles). As in John 2: 11, the issue of *semeia* is raised in a conflictual situation, in which the *semeia* are presumed to legitimate the true messenger of God.

To be sure, it is often overlooked that *semeion* is also used in the Greek Bible to translate the Hebrew *nes*. The usage of this term in several key passages is eschatological: it is the war standard to be raised on the mountain to call the tribes into battle. Jonathan A. Draper has argued persuasively that, although Mark seems to lack this notion, it is clearly influential in such passages in John as the raising of the serpent at 3: 14–15 (cf. Num 21: 4–9) and 12: 31–33.[12] Although this meaning of *semeion* can be found elsewhere in early Christian texts (Matt 24: 29–31; *Didache* 16.6–8), it is probably not the meaning found in the *early* traditions in John or in Mark. Thus our search for an early gospel tradition of signs should focus on the authenticating signs of the prophet (that is, Hebrew *ot*, not *nes*).

Although the "prophet like Moses" passage of Deut 18: 15 is never quoted in the gospels, it is quoted at Acts 3: 22 and 7: 37, and seems to have influenced John as well. As Wayne Meeks and others have made clear, Moses traditions are very strong in John.[13] For instance, Jesus gives true manna (John 6), promises water from the rock (John 7), and uses words as if he were Moses (John 7: 16–17; 8: 28–29; 12: 48–50; 14: 10; 17: 6–26; compare 1:

21; 45; 5: 46). It has been quite plausibly suggested by Robert Houston Smith that the sign-miracles in John are intended to mirror seven of the plagues in Egypt.[14] The ten plagues are not all reflected in John, but there is a good case for seven of them (of these, only the official's son is a weak comparison):

Ex 7: 14–24	water into blood	Jn 2: 1–11	water into wine
Ex 7: 25–8: 32	three miracles: frogs, gnats, flies	no parallel	
Ex 9: 1–7	domestic animals	Jn 4: 46–54	official's son
Ex 9: 8–12	sores	Jn 5: 2–9	lame man at Bethzatha
Ex 9: 13–35	hailstorm	Jn 6: 16–21	stilling the storm
Ex 10: 1–20	locusts and famine	Jn 6: 1–15	feeding of 5,000
Ex 10: 21–29	darkness makes "blind"	Jn 9: 1–41	healing blind man
Ex 11: 1–12: 32	striking first-born	Jn 11: 1–44	raising Lazarus.

The destructive nature of the plagues now becomes life-giving in John: turning the Nile into blood becomes turning water into wine, the hailstorm becomes the stilling of the storm, and so on. Although it may be considered a leap from a Moses typology to a *prophet*-like-Moses typology, the latter probably underlies the Moses imagery in John. In 6: 14 and 7: 40, the prophet who is to come is discussed in the same context as Moses.[15]

The Gospel of Mark is more ambiguous. The word "prophet" is rarely used in Mark, but the prophetic nature of the gospel is often asserted by scholars nevertheless.[16] Mark's interest in the prophetic writings is patent: they are quoted or alluded to more often than the rest of the Bible. Jesus notes that "A prophet is not without honor except in his own country" (6: 4), and there is a question on people's minds as to whether Jesus is a prophet (6: 15; 8: 28). It is easy to see why. Jesus announces the approach of the rule of God (1: 15), which necessitates a new charismatic lifestyle that cuts the Christian off from the family (1: 20; 3: 20–21, 31–35; 6: 4; 10: 28–30), and he condemns the ruling authorities in the temple. Mark also associates John the Baptist with Elijah by noting that John appears in the garb of Elijah (1: 6; compare 8: 28; 9: 4, 11–13; 2 Kgs 1: 8). Mark, like John, also associates Jesus with Moses indirectly, when the voice from heaven at Mark 9: 7 says, "Listen to him" (compare Deut 18: 15). Other Moses parallels can be seen in the transfiguration on the mountain, and Exodus motifs in the feeding of the 5,000 that would call to mind a new Moses.[17] Klaus Baltzer also asserts that in the very structure of Mark there are close parallels to the biography of the prophet as found in the Hebrew Bible.[18] Mark recounts the story of Jesus not in the manner of Greco-Roman biographies, which emphasize the particular virtues of an important person, but in terms of the function of Jesus as the one called by God.

But when all is said and done, Mark still refrains from depicting Jesus *clearly* as a prophet. There are many more sayings in Q that focus on Jesus or his followers as prophets. Mark downplays the *semeia* as signs that confirm that a prophet is sent by God. At 8: 11–12, the request for a sign is met with a refusal on Jesus' part – compare the response of Jesus in John 2: 18–19 – and elsewhere Mark uses the word *dunameis* rather than *semeia* to emphasize the healing miracles that Jesus performs to signal the coming of God's rule and the victory over demonic rule. Some scholars would deny to Mark any prophetic element. Morton Smith asserts that since there is no specifically *eschatological* prophet expected in Deut 18: 15–18, the hope of a prophet like Moses cannot be ascribed to Mark (or anyone else).[19] Further, Mark's Gospel presents a miracle worker who refuses to do the signs of the eschatological prophet, that is, he does not assemble the people, wage a war against Gentiles, declare the revelation of the temple vessels, effect a victory over the demonic (except in secondary levels of the texts), prophesy, preach repentance or preparation for the end, or teach. But Smith here greatly overstates the discrepancies. However the role of the prophet was envisioned in the pre-exilic period, Deuteronomy 18 was considered an eschatological prophecy by some in the first century, and most of these expected signs of the prophet had been supplanted by others. And when in Mark Jesus refuses to perform the sign of the prophet, we can only surmise that the *reader* is perceiving here an implicit challenge to understand the usual signs of the prophet anew.

The traces of Mark's redactional shift on the issue of signs can be found at a number of points, not least in chapter 13; here the expectation of the return of the Messiah has evidently given rise to a new search among early Christians for signs of the Endtime (13: 4), an expectation that Mark does not want to encourage (13: 22).[20] As a result, Mark the redactor does not develop the theme of prophet, and may in fact suppress it in favor of a depiction of Jesus as the suffering Son of Humanity. Mark has introduced the parables in place of the *semeia* to serve the same purpose: the parables in Mark become interpretive keys to the meaning of the kingdom (4: 10–12), and therefore they point to the kingdom for the one who perceives.[21] Nevertheless, if these changes can be ascribed to Mark's *redaction*, then it is likely that the prophet, and specifically the prophet like Moses, had a role in Mark's *source*. Further, the Longer Ending of Mark may retain the earlier emphasis on *semeia*: "These signs will follow those who believe . . . They went out and preached everywhere, as the Lord worked with them, confirming their preaching through accompanying signs" (16: 17, 20). Ultimately, however, the question is not whether Mark utilizes some particular motifs of a "prophet christology," but whether in this narrative we see in Jesus a literary type. And in a quite general sense, Jesus is *depicted* as one who foresees, speaks the will of God, and condemns. Further, he is executed for it. The characterization as a prophet remains, but the prophetic christology became the "lost christology." It is a primitive christology that utilizes native traditions, but is finally too "low" a christology for the church, and is supplanted by such terms as "Lord," "Son of God," and "Christ."

The discernment of true prophets by authenticating *semeia*, then, had long been part of the Jewish conception of the prophet, and Mark and John both reflect an older gospel tradition in which the prophet sent from God is marked in this way. In Mark the *semeia* are suppressed as an issue, while in John they are elevated to become the signs of recognition of the cosmic redeemer; those who recognize the redeemer through these signs are saved, and those who do not are judged. John could hardly have developed the positive meaning of signs from Mark. The similarity of the *background* of the *semeia* theme can be seen in the request for a sign (Mark 8: 11–12/John 2: 18–19), treated in very different ways in the two gospels, and equally, the similar background of the prophet theme is seen in such passages as the prophet who is without honor in his own homeland (Mark 6: 4/John 4: 44), again, treated very differently. The older gospel tradition saw Jesus' identity as a prophet as the reason for his outsider status, the reason for his death, and the reason for his eventual cult. But the depiction of Jesus as prophet need not correspond precisely to what we know of prophets in the first century. It is a narrative topos, influenced by Jewish prophets and revered men and Greco-Roman views of the sage-outsider. Jesus is a prophet, and more than a prophet. His role is akin to that of Socrates, Aesop, Elijah and Elisha, and the high priest Onias III as depicted in 2 Macc 3–4.

B. MIRACLES, SABBATH CONTROVERSY, AND THE CAUSE OF CONFLICT

It is striking that there are so few healing miracles in common between Mark and John. In chapter 3 I posited some similarities of theme between Mark 2: 1–12 and John 5: 1–16 and 7: 19–23, and some similarities of story structure between Mark 5: 21–43 and John 4: 46–54. The feeding and water miracles of Mark 6 and John 6 are clearly parallel, but the healing miracles represent a small intersecting set. It is also significant that the overall parallel *order* between Mark and John is fairly close throughout the gospels, *except in the sections of the teachings and healing miracles*. The discrepancy with respect to the teachings is quite understandable: Jesus' teachings, such as the parables in Mark and the core of the discourses in John, were likely transmitted early on in sayings collections like Q.[22] The healing miracles, however, represent a more complicated problem. John has two numbered signs, the existence of which formed the basis for Robert Fortna's reconstruction of the entire Signs

Gospel.[23] However, only one of them (John 4: 46–54) is paralleled in Mark. It should also be noted that Mark includes a number of exorcisms, a category of miracle which John lacks.

Burton Mack suggests that there is perhaps a stronger overlap than at first appears.[24] He begins by simplifying Fortna's rather complicated list of seven miracles in the Signs Source to the following seven:

1 Water into wine (2: 1–11)
2 The official's son (4: 46–54)
3 The lame man at Bethzatha (5: 1–9)
4 Feeding of the 5,000 (6: 1–14)
5 Walking on water (6: 16–21)
6 Healing the blind man (9: 1–34)
7 Resurrection of Lazarus (11: 1–44).

Mack then argues that the first and last of these are strange and out of place: the changing of water into wine is a merely "symbolic" miracle, and the resurrection of Lazarus *becomes* symbolic in John's schema. It is possible that both were added when the Signs Source was incorporated and interpreted symbolically. If that was the case, then the five remaining miracles are very similar to the two "miracle catenae" often postulated as sources for Mark: a sea crossing, a feeding, and three healing miracles (in different order). His reconstruction remains speculative, but intriguing (even though I have argued against it in chapter 3), but even if some such grouping of miracles is granted, the intersection of miracles in Mark and John is not extensive, and they have both added separate and quite different miracles of their own.

Despite the lack of overlap of miracles in general, however, there is one place where the miracle tradition is at least parallel *in function*. Both gospels open up a miracle story to create a story of conflict (Mark 2: 1–12/John 5: 1–16; 7: 19–23), even though the story itself is not similar. The tendency to "create conflict" was probably already in place in the gospel tradition, and at some point in the Mark and John traditions this tendency was exercised in a parallel fashion using different materials. Anitra Bingham Kolenkow would see in these passages the entire gospel in miniature.[25] She argues that the controversy that arises from the healing on the Sabbath is not just a foreshadowing of the passion, but is rather the short narrative that gives rise to the long narrative. Although I believe that she has overemphasized the centrality of these particular passages, she rightly draws our attention to the important theme of conflict in the early tradition. This provides a clue to a significant similarity between the gospels, to which I shall turn below.

Corresponding to the question of the role of miracles common to Mark and John is the question of the use of the verb *pisteuo*, "to believe." Fortna rightly emphasizes the connections between the signs-miracles and believing, and suggests that in the source the signs are seen to lead naturally to belief, while in John's redaction this is considered an immature form of faith.[26] The later level points instead to the deeper meaning of the signs. Since it is the thesis of the present study that Fortna's reconstruction does not coincide precisely with the early gospel tradition, it is necessary to examine what role the verb "to believe" might have had in Mark as well. The miracle of the healing of the synagogue leader's daughter (Mark 5: 22–24, 35–42) and the official's son (John 4: 46–54) contains a circumspect attitude toward belief, but Mark in general has fewer uses of the verb "to believe." It does occur, however, in the Longer Ending of Mark in connection with signs; it is possible that these two passages are what remains of a common tradition of signs and belief, but it is not clear from the present evidence. At any rate, the use of the verb *pisteuo* in John is not likely to have come from knowledge of Mark; the latter has a preference for the noun form, *pistis*, especially in redactional passages, which John never uses. Fortna's judgment concerning *pisteuo* in the source of John may have applied to the source of Mark as well, though neither gospel has retained it in its original form.

C. CONFLICT AND THE DECISION TO KILL JESUS

When we turn to the category of pronouncement stories or *chreiai*, we find that Mark and John share much more material than was the case in regard to the miracles. Some of the *chreiai* are not actually conflictual, but often function nevertheless to characterize the protagonist as an outside commentator, a figure who is prophetic in the broad sense of the term. The *chreiai* have received a great deal of attention in recent years by New Testament scholars, and deservedly so. Rudolf Bultmann and Martin Dibelius drew attention to their importance in the first half of the century (Bultmann called them apophthegms and Dibelius paradigms),[27] but the comparative work of recent years has altered the terminology and the division of the *chreiai* into subcategories. Especially informative has been volume 20 of the journal *Semeia*, devoted to this form. There Robert C. Tannehill divided ancient *chreiai* into six types: correction stories, commendation stories, objection stories, quest stories, inquiry stories, and description stories.[28] Tannehill finds examples of the first five types in the synoptic gospels, but no description stories.

However, what he does not note is more important for the present analysis: almost all of the *chreiai* found in both Mark and John fall into one category, the objection story. Although only vestiges of some can still be seen in John, I would include the following: on fasting (Mark 2: 18–22/John 3: 26–30); Beelzebul controversy (Mark 3: 22–30/John 7: 19–20; 8: 48–52); healing on the Sabbath (Mark 3: 1–6/parallel theme at John 5: 1–18); prophet in his own land (Mark 6: 1–6/John 4: 43–45); and on eating with hands defiled (Mark 7: 1–15/John 3: 25). The two *chreiai* common to Mark and John that are not objections in Tannehill's assessment are also interesting, since they depict the same conflictual relations as the objection *chreiai*. First, Tannehill classifies Jesus' action in the temple, Mark 11: 15–18/John 2:

13–17, as a correction story. The words of Jesus differ in Mark and John, however, and as Bultmann argues, they may have been added to an older report of a prophetic action.[29] Thus, it has an unclear relation to the *chreiai*. Also, Tannehill classifies the question of authority in Mark 11: 27–33 as an inquiry story, while Bultmann included it as a controversy apophthegm. An interesting question here is whether Bultmann's classifications or Tannehill's are more helpful in identifying the form of the material common to Mark and John, but to avoid the problems of circularity in reasoning – that is, searching out a hybrid system that will confirm my hypothesis – I adhere more closely to Tannehill's divisions.

The import of this is significant. Either John eliminated *chreiai* of the other subcategories, or the narrative tradition common to Mark and John contained only objection-*chreiai*. I consider the latter conclusion more likely. In this case, the objection-*chreiai* would constitute the bulk of the teaching ministry that Mark and John have in common, and would have set the tone of conflict that preceded the final act of the passion narrative. They would have been roughly equivalent to the barbed teachings of Aesop that led ultimately to Aesop's opposition to the authorities in Delphi. Whereas Kolenkow emphasizes the miracle-as-controversy as the short narrative that gives rise to the long narrative of the passion, James G. Williams argues that the *chreia* is the key to understanding the conflict that gives rise to the passion-oriented gospel.[30] More precisely, Williams says that the parable and the *chreia*, both of which are found in Q, can be seen in their combined effect to give rise to the narrative gospel. Although Mark the redactor is interested in the parables, and perhaps molds the gospel with them in mind, I do not believe that the parable is in any way constitutive of the early gospel genre, end evidently neither did John. The *chreia* is another matter. For instance, of the eleven *chreiai* in Q that Williams discusses, five contain some parallel in John: Luke 3: 7–8; 7: 1–10, 7: 18–23, 7: 24–35; and 11: 14–26. At any rate, there are fewer healing controversies in common between Mark and John than there are objection-*chreiai*. However, both categories are used in a similar way to structure the gospel around the theme of the small conflicts that lead to the great conflict, and in this they both contribute, as Mack argues.[31]

Having surveyed this beginning of conflict, one might also ask what is the precise reason given for the authorities' desire to kill Jesus, but this is not clearly and consistently stated in either gospel. In Mark, the reasons given include the popularity of his teaching (11: 18), the threat to the temple (14: 58), and "blasphemy" (14: 64); in John, breaking the Sabbath (5: 16), the "blasphemy" of making himself equal to God (5: 18; 10: 31–33), and fear of the Romans (11: 48). It is possible that a tradition common to Mark and John lurks in the issue of "blasphemy." When Jesus is being interrogated by the high priest at Mark 14: 61–64, he is asked whether he is "the Messiah, the son of the Blessed One." Jesus replies, "I am" (*ego eimi*), and then quotes Dan 7: 13 and Ps 110: 1 together: "and you shall see the Son of Humanity (or of a human being) sitting on the right hand of the Power, coming with the clouds of heaven." This utterance immediately provokes a cry of "blasphemy" by the high priest and a judgment of death by the Sanhedrin. (Compare here the judgment by the Delphians against Aesop on a charge of blasphemy, *Aesop* 132.[32]) Part of Jesus' self-identification here should not escape notice. In his response, Jesus says *ego eimi*, which is the formula of God's self-revelation in the Greek translation of Exod 3: 13–15 (compare Mark 13: 6). John elsewhere uses *ego eimi* as a self-predication of Jesus (John 8: 24, 28, 58; 13: 19), and although some of John's "blasphemies" occur outside the trial scene (5: 18 and 10: 31–33), they are equally concerned with Jesus' claim to be the Son of God (compare Mark's "son of the Blessed One"), and this can still be seen in the accusations in John's trial scene: "The Judeans answered him, 'We have a law, and according to this law, he must die, because he claimed to be the Son of God'" (19: 7). In both gospels this blasphemy is connected with the decision to kill Jesus, although in Mark it is more intensely focused at the climax of the trial.

Thus, even if it was the Roman authorities who were mainly responsible for killing Jesus, which was likely the case, opposition in both gospels was initiated by Jewish leaders. The narrative tradition is not interested in an execution by Roman but by Jewish authorities. Despite the efforts of some scholars to postulate the real reasons why Jesus was crucified,[33] the texts of Mark and John do not provide adequate answers. The authors evidently felt very little need to do so, but from the narrative point of view, a precise dogmatic statement hardly matters. A tension arose between Jesus and the authorities, a tension that was inevitable for the paradigm of the prophet, and that had inevitable results. In an earlier work, I argued that in the Jewish wisdom court narratives of Daniel and Esther, the *content* of wisdom is not nearly so important (if it is present at all) as the mere fact that the hero who is "marked" by wisdom succeeds.[34] In a similar way, the content of the antagonism between Jesus and the authorities is perhaps less important than the narrative truth that the genre demands: Jesus will inevitably be opposed and put to death.

Now we must turn to a further distinction in the conflict material: many of the scenes of conflict in Mark and John result in a resolve on the part of the authorities to arrest or kill Jesus, while others do not. The first two lists below indicate the scenes of conflict in Mark and John that contain no reference to a plot to arrest or kill Jesus; the Jewish groups named as opposing Jesus are also shown:

Mark

	conflict	*opponents*
2: 1–12	forgiving sins	scribes
2: 15–17	eating with sinners	scribes of the Pharisees
2: 18–22	question about fasting	disciples of John and Pharisees
2: 23–28	plucking grain on Sabbath	Pharisees
3: 21, 30	Jesus insane	Jesus' family[35]

168

3: 22–29	Beelzebul	scribes
3: 31–35	Jesus' true family	Jesus' family
6: 1–6	prophet without honor	hometown
7: 1–15	eating with unwashed hands	Pharisees and some scribes
8: 11–12	request for sign	Pharisees
8: 14–15	leaven of Pharisees, Herod	Pharisees, Herod
10: 2–9	question on divorce	Pharisees
12: 13–17	question about taxes	Pharisees, Herodians
12: 18–27	question on resurrection	Sadducees
12: 35–40	question about David's son	scribes (not present)

John

	conflict	*opponents*
1: 19–28	question to John Baptist	Judeans, priests, Levites, Pharisees
3: 25–30	question on fasting	a Judean
4: 1–3	Jesus and John baptizing	Pharisees
6: 22–59	bread from heaven	Judeans
8: 12–20	Jesus' false testimony	Pharisees, Judeans
9: 13–34	blind man	Pharisees, Judeans
9: 35–41	blindness of Pharisees	Pharisees
12: 12–19	resentment of Jesus	Pharisees
12: 42–43	fear in synagogue	Pharisees

The next two lists indicate scenes of conflict in which some reference is made to a plot to arrest or kill Jesus:

Mark

	conflict	*opponents*
3: 1–6	healing on Sabbath	Pharisees, Herodians
8: 31–33	passion prediction	elders, chief priests, scribes
9: 30–32	passion prediction	"betrayed into human hands"
10: 32–34	passion prediction	chief priests, scribes
11: 15–19	prophetic action in temple	chief priests, scribes
11: 27–33	question on authority[36]	chief priests, scribes, elders
12: 1–12	parable of wicked tenants[37]	chief priests, scribes, elders
14: 1–2	plot to kill Jesus	chief priests, scribes
14: 10–11	Judas' betrayal	chief priests
14: 43–50	Jesus' arrest	chief priests, scribes, elders
14: 53–65	Jesus before Sanhedrin	high priest, chief priests, elders, scribes, Sanhedrin

John

| | *conflict* | *opponents* |
| 5: 1–18 | healing on Sabbath (continues in 7: 14–31)[38] | Judeans, crowd |

6: 41–42	"Is not this Jesus?"	Judeans
7: 1	Judeans intend to kill Jesus	Judeans
7: 32–36	attempt to arrest Jesus	Pharisees, chief priests
10: 22–39	Judeans try to stone Jesus	Judeans
11: 45–53	one man should die	chief priests, Pharisees, Sanhedrin, high priest
12: 9–11	intent to kill Lazarus	chief priests
18: 1–11	Jesus' arrest	chief priests, Pharisees
18: 12–24	Jesus' trial	high priest

Two of the groups of opponents in these lists are likely redactional: Mark alone of the gospel authors introduces the Herodians, and John often describes the opponents as "the Judeans," even when the episode begins with some more specific designation. Granting that these two sets of opponents are likely Markan and Johannine respectively, we turn to the other designations which the two authors share. An important pattern can be discerned here: where the opposition culminates in an attempt to arrest or kill Jesus, the opponents are almost always chief priests and some other group, and the location is in Jerusalem; where the opposition does not culminate in a threat to Jesus' life, the opponents are almost always the Pharisees, and the location is in Galilee. Interestingly, the word "Pharisee" does not occur in either of the two passion narratives except at John 18: 3, and there it is used with "the chief priests." Instead, the opposing group in the passion narrative is generally designated as "chief priests, scribes, and elders" in Mark (the three classes that make up the Sanhedrin), and chief priests in John. In other words, less severe opposition to Jesus is correlated with Pharisees as opponents, and more severe opposition to Jesus is correlated with chief priests. Further, in both gospels, where opposition with the threat of death occurs outside the passion narrative, a clearly redactional term for the opponents is generally used.

It is also interesting that, in both gospels, when there is serious opposition to Jesus in the first part of the gospel – that is, opposition to the point of plotting Jesus' death – it is over the issue of healing on the Sabbath. No other halachic (that is, legal) issue elicits this kind of opposition. Although one might assume that this motif was part of a later, antinomian or even "anti-Jewish" redaction, it may well be an early tradition, and one that is not, strictly speaking, "antinomian." This early critique is not concerned with all Sabbath laws, or with a constitutional rejection of Mosaic law, but with the symbolic "inbreaking" of Jesus' healing on the Sabbath and a new, "purified" religion, analogous perhaps to the critique of oaths that is found in various religions at the turn of the era.[39] To be sure, this motif may indeed have been added to pre-existing miracle stories, for example, in John 5 and 9 (see synopsis), but at a period *before* the composition of Mark and John.

A very different approach to the question of the varied opponents in Mark is that of Michael J. Cook.[40] Using only Mark, with no comparison to John, he suggests that Mark uses three different sources regarding conflict between Jesus and Jewish authorities, and that the three sources, naming three different sets of opponents, take different geographical settings: (1) chief priests, scribes, and elders; set in Jerusalem (= passion narrative); (2) scribes; set in Jerusalem; (3) Pharisees and Herodians; set in Galilee. When one examines the passages in Mark that fall into these three categories, one notes that (1) chief priests, scribes, and elders in Mark overlaps a great deal with chief priests (plus others) in John; (2) Cook's scribes passages (Mark 12: 18–27, 28–34a; 9: 11–12a, 13ab; 12: 35–37, 38–40) have no counterpart in John. Although his "scribes source" is somewhat speculatively derived (he omits, for example, Mark 3: 22–29, which is paralleled in John), it does call attention to the fact that John never mentions scribes and lacks these particular episodes. This constitutes evidence that John did not know Mark, since John would not be likely to omit so completely the scribes passages – change them, perhaps, even significantly, or change the opponents to Judeans or Pharisees, but not simply drop this group of passages.

The Pharisees material requires special attention. Cook proposes that Mark derives this material from a source that included the following narratives in this order:

Mark 7: 1–13	washing hands
Mark 2: 15–17	eating with tax collectors and sinners
Mark 2: 18–22	question on fasting
Mark 2: 23–28	plucking grain on Sabbath
Mark 3: 1–6	healing on Sabbath
Mark 12: 13–17	question on taxes

These are all narratives about halachic disputes, and Cook's suggestion that they derive from a single source is possible. Yet they are also all *chreiai*, and several have parallels with material in John, as noted above. It is significant that Cook's collection of conflict stories contains a number of boundary-defining disputes – washing hands, authority to forgive sins, eating with sinners and tax collectors, fasting, Sabbath observance, and so on – some of which overlap with the *chreiai* that are attested in both Mark and John. Although the latter group of *chreiai* are not restricted to halachic questions, it is a common enough theme among them. It would be a mistake to posit an earlier gospel narrative with a fixed text; perhaps Cook's list and the set of *chreiai* common to Mark and John both provide evidence of what was included in the earlier gospel controversies.

D. GALILEE

Although Cook perhaps goes beyond the evidence in arguing that there was a separate source for the Pharisees material, it is certainly true that the Pharisees have a special role in the narrative: to question Jesus in Galilee. The chief priests, scribes and elders, on the other hand, are the Jerusalem authorities who will ultimately press to have Jesus killed. This division may make perfect sense considering the roles of these groups in the first century. Anthony Saldarini suggests that the Pharisees were not "native" to Galilee, or leaders within the synagogue, but "retainers" from Jerusalem, that is, officials with governmental authority sent from the temple authorities, and appearing in Galilee. We note, for example, that Pharisees were dispatched from Jerusalem (Mark 7: 1, perhaps reversed in John 1: 19, 1: 24). Thus the drama of the gospel narrative, with the Pharisaic opponents in Galilee, reflects the actual social conditions of the mid-first century.[41] Perhaps corresponding to its marginalized status vis-à-vis Jerusalem, Galilee is a region rich in a different kind of religiosity. There are many sacred tombs there, it is the home of many wonder-workers from Elijah to Hanina ben Dosa, and it is the locus in other texts of important visions.[42]

Mark and John both move Jesus generally from Galilee to Jerusalem, but John's historical and geographical outline is much more complicated than Mark's. It involves a three-year ministry of Jesus, as opposed to Mark's one-year ministry, and in John, Jesus moves in and out of Galilee a number of times before going finally to Jerusalem. Mark's simpler account portrays Jesus as beginning his ministry with teaching and miracles in Galilee, moving inexorably toward crucifixion in Jerusalem, with the disciples returning to Galilee to await Jesus' return. Jerusalem is the center of opposition to Jesus; Galilee is the center of hope. In 1936, Ernst Lohmeyer analyzed this opposition between Galilee and Jerusalem, and suggested that there were two locales for the growth of the early Christian tradition, Galilee and Jerusalem.[43] The former was a hotbed of discontent and apocalyptic fervor, and so it was understandable that one of the two foci would be located there. He was clearly correct in pinpointing an opposition in the text, although others have nuanced his findings. To Willi Marxsen, Galilee was not the home of a continuous Christian community that had gone back some decades, but had only recently become a center for Mark's community.[44]

In the case of John, several scholars who have analyzed the proposed Signs Source have divided the miracles there into signs in Galilee and signs in Judea. It has been suggested by some that John's miracles are intentionally arranged in a pattern of four miracles in Galilee, three in Judea. The numbered signs, in fact, are specifically said to be signs occurring *in Galilee* (John 2: 11; 4: 54).[45] Interestingly, Jesus' resurrection appearances in John at first mention nothing about Galilee, but John 21, a chapter most likely added to the gospel, includes a separate appearance of Jesus to the disciples in Galilee. And although canonical Mark ends with a resurrection appearance tradition in Galilee, the Longer Ending of Mark 16: 9–20 contains no such reference. Thus in Mark and John we have analogous problems of secondary endings that may retain alternative traditions, creating a difficulty in establishing possible parallels: the presumably original ending of Mark contains a reference to

Galilee, but the secondary ending does not; the presumably original ending of John does not contain a reference to Galilee, but the secondary ending does. As noted in the synopsis of chapter 3, it is possible that the secondary endings in both cases contain older material that might have been part of the earlier gospel traditions. As a result, we cannot be certain whether both gospels ended with a resurrection appearance in Galilee or not. Because of the early growth of the Christian community in Galilee, the Galilean locus may have been added to an early tradition that envisioned reconciliation in Jerusalem. This, however, is now impossible to tell. Granting this uncertainty concerning the end of the gospels, we can still detect a common tradition in the Galilee-to-Jerusalem movement.

If we are to postulate a pre-Markan and pre-Johannine gospel tradition that depicts Jesus as moving between Galilee and Judea, then it is necessary to identify the redactional elements that may account for the differences between the two gospels. Jouette Bassler observes that John begins with a fairly clear pattern of a positive reception of Jesus in Galilee, and a rejection in Judea (a pattern not unlike Mark's).[46] Not all the interactions with Jesus in Galilee are positive, however. Bassler proposes that the key to John's symbolic universe is the focus on Galilean and Judean *people*, not the places *per se*. Those who oppose Jesus are generally called simply "the Judeans," wherever they occur, and likewise "Galileans" are people who are receptive to Jesus. Thus we may gain some insight into the peculiar statement in John 4: 44–45 that, despite the fact that the prophet has no honor in his own homeland, the Galileans welcomed him. The positive valuation of the Galilean reception has overridden the older traditional saying about rejection, and we are perhaps to see Jesus' "homeland" as Judea (see chapter 3). John's pattern of moving Jesus back and forth between Galilee and Judea can on this theory be explained as an attempt to problematize the real and metaphorical boundary issues of Galileans versus Judeans. John plays with this boundary issue by having various characters accused of being something they are not: Jesus is accused of being a Samaritan (8: 48–49), Nicodemus is accused of being a Galilean (7: 52), and Pilate is accused of being a Judean (18: 35).

In both Mark and John, one city in Galilee, Capernaum, is also highlighted as a special site of Jesus' activity. Mark places two miracles there: the man with the unclean spirit (Mark 1: 21–28) and the healing of a paralytic (2: 1–12), in addition to one of the three passion predictions (9: 33). In John, Jesus at one point repairs to Capernaum with his mother, brothers, and disciples (2: 12), and the healing of the official's son also takes place there (John 4: 46–54; compare Mark 5: 21–43), Jesus walks on the water as the boat is en route to Capernaum (6: 17, 24), and he teaches in the synagogue there (6: 59, perhaps added). The coincidence of Capernaum as the site of early miracle stories in both gospels is intriguing. However, aside from this city, place names in Galilee unique to John are southern, while northern places mentioned by the synoptics are absent from John.[47] This indicates that part of the Galilee

173

tradition is common to the two gospels, and part is the product of a separate community history that has given rise to two sets of place names. It is quite possible that the early gospel tradition centered the beginnings of Jesus' ministry not just in Galilee, but specifically in Capernaum. But be that as it may, the *region* of Galilee is now emphasized by Mark and John, as Jesus makes a point of moving from area to area within Galilee. Both gospels are thus dependent upon a tradition that begins in Galilee and moves toward Jerusalem, and which included, among other things, the negative saying about a prophet who is without honor in his own homeland (Mark 6: 1–6/John 4: 43–45). Only by an awkward redaction can John make this a positive statement about Galileans. Jesus was probably depicted as being rejected in his homeland, but the movement of the narrative, at any rate, would have been from Galilee to Judea.

E. SON OF HUMANITY

The Son of Humanity (or "Son of Man") sayings in the gospels are generally divided by scholars into three categories: (1) sayings that describe the earthly activity of the Son of Humanity; (2) sayings that refer to a coming, judging Son of Humanity of the Endtime; and (3) sayings that emphasize the suffering Son of Humanity. Q contains sayings of the first and second types. The second type is often regarded as more primitive, that is, as arising earlier in the tradition, and may even derive from pre-Christian speculation. Mark, however, is noteworthy for introducing sayings of the third kind, and also for rearranging some of the material in very profound ways. Mark takes Son of Humanity sayings and places them together in chapters 8, 9, and 10; connects them with suffering, not exaltation; and follows these with the theme of the disciples' misunderstanding, which occasions lectures on the meaning of discipleship.[48] Gerd Theissen, for example, emphasizes the variety of functions of the Son of Humanity in Mark, from the active (breaking the Sabbath, 2: 28) to the passive (suffering, 9: 31), and being a "ransom for many" (10: 45), all drawn into one conception. The Son of Humanity "both shatters and is betrayed, transcends society's norms on one hand and suffers by being rejected by them."[49] It is clear that Mark develops the Son of Humanity concept in a unique way, as a new multi-dimensional figure is created out of the primitive Christian (and perhaps Jewish) understanding. It is even more significant, then, that John does not contain any Son of Humanity sayings of the third type; it lacks this characteristically Markan form. Even Norman Perrin, who argues that John knew Mark, grants that the Son of Humanity is different in the two gospels.[50]

At first sight, the fact that the Son of Humanity is associated in Q with the idea of the kingdom of God would suggest that we might also find these concepts connected in the early narrative gospel tradition as well. However, this does not appear to be the case. First, John Kloppenborg has argued that Q should be divided into two layers, an early sapiential collection of sayings that emphasize the kingdom, and a later apocalyptic layer that emphasizes the coming Son of Humanity.[51] If Kloppenborg is correct, then the close association of the kingdom and the Son of Humanity in Q disappears. Adela Yarbro Collins and Horsley, however, have disputed Kloppenborg's division of Q into two layers, and with it the isolation of the Son of Humanity sayings in the later layer.[52] Even if they are correct, however, the association of the kingdom with the Son of Humanity might be argued for Mark and Q, but not for John. In the latter gospel, we find only one mention of the kingdom, in the discussion with Nicodemus in chapter 3. This is likely a pre-Johannine tradition,[53] but in any case is hardly enough to suggest an association of these concepts in an earlier form of John. Although the presence of the kingdom doctrine in the early gospel tradition cannot be ruled out, it cannot be argued on the basis of a comparison of Mark and John. We should also be cautious in equating the language of Jesus as king, which does appear in Mark and John, with the language of the kingdom that is found in Mark and Q. The two theological affirmations, king and kingdom of God (or perhaps we should say "rule of God" for the latter), may in fact reflect different social configurations: general notions of Jesus as royal Messiah for the former, and the community as a sectarian entity for the latter.

What John does indicate about the Son of Humanity tradition is very difficult to ascertain clearly, because the figure has become a pre-existent, cosmic redeemer in many passages. As Wayne Meeks has observed, several of the usages in John emphasize the Johannine theme of the descending and ascending heavenly redeemer (3: 13; 6: 62; 9: 35; 12: 23).[54] This may have a background in older religious speculation, but may also derive from John's own redaction. In one passage, however, John clearly associates the Son of Humanity with eschatological judgment:

> Very truly, I say to you that an hour is coming, and now is, when the dead will hear the voice of the Son of God, and those who hear will live. For just as the father has life in himself, so also has he given life to the son to have in himself. He has also given him authority to pass judgment, because he is the Son of Humanity. But do not be surprised at this, for an hour is coming when all who are in the tombs will hear his voice and come out, those who have done good to resurrection of life, those who have done evil to resurrection of judgment. (John 5: 25–29)

Despite John's introduction of present eschatology ("and now is"), the passage clearly has a background in the coming, judging Son of Humanity tradition. This corresponds with pre-Markan tradition, and there is nothing in John's Son of Humanity that betrays any awareness of Mark's own redaction.[55]

In addition to the three-fold division of the Son of Humanity sayings posited above, Collins offers another that has implications for the present study.[56] She points out, first, that not all Son of Humanity sayings can be placed neatly within the usual three-part division as outlined above, and proposes instead a division of the Son of Humanity sayings into those that allude to Dan 7: 13 ("I saw one like a son of a human being coming with the clouds of heaven"), and those that do not. This division in no way invalidates the former one, but brings attention to bear on the fact that much of the Son of Humanity tradition was, in fact, exegetical, that is, it applied the apocalyptic meaning of Dan 7: 13 to the contemporary situation. John 5: 25–29, quoted above, similarly betrays an exegetical relationship to Dan 7: 13, and the *descending* Son of Humanity that Meeks analyzes may be based, directly or indirectly, on this *coming* Son of Humanity tradition.[57]

From this examination of John's Son of Humanity sayings, we see that John often depicts a Son of Humanity who is a descending/ascending redeemer, but when other passages are examined and the Johannine redaction is stripped away, what is left corresponds to only one of the three types of Son of Humanity sayings found in Mark, the Son of Humanity as eschatological judge. The background of this motif lies in a tradition that explicates Dan 7: 13, and is not directly influenced by Mark. Similarly, Mark's characteristic redaction, found principally in the third type of sayings, is not reflected in John. The tradition common to Mark and John utilized a concept of the Son of Humanity as a coming eschatological judge, derived from Dan 7: 13, and this coming Son of Humanity was probably not identified with Jesus.[58]

F. SON OF GOD

A more ambiguous case is the comparison of the Son of God in the two gospels. Mark uses this designation at three very pointed locations in the text: at the beginning (baptism, 1: 11), the middle (transfiguration, 9: 7), and the end (crucifixion, 15: 39).[59] John has some references to the Son of God that are similar: beginning (1: 49 and perhaps at the baptism, 1: 34), a number of highly developed discourses in the body of the gospel (see especially 3: 18; 5: 17–25; 10: 31–39; 11: 4, 27), and at the end (17: 1; 19: 7; 20: 31). John has clearly developed the Son of God motif in a particular way. As noted above, Jesus' claim to be Son of God, called a blasphemy by his interlocutors, is given an extra christological development at John 5: 18 when the interlocutors interpret this to mean – rightly? – that Jesus claims to be *equal* to God, or, in fact, God (10: 33). John, however, has not expanded the statement at the trial that Jesus is crucified because he claimed to be the Son of God (19: 7); it apparently remains more or less as it was in the tradition (see above). Mack has pointed out that Mark may have repositioned the Son of God references, or the episodes that contain them, for redactional purposes: one at the beginning, one in the middle (at the turning of the story), and one at the end, in order to "frame" the two phases of Jesus' activity with the myth of divine entrance into the world. This may very well be the case, although Mark may have been altering a pattern that already existed in the tradition – Philipp Vielhauer, in fact, traces this pattern to ancient Egyptian sources.[60] It is not clear whether John reflects this placement of the Son of God pronouncements, but it is interesting to note that they are in that gospel usually uttered as accusations of blasphemy.

G. DISCIPLES

The disciples were likely featured prominently in the earlier narrative. The call of the disciples occurs in Mark and John near the beginning, though described in very different ways. In Mark they are called and follow immediately without any questioning; in John they are more reflective, and it is they who approach Jesus. According to Mack,[61] the disciples often figure in Mark as "understudies of Jesus." The same can basically be said for the Gospel of John. The obtuseness of the disciples may have played some role in the earlier stage of development; it is a common theme, almost a required element, of dialogues between sages and disciples in the Greco-Roman world, but Mark develops it in a much more taut, ironic way. In Mark the disciples remain quite dense even after the miracles, and are supplanted by the women in key scenes near the end.[62] The earlier tradition contained Peter's denial at the trial of Jesus, along with the theme of the obtuseness of the disciples and their abandonment of Jesus, but it did not tie these as directly as Mark did to the suffering of Jesus, or with the demotion, even "demonizing," of Peter (Mark 8: 33).

CONCLUSION

The synopsis of Mark and John in chapter 3 allowed for a number of observations here concerning the way in which certain motifs and themes were likely treated in the earlier gospel tradition and in Mark and John. My main objective, once again, was to present an argument of plausibility; that is, to argue that the complicated relationships of certain elements in Mark and John are perfectly understandable on the assumption of a third party to the ancient discourse, a previously existing gospel narrative. The motifs chosen here are certainly among the most important, although others could also have been chosen: Jesus as king, the role of Pilate, or the Last Supper, which may provide the blueprint for the actual cultic activity of the group. Here, however, I wanted to establish an overall generic pattern, not reconstruct an earlier gospel in detail. Even if my hypothesis is true, a complete reconstruction could never be achieved, and would be a chimerical goal. Many current reconstructions of John's sources go far beyond the reasonable limits that the method allows.

In this study I have laid out a very broad argument that runs along two parallel, but ultimately independent lines: first, the *Life of Aesop*, an aretalogical biography related to the foundation of a cult, is the closest parallel to Mark and John, and second, John is independent of Mark, and therefore both gospels must depend on an earlier gospel narrative. There are, to be sure, important differences between Mark and John and the earlier gospel tradition. Mark and John may have become "post-Jewish," in the sense that the community of the two gospels may no longer be composed mainly of ethnic Jews, while the older narrative was probably still well within the boundaries of what was considered sectarian Judaism. The hero/people antagonism in the earlier narrative is an unbearable tension, but not a rupture. As in the Greco-Roman hero narratives, the tension was also seen as being reconciled in cult. For Mark and John, the "people" who are reconciled in cult may have shifted considerably from those intended in the earlier narrative, from a Jewish group to a Jewish–Gentile mix, but there may have been more flexibility on this point than we usually grant. Though the authors of Mark and John may have explored new directions for the cult narrative, their gospels still qualify as exemplars.

Jon Levenson's study of the sacrifice of the beloved son in the Hebrew Bible, early Christianity, and rabbinic Judaism uncovers some of the same patterns as does the present analysis.[63] His principal interest is in the transmutation of the sacrifice of the son into such motifs as the redeeming of the first-born son through the substitution of a lamb in Israelite law (Exod 34: 20), the near-sacrifice of Isaac (again with the substitution of a ram), the persecution of the servant of God in Isaiah 42–53, and the sacrifice of Jesus as the beloved son. Levenson is probably right that the biblical concept of the sacrifice of the first-born influenced the tradition of the death of Jesus, but the present study has aimed at more specificity, especially in regard to genre. I have stated the various planks of my theory as clearly as possible to begin the process of reflection on the theory and to facilitate debate. It will not be difficult to identify the terms of the debate, as the past decade has witnessed a move away from the cultic and mythical in the earliest gospel traditions. Mack represents that point of view well when he says, "Movements in the name of Jesus as a teacher, sage, or charismatic reformer must have been the normal formation, the Christ cults a peculiar aberration."[64] But even if Jesus himself was a teacher or sage, the operative metaphor for his *vita* was cult – compare here Aesop as fabulist and Aesop as hero of cult. And even if the cultic practice of his followers was limited – a question I find undecidable – the literary form of the *vita* was couched in terms of the cultic metaphor.

It also becomes clear from this study that a number of aspects of Mark and John are better explained by recourse to their genre than by appealing to the overly subtle redaction of the two authors – profound as that often is. The smaller constituent parts of the gospel, such as miracle story and pronouncement story, may very well have originally circulated independently, but they are now found in the gospel with a new narrative purpose: they help to characterize the protagonist and to dramatize his relationship with others. The *content* of the miracles and of the pronouncement stories is not as important in the narrative as the *fact* that they occurred. If the content of the miracle stories were the main message that the reader was to take away, we would expect a stronger statement of a theme in them. Yet in one recent analysis of the miracle stories in Mark, we find that of the twenty-seven motifs that occur, the two most common by far are "miracle worker comes" (found in nineteen of twenty-one miracle stories) and "miracle worker goes" (eighteen of twenty-one).[65] Likewise, the pronouncement stories may communicate a theological content – "Render unto Caesar" could well be an important political program to the redactor – but in addition, the stories *function* to characterize the protagonist as a prophetic critic, just as Aesop is characterized regarding the abuse of rituals at Delphi, or even Peregrinus is characterized in Lucian's satire. Regarding other themes as well, we find that the obtuseness of the disciples is fraught with a profound irony in Mark, and yet, as Jonathan Z. Smith has shown, the misunderstanding of the disciples is found in other biographies of sages, even where the teaching is a series of commonplaces.[66] The "meaning" of Jesus' life and death is thus made clear, not only in the individual messages of his words and deeds, but in the overall pattern of the gospel. Though this pattern is by no means trivial, it is not unique.

The gospel participates in a genre with parallels already existing in the eastern Mediterranean, which have the same function: the justification of a cult. It has a large theological program already attached to it. In other words, it is not a unique or sectarian genre, but a communication within the broader world of the eastern Mediterranean; it begins as public discourse. The gospel genre likely arose as a fluid, often-copied, entertaining prose narrative used to tell the "charter myth" of the foundation of the group.[67] In competing with the *vitae* of other sages, it speaks to a broad social world, but in justifying the beginnings of a worshiping community, it speaks to its own.

APPENDIX
ENGLISH TRANSLATION OF THE
LIFE OF AESOP

Because the *Life of Aesop* is so important to the arguments of this book, and is relatively unknown even to scholars of the New Testament, I have included here a translation of the text. There are two important texts of the *Life*, the Westermann, or W, and the G, which is apparently an arbitrarily chosen letter.[1] Since the researches of B. E. Perry, it has been generally agreed that the G text represents the earlier and better text tradition. Lloyd Daly's excellent English translation of the G text,[2] based on the edition of Perry,[3] was not available because of copyright restrictions, and there being no other English translation of the G text, I have provided my own fresh translation, using the more recently established G text of Manolis Papathomopoulos.[4]

THE BOOK OF XANTHOS THE PHILOSOPHER AND AESOP, HIS SLAVE, CONCERNING THE COURSE OF HIS LIFE

1 Aesop, the story teller and composer of fables and great benefactor of humanity, was born in Amorium of Phrygia, as fate would have it, a slave. He was truly horrible to behold: worthless, pot-bellied, slant-headed, snub-nosed, hunchbacked, leather-skinned, club-footed, knock-kneed, short-armed, sleepy-eyed, bushy-lipped[5] – in short, an absolute miscreant. Worse than this, he had one other defect, even greater than the overall disharmony of his bodily appearance: he was dumb and could not utter a word.

2 Since his master considered him to be thoroughly loathsome, and thus singularly unsuited for affairs in town, he sent him to the country to labor there on his estate. [And once, when his master was visiting his farm, a farm hand who had picked some beautiful figs brought them to him and said, "Master, take these first fruits of your harvest."

The master was quite pleased and said, "Bless me, these are beautiful figs!" He turned to his house steward and said, "Agathapous, take these and put them away for me. After my bath and supper, bring this fruit out for me to eat."

At about that time Aesop quit work and came into the house for his daily meal. Agathapous, who had just brought in the figs, began to feel hungry and ate one or two of them. "I want to eat my fill of these figs," he said to himself, "but I do not dare."]

The other slave saw his pained expression, and said to him, "Fellow slave, I can tell what is on your mind. You want to eat those figs."

"Yes, by Zeus, I do," he answered, "but how did you know?"

"From the expression on your face," said his comrade, "one can tell plainly what you are thinking. But I've got a scheme for the two of us to eat them."

"I don't trust your schemes," said the first. "When the master returns he will ask for the figs, and when we don't have them, what then?"

His comrade replied, "Just tell him that Aesop found the storeroom open, went in, and ate the figs. Since Aesop can't speak, you'll have your wish and he'll get whipped."

Thus they agreed, and sat down to feast on the figs. "Woe to Aesop," they said. "He is truly a worthless slave, good for nothing but a beating. So let's make an agreement here and now: when anything is lost or broken or spilled, let's say that Aesop did it. We'll always get off scot-free." And with that, they consumed the rest of the figs.

3 Soon the master appeared, bathed and fed, his mouth watering for his figs. "Agathapous," he said, "bring the figs!"

Agathapous turned and said, "Hermas, bring the figs!"

But when the master learned that for all his efforts he had been cheated of his figs, and that Aesop had eaten them, he said, "Bring in Aesop!" Aesop was summoned, and came before him. The master said to him, "Tell me, you cursed wretch, do you despise me so much that you would sneak into my storeroom and eat the figs I had set aside for myself?" Although Aesop heard what they were saying about him, and could see his accusers face to face, he was unable to respond because of his impediment. Knowing that he was about to be whipped, he fell at the knees of his master to beg him to hold off punishment for just a moment. When the master agreed, Aesop took a pitcher he saw lying at hand, and indicated by gestures that he wanted some warm water. He then placed a basin in front of him, drank the warm water, and placing his fingers down his throat, regurgitated the water that he had drunk. It was clear that he had not eaten a thing. Having thus provided tangible proof through his great resourcefulness, he then asked the slaves who had accused him to do the same. The master, pleased by this notion, commanded that the other two slaves should also drink water and vomit.

They said to themselves, "What shall we do? Let's drink, but instead of placing our fingers down our throats, we'll place them in our cheeks." But as soon as they drank the warm water, the figs, mixed with bile, began rising up, and when they placed their fingers in their cheeks, they poured out.

The master said, "Just look how you lied against someone who can't even speak. Strip them!" They were whipped, and thus learned that

A person who connives an evil scheme against another
will often find later that he has brought it upon himself.

4 As a result, they paid the penalty for the wrongs they had committed against a man who could not speak.

The next day the master returned to the city. As Aesop was digging in the field, a priestess of Isis happened to wander away from the road and into the field where he was working. She saw him working away in his drudgery, and unaware of the circumstances of his condition, said to him, "Good man, if you have any pity for another human being, show me the way back to the road that leads to the city."

Aesop turned and saw her, dressed in the clothes of a goddess. Being a pious man, he bowed down to her. He then motioned to her, as if to ask, "Why did you leave the main road and wander out into the field?"

She realized that he could hear but could not speak, but all the same began to gesture as she spoke, "I am a stranger to these parts, and as you can see, a priestess of Isis. Since I have wandered from the road, would you please show me the way back?" Aesop picked up his mattock, took her by the hand, and led her to a grove of trees. There he placed before her bread and olives, and cut wild greens and brought them to her. He urged her to partake of his food, which she did. Then he led her to a spring, and offered her a drink. She shared both his food and water, and then prayed that Aesop should receive the greatest possible blessings. She then asked by signs that he bestow one final gift, and show her the way back to the road. He led her to the main road, and when he had pointed it out to her, returned to his labors.

5 The priestess of Isis, however, on her way again, did not forget Aesop's kindness. She raised her hands to heaven and said, "Diadem of the whole world, many-named Isis, have mercy on this poor worker, who suffers and is yet pious. He has exhibited this piety not to me, O Mistress, but to your image. And if it is not your will to reward this man with great wealth, recompensing him for what the other gods have taken away, at least grant him the power of speech, for you can bring into the light those things that have fallen into darkness." When the priestess of Isis finished her prayer, the heavenly mistress consented, for any report of piety quickly makes its way to the ears of the gods.

6 Since it was very hot, Aesop said to himself, "I am allowed two hours rest by my overseer. I'll take my rest now and sleep while it's hot." He chose a pleasant spot, green and secluded, a shaded grove of trees surrounding a blanket of green grass and all sorts of flowers, encompassed by a brook. Aesop threw his bag down beside his mattock, and using his sheepskin for a pillow, stretched out on the grass and took his rest. The brook echoed the rustling of the branches of the trees round about. As a sweet, gentle wind began to blow, the verdant limbs were gently moved and wafted over him a cool breeze, creating in the many-blossomed wood a fresh and restful spot. The hum of cicadas in the branches filled the air, and the chorus of many different kinds of birds could be heard. While a nightingale lamented, the olive branches sang back

in sympathy, and the slenderest branches of the pine trees fluttered in the wind, mimicking the blackbird. And Echo, the imitator of voices, uttered her responsive sounds in harmony. All of these voices conspired to lull Aesop into a deep and blissful sleep.

7 Our lady, the goddess Isis, then made her appearance, together with the nine Muses, and said, "You see here, my daughters, the very image of true piety, a man who may be ill-proportioned on the outside, but is above all reproach in regard to his inner spirit. He once gave guidance to my servant when she had lost her way, and now in your presence I shall reward him. I myself shall restore his voice, while you bestow upon that voice the most noble ability in speaking." When she had said this, Isis removed from Aesop's tongue the impediment that had prevented him from speaking, and gave him back his voice. She also persuaded each of the Muses in turn to grant Aesop something of her own gifts. They bestowed upon him the power to compose and elaborate Greek tales. The goddess prayed further that Aesop might achieve fame, and then she withdrew. The Muses each in turn then conferred upon him her own gift, and ascended to Mount Helicon.

8 When Aesop had finished the dream that had been planted by Isis, he awoke and said, "What a pleasant rest!" He then began to name each item he saw – mattock, pouch, sheepskin, ox, ass, sheep – and said, "By the Muses, I am speaking! Where did I get the power of speech? It must have come to me because I helped the priestess of Isis. Surely it is a good thing to be pious. No doubt I can expect to receive even more rewards from the gods!"

9 Overjoyed with his new powers, Aesop picked up his mattock and set back to work. But when the overseer arrived and began to beat one of Aesop's fellow slaves with a stick, Aesop could not restrain himself. "My good man," he said, "why do you beat this man so mercilessly, even though he has done nothing wrong, while you yourself constantly do wrong, and yet never get a beating?"

"What is this?" said Zenas to himself. "Aesop is speaking! But by the gods, no sooner has he begun to speak than he strikes out at me, the very one who should do the speaking, giving him his orders! If I don't find some way to accuse him, he will have me removed from my position. Even when he was dumb, he would gesture as if to say, 'When the master comes I shall get him to remove you. I can condemn you with signs!' If he could accuse me with signs, even more could he persuade with words! I'll have to beat him to the punch." 10 The overseer then got on his horse and rode quickly back to the city. When he came to his master's house, he found him and said, "Master!"

"What is it?" said his master. "Why are you so troubled?"

Zenas replied, "A most terrible and portentous thing has occurred on your estate!"

"Has some tree borne fruit out of season?" he asked.

"No, master."

"Or some animal borne young that have human form?"

"No," said Zenas.

"What is so portentous, then? Tell me the truth."

"Aesop, that worthless slave whom you sent out to the field to dig, that pot-bellied . . ."

"What? Has he given birth?"

"No, nothing like that. It's that he was dumb, and now speaks!"

"You won't receive any reward for bringing that news. What? Do you think this is a portent?"

"Oh, but it is, and a very awesome portent."

"But why is that? If the gods were once angry with someone and deprive him for a while of the power of speech, but have now become reconciled to him and bestow this power on him – which is what has evidently occurred – why do you consider that a portent?"

"But master," the overseer replied, "as soon as he began to speak, he started uttering inhuman things. Most of all, he has wrongly accused me – and you too, sir – of things I cannot bear to hear. And though I need scarcely mention that you have no earthly use for him, I still cannot bring myself to utter what he has said about you, simply because you sent him away to the fields as unsuitable for city work."

11 Now agitated, his master said, "Go sell him."

"Are you joking, master?" said Zenas. "Do you not know how ugly and misshapen he is? Who would want to buy him and end up with a baboon instead of a man?"

"In that case," said his master, "give him away. If no one will have him, take him out and beat him to death."

Zenas, now possessing absolute power over Aesop, jumped on his horse and rode back to the estate. He said to himself, "My master has granted me authority over Aesop – to sell, to give away, to kill. But what wrong has he done that I should kill him? I'll sell him instead." Thus all the blessings of the gods worked to Aesop's advantage.

12 It happened at that time that a slave dealer was going from the countryside to the city. He had wanted to lighten the burden of his slaves by hiring pack animals, but when he could not procure any, decided to head back to the city. When Zenas, who knew the dealer, met him, he said, "Greetings, Ophelion, noble merchant!"

"Greetings, Zenas, noble farmer!" he replied. "Do you have any animals to hire out or sell?"

Zenas answered, "No, by Zeus, I do not. But I do have a male slave to sell cheap, if you are interested."

Ophelion, who made his living in this way, said, "You ask me, a slave dealer, whether I want to buy a slave cheap?"

"Come over to our field, then."

13 So they went to the field, and Zenas said, "Send one of the slaves to get Aesop."

One of the slaves then went out, and when he saw Aesop digging, said, "Aesop, drop your mattock and come with me, for the master wants you."

But Aesop said, "Which master, my real master or the steward? Tell me clearly which you mean, and say 'the steward' and not 'the master,' for the steward is also under the yoke of slavery, and is also ordered about as a slave."

"Well!" said the slave. "This is a marvelous turn of affairs! Ever since he began to speak, he has become a know-it-all."

So Aesop dropped his mattock and said, "How horrible it is to be a slave to a slave. Surely this is loathsome to the gods. 'Aesop, set the table,' 'Aesop, heat up the bath,' 'Aesop, fill the water basin,' 'Aesop, feed the livestock.' Anything that is wretched or wearisome or painful or menial, Aesop is the one who is ordered to do it. But now, do I not also have the power of speech, granted to me by the gods? The master will come soon, and I shall condemn the overseer and have him removed from his position. Now, however, I must obey, so lead on, fellow slave."

Soon they arrived, and Zenas said, "Look him over, noble merchant."

14 When the slave dealer turned and saw what a specimen of human garbage Aesop was, he said, "What? Is this the trumpeter in the battle between pygmies and cranes [*Iliad* 3.3–6]? Is this a man or a turnip? If he did not speak, I would have said he was a pot or a jar or a goose egg. Zenas, I am surprised at you! I could have been home by now, but you have dragged me back here as though you had something good to sell, and not this human refuse."

And with that, he turned to go. **15** But Aesop came along behind him and tugged at the mantle of his cloak. "Listen," he said.

The slave dealer yelled, "Let me go, damn you! Why did you call me back?"

"Why did you come here?" asked Aesop.

"For you – to buy you," answered the dealer.

"Why don't you buy me, then?" Aesop asked.

"Tell me why I should, since I have no desire to," said the dealer. "I don't want to buy you."

"Do you not have in your market any undisciplined slaves always asking for food?" asked Aesop. "Buy me and make me their trainer. Out of fear of my ugly face they will stop acting like base slaves."

The dealer replied, "A splendid idea, by your murky nature!" He turned to Zenas, "How much for this worthless slave?"

184

The latter replied, "Take him for three obols."

"No, in truth, how much?" asked the dealer.

"Give me whatever you will," said Zenas. So giving him a few coins, the slave dealer bought him.

16 Upon returning to the city, the dealer took Aesop to the slave market. Two young boys, still in the care of their mother, saw Aesop and began to cry and hide their faces. Aesop said to the dealer, "Here you already have proof of what I promised. You have in me a ready cure for churlish young slaves."

The dealer laughed and said, "There is the dining room where your fellow slaves are gathered. Go say hello to them."

Aesop went in and saw many handsome lads, all carefully chosen, each like a Dionysus or an Apollo. He greeted them, "Hello, boys!" They answered back hello. "Gentlemen," he said, "I am your fellow slave, even though I am loathsome."

"That he is, by Nemesis," the slaves said to each other, "but what has come over the master to buy such a wretch?"

One slave asked another, "Do you know why he bought him?"

"No, why?" the second responded.

"To scare away the evil eye!" said the first.

17 The slave dealer then came in and said, "Boys, pray for better luck and good health, but unfortunately, I could not procure pack animals. You'll have to divide the gear among you, for tomorrow we are going to Asia Minor." So they paired off and began to divide up the baggage.

Aesop fell to his knees before them and said, "I beg you, fellow slaves, since I was just purchased and am very weak, let me carry the lighter gear."

They answered, "Don't carry anything, then."

But Aesop responded, "I would be ashamed to appear so useless to the master while all of my fellow slaves were working so hard."

So they said to him, "What is this? Is he a showoff? Carry whatever you want."

18 So Aesop looked around at all the baggage the slave dealer had assembled for the journey: a trunk, reed mats, bags full of gear, bedding, jars, and wicker baskets. Aesop spied one basket, loaded with bread, that four men were preparing to carry, and said, "Men, just set this basket on my back."

The slaves said to each other, "Have you ever seen a bigger fool? He begged to carry the lightest load of all, and now he's chosen the heaviest."

But another said, "He's no fool, but starved. He wants to break off pieces of bread and eat more than any of us. But let's give him the basket." And they all gathered round and hoisted it onto his back. Aesop went out carrying the basket like an Atlas – albeit a shaky Atlas.

But when the slave dealer saw him, he was astonished and said, "Just look at Aesop, how eager he is to work, and ready and willing to take on the burdens of the others. I've already gotten back what I paid out for him. That is a load for a mule." **19** His fellow slaves laughed at him as they hauled their burdens, for as he went along the road, he taught his basket how to walk, so to speak. When going uphill, he would tip the basket over and pull with his teeth until he reached the top of the hill, and on the way down he would coast by rolling the basket down the hill and riding on top.

After a tiring trip, they came to an inn. The slave dealer said, "Innkeeper, give to each a farthing's worth of stew, for we have bread. Aesop, give bread to each pair of slaves." The number of slaves was such that when they received this ration, the basket became half empty. They again took up their loads and set out, but now Aesop's step was lively. Once again they came to an inn, and again Aesop gave out bread to the slaves, and his basket was now empty. So throwing the basket on his shoulder, he ran out ahead of everyone.

The slaves said to each other, "Who is that up ahead, one of our party or a stranger?"

One said, "I don't know. I believe it is that new slave who is worthless, the one who carried a basket that a mule couldn't bear."

Another said, "You don't know how clever the little fellow is."

Still another: "These little fellows who are short on looks are long on brains. He asked to carry the bread that would be used up, while we carry the baggage, the bedding, the brassware – things that will not be used up."

And another: "This little fellow should be crucified!"[6]

20 When they arrived at Ephesus, the dealer sold the slaves for a profit. However, he had three slaves left, two striplings, one a schoolteacher and the other a harpist, and Aesop. The two other slaves did not bring a decent bid, and Aesop brought no bid at all, for no one wanted to buy him. Then a friend of the slave dealer said, "If you want to get a fair price for your slaves, go over to the island of Samos. Business is good there. Xanthos the philosopher has established his school, and many people come from Asia Minor and Greece to study with him. Someone will buy the teacher to get help with their studies, and some man about town will buy the musician, to party with his young friends. And someone with whom the gods are angry will even buy this one, and make him a butler or doorman or cook."

Persuaded by his friend, the slave dealer boarded a small boat with his slaves and sailed for Samos. When he arrived, he found lodging, and dressed his slaves up for the market. **21** He dressed the musician, who was quite handsome, in a white robe, put delicate sandals on his feet, combed his hair, put a kerchief about his shoulders, and stood him on the auction block. The teacher, however, had spindly ankles, so he dressed him in a long robe and high boots, in hopes that his clothes would hide his ugly legs. He also combed his hair, gave him a scarf, and stood him on the auction block. When he turned to Aesop, however, he could not hide or improve him in any way, since he was but a heap of disharmonious parts. He therefore dressed him in a sackcloth robe, tied a piece of cloth around his middle, and stood him between the two handsome slaves. When the auctioneer announced the sale of the slaves, many people began to examine them, and said, "Well, these two are handsome enough, but where did they find this ugly thing? He ruins the appearance of the other two. Get him off the block!" All the while they jeered at him, however, Aesop was not perturbed.

22 It happened that the wife of Xanthos the philosopher passed by, riding in a litter, and heard the auctioneer announcing the sale. When she got home, she said to her husband, "Dear, we don't have many male slaves, and you are generally waited on by my maids. Fortunately, there are some male slaves being auctioned right now. Go there and buy me a nice slave."

"I shall," said Xanthos, and went out. He first met with his students and engaged them in discussion. When his class was over, he took them with him to the market. **23** When Xanthos saw from a distance the two handsome slaves with the ugly one, he marveled at the slave dealer's intelligence, and exclaimed, "Well done, by Hera! A keen and philosophical, I would even say an awe-inspiring and superior, expert in these matters!"

"Professor, what are you saying?" asked the students. "What here is worthy of your admiration? Tell us, so that we may share your experience."

"Scholars and gentlemen, do not assume that philosophy can only be expressed through words; it can be expressed through actions as well. Often, in fact, unspoken philosophy surpasses that which is spoken, far more than you would think. This can be seen in the case of dancers, when the movements of their hands surpass the things communicated by long speeches. Philosophy is especially communicated through deeds, and this scene demonstrates that philosophy is silent. This man had two handsome slaves and one ugly, and he placed the ugly one between the handsome ones so that the ugliness of one would make the beauty of the other two stand out even more. For if the ugly had not been placed side by side with the beautiful, the superiority of the beautiful would not have been so evident."

The students responded, "You have extraordinary perception, Professor, and have caught the intention of the dealer most accurately."

"Well, come along," said Xanthos, "and I shall buy one of these slaves, for I need a servant."

24 Xanthos stepped up to the first slave and said, "Where are you from?"

"Cappadocia," he replied.

"What is your name?" asked Xanthos.

"Liguris," said the slave.

Xanthos then asked, "What do you know how to do?"

"I can do everything," he replied. Aesop suddenly burst out laughing.

When the students saw him laughing, [his face so sharply contorted that only his teeth were visible, they thought they were witnessing some portent. They said to each other, "Could this be a hump with teeth?"

"What did he see to laugh at?" asked another.

Yet another said, "He is not laughing; he is shuddering. Let's find out what he has to say." He went up behind him, tugged at him, and said, "My good man, what are you laughing at?"

Aesop turned to him and said, "Get out of here, you flounder!" The student was taken aback and stepped away.

Xanthos said to the merchant, "How much for the harpist?"

"A thousand denarii," he replied.

When Xanthos heard this high price, he went over to the other slave and said, "Where are you from?"

"Lydia," he replied.

"What is your name?"

"Philokalos."

"What do you know how to do?"

"Everything."

Aesop laughed again.

When the students saw this, they asked, "Why is he laughing at everything?"

Another said, "If I want to be called a flounder again, I'll ask him!"

Xanthos said to the merchant, "How much are you asking for the teacher?"

"Three thousand denarii," said the merchant. When Xanthos heard that, he lost interest and turned to leave.

"Professor," said the students, "Didn't you like the slaves?"

"Yes," he said, "but it is a rule with me not to buy expensive slaves, but to be served by cheap ones."

One of the students said, "If it is your rule not to buy expensive slaves, buy the ugly one. He will provide the same service, and we'll all chip in to pay his price."

"It would be ludicrous," said Xanthos, "for you to chip in or for me to buy this slave. At any rate, my wife is too fastidious and would never stand for being served by an ugly slave."

"Professor," said the students, "most of your teachings emphasize that one should not be influenced by a woman."]

25 Xanthos said, "Very well, let's find out whether he knows anything. *Caveat emptor!*" Xanthos proceeded up to Aesop and said, "Good day."

"What is wrong with my day so far?" replied Aesop. "Why do you say that?"

"By the Muses, he's right!" exclaimed the students. "What was wrong with his day?" They were astonished at his well-aimed retort.

Xanthos said to Aesop, "Where do you come from?"

"From the flesh."

"That's not what I meant. Where were you born?"

"Inside my mother's womb."

"Damn you! That's not what I asked you. In what *place* were you born?"

"My mother never told me whether it was in the bedroom or in the dining room."

"I'm asking you what nation are you from?"

"Phrygia."

"What do you know how to do?"

"I know nothing at all."

"Why nothing?"

187

"Because these other two slaves know everything."

The students exclaimed, "Yes, indeed! He is marvelous! These other two were wrong, for no one knows everything. That's why he said that he knew nothing, and that's why he laughed."

26 Xanthos asked him, "Do you want me to buy you?"

"Do you have some notion that you already own me, and I am one of your advisers? If you want to buy me, then buy me. Otherwise, move along. It doesn't matter to me. The man who is selling me doesn't need to drag in the unwilling, and you are not bound by any contract, but have total authority to make your own choice. If you want to buy me, open up your money bag and pay my price. If not, don't tease me."

Xanthos then asked him, "What is this? Are you a blabber-mouth? To hell with you!"

Aesop replied, "A talking bird fetches a higher price."

The students exclaimed, "Well said, by Hera! Aesop has shut the professor's mouth!"

Xanthos said, "I want to buy you, but you won't try to run away, will you?"

"If I do decide to," said Aesop, "I won't take you on as my privy counselor, as you are me. But my running away – who does it depend upon, you or me?"

"Clearly on you."

"Oh, no, on *you*."

"How on me?"

"If you treat your slaves well, no one will run away from that which is good to that which is bad, willingly giving himself over to a homeless existence, with only fear and starvation to look forward to. But if you are cruel to your slaves, I won't remain with you for one hour, not for a half-hour, not even for a minute!"

Xanthos said to his students, "This man can't face the consequences of his actions." Turning to Aesop, he said, "Everything you are saying is true for a human being, but you are a miscreant!"

"Do not look at outward appearances," said Aesop, "but examine the soul."

"What is outward appearance?"

"It is like this: when we go into a wine shop to buy wine, the wine jars appear ugly, but the wine tastes good."

27 So Xanthos, praising Aesop's ability with words, went to the slave dealer and said, "How much do you want for this one?"

The dealer replied, "Are you ridiculing my profession?"

"Why do you ask?" said Xanthos.

The dealer replied, "You've passed on these valuable slaves and are interested in this abominable piece of chattel. Buy one of the good ones and I'll throw in this one for free."

Xanthos responded, "No, how much for *him*?"

"I paid sixty denarii for him, and he's cost me fifteen more in expenses, so just pay what he cost."

The tax collectors heard that a sale of slaves had taken place, and so inquired who the seller was and who the buyer. But Xanthos hesitated to admit, "I bought this slave for seventy-five denarii," and the dealer was also embarrassed.

As they stood silent, Aesop cried out, "I am the one who was bought, this man is the seller, and that man is the buyer. If they are totally silent, it's clear I must be a free man."

Xanthos said, "I bought him for seventy-five denarii." The tax collectors laughed, waived the tax on Aesop for Xanthos and his students, bade good-bye, and left.

28 So Aesop followed along after Xanthos. It was high noon, the hottest part of the day, and since the road was now deserted because of the heat, Xanthos lifted up his robe and began to urinate as he walked along. When Aesop saw this, he became furious, seized the hem of Xanthos' robe, and pulled it. "Sell me," Aesop demanded, "since you won't allow me to run away!"

"Aesop, what's come over you?" Xanthos responded.

"Sell me. I can't be your slave."

"Has someone turned you against me – one of those people who go about upsetting respectable homes with their slander? Has someone said something wicked about me, that I mistreat slaves and beat them, or am a drunkard or hot-tempered? Do not pay any attention to vicious rumors. 'Slander pleases the ear, but provokes for no reason.' That is certainly my belief."

"Your own puddle accuses you, Xanthos! For if you, a person who is master of his own fate, and does not live in fear of blows and punishments, cannot take just a minute to see to his physical needs but urinates while walking, what am I, a slave, supposed to do when I'm sent out on some errand – defecate on the wing?"

"That is what upset you?"

"I should say so!"

"I urinated while walking along to avoid three unpleasant consequences."

"What are they?"

"The heat of the earth, the smell of the urine, and the burning rays of the sun."

"How is that?"

"Do you see that the sun is directly overhead and has scorched the earth? If I stop to urinate, the hot ground burns my feet, the smell of the urine rises up to my nose and irritates my nostrils, and the sun burns my head. Thus, by urinating while walking, I avoided these three unpleasant consequences."

"That's reasonable. You've convinced me. Walk on, then."

"I didn't realize that I had purchased a master."

29 When they reached the house, Xanthos said, "Aesop, the little woman is very fastidious. Wait here until I tell her about you, or else she may take one look at your pathetic form, demand back her dowry, and leave me."

"If you're so dominated by her," said Aesop, "go and get it over with."

So entering, Xanthos said to her, "Dear, you no longer have reason to complain that I am only waited on by your maids. Now I've gone out and bought a male slave."

"Thank you, Lady Aphrodite!" said Xanthos' wife. "You are great, and your messages are true. For when I was sleeping, I dreamed that you, my good husband, had bought a beautiful slave and given him to me as a gift."

"Just wait," said Xanthos, "and you shall see a kind of beauty such as you have never seen. I would almost say that you will see an Apollo or an Endymion or a Ganymede."

30 The maidservants rejoiced, and one said, "The master has bought a husband for me."

"Oh no, for me!" said another, "for I saw him in my dreams."

And another: "Whoever is the most persuasive will get him."

"Are you more persuasive than I?" asked the first maid.

"Well, are *you*?" asked the second. And thus they began to quarrel.

Xanthos' wife then asked, "Where is this paragon?"

"Outside the door, my dear," replied Xanthos. "It is a cardinal rule of good training not to enter into another person's home until called. He accompanied me to the door, but is waiting there for you to send word."

"Someone call in this new slave," said Xanthos' wife.

While all the other maids were arguing, one of them, also looking for a husband, said to herself, "I shall go out first and get myself engaged to him." She went out and said, "Where is the new slave?"

Aesop turned to her and said, "Here I am, sister."

"Are you the new slave?" she asked.

"Yes, I am," said Aesop.

"Then where is your tail?" she asked.

Catching her joke about his dog's head, Aesop replied, "My tail does not grow behind, as you would expect, but here in front."

"Stay here," she said. "Don't enter or they will all flee when they see what a horror you are."

189

She went back in, and when she saw her companions still fighting, she said to them, "It pains me to spoil the dreams that your Muses have brought you, but before you attack each other, you had better have a look at his 'beauty.'"

One of them went out and said, "Where is my husband, the one who was just bought, my beauty?"

"Here I am!" answered Aesop.

"May Aphrodite strike your ugly face!" she said. "I was fighting over you, you human garbage! Damn you! Go in now, but don't even touch me. Stay away from me!" So Aesop entered and stood before his mistress.

31 When Xanthos' wife beheld Aesop's ugly face, she turned and said to her husband, "Well, Xanthos, you have acted like a true philosopher and gentleman. You wanted to take a new wife, but did not dare to say to my face, 'Leave me.' Knowing how fastidious I am, you brought me this creature whom I could not bear to have as a servant as part of a scheme to get me to flee this house on my own accord! Give me back my dowry and I'll go on my own way."

Xanthos said to Aesop, "You had all those fancy words for me when I was urinating along the way, but now you have nothing to say to her?"

"Let her go her way and be damned!" said Aesop.

"Silence, you refuse!" said Xanthos. "Don't you realize that I love her more than my own life?"

"So, you love the little woman?"

"Yes, certainly."

"Do you want her to stay?"

"I do, you wretch."

"Is that what you really want?" Aesop stamped his foot and cried out, "If Xanthos the philosopher is henpecked, tomorrow in the lecture hall I shall clearly demonstrate how contemptible he is!"

"Well done, Aesop!" said Xanthos.

32 Aesop turned to Xanthos' wife and said, "Woman, I take it that what you want is for your husband to go out and buy you a very beautiful young slave, with a handsome face, pleasing form, good eye, and blond hair."

"Yes, why?" replied Xanthos' wife.

Aesop said, "So this beautiful slave would go with you into the bath, then this beautiful slave would take your clothes, and when you come out of the bath this beautiful slave would put your robe around your shoulders, and stoop down and put your sandals on, then play with you and gaze into your eyes as though you were a maid who had caught his fancy. Then you will smile back at him and try to look young, and become aroused and call him into your bedroom to massage your feet, then in a fit of passion you will draw him to you and kiss him and do all the things in keeping with your shameful impudence, and the philosopher here will be disgraced and cuckolded. Well done, Euripides! Your lips should have turned to gold when you said something so true:

> Danger there is in angry waves of the sea,
> Danger also in the raging river and burning fire,
> Danger in poverty, and in a thousand other things,
> But no evil is so dangerous as woman.
> (Euripides, fragment 1059 Nauck)

But you are a foolish philosopher's wife, who wishes to possess handsome male slaves. You bring a great shame and dishonor upon your husband. I'll bet you are constantly on the prowl, never minding your own business. Be careful, or I'll show you the righteous indignation of a new slave, you whore!"

"What brought this on?" asked Xanthos' wife.

"You see how much he has said to you already, dear," said Xanthos. "By all means, don't let him see you defecating or urinating, or you'll meet Aesop, the true Demosthenes."

190

"By the Muses," said Xanthos' wife, "this little fellow appears to be spirited and clever. I'd better make up with him."

"Aesop, your mistress has made up with you," said Xanthos.

"Some achievement," said Aesop, "to tame a woman by impressing her!"

"You runaway!" said Xanthos.

33 "Aesop," said Xanthos' wife, "from what you have said, it is obvious that you are astute, but I was misled by my dream. I thought I was to receive a good-looking slave, but you are loathsome."

"Do not be surprised," said Aesop, "that you were tripped up by a dream, for not all dreams are true. At the request of Apollo, the head of the Muses, Zeus granted him the gift of prophecy, so that he excelled everyone in divining oracles. Since Apollo was marveled at by all people, he thought himself superior and became boastful in other ways as well, both because his prophecies were accurate and because they gave him such authority. This angered Zeus, who did not want him to possess this much power over people. Zeus then created dreams, which accurately told people during their sleep what was about to happen. When Apollo realized that people would no longer have any need of his prophecy, he asked Zeus to forgive him and not undermine his oracles. Zeus relented, and so created other dreams for people which were not true, and the human race, once thus deceived, would again be forced to rely on Apollo's prophecy. And so for this reason, the false dreams, when they come, appear like the true ones. Don't be surprised, therefore, when many things appear one way in your dreams, but turn out another way. It was not the first kind of dream you saw, but one of the lying ones, which has come to deceive you with false visions."

34 Xanthos praised Aesop, noting how intelligent and articulate he was. He said to him, "Aesop, bring a carrying bag and come with me. We will buy some vegetables from the gardener for dinner. So Aesop threw the bag over his shoulder and followed along. When they came to the garden and found the proprietor, Xanthos said, "Give me some cooking vegetables." The gardener took his knife and cut some stalks of kale, beets, asparagus tips, and other savory vegetables, tied them in a neat bundle and handed them to Aesop.

Xanthos opened his money bag and was about to pay the man, 35 when the gardener said, "What's that for, Professor?"

Xanthos replied, "I'm paying you for the vegetables."

"Why bother?" said the gardener. "As far as the garden and the produce are concerned, you can have this garbage. Just tell me one thing."

"Well, by the Muses," said Xanthos, "I won't take the money or the vegetables unless you explain to me first how anything I can tell you would be of value to a gardener. I'm not a handyman or a smith to make you a hoe or a leek slicer. I am a philosopher."

"But sir," said the gardener, "that is very useful for me. There's a small matter that has been bothering me so much I can't sleep at night. I have been pondering and pondering why it is that I put seeds into the ground, hoe them and water them, give them the best of attention, and yet the weeds still come up faster than what I planted." Xanthos listened to this philosophical question, but when he could not answer it on the spot, said, "All things come to pass through divine providence." 36 Aesop, standing behind Xanthos, began to laugh. "Are you laughing with me or at me?" asked Xanthos.

"Oh, not at *you*," replied Aesop.

"At whom, then?"

"At the professor you studied under."

"You abominable wretch, you are uttering blasphemy against the entire Greek world! I studied in Athens, under philosophers, rhetoricians, learned professors. Are you able to ascend Mount Helicon, where the Muses hold forth?"

"If you speak gibberish, you can expect to be ridiculed."

"Does this problem he posed have some other solution? Things that happen by divine providence cannot be investigated by philosophers. Are you, then, capable of solving it?"

191

Aesop said, "Agree to do it, and I will solve it for you."

37 Xanthos was embarrassed and said, "It would be highly irregular for me – a philosopher who has debated in the greatest lecture halls – to engage in debate here in a garden. But so be it." He turned to the gardener and said, "My slave-boy here is very worldly. Put the question to him and he will solve it."

"Where is he?" asked the gardener.

"Here he is," said Xanthos.

"This worthless slave has learning?" asked the gardener.

Aesop laughed and said to him, "You should talk, you miserable wretch!"

"I'm a miserable wretch?" exclaimed the gardener.

"You're a gardener, aren't you?"

"Yes."

"How can you object to being called a miserable wretch if you are a gardener? But do you want to know why you plant seeds in the ground, you hoe them, water them, tend them with loving care, and yet you say the untended weeds come up quicker than your vegetables? Listen carefully to what I say. It's like what happens when a woman is married a second time, and has children from her first marriage, but also finds that her new husband has children from his first wife. She is now mother of those children she bore, but stepmother of her husband's children. The difference between them is great. She lavishes great care and affection on those whom she bore, but she is jealous of those who were brought into this world through another woman's labors, and hates them, cutting back on their food and provisions to give more to her own children. It is only natural that she love her own children and hate her husband's, and treat them as strangers. In the same way, the earth is the mother of the plants that come up on their own, but stepmother of those planted by others; nourishing her own, she causes them to grow faster than the orphans which you plant."

Upon hearing all this, the gardener said, "You have taken a load off my shoulders. Here, take the vegetables as a gift, and if you ever need any more, come and treat the garden as your own."

[There is a gap at this point in the manuscript. From later references in the text, it appears that Aesop took the vegetables home and provoked Xanthos' wife to anger; she then trampled the vegetables underfoot. The manuscript resumes in the middle of a speech by Xanthos.]

38 "In the future, do not cause me grief by doing any more or less than what you are told. Pick up the oil flask and towels, and we'll go to the bath."

Aesop said to himself, "Masters who are overly severe about the service they expect have only themselves to blame when things go wrong. I'll give this philosopher a real lesson in how best to give orders." So Aesop took the flask and towels, but did not take any oil, and set off after Xanthos to the bath.

There Xanthos undressed, handed Aesop his clothes, and said, "Give me the flask," which Aesop did. When Xanthos turned the flask over and found it empty, he said, "Aesop, where is the oil?"

"At home," said Aesop.

"Why is that?" asked Xanthos.

"Because you said to me, 'Take the flask and towels.' You did not mention oil. I was not supposed to do anything more than what I was told. If I had failed in my instructions, I would have been liable for a beating." Then he was silent.

39 Xanthos then found some of his friends at the bath, and commanded Aesop to hand the clothes to their servants, and said to him, "Aesop, go home now, and since my wife trampled the vegetables in a fit of rage, cook lentil for us. Put it in the pot, add some water, put it on the hearth, place some wood under it, and light it. Now do as I say."

"I'll do it," said Aesop. So he went home, entered the kitchen, placed one lentil in the pot, and cooked it.

When Xanthos and his friends had finished their bath, he said, "Gentlemen, will you share a simple meal with me? We are having lentil. We should not judge our friends by the lavishness of their victuals, but by the quality of their intentions. For indeed sometimes the humblest offerings provide more enjoyment than the richest banquet, especially if the host offers them with a gracious welcome."

"Let us proceed," said the friends.

40 Xanthos led them to his home and said, "Aesop, bring something to drink for men straight from the bath!" Aesop ran to the baths and filled a jug with warm water and gave it to Xanthos.

"What's this?" he asked.

"Something to drink, straight from the bath."

Xanthos' countenance fell, and after a moment, he said, "Bring me a foot bath." Aesop brought the foot bath without water in it and set it before him.

"What is this?" asked Xanthos.

"You said, 'Bring me a foot bath,' but you didn't say, 'Fill it with water and wash my feet.'"

"Take off my sandals and get on with it," said Xanthos, and then turned to his friends. "Gentlemen, it seems that I have not bought a slave, but a professor. Now, if you wish, let us rise and go to the table." 41 When the drinking had proceeded for some time, Xanthos said, "Aesop, is the lentil cooked?"

"Yes," said Aesop.

"Bring it in," said Xanthos, "and I shall see if it is done."

Aesop brought the one lentil in a spoon and gave it to Xanthos. He tasted it and said, "It's done. Bring it in and serve it." Aesop set down a bowl and poured the soup and said, "Enjoy your meal."

"You have only served soup," said Xanthos. "Where is the lentil?"

"You've eaten it," said Aesop.

"You only cooked one lentil?"

"Yes. Did you not say, 'Cook lentil,' and not 'Cook lentils'?"

42 "I don't want to insult the guests. Go quickly and cook with vinegar the four pig's feet you bought." Aesop put the pig's feet in a kettle and began to cook them. Xanthos, meanwhile, was searching for some pretext to have Aesop whipped, and so he got up and said to him, "Aesop, go bring in some vinegar from the storeroom and put it in a kettle." But while Aesop was gone, Xanthos went into the kitchen, took one of the pigs' feet from the kettle, and hid it. When Aesop came back and found only three feet in the kettle, he realized that Xanthos had deliberately taken the foot in order to get the best of him. He had noted that a pig was being kept for the birthday of Xanthos' wife, so he quickly tied the pig's snout with a rope, cut off one foot, roasted it over the fire until it was singed, and threw it into the kettle to replace the one taken. Xanthos, however, suspecting that Aesop would run away when he saw that a foot was missing, retrieved it, went back into the kitchen, and threw it into the kettle. Now there were five feet, but neither Aesop nor Xanthos knew it.

43 A bit later Xanthos said to Aesop, "Have you cooked the pig's feet?"

"Yes," said Aesop.

"Well, bring them in," said Xanthos. Aesop set down a bowl and emptied the kettle into it, and out poured five pigs' feet. Xanthos' face went white. "How many feet did this pig have?" he asked.

"How many feet do two pigs have?" said Aesop.

"Eight."

"It all balances out, then. This pig had five feet, and the one we're tending in the pen outside has only three."

"Gentlemen," said Xanthos, "this slave will soon drive me mad!"

"If you had not hemmed me in with so many rules," said Aesop, "I would have served you much better. But do not despair, master, for your way of prescribing rules will turn out to be a valuable lesson for you. It will teach you not to make mistakes in the classroom. Statements that

193

are too vague, and either include too much or exclude too much, cause serious problems." Xanthos could find no excuse to have Aesop beaten, and kept his silence.

44 In the days that followed, Aesop accompanied Xanthos to the lecture halls and became known to everyone. Once one of the students prepared a dinner, to which he invited Xanthos, along with the other students. Xanthos said to Aesop, "Get everything I shall need for a dinner party – by that, I mean a basket, a plate, a napkin, a lantern, sandals, and anything else I may have forgotten to mention – and come with me." Aesop collected them and went along with Xanthos. During the meal, Xanthos took portions of food and gave them to Aesop, who placed them in his basket. Xanthos turned to Aesop and said, "Do you have all the portions?"

"Yes, I do," he said.

Then Xanthos said, "Now take them to the one who adores me."

"I will," said Aesop. As he left, he said to himself, "Now is my chance to exact my revenge on my mistress. I'll pay her back for the way she mocked me and made fun of me when I had just been purchased. She also tore up and trampled the vegetables the gardener gave me, and would not allow my gift a chance to please my master. I'll show her that a woman cannot compete with a household slave for the affections of his master. My master said, 'Give the portions to the one who adores me'; well, now he is going to find out who really adores him." **45** When Aesop had returned home, he placed the basket down and called Xanthos' wife. He showed her all the portions, and said to her, "Note carefully, Madam. Nothing is missing; nothing has been eaten."

"Everything looks just fine, Aesop," said Xanthos' wife. "Did the master send these to me?"

"No," said Aesop.

"Then to whom did he send them?"

"To the one who adores him."

"And who adores him, you runaway slave?"

"Bear with me just a little, and you will see who adores him." Aesop looked at the prize pedigreed dog which lived in the house with them, and called her to him, "Here, Lycaena, take this." The dog immediately came to him, and Aesop fed her the portions. When the dog had eaten all the food, Aesop returned to the dinner party and took his place at Xanthos' feet.

46 Xanthos said, "Did you give her the food?"

"Yes," said Aesop.

"Did she eat it?" asked Xanthos.

"Yes, she ate all of it."

"Could she really eat all of it?"

"Yes, she was hungry."

"Did she enjoy it?"

"Yes, she did."

"What did she say?"

"She didn't say anything, but she certainly expressed her thanks in her own way."

"I'll get back at her for this!"

Meanwhile, Xanthos' wife was saying to her maids, "Girls, I cannot remain with Xanthos another minute. Let him give me back my dowry and I'll be gone. If he prefers his dog to me, how can I stay here with him any longer?" So she went off to her bedroom and brooded.

47 As the drinking at the banquet proceeded, there was much conversation, and as is typical at a gathering of scholars, many different topics were touched upon. One of the students said, "What circumstances would provoke a great consternation among people?"

Aesop, who was now standing behind his master, said, "If the dead were to rise up and demand back their property."

There was much laughter and not a little whispering among the students, and they said, "This is the new slave whom Xanthos bought when we were with him."

"He once said I was as stupid as a flounder," said one of the students.

Another said, "Though some of the things he says are his ideas, many he has learned from Xanthos."

"You all certainly have a good nose for others' ideas!" said Aesop.

The students said, "Professor, by the Muses, allow Aesop to join us for a drink." Xanthos agreed and Aesop began to drink.

48 One of the students said to the others, "Why is it that when the sheep is led to the sacrifice, it does not make a sound, while the pig squeals loudly?"

When none of them could answer the question, Aesop said, "Because the sheep has milk, which is useful, and wool, which is beautiful. At the appropriate time, the wool is shorn, which is heavy, and when the sheep is milked, it is unburdened. Therefore, when it goes to the slaughter, it does not expect any harm, but rather follows happily and does not flee the altar. But the pig does not have beautiful wool, or milk, and so quite naturally it squeals, knowing that it is being led away for the use that is made of its meat."

"By the Muses," said the students, "well put!"

49 When everyone had parted company, Xanthos went home and entered his bedroom, where he began to speak sweetly to his wife and kiss her. She turned to him and said, "Don't come near me, you slave-lover, or better yet, you dog-lover! Give me back my dowry!"

"What rotten luck!" said Xanthos. "What has Aesop done now?"

His wife replied, "Go and have your way with the one you sent all the food!"

"Didn't I tell you that Aesop had stirred up more trouble for me? Someone call him!" **50** Aesop came, and Xanthos said to him, "Aesop, to whom did you give the portions of food?"

Aesop replied, "You said to me, 'Give them to the one who adores me.'"

"I received nothing," said Xanthos' wife. "There he is. Let him deny it to my face."

"You runaway slave," said Xanthos. "She says she received nothing."

"But to whom did you tell me to give the portions?" asked Aesop.

"To the one who adores me!" said Xanthos.

"Well, in what way does she adore you?"

"Well, who does, you runaway slave?"

"Let's find out who adores you." Aesop called the dog and said to Xanthos, "She is the one who adores you. Your wife says she does, but doesn't, and here's proof: you thought she adored you, but she demanded back her dowry and threatened to leave you over a trifling amount of food. But beat your dog, thrash her within an inch of her life, knock her down, chase her away, and she won't leave you. She'll forget all your abuse, and return to her master, wagging her tail. You should have said to me, 'Take this food to my wife,' and not, 'to the one who adores me,' for she is not the one who adores you. The dog is."

Xanthos said, "Do you see, Dear, it was not my fault at all, but the maddening chatter of this slave who brought it." Xanthos turned to Aesop: "I'll find some excuse to beat you and will punish you soundly!"

[**50a** His wife said, "I won't live with you any more!" And with that she slipped out of the house and went to her parents.

Aesop said to his master, "Didn't I tell you the dog adored you and not your wife?" But when several days had passed and she was still not over it, Xanthos sent friends around begging her to return to him, but she was not persuaded. Lonely for his wife, he sank into a deep depression. Aesop came to him and said, "Don't be so upset, master; tomorrow I shall make her come back to you of her own accord." So Aesop took some money and went to the marketplace, and bought there some birds, geese, and other things. He then carried them as he passed by the house where his mistress was staying, pretending all the while that he did not know she was there. He found one of her parents' servants, and said to him, "Brother, is it possible that anyone in this house would have some geese or anything else that would be fitting for a wedding?"

"And why do you need them?" asked the servant.

"Tomorrow," said Aesop, "Xanthos the philosopher is going to be married."

The servant ran into the house to inform Xanthos' wife. When she heard, she immediately returned to Xanthos and shouted at him, "Xanthos, how can you marry again while I'm still alive?"]

51 On the next day, Xanthos invited to dinner the students who had entertained him, and said to Aesop, "I have invited my friends to dinner. Go and buy the best thing in the whole world."

Aesop said to himself, "I'll show him not to give stupid orders." He went to the butcher's shop and bought pigs' tongues, then returned home and began to prepare them: some he boiled, some he roasted, some he spiced.

Xanthos said, "Aesop give us something to eat." Aesop brought each of them a boiled tongue, served with spicy sauce.

The students said, "Indeed, even your dinner expresses your philosophy! You never do anything that isn't carefully thought out, for at the very beginning of the dinner, tongues are served."

52 And after two or three drinks, Xanthos said, "Aesop, give us something else to eat." Aesop again gave each a tongue, this time roasted, served with salt and pepper. The students exclaimed, "Inspired, Professor! By the Muses, this is excellent! Every tongue is sharpened by fire, and even better, by salt and pepper, for the salt is mixed with the sharpness of the tongue to bring out a razor-sharp wit."

After they had drunk again, Xanthos said for the third time, "Bring us something else to eat." Aesop brought each a spiced tongue.

"Democritus!" said one of the students to another, "I have worn out my tongue eating tongues."

"Is there anything else to eat?" asked another. "Wherever Aesop labors, nothing good can come of it."

When the students tasted the spiced tongues, they became nauseous. Xanthos said, "Aesop, bring us each a bowl of soup." Aesop served them tongue soup.

The students did not even touch this, but said, "This is Aesop's final blow. We have been beaten by tongues."

"Aesop, do we have anything else?" asked Xanthos.

"No, nothing else," he replied.

53 "Nothing else, you wretched slave? Did I not tell you to buy 'the best thing in the whole world'?"

"I'm glad that you find fault with me in the presence of so many learned men," responded Aesop. "You told me to buy 'the best thing in the whole world.' Well, what is better or finer than the tongue? You will note that all philosophy and all education depend on the tongue. Without the tongue, nothing could happen – no giving, no receiving, no enterprise. Through the tongue cities are constituted and ordinances and laws are established. If, therefore, all living depends upon the tongue, nothing could be greater."

The students said, "By the Muses, he speaks well! You were mistaken, Professor!" The students then got up and went home, but all night long they suffered from bouts of diarrhea.

54 On the next day, the students complained to Xanthos, but he said, "Gentlemen and scholars, it was not my fault, but the fault of that worthless slave Aesop. But tomorrow I'll make good on my dinner, and I'll give him his instructions in your presence." So calling Aesop, he said to him, "Since you seem determined to turn my words upside down, go into the marketplace and buy the worst, the vilest thing in the whole world." Aesop readily agreed and went to the butcher, and again he purchased pigs' tongues. He then brought them home and prepared them for dinner. When Xanthos arrived with his students, they all took their places at the table. After their first drink, Xanthos said, "Aesop, bring us something to eat." Aesop served each of them a pickled tongue with hot sauce.

The students said, "What is this, tongue again?" Xanthos blanched. The students continued, "Maybe he wants the vinegar to soothe our stomachs from yesterday's diarrhea."

After they had a second round of drinking, Xanthos said, "Bring us something to eat."

Aesop served each of them a roast tongue. "Oh no, what's this?" said the students. That idiot from yesterday is trying to make us sick again with tongues!"

55 Xanthos said, "Not again, you scum! Why did you buy these? Didn't I tell you to buy 'the worst, the vilest thing in the world'?"

Aesop replied, "And what bad thing does not come about through the tongue? On account of the tongue there are enemies, plots, conflicts, battles, jealousy, strife, wars. Surely there is nothing worse than this most abominable tongue."

"Professor," said one of the students, "if you pay attention to him, he will soon drive you crazy. Like body, like mind. This slave is abusive and mischievous. He isn't worth a copper!"

"Silence, student!" said Aesop. "You seem to me to be much more mischievous than I. You lack my master's status, yet you incite his anger with your inflammatory tone, and turn him against his slave. This is not the action of a person who minds his own business, but of a busybody, sticking your nose into other people's business!"

56 Now Xanthos, looking for an excuse to give Aesop a beating, said to him, "Aesop, since I am forced to discuss philosophy with my own slave, you have called my friend a busybody. Prove to me there is such a thing as a man who is *not* a busybody."

"There most certainly is," said Aesop. "To be sure, many people eat and drink at others' tables, and stick their noses into other people's business, but there are others who are concerned only with their own troubles, and don't meddle in everyone else's."

Xanthos said, "If you say that there is a person who is not a busybody, I'll give you a new set of orders and cancel your previous ones. Someone else will prepare tomorrow's dinner. You go find a person who is not a busybody and invite him to dinner. If he meddles in other people's business in any way, the first time I shall keep silent, the second time I'll also excuse, but the third time you will get a beating and be placed in the stocks."

57 The next day, Aesop, responding to his new orders, went to the marketplace to find someone who was not a busybody. [There he saw a fight going on, and a large crowd standing around watching. One man, however, was sitting off to the side, reading. "I'll invite him," said Aesop to himself, "For he is evidently no busybody, and I'll avoid a beating." So he approached him and said, "Kind sir, Xanthos the philosopher has heard of your gentle manners, and invites you to dinner."

"I shall come," he responded. "You will find me at your gate." So Aesop went home and prepared dinner.

Xanthos said, "Aesop, where is this man who is not a busybody?"

"He is standing at the gate."

At the appointed hour, Xanthos brought him in and sat him at the table with his friends. **58** Xanthos ordered the honeyed wine to be served to his guest first, but the man said, "Oh no, sir. You drink first, then your wife, then we, your friends."

Xanthos nodded to Aesop, "That's once," for the man had by this proven himself to be something of a busybody. Next, a fish dish was served. Xanthos, looking for some pretext, said, "All of these condiments can't help this main dish. It has no spices, no oil, and the sauce is lumpy. Have the cook beaten!"

"Wait, sir!" said the guest. "He hasn't done anything wrong. Everything is fine!"

Xanthos nodded again to Aesop, "See – twice." Then a sesame cake was served. Xanthos tasted it and said, "Call the baker! Why doesn't the cake have any honey or raisins?" The man again said, "Sir, the cake is fine, and there is nothing wrong with the dinner. Don't beat your slaves without reason!"

Xanthos then nodded to Aesop, "That's the third."

"I concede," said Aesop. When the guests left after dinner, Aesop was strung up and beaten. Xanthos said to him, "That's what you get now. If you do not find a man who is not a busybody to invite to dinner, I'll shackle you and break you in two!"

59 On the following day, Aesop went outside the city to look for a man who was not a busybody. He saw many people pass by,] and at last he spotted a man who was rough in his appearance, but seemed to have a civil manner. He was leading a small donkey loaded with wood, keeping out of the way of the bustling crowds, and speaking to the donkey as he went along. Taking this man to be a person who would clearly mind his own business, Aesop followed him. The crude man was riding the donkey, saying to him as they proceeded, "Let's go. The sooner we arrive and sell the wood for twelve coppers, the sooner you'll get two coppers for fodder. I'll take two as my share, and put away the rest for a rainy day, for if you eat the good barley today, and some unforeseen bad luck happens your way, you'll end up with neither barley nor hay."

60 When Aesop heard all this, he said to himself, "By the Muses, this man does not seem to be a busybody. I'll approach him." Aesop walked up to him and said, "Greetings, sir." The man returned his greetings. Aesop then asked him, "How much do you want for the wood?"

"Twelve coppers," said the man.

"He's telling the truth," Aesop said to himself. "He's asking just the same price he mentioned to his donkey." Then Aesop said to the man, "Sir, do you know Xanthos the philosopher?"

"No, son, I don't," he replied.

"Why not?" asked Aesop.

"Because I'm no busybody. I've *heard* of him."

"Well, bless you! I'm his slave."

"Did I ask you whether you were a slave or a free man? What do I care?"

Aesop said to himself, "Indeed, he is no busybody," and turned to the man, "Sir, your wood is now sold. Drive your donkey to Xanthos' house."

"But I do not know where his house is," said the man.

"Follow me and you'll find out."

61 After leading him to Xanthos' house, Aesop unloaded the wood, paid him, and said, "Sir, my master would like for you to dine with him. Leave your donkey in the yard and it will be fed." So the man entered into the dining room just as he was, his feet covered in mud, without even inquiring why he should be invited.

Xanthos said, "Is this the man who is not a busybody?" When Xanthos heard what great things Aesop said about the man, he said to his wife, "Dear, would you like to see Aesop taught a lesson?"

"This is what I pray for," his wife responded.

"Then do as I say," said Xanthos. "Get up and take a basin over to the stranger as though you were about to wash his feet. He will assume from your appearance that you are the lady of the house and will not allow you to do it, but will ask you, 'Madam, do you not have a slave to wash my feet?'"

So Xanthos' wife, out of hatred for Aesop, tied a towel around her waist, took another over her arm, and brought over the basin to the stranger. The man realized that she was the lady of the house, but said to himself, "Xanthos is a philosopher. If he wanted my feet to be washed by a slave, he would have ordered it. And if he has ordered his wife to wash my feet in order to show me honor, I do not want to bring dishonor on myself, so I won't be a busybody. I'll just hold out my feet and let her wash them." So as Xanthos' wife washed his feet, the man settled in and relaxed.

62 "By the Muses," said Xanthos, "he's clever!" Xanthos then ordered the honeyed wine to be served to their guest first. The rustic said to himself, "It is customary for the hosts to drink first, but if the philosopher has ordered that I should drink first in order to show me honor, I won't be a busybody." So he took the cup and drank.

Xanthos then called for the dinner to be served, and a plate of fish was brought in. Xanthos said to the crude stranger, "Eat." The man began to wolf down the fish like Charybdis. Xanthos tasted the food, and wishing to engage the man in conversation to show him up as a busybody, said to his servant, "Go call the cook." The cook came in, and Xanthos said, "Tell me, you runaway slave, when you got all the ingredients, why didn't you add enough oil, fish paste, or pepper? Strip him and beat him."

The visitor said to himself, "It tastes well seasoned to me, with nothing missing. Still, if Xanthos is so mad at his cook that he wants to beat him, I won't be a busybody."

The unfortunate cook was whipped, and Xanthos said to himself, "This man appears to be deaf or dumb and doesn't speak at all." After dinner, the cake was served. The rustic, who had never seen a picture of cake, much less eaten it, began to break off square pieces the size of bricks and gulp them down. **63** Xanthos tasted it, and once again called out, "Someone call the baker." He came in and Xanthos said, "Damn you! Why does the cake not have any honey or pepper or pine nuts, but is instead so sour?"

The baker said, "Sir, if the cake is raw, blame me, but if it doesn't have enough honey and is sour, it's not my fault but the mistress's. When I was making the cake, I asked her for honey, and she said, 'When I return from the bath I'll fetch some.' She was late, however, and I didn't get the honey in time, and so it is sour."

Xanthos said, "If this came about as a result of my wife's carelessness, I'll burn her alive this minute!" Xanthos then whispered to his wife, "Now, dear, play your part." Turning to Aesop, he said, "Aesop, go get some brushwood and build a fire right here." Aesop brought it in and built a large fire. Xanthos took his wife and put her into the fire, watching the guest to see whether he would jump up in anger and stop the whole display. **64** The rustic, however, did not show any concern, but kept to his seat and finished his drink. He knew by this time that Xanthos was testing him, so he said, "Sir, if you are determined to carry this through, wait just a bit, until I run to my farm and bring back my wife. You can burn the two of them."

Xanthos, marveling at the implacability of this man, who was clearly no busybody, said, "Aesop, I admit defeat. Let's call a truce. Stop making fun of me, and serve me in earnest from now on."

"You won't see any cause for complaint in me, master," said Aesop, "but you will find me a dutiful servant."

65 On the next day, Xanthos said to Aesop, "Go and see whether there are many people at the bath."

On the way to the bath, Aesop met the governor. The governor knew Aesop, and said to him, "Aesop, where are you going?"

Aesop said, "I don't know."

The governor said, "I ask you where you are going and you say, 'I don't know'?"

Aesop answered, "By the Muses, I don't."

The governor ordered him to be taken off to jail. Aesop said, "Sir, now you can see that I answered you correctly, because I didn't know I was going to be taken off to jail."

The governor was so struck by his response that he released him.

66 Aesop proceeded on his way to the bath, and saw there a large crowd of bathers. At the entrance of the bath Aesop also saw a stone that happened to be lying there. Each bather who entered stumbled on the stone and cursed it, but no one moved the stone aside. While Aesop was marveling at the stupidity of those who were continually stumbling on it, one man who stumbled said, "A curse upon the man who left this stone here," and then moved the stone aside and went in.

Aesop returned home and told Xanthos, "Master, I found only one man at the bath."

"One man?" said Xanthos. "Now I have my chance to bathe without the crowds. Bring my things for the bath." But when Xanthos entered the bath and saw all the people there, he said, "Aesop, didn't you say, 'I found one man at the bath'?"

"Yes, indeed," replied Aesop. "Do you see this stone? It was lying at the entrance and everyone who was bathing tripped on it, yet no one had the good sense to move it. Only one man out of all those who tripped moved the stone so that others who entered wouldn't suffer the same fate. I consider him alone out of all these people to be a man, and thus I told you the truth."

Xanthos said, "Aesop is never lacking for a sound defense whenever he does something wrong."

67 When Xanthos had bathed, he called Aesop to bring his belongings and went to dinner. After a few glasses of wine, rumblings in Xanthos' bowels indicated to him that it was time to answer the call of nature. He went out, and Aesop stood beside him holding a towel and pitcher of water. Xanthos asked him, "Can you tell me why it is that when we defecate, we often examine our own feces?"

Aesop replied, "Because long ago there was a king who had a son who, because of his indulgent and wanton way of life, sat relieving himself once for so long that he defecated out his own brains. From that day on, when people defecate they look back at it out of fear that they may also have passed their own brains. But don't worry about this. You will never defecate out your brains, because you haven't got any."

68 Xanthos went back in to the dinner and took his place at the table. When the drinking had proceeded apace, and Xanthos was becoming drunk, they began to pose questions and problems, as philosophers are wont to do. When an argument erupted over one issue, Xanthos began to engage in the debate, as though he were in a lecture hall and not at a drinking party. Aesop saw that Xanthos was about to get into a real scrape, and said, "When Dionysus discovered wine, he mixed three cups to demonstrate to humans how wine is to be used: the first cup is for pleasure, the second for a warm and pleasant feeling, and the third for rashness. So, master, drink the first cup, which was given for pleasure, when you return from the steam room at the baths or from any labor, and the second cup, of warm and pleasant feeling . . . [lacuna in text] when you find yourself insatiable, the third cup for rashness. Therefore, master, since you have drunk the cup of pleasure and the cup of warm feeling, pass the cup of rashness on to the younger men. You can demonstrate your talents in the lecture halls."

"Will you never shut up, you goatherd?" said Xanthos, who was now quite drunk. "You are the scourge from hell."

"Just wait," said Aesop, "And you'll end up in hell."

69 One of the students, seeing that Xanthos was going to continue in his arguments, said, "Professor, are all things possible for a human being?"

Xanthos replied, "Who brought the conversation around to human beings? A person can do anything."

The student then pushed the argument to an impossible conclusion by asking, "Can any person drink the sea dry?"

"That's easy," said Xanthos. "I'll drink it dry."

The student said, "But if you can't, what then?"

Xanthos, totally undone by all the strong wine he had drunk, said, "I'll wager all my fortune on it. If I cannot drink it dry, I shall lose everything." They both threw in their rings to guarantee the wager.

Aesop, standing at Xanthos' feet, slapped his hand and said, "What are you doing, master? Are you out of your mind? How are you going to drink the sea dry?"

"Shut up, you human refuse!" said Xanthos, but he did not realize what he had wagered.

70 Early the next morning, Xanthos got up, and wanting to wash his face, called Aesop.

Aesop replied, "What is it, master?"

"Pour some water on my hands," said Xanthos. Aesop took the pitcher and poured. When Xanthos had washed his face, he noticed that his ring was missing and said, "Aesop, what has become of my ring?"

"I don't know."

"Bah!"

"You'd better take whatever you can of your fortune and hide it for a rainy day, because it isn't yours any more."

"What are you saying?"

"During the drinking party last night, you bet that you could drink the sea dry, and you threw in your ring as a guarantee against your entire fortune."

"And how am I going to drink the sea dry?"

"I stood at your feet and said, 'Wait, master, what are you doing? It is impossible,' but you wouldn't listen to me."

Xanthos fell at Aesop's feet and said, "I beg you, Aesop, if you can, use your cleverness to find some way for me to win the bet or get out of it."

"Although you can't win it," said Aesop, "I shall arrange it so that you can get out of this mess you're in."

"How? Tell me your idea."

71 "When the stakeholder comes with the challenger and tells you to drink the sea dry, don't put them off, but now that you're sober, restate the bet you made when you were drunk. Then call for a table, command that it be placed on the shore, and have servants standing by. This is certain to make an impression, and a large crowd will gather to see the spectacle, thinking that you are about to drink the sea dry. When you see that everything is ready, fill a cup with sea water, call for the stakeholder and say, 'What was the bet I made?' He will say, 'That you will drink the sea dry.' And you say, 'Is that all?' and he will say, 'That is all.' Then before everyone you say, 'Fellow citizens, there are many rivers and streams that pour a great effluence into the sea. I wagered that I could drink the sea alone, not the rivers and streams that flow into it. Let the challenger close the mouths of the rivers, so that I may drink up the sea alone. It is impossible, however, to stop up the mouths of all the rivers, and it is impossible to drink the sea dry.' One impossibility will thus be canceled out by another, dissolving your bet."

72 Xanthos was astonished at his intelligence and now looked forward to the contest. The man with whom Xanthos had made his bet arrived at Xanthos' doorstep with some of the leading citizens of the city. He called Xanthos and said, "Fulfill your end of the wager or hand over your entire fortune."

Aesop answered him, "Give us an accounting of *your* fortune, for we've already drunk up half the sea."

The student said, "Aesop, you're my slave now, not Xanthos'!"

"You'd better hand over your fortune to my master, and stop talking nonsense." After he said this, he ordered a couch brought out and placed upon the beach, then placed a table before it, with some cups on it. Everyone ran out to watch as Xanthos came and sat down. Aesop stood beside him and filled a cup with sea water and gave it to his master.

The student said, "Curse me! Is he really going to drink the sea dry?"

Said another, "I'm afraid so!"

73 But when Xanthos was about to put the cup to his lips he said, "Stakeholder, come forward." He stepped up. Xanthos said, "What was my wager?"

The student answered, "That you would drink the sea dry."

"Nothing else?" asked Xanthos.

"No," said the stakeholder.

Xanthos said to the crowd, "Fellow citizens, you know that there are many rivers, freshets, and other streams that flow into the sea. My bet was that I would drink up the sea only, not the rivers too. Therefore, let my challenger close up the mouths of the rivers, so that I do not have to drink up the rivers along with the sea." The philosopher had vanquished his opponent. A cry went up from the crowd acclaiming Xanthos as victor. The student fell at Xanthos' feet and said, "Professor, you are magnificent! I confess that you have vanquished me. I beg you to call off the bet." And they dissolved the bet.

74 Aesop said to Xanthos, "Master, I saved your fortune. I should now receive my freedom."

Xanthos replied, "Will you not be quiet? I certainly did not intend to grant it."

Aesop was very grieved, not for failing to gain his freedom, but at Xanthos' ingratitude. However, he did not press it, [but said to himself, "Just wait. I'll get even with you."

75 One day when Aesop was out by himself, he lifted his garments and began to rub himself with his hands to stimulate himself in a rude and lascivious manner. When Xanthos' wife came unexpectedly out of the house, she said, "Aesop, what is this?"

"Ma'am," he answered, "I'm performing a good deed for myself. This helps my stomach."

When she saw how long and thick his member was, she was stricken, and forgetting all about his deformities, was overcome with lust. She called him into her private quarters and said,

"If you do what I want and don't resist, you will have more pleasure than your master."

He responded to her, "You know that if my master finds out about this, he will be justified in punishing me severely."

But she laughed and said, "If you lie with me ten times, I'll give you a shirt."

"Give me your oath," he said. She was so aroused that she gave him her oath. Aesop took her word, and since he wanted to get back at his master, he lay with her nine times, but then said, "Ma'am, that's all I can do."

She, however, continued to press him, saying, "Unless you complete the full ten times, you won't get anything from me."

So he struggled once again, but his semen fell on his thigh, and he said, "Give me the shirt, or I'll take my case to the master."

The woman said, "I hired you to plow my field, but you crossed over the fence and plowed someone else's. Fulfill your end of the bargain, and you can have the shirt."

76 When Xanthos returned, Aesop went to him and said, "Judge between your wife and me."

He agreed and said, "What is the problem?"

"Master," said Aesop, "when your wife was walking with me she saw a plum tree with ripe fruit. One particular branch full of plums caught her eye, so she became hungry and said, 'If you can take a stone and knock down ten plums, I'll give you a shirt.' I took a stone and knocked down ten, but one happened to fall into a dung heap, and now she does not want to give me the shirt."

Xanthos' wife said in response, "I admit that he gave me the nine, but I can't count the one that fell into the dung heap. Let him throw yet once more and knock down a plum for me, and he will receive his shirt."

Aesop said, "I'm not sure whether the 'fruit' is still 'ripe.'"

Xanthos decided that Aesop should get the shirt, but said to him, "Aesop,] since I am completely indifferent on this issue, come with me before dinner and we shall wander together down to the marketplace, and when we return, you can knock down the last plum for your mistress, and then you'll get your shirt."

Xanthos' wife added, "As you insist, I'll give him the shirt, but don't get the idea that he will knock off any plums for you."

77 Xanthos said to Aesop, "Since you are but a newly bought slave, go out and see whether there is any ominous bird sitting at the gate. If you see two ravens sitting at the gate, call me, for this is a good sign for the one who sees it."[7]

So Aesop went out, and fortune had brought two ravens to the gate. He went back in and said to Xanthos, "Master, it's a good time to go out, for there are two ravens out there."

"Let's go, then," said Xanthos. But as they were going out, one flew away. When Xanthos saw it, he said, "Curse you! Did I not say, 'If you see two ravens, call me'? But you saw one raven and called me."

"But master," said Aesop, "one flew away."

"Now you have really fouled up. Strip him and bring the straps." Aesop was whipped soundly, but before it was over, a slave of one of Xanthos' friends arrived with an invitation for Xanthos to come to dinner.

"Master," said Aesop, "you have beaten me unjustly."

"Why unjustly?"

"Because you said that two ravens are a good omen. I saw two ravens, and while I came to tell you, one of them flew away. Now you, who went out and saw one raven, were invited to dinner, while I, who saw two ravens, received a beating. Doesn't that prove that signs and omens are useless?"

Xanthos was struck by this reasoning, and said, "Let him go. Stop beating him." Then Xanthos said that Aesop should accompany him to dinner.

[**77a** A few days later, Xanthos called Aesop in and said, "Make a good dinner for us. I have invited my students over."

Aesop prepared everything for dinner, and said to his mistress, who was lying there on the couch, "Keep a close watch on the table, so that the dog doesn't come in and eat any of the food."

But she replied, "Go ahead and don't worry about a thing. I even have eyes in my bottom." Aesop left to attend to his other duties, and when he returned, he found his mistress asleep on the couch, with her back to the table. Fearing that the dog would come in and get at the table, he remembered that his mistress had said, "I even have eyes in my bottom," so he raised up her robe and exposed her backside, and left her there. When Xanthos came in with his students, they went directly in to dinner. When they saw her, asleep on the couch with her bottom exposed, they turned their eyes away in shame.

Xanthos said to Aesop, "What is this, you wretch?"

"Master," said Aesop, "I was busy with the preparations for your dinner, so I told the mistress to keep a close watch on the table so that the dog would not come in and eat anything. She said to me, 'Go ahead and don't worry about a thing. I even have eyes in my bottom.' She fell asleep on the couch, master, just as you see her there, and so I uncovered her bottom so that her eyes could see the table."

"You runaway!" said Xanthos, "You have damaged my reputation many times, but you have never done anything worse than this! You have disgraced both me and your mistress, but for the sake of my guests, I won't get angry now. I will find an opportunity, however, to beat you half to death."

Some time later, Xanthos invited some rhetoricians and philosophers to dinner, and said to Aesop, "Stand at the door, and do not let any idiots enter here, but only wise men."

At the appointed hour, Aesop closed the door of the house and sat inside. When one of the guests arrived and knocked on the door, Aesop said, "What does a dog shake?" The man thought that he was calling him a dog, and walked off in a huff. And when Aesop addressed the other guests in the same way, they all left, thinking that they had been insulted. When one man arrived, however, and Aesop asked him, "What does a dog shake?" he answered, "Its tail." When Aesop heard him answer correctly, he opened the door and let him in. He went in to Xanthos and said, "Master, no other philosopher came to dine with you tonight except for this man." Xanthos was very upset to hear this, since he thought that he had been stood up. But the next day when the men came to his lecture, they said to Xanthos, "Professor, evidently you wanted to humiliate us, but were ashamed to do it yourself, so you posted that worthless Aesop at the door to insult us by calling us dogs."

"Did you dream this," asked Xanthos, "or did it really happen?"

"If we are not asleep," they answered, "it must have really happened."

"Somebody call Aesop," said Xanthos. When Aesop arrived, Xanthos said, "Tell me, you piece of garbage, when my friends and students arrived, why, instead of showing them in with all due respect to have a pleasant dinner with me, did you treat them with contempt and chase them away by insulting them?"

"Master," said Aesop, "did you not say, 'Do not allow any stupid men to enter my house, but only rhetoricians and philosophers'?"

"Yes," said Xanthos, "and what of it, you hobgoblin? Aren't these men wise?"

"No," said Aesop. "Indeed, they are very stupid, for when they knocked on the door, and from inside I asked them, 'What does a dog shake?' not one of them knew the answer. Since they were such idiots, I did not allow them to enter, all except for this one man who answered wisely." He pointed to the man who had dined with Xanthos. And so when Aesop had thus defended his actions, they said that he was right.

78 A few days later, Aesop accompanied Xanthos to the outer edges of the city, the two of them engaging in pleasant conversation as they went. When they came to the cemetery, they entertained themselves by reading the gravestones. Aesop found engraved on one stone the following letters: A B Δ O E Θ X. He pointed them out to Xanthos and asked, "What can these mean?"

Xanthos tried to discern the meaning of the letters, but could not. He was quite perplexed and troubled, because although he was a philosopher, he could not decipher their meaning. "Aesop," he asked, "what does it mean?"

Aesop could tell that Xanthos was straining to comprehend it, and since he had received a divine gift, and possessed the wisdom of the Muses, he said, "Master, if I find a treasure of gold by means of these letters, what will you give me?"

"Half of the treasure and your freedom."

79 When Aesop heard this, he immediately picked up a good-sized potsherd, counted off four paces from the gravestone, and began digging in the ground. He uncovered a treasure of gold, gave it to his master, and said, "Master, give me what you promised."

Xanthos replied, "By the gods, I will not give it to you, unless you tell me how you knew the treasure was buried there. Learning that is much more valuable to me than acquiring the treasure."

"Master," said Aesop, "the person who hid this treasure was a philosopher, and protected his treasure by concealing its location with the enigmatic letters. You can see how he inscribed the first letter of each word in the stone: A: stepping off (*apobas*), B: paces (*bemata*), Δ: four (Δ is the Greek letter for four), O: dig (*oruxon*), E: you will find (*[h]eureis*), Θ: treasure (*thesauron*), X: of gold (*chrysiou*)."

"Well," said Xanthos, "since you are intelligent and much more clever than I, you won't get what I promised."

When Aesop realized that he was being cheated of his reward, he said, "Master, I urge you to give the gold back immediately to its rightful owner."

"And who is the rightful owner of this treasure?"

"Dionysius, king of Byzantium."

"And how do you know that?"

"Listen again to what it says: A: give back to (*apodos*), B: King (*basilei*), Δ: Dionysius, O: what you have found (*[h]on heures*), E: here (*enthade*), Θ: treasure (*thesauron*), X: of gold (*chrysiou*)."

80 When Xanthos saw that Aesop had interpreted it well, he said, "Aesop, take half the treasure and keep quiet about it."

But Aesop added, "Don't give it to me as a gift from you, but as a gift for the two of us from the one who buried it here."

"Why?"

"Because the letters also say: A: take up (*anelesthe*), B: go away (*badisate*), Δ: divide (*dieles-the*), O: what you have found (*[h]on heurate*), E: here (*enthade*), Θ: treasure (*thesauron*), X: of gold (*chrysiou*)."

Xanthos said, "You are endowed with a great spirit. Let's go home and divide the gold, and you will receive your freedom." But when they reached home, Xanthos was afraid that Aesop would look for some opportunity to inform King Dionysius that they had the treasure, and commanded that Aesop be bound and locked up. Aesop said, "Give me my freedom, and keep the gold!"

But Xanthos said, "Not likely! As a free man, you would be in a more credible position with King Dionysius to demand back the gold. You'll never convince me to do that!"

"Take heed, master. If you do not free me of your own accord, you will be forced to do it!"

"You're contemptible, so shut up!"

81 At about that time there was an election in the city, and the populace gathered into the theater. The keeper of the laws brought in the city constitution and the official ring of the city, and placed them in the middle, saying, "Fellow citizens, now you must elect a new keeper of the laws who will uphold the constitution and use the official ring to transact all the business of the city." While they were deliberating over whom they would entrust with this position, an eagle swooped down, took the ring in its talons, and flew away. The Samians were seized with fear, viewing the evil omen as a disaster.

They immediately called forth the seers and priests to interpret the omen that had occurred, but when no one was able to interpret the sign, an old man of the city got up and said, "Fellow Samians, we are about to give heed to men who fill their bellies with the cult offerings, and though they appear respectable enough, they gamble away their own fortunes. Are you not aware that it is no easy feat to interpret an omen? If a person is not well versed in these matters, he cannot correctly analyze a portent. But among us we have Xanthos the philosopher, known to all of Greece. Let us ask him to interpret the sign."

When the old man sat down, they all called out and appealed to Xanthos to interpret the sign. **82** Xanthos stepped forward, but could not think of anything to say. He therefore asked for a brief delay in order to give his interpretation. But as the crowd was about to disperse, the eagle swooped down again and dropped the ring into the lap of a slave who belonged to the city. They asked Xanthos to give an interpretation of this sign as well, and he agreed, but left with a troubled look on his face. **83** Retiring to his home, he said, "I am going to have to beg a favor of Aesop again in order to arrive at an interpretation of the omen." He called for Aesop, who entered in chains, and said, "Release him."

But Aesop said, "I don't want to be released."

"I am releasing you so that you may in turn release me from a problem."

"Then it is for your own interest that you are releasing me."

"Stop, Aesop. Get over your anger and solve this problem."

"What is it you want, master?" said Aesop, now released. Xanthos described the omens, and Aesop agreed to undertake the interpretation.

84 On the next day, however, Aesop decided to turn the screws on Xanthos, and said to him, "Master, if it were a question concerning words, I would readily solve it, but what you described is in the realm of the inexplicable, and I am no prophet."

Upon hearing this, Xanthos lost all hope, and since he would be shamed before the Samians, contemplated taking his own life. He said to himself, "Now it is time for me to interpret the omen, but I can't bear the shame of being a philosopher who is unable to do what he promised." After he said this, Xanthos waited for nightfall, then took a rope and went out of the house. **85** Aesop, lying in his room, saw his master leaving at an odd hour, and realized what he intended. He followed him, forgetting all about their squabble over the gold. Aesop saw Xanthos outside the gate, tying the rope to a tree branch.

Xanthos was about to put his neck into the noose, when Aesop cried out from afar, "Wait, master!"

Xanthos turned, and in the moonlight could see Aesop running toward him. "I've been found out by Aesop!" said Xanthos. "Why do you call to me to forsake the path of justice?"

"Master," said Aesop, "where is your philosophy? Where is your pride in your education? Where is your teaching about self-control? Have you become so slack-hearted and irresponsible that you rush toward death, ready to forsake all the pleasures of life by hanging yourself? Stop and think about it, master!"

"Leave me alone, Aesop! I prefer death with honor to a life spent in shame."

"Put down the rope, master, and I'll try to interpret the omen for you."

"How would you do that? What reasoning would allow you to interpret it?"

"Take me into the theater with you and make up some pretty speech about the dignity of philosophy. Then put me forward as someone you yourself have instructed. I shall come, and at the opportune time will be called up to speak." **86** With these words, Aesop persuaded Xanthos to change his mind.

The next day Xanthos came forward and said, "Your assembly is pushing the limits of what can be treated by rational philosophy, but this particular interpretation should nevertheless come from within my own household. I have attained a certain renown as a philosopher – though, to be sure, I no longer investigate the meanings of portents or bird-omens. Yet I can commend to you a slave whom I have carefully trained in these matters. He will interpret the sign." So saying, Xanthos brought out Aesop.

205

87 But when the Samians saw him, they began to laugh, and shouted, "Bring us some other interpreter of omens to explain this sign."

Aesop was unperturbed by all this, and when he had calmed them, began to speak: **88** "Fellow Samians, you should admit that when you stare at me, you are really seeing a reflection of yourselves."

But the Samians said, "Look how ugly he is! He must be a frog, or a hedgehog, a misshapen jar, the captain of the monkeys, a flask, a cook's pot, or a dog in a wicker-basket!"[8]

Aesop retorted, "You should consider my intelligence, not my appearance. It is absurd to condemn someone's mind based on appearances alone; many people with the worst appearance are intelligent. No one should find fault with a person's mind if he has not examined it. A doctor does not give up on a patient immediately after first laying eyes on him, but takes his pulse to know the patient's condition. Would you claim to know the quality of a wine without tasting it? The Muse is judged in the theater, and Aphrodite in bed; so also Intelligence is judged by her words. She is not within my power, as is often the case,[9] working together with me, but she does allow me to hear the words that will persuade you. Just as she knows when to speak, she also knows when to be silent, for knowing the right time is the beginning of wisdom."

When the Samians realized that Aesop's words did not correspond to his appearance, they said to each other, "He is clever, by the Muses, and quite capable of speaking well." They called out to him, "Go ahead, interpret!"

Upon hearing himself praised, Aesop presumed to speak openly, and said,[10] **89** "Fellow Samians, it is not a sensible arrangement to have a slave interpret an omen for a free people. Therefore, grant me the right to say what I am about to say openly and freely, so that if I succeed, I shall receive the appropriate honors as a free man, and if I fail, I shall be punished as a free man and not as a slave. If, indeed, you grant me the right to speak as a free man, I shall begin to interpret with full confidence."

90 The Samians said to Xanthos, "We entreat you, Xanthos, free Aesop."

The presiding officer added, "Make him a free man."

Xanthos replied, "I shall not free a slave who has only served me a short time."

When the officer saw that Xanthos would not relent, he said, "Accept the price you paid for him, give him to me, and I shall release him on behalf of the city."

But when Xanthos considered that he had only paid seventy-five denarii for him, in order not to appear stingy to the gathered crowds, he decided to free Aesop. He stood Aesop before them all and said, "I, Xanthos, in response to the request of the people of Samos, grant Aesop his freedom."

91 Now Aesop turned to them and said, "Fellow Samians, come to each other's aid and take counsel over your own freedom, for this omen concerns the siege of the city, and the portent is of enslavement. First, there will be war. Mark this well, because the eagle is the king of birds, stronger than all the others. It swooped down, seized the ring of leadership away from its place with the constitution, and dropped it into the lap of a slave of the city, consigning the guarantee of the citizens' freedom to the yoke of slavery. This is the interpretation of the portent. Surely there is some neighboring king who wants to deprive you of your freedom, strip you of your laws, and set his own seal upon you."

92 Just as Aesop was saying this, an emissary arrived from King Croesus, wearing a white-bordered robe, asking to speak to the officials of Samos. When he learned that an assembly was at that moment being held in the theater, he came there and handed over a letter to the officials. They opened it and read it aloud: "Croesus, king of the Lydians, to the officials, council members, and people of Samos: greetings. I command you from this day forth to pay tribute and taxes to my office. If you do not do so, I shall attack you with the full power of my kingdom."

93 The city officials took counsel with the people, and advised them to accede to the demands to avoid making such a king an enemy of the city. At the same time, they honored Aesop as a true prophet of the omen, and asked him to give them his opinion as to whether they should hand over tribute or refuse. Aesop said to them, "Fellow Samians, although your own civic leaders have advised you to pay tribute to the king, you should have asked me first before they rendered their opinion. If I say to you, 'Don't pay,' I make myself an enemy of King Croesus."

But the crowds shouted, "Give us your opinion!"

Aesop said, "I shall not give you my opinion, but tell you a fable instead. **94** Once Zeus commanded Fortune to show human beings two alternative ways, the way of freedom and the way of slavery. The way of freedom was at the beginning rugged, difficult to negotiate, steep, barren, full of brambles, beset with constant perils, but opening up finally into a level plain, with gardens, groves of fruit trees, and pools and streams, where the difficult journey ends in rest for those who have chosen this path. The way of slavery, however, begins in a level plain, flowery and pleasant to look at, delightful in every way, but ending in a narrow path, rugged, with sheer cliffs." **95** The Samians realized from Aesop's fable which path they should choose, and shouted out with one accord to the emissary that they would choose the rough road. He departed and went back to King Croesus, and informed him what Aesop had said.

When Croesus heard this, he called out his army and commanded them to prepare for battle. His advisers encouraged him, saying, "Master, let us go to this island, subdue it, and drag it to the Atlantic Ocean as an example to others who would oppose so great a king." But a close relative of the king was given permission to speak, and said, "I swear to you by the sacred crown upon your head that you are arming yourself against them in vain,[11] since indeed you will never be able to capture the Samians while the man called Aesop, who gives them advice, is still alive, for the emissary said that it was he who prevented them from paying the tribute. Send a letter to them and demand that they hand over Aesop. Say, 'Whatever you want for him, ask it, and I shall give it to you.'"

96 When Croesus heard this, he commanded the man who had given him this advice to go to Samos, since he had no adviser more devoted to him and wise. Without delay, the man sailed to Samos, called an assembly, and persuaded the citizens that it would be better to save themselves by handing over Aesop than to lose the friendship of the king. The people shouted out, "Take Aesop away! Let the king have him!"

But Aesop stepped up before the crowd and said, "Fellow Samians, I would agree to die at the foot of the king, but I want to tell you a story, so that you can engrave it on my tombstone when I am dead. **97** There was a time when animals spoke the same language as people, and the wolves and sheep were at war with each other. The wolves, who were winning, were harassing the sheep at every turn. When the dogs came and took the side of the sheep, however, they routed the wolves. While the wolves were being beaten back by the dogs, they sent an emissary to the sheep, who stood before them and spoke like a true politician: 'If you want to avoid fighting and being attacked, hand over the dogs to us, and you can sleep peacefully, with no fear of war.' The foolish sheep were convinced and handed over the dogs, and the wolves tore them to pieces. Soon after the wolves also conquered the sheep. So the lesson of this fable is that you should not so readily hand over people who contribute to your welfare."

98 The Samians realized that this fable had been told with them in mind, and decided to keep Aesop. Aesop, however, did not remain with them, but left with the emissary to Croesus. When the king saw Aesop, he was angry and said, "Just look at the man who prevented me from subjugating the city, and kept me from collecting my tribute! If he were a man it would not be so bad, but he is an enigma, a monstrous portent among men!"

"Your highness," said Aesop, "I was not brought here by force, but I came here of my own free will, and fall at your feet. You respond like a man who is suddenly wounded, crying out in rage. Wounds incurred in battle are healed by the special knowledge of doctors, but my words will cure your wrath. If I were to be killed here at your feet, I would bring shame to your rule, for you would continually have your court counselors giving you bad advice. Were they to see that those who give you good advice are executed, they would always speak against your best interests."

99 The king marveled at his words and smiled. He then asked Aesop, "Can you say more, and tell me fables about human destiny?"

Aesop answered, "There was a time when animals spoke the same language as people, and a poor man who had no food would catch locusts and pickle them to sell at a fair price. Once he held one of these in his hand, called 'sweet-humming cicada,'[12] and was about to kill it. It saw what was about to happen and said, 'Do not be so quick to kill me. I have not harmed the wheat or eaten the new shoots, nor have I destroyed the branches, but by moving my well-adapted wings and feet in harmony, I make a marvelous sound, and give rest to the traveler.' The man was moved by these words and released it to fly away. In the same way, I fall at your feet. Have mercy on me. I am not powerful enough to attack your army, or distinguished enough in my bearing to bring false charges against anyone and make them stick. My worthless body is my instrument, by which I utter wise sayings to benefit the lives of mortals."

100 The king was moved by these words, and said, "I grant you your life. Ask what you will, and I will give it to you."

Aesop said, "Make peace with the Samians."

"Done," the king replied. Aesop fell at his feet and thanked him. He then wrote down for the king all the sayings and fables that are even now still recounted, and deposited them in the library.

Aesop prepared to return to the Samians with a letter from the king stating that he agreed to keep peaceful relations for the sake of Aesop. With many gifts from the king in hand, Aesop sailed for Samos. Upon arriving, he called an assembly of the people and read the letter from the king. The Samians now recognized that Croesus had made peace with them for the sake of Aesop, and voted honors for him. They named the spot where he was turned over to King Croesus the Aesopeion. There Aesop erected a shrine for sacrifices to the Muses, and set up in the middle a statue of himself as a memorial, but not one of Apollo, the head of the Muses. As a result Apollo was angered, just as he had once been with Marsyas.[13]

101 After spending many years in Samos and receiving numerous honors, Aesop decided to tour the world. He procured a large income through his lecturing, and in his travels came ultimately to Babylon, ruled over by Lycurgos. Aesop exhibited his philosophy there, and as a result was proclaimed a great man. Because of his intelligence even the king became enamored of his teaching and made him chief counselor.

102 In those days the kings had a practice of receiving tribute by means of contests of valor, but rather than engage in wars and battles, they would send letters containing philosophical conundrums, and the one who could not discover the solution would send tribute to the one who sent it. Aesop solved many of the problems sent to Lycurgos, acquiring great honors for the king. He also sent many problems to other kings in the name of Lycurgos, forcing them to send tribute when they could not solve them. Thus the kingdom of the Babylonians expanded, so that it included not only the barbarian peoples, but most of the lands up to Greece.

103 While in Babylon, Aesop came to know a certain young man of noble family named Helios, and since Aesop himself was childless, he adopted this young man as his son. He presented him to the king as the heir of his own wisdom, and took every care in his education. Helios, however, soon began to think too highly of himself. He became involved with the king's concubine, and was reveling in the affair. When Aesop learned what was going on, he became angry and threatened him, saying that anyone who touched a woman of royal birth was forging his own death on the anvil. **104** The young man, however, could no longer bear Aesop's criticism, and was persuaded by his friends to accuse Aesop falsely before the king. He forged a letter from Aesop to the king's enemies, giving his pledge that he would help them, and sealed it with Aesop's ring. The young man showed it to Lycurgos and said, "Just look how your trusted adviser has now plotted against you!"

Convinced by the seal, the king in a rage commanded Hermippos, the captain of his guard, to execute Aesop as a traitor. The captain did not carry out the order, however, because he was a true friend of Aesop. Since no one inquired about Aesop, the captain was able to keep him hidden in the prison, and reported to the king, "I have killed Aesop." Helios then succeeded to Aesop's position as chief counselor.

105 Some time later, King Nectanebo of Egypt heard that Aesop had died. He therefore sent an emissary to Lycurgos with a letter containing a conundrum for him to solve, knowing that after Aesop's passing no one could be found among the Babylonians to solve it. The letter and conundrum was this: "Nectanebo, king of Egypt, to Lycurgos, king of the Babylonians: greetings. I wish to build a high tower that touches neither earth nor heaven. Send me people to build it who will also answer whatever question I put to them. If you can do this, you will receive ten years' tribute on behalf of all the lands under my control. But if you cannot, I shall receive ten years' tribute on behalf of all the lands under your rule."

106 When Lycurgos read the letter, he became very upset over this sudden calamity. He called for all his advisers, including Hermippos, and said to them, "Can you solve the problem of the tower, or shall I chop off your heads?"

The advisers said, "We do not know how a tower can be built that touches neither heaven nor earth."

And another adviser dared to add, "Your highness, we want to do everything you command, but we are powerless and inexperienced in these matters. We beg you to forgive us."

But the king, in a rage, commanded the guard to execute them all. Now lamenting the loss of Aesop, he held his head, beating his brow and pulling his hair. "Because of my rashness," he moaned, "I have destroyed the pillar of my kingdom!" And he neither ate nor drank.

107 When the captain of the king's guard learned of the king's difficulties, he sought an opportunity to inform the king of his disobedience concerning Aesop. He said to the king, "Your highness, I know that today is my last."

"Why is that?" asked Lycurgos.

The captain replied, "I did not carry out the king's order, and have brought disaster upon myself."

The king asked, "What do you have on your conscience?"

"Aesop is alive," answered the captain.

The king's countenance changed from despair to joy when he heard this, and said to the captain, "I wish I could make this last day you speak of an everlasting day, a beacon of hope for all people forever, if you are telling the truth and Aesop is alive. In preserving him alive you have safeguarded my welfare. And I'll not let you go unrewarded, but declare you to be my savior and benefactor." The king then ordered Aesop to be brought in. When he appeared, covered with filth, his hair long and shaggy, his skin pale from a long imprisonment, the king turned aside and wept. He then commanded that Aesop receive special care and new clothing, and be brought in to receive the king's embrace. **108** When Aesop had recovered, he came in to embrace the king, and to defend himself against the slander of his adopted son; he confirmed his testimony with an oath. The king wanted to execute Helios for betraying his father, but Aesop asked for clemency, saying that if the young man died, he would escape the shame that he deserved for the way he lived his life. On the other hand, if he lived, he would be a continual monument to his own guilt. The king agreed to this, and said to Aesop, "Read this letter from the king of the Egyptians."

Aesop reflected on the problem, then smiled and said, "Write back to him and say, 'I am sending you people who will build your tower and answer your questions, when winter is over.'" The king wrote the letter and sent it by emissaries to Egypt. Lycurgos also restored Aesop to his position over all the administration of his affairs of state, and placed Helios under his control. Aesop took his son aside and instructed and exhorted him by means of the following sayings: **109** "Heed my words, my son, Helios, with which you were once instructed, even though you paid me back with a kind of gratitude that is false. First of all, revere God. Honor your king, for his rule deserves equal honor. Honor the one who adopted you as your own parents; you are obligated to honor your parents by nature, but you should give double honors to the person who loves you by choice. Procure food for today, as much as you can. Pray that your enemies live long, but are both weak and poor, so that they are unable to harm you, and at the same time pray that your friends prosper, for they will help you, either by word or by deed. Avoid envy, and do not try to bring down those who live above you.[14] Do not try to show off your learning while drinking wine, or you may trip over your own tongue and become a laughing stock. Do not envy those who are successful, but rejoice with them. Take care of your slaves, sharing with them what you have. Control your passions. Do not be ashamed if you learn something late in life; it is better to be called a late-bloomer than a dolt. Do not entrust to your wife your secrets and private affairs. **110** Be friendly and cordial with those you meet, knowing that a dog's tail gets him food, his mouth, a licking. If you prosper, do not bear a grudge against your enemies; it is better to treat them well, so they may come around when they realize what kind of man they have wronged. Thus both what you have done and what you have said will become clear to others."

When Aesop had finished speaking these proverbs to the young man, he left. But Helios, wounded by these words, was consumed with grief for his past actions toward Aesop. As a result, he refused all food and quit this life by starving himself to death. Aesop gave his son a grand funeral, and observed a period of mourning.

111 After this, Aesop called for some bird-catchers and ordered them to capture four eagles. When the eagles were caught, he plucked out the last row of tail-feathers, with which it is thought that they fly. He commanded that they be nurtured and taught to carry boys. When they were mature, the eagles, carrying the boys on their backs, flew up into the air, reined with cords which the boys held. The eagles would then fly wherever the boys wished. When summer came, Aesop said good-bye to the king and sailed for Egypt, taking with him the boys and the eagles. They also brought along many servants and equipment to make a strong impression on the Egyptians.

112 Aesop's arrival in Memphis was announced to King Nectanebo. Nectanebo was displeased to hear this, and called for his advisers. "Men," he said, "because I had heard that Aesop had died, I find that I am now trapped. I have challenged Lycurgos by letter." He then commanded that Aesop be allowed to disembark. On the next day Aesop came and greeted the king. Nectanebo commanded that the generals and governors put on white robes, while he himself put on a robe of pure linen, a tiara, and a crown with horns on it. Thus seated upon his throne, he ordered Aesop to enter. **113** When Aesop saw all of the courtly pomp, he was overwhelmed. "What do I resemble?" asked Nectanebo. "How do you perceive all those around me?"

"You are like the moon," said Aesop, "and those about you like the stars. [For just as the moon is greater than the stars, in your horned crown you are also like the moon, and your officials like stars around it." When Nectanebo heard this, he was amazed, and gave Aesop gifts. **114** On the next day, Nectanebo dressed in splendid purple and carried many flowers. He stood with his officials and commanded that Aesop be brought in. When he entered he asked him, "What do I resemble, and those around me?"

Aesop answered, "You are like the sun in springtime, and those around you like the fruits of the earth, for as king you have the beautiful radiance of your purple robe, and draw to yourself all of the flowering fruits of the earth." The king was once again amazed at his intellect, and bestowed gifts upon him.]

115 On the next day, Nectanebo sat on his throne dressed in a white robe, while his advisers were dressed in scarlet robes. When Aesop entered, Nectanebo asked him, "What do I resemble?"

Aesop replied, "You are like the sun, and those about you like its rays. Just as the sun, bright and undefiled, dulls the other stars by the light of its rays for those who wish to behold them, in the same way you, wearing a white robe, present yourself pure to those who enter at the appropriate time to look upon you. You are bright as the sun, while these men are fiery red like its rays."

The king was impressed, and said, "As long as my court is thus arrayed around me, no good can come to Lycurgos."

Aesop smiled and said "You treat him too lightly, and do not show him proper respect when you mention his name, for Lycurgos is as much greater than you as Zeus is greater than the things of this world. Zeus, indeed, can keep the sun and moon from shining, and the stars from moving in their appointed times, if he becomes angry. He causes his own domain to tremble, and brings terrible thunder and lightning and dreadful earthquakes, but by resting the earth on a solid firmament, he prevents it from being plunged into the ocean when it moves. In the same way, Lycurgos, by the brilliance of his rule, makes your bright kingdom dark and the dark light.[15] Thus he brings your prominence to naught."

116 Nectanebo, now aware of Aesop's brilliance and cleverness with words, pressed him further and said, "Have you brought me men to build the tower?"

Aesop answered, "They are ready, as soon as you show me the place."

The king was again surprised, and went with Aesop to a place outside the city, and showed him the location for the tower. Aesop placed the eagles at the corners of the plot of land indicated to him, and ordered the boys to mount the eagles and fly into the air. Once in the air, they called down to those below, "Give us the clay, bricks, wood, and the other materials we shall need to build the tower."

Nectanebo asked, "Where am I to get winged men?"

"Lycurgos has winged men," said Aesop. "Do you, who are only a man, wish to contend with a king who is equal to the gods?"

"Aesop, I am beaten. Just answer one question."

"What is that?"

117 "I have imported brood mares from Greece, but when they hear the horses neighing in Babylon, they miscarry."

"Tomorrow I shall provide a solution to this problem." When Aesop got home, he ordered his servants to catch a cat alive. (Now the cat is a holy symbol of the goddess Bubastis.) They caught a large cat and began to beat it in public. When the Egyptians saw this, they ran to Aesop's house and cried out in protest. Aesop then ordered the cat to be released. Still the Egyptians went to the king and continued to cry out against Aesop.

The king called for Aesop, and when he arrived, he said, "What you have done is wrong. This animal is a holy symbol of the goddess Bubastis, a deity whom the Egyptians especially revere." 118 Aesop replied, "Yes, but Lycurgos was wronged by it tonight. He had a prize fighting rooster, which also crowed to tell him the time, and this cat killed it tonight."

Nectanebo said, "Aren't you ashamed to tell such a bald-faced lie? How could a cat get from Egypt to Babylon in one night?"

Aesop answered, "And how can your horses in Egypt hear horses in Babylon and miscarry?"

The king now realized how clever Aesop was, and began to be afraid that he would be bested and forced to pay tribute to King Lycurgos. 119 Nectanebo immediately sent for prophets from Heliopolis who were very knowledgeable about questions of science. After they had discussed Aesop with him, he ordered them to come to a dinner, together with Aesop. At the appointed hour, they arrived and reclined at dinner. One of the prophets said to Aesop, "We have been sent from god to present some propositions for you to interpret."

Aesop replied, "You condemn yourselves and your god, for if he is a god, he should be able to discern the thoughts of every person. But at any rate, proceed to ask whatever you like."

120 They said, "There is a certain temple with one column on the temple, and on top of the column are twelve cities, and each city has a roof composed of thirty beams, and around each of them run two women."

"In our country," said Aesop, "this sort of problem is solved by children, and those who have learning laugh at those who propose such problems. The temple is the universe, which encompasses all things. The column is the year, for it stands firm. The cities upon the column are the twelve months, for they are continuously governed. The thirty beams are the thirty days of the month, which cover all time. The two women who run about are night and day, one always proceeding after the other, directing the daily life of the people." After this, they all rose up from dinner.

121 On the next day, King Nectanebo met privately with his advisers, and said, "As I see it, on account of this unsightly and accursed fellow, I am going to have to send tribute to King Lycurgos."

But one of his advisers said, "Let us pose to him the following problem: What is there that we have neither seen nor heard of? Whatever answer he proposes, we shall say that we have seen it or heard of it. He will not be able to contradict us and will admit defeat."

The king was very pleased with this plan, supposing that by this device he would finally attain victory. When Aesop arrived, King Nectanebo said to him, "Solve just one more problem, and I will pay tribute to Lycurgos. Tell us something we have neither seen nor heard of."

Aesop answered, "Give me three days, and I will answer you." He departed from the king, and began to turn the problem over in his mind: "Whatever I say, they will say that they are familiar with it."

122 But Aesop, always very clever in such matters, sat down and wrote a record of a loan which read, "Loaned to Nectanebo by Lycurgos, a thousand talents of gold." He then included the date on which it was due. After three days, Aesop returned to King Nectanebo and found him with his advisers, awaiting Aesop's concession of defeat. Aesop, however, brought forth the false note and said, "Read this record of an agreement."

The advisers of King Nectanebo lied and said, "We have seen this and heard of it many times."

But Aesop said, "I am glad that you will testify to its authenticity. Let King Nectanebo pay it back immediately, for it is overdue."

When King Nectanebo heard this, he said, "How can you testify to the authenticity of a loan I never received?"

The advisers said, "We have never seen or heard of this."

"If that is your conclusion," said Aesop, "then the problem you posed to me has been solved."

123 Nectanebo said, "Lycurgos is truly blessed to have procured such wisdom for his kingdom." Handing over to Aesop ten years' worth of tribute,[16] Nectanebo sent him back to Lycurgos with a letter bearing greetings of peace. When Aesop arrived in Babylon, he recounted to Lycurgos everything that had happened in Egypt, and presented him with the money. Lycurgos then commanded that a golden statue be erected of Aesop with the Muses, and held a great festival in honor of Aesop's wisdom.

124 Aesop decided that it was time to go to Delphi, so he said good-bye to the king, but promised that he would return to him again and reside in Babylon for his remaining days. He traveled by way of many other cities, demonstrating his wisdom and learning, and finally came to Delphi and began to exhibit his wisdom there as well. Although the crowds enjoyed his presentations at first, they gave him nothing. When Aesop noted that the people there were the color of table greens,[17] he said to them, "Like the generation of leaves, so also that of people" [*Iliad* 6.146]. **125** Intent on offending them further, he also said, "O Delphians, you are like driftwood afloat on the sea. Seeing it from afar, bobbing about on the waves, we think it is something valuable, but as we approach it we find that it is an insignificant thing, worth nothing. Similarly, while I was living at a distance from your city, I was quite impressed with your wealth and magnanimity, but now that I see how inferior you are to other people, both in your leading families and in the constitution of your city, I realize that I erred in holding a positive opinion of you. Indeed, you act in a way not unworthy of your ancestors."

126 "And who are our ancestors?" asked the Delphians.

"Freed slaves," replied Aesop. "And if you are unaware of this, then listen carefully. There was a law among the Greeks in ancient times that when they captured a city, they would send a tenth part of the spoils to Apollo, so that out of a hundred oxen, they would send ten, and similarly with goats and with everything else – money, male slaves, female slaves. It was from these slaves that you are descended and you are thus like bondsmen and women, slaves of all Greeks."

When he had said this, he prepared to depart, **127** but the city officials, smarting at his abuse, reasoned among themselves: "If we allow him to depart, he will make a round of the other cities saying even worse things about us." They decided, therefore, to kill him through deceit.[18] Apollo was also angry, because Aesop had slighted him in Samos by not including him with the statues of the nine Muses.

Since the Delphians had no legitimate charge against Aesop, they devised a cunning plan, so that visitors to their city could not help him. They kept a close watch on Aesop's slave resting at the city gate, and when he fell asleep, they took a golden cup from the temple, and hid it in Aesop's baggage. The next day, Aesop set out for Phocis, unaware of what he was carrying. **128** Some of the Delphians caught up with him, bound him, and dragged him back to the city. He called out, "Why are you hauling me away in bonds?"

They answered him, "You have stolen vessels from the temple."

"Let me die if I am found guilty of any such charge!" said Aesop, whose conscience was clear. The Delphians searched through his bags and found the cup, then showed it to the city as they dragged Aesop about for all to see. Aesop realized that the cup must have been planted among his belongings as part of a plot, and pleaded with the Delphians to release him, but they would not listen. Aesop said, "Since you are but mortals, do not consider yourselves higher than gods!" But they locked him in jail to await punishment. Aesop found himself unable to devise any means of escape, and said, "If I am but a mortal man, how shall I be able to escape what is about to happen?" Aesop cried to himself and said,

> Do not despair, my heart, if you are too weak to flee.
> My eyes beheld beforehand what is in my soul,
> That the Delphians would act without just cause.

129 A friend of his came to the jail, and obtaining permission from the guards, entered into the place where Aesop was kept. When he saw Aesop crying, he said, "How did this happen, my miserable friend?"

Aesop told him a fable: "A woman who had buried her husband was sitting at his tomb, weeping and overcome with grief. A plowman saw her and began to desire her, so he left his oxen standing with the plow and came over to her, pretending to weep. She paused and asked, 'Why are you crying?' The plowman answered, 'I have just buried a good and wise wife, and when I cry, I find it makes my grief easier to bear.' The woman said, 'I have also lost a good husband, and when I do as you do, I also find it takes away some of the grief.' So he said to her, 'If we have suffered the same fate, why don't we get to know each other better? I shall love you as I did her, and you will love me as you did your husband.' He thus persuaded the woman, but while he was lying with her, someone untied his oxen and led them away. When the plowman got up and discovered that his oxen were gone, he began to wail in genuine grief. The woman asked, 'Why are you crying again?' And he replied, 'Woman, now I really do have something to mourn!' So you ask me why I am grieving when you see my great misfortune?"

130 The friend, saddened by Aesop's predicament, said, "Why did you get it into your mind to insult them in their own country and city, while you were under their authority? Where is your training? Where is your learning? You have advised cities and entire peoples, but when it comes to yourself, you are a fool!"

131 Aesop then told him another fable: "Once a woman had a foolish daughter. She prayed to all the gods for her daughter to get some sense, and her daughter often heard her when she prayed. One day they went out into the field, and the daughter wandered away from her mother outside the farmyard and saw a man having sex with a donkey. She asked the man, 'What are you doing?' He replied, 'I'm putting some sense in her.'[19] The simple-minded girl recalled her mother's prayer and said, 'Put some sense in me too.' But he refused to lie with her, saying, 'There is nothing more thankless than a woman.' But she said, 'There's nothing to worry about, sir. My mother will thank you, and pay you whatever you want. She has prayed for me to get some sense.' So he robbed her of her virginity. The girl, overjoyed, ran to her mother and said, 'Mother, I have sense.' Her mother said, 'The gods have heeded my prayers!' 'Yes, mother,'

said the girl.' 'How did you get sense, my child?' asked the mother. The foolish young girl explained to her: 'A man put it inside me with a big, red, muscular thing that went in and out.' When her mother heard her explanation she said, 'Oh, my child, you have lost even the little sense you already had.' It has now happened to me in the same manner; I have lost even the little sense I already had in coming to Delphi." Aesop's friend shed many tears for him, and then left.
132 Afterward, the Delphians came in and said to Aesop, "By a vote of the city, today you will be executed by being thrown off a cliff, as is fitting for a temple-robber, a huckster, and a blasphemer. You won't even be deemed worthy of a burial. Prepare to meet your end."

When Aesop saw that they were now ready to kill him, he said, "Just hear one fable." They allowed him to proceed. Aesop said, **133** "When animals all spoke the same language, a mouse became friends with a frog and invited him to dinner. He brought him into a very rich store-room, in which there were bread, meat, cheese, olives, and figs, and said, 'Eat!' The frog indulged himself gladly, and then said, 'Now you must also come to my house for dinner, and I shall receive you well.' He took the mouse to his pond and said, 'Dive in!' The mouse said, 'I don't know how to dive.' The frog said, 'I'll teach you,' and tying the mouse's foot to his own with a string, jumped into the pond, pulling the mouse with him. As the mouse was drowning, he said, 'Although I am dead, I will take my revenge on the living.' When he had said this, the frog dove down and finished off the mouse. But as the dead mouse lay floating on the water, a raven seized it and carried it away, with the frog still tied to it. The bird devoured the mouse, then turned and tore the frog apart as well. Thus the mouse got his revenge on the frog. So also, men of Delphi, although I die, I shall be the death of you as well. Indeed, Lydians, Babylonians, and practically all of Greece will reap the fruits of my death."
134 All his words failed to persuade the Delphians, but as they were leading him away to the cliff, he took refuge in the temple of the Muses. They had no mercy on him, however, but dragged him away against his will. He said to them, "Men of Delphi, do not scorn this temple! At the right time it will proclaim my innocence! Listen to this fable: **135** The rabbit, pursued by an eagle, took refuge with a dung-beetle and begged him to save him. The dung-beetle pleaded with the eagle not to disregard the rabbit's request, adjuring her in the name of Zeus not to scorn him because of his small size, but the eagle knocked over the beetle with her wing, grasped the rabbit in her claws, and tore him apart and ate him. **136** The beetle became angry and flew off after the eagle, observing the location of the nest where the eagle safeguarded her eggs. The beetle returned later and smashed the eggs. When the eagle arrived back at the nest, she moaned and wailed, and set out to find the one who did this in order to tear him apart. When it was nesting season again, the eagle laid an egg in an even higher nest, but the dung-beetle returned again, did as before, and departed. The eagle mourned the loss of her eggs, saying that this bitterness was ordained by Zeus in order to make eagles an even rarer species. **137** When the nesting season again returned, the eagle was so despondent that she did not even place the eggs in the nest, but instead flew up to Mount Olympus and dropped them in the lap of Zeus, saying, 'Twice now my eggs have been broken, so now I am depositing them with you to safeguard them for me.' The dung-beetle found this out, and covering himself with dung, flew up to Zeus and circled around his head. Zeus was so startled by this filthy bug that he jumped up, forgetting the eagle eggs in his lap, and broke them. **138** Zeus later learned that the dung-beetle had been wronged, so when the eagle returned, Zeus said to her, 'You deserved to lose your eggs, for you have wronged the dung-beetle.' The beetle added, 'Not only has she wronged me, but she has been very impious toward you as well. I had adjured her in your name, but she was unconcerned and killed the one who sought my protection. I will never stop until I have punished her to the fullest extent.' **139** Zeus did not want the species of eagles to die out entirely, and tried to persuade the dung-beetle to be reconciled, but the beetle would not listen. Therefore, Zeus altered the laying season of eagles to the time when the dung-beetles do not appear on the earth. In the same way, men of Delphi, you should not despise this temple where I have taken refuge, even though it is a small shrine, but remember the dung-beetle, and revere Zeus, god of strangers and Olympus."

140 The Delphians once again were unmoved, but led Aesop to the edge of the cliff. When Aesop saw that his end was near, he said, "Since I have addressed you in many different ways and not convinced you, hear just one more fable: A farmer who had grown old in the country, but had never seen the city, asked his children to let him go away to see the city before he died. So his children hitched up the wagon to the donkeys for him, and said, 'Just drive the donkeys, and they will take you to the city.' But when a storm came up and it became dark, the donkeys went astray and took him to a place surrounded by cliffs. When the man saw the danger, he said, 'O Zeus, how have I wronged you so that I am going to die? And I am not being killed by horses, but by these wretched donkeys!' Just so, I am upset that I shall die, not at the hands of reputable men, but at the hands of these wretched slaves!"

141 And just as Aesop was about to be thrown from the cliff, he told them yet another fable: ["A certain man fell in love with his own daughter, and was so consumed with passion that he sent his wife to the country and forced himself upon his daughter. She said to him, 'Father, this is an unholy thing you have done! I would rather have submitted to a hundred men than to you.' That is how I feel toward you,] men of Delphi – I would rather wander through Syria, Phoenicia, and Judea than be killed by you here, where one would least expect it."

142 Aesop cursed them, called upon Apollo, the head of the Muses, to bear witness that he was dying unjustly, and threw himself off the cliff. In this way he ended his life. But when the Delphians were afflicted with a plague, they consulted an oracle from Zeus, which stated that they should expiate the death of Aesop. And when the Greeks, Babylonians, and Samians heard of Aesop's execution, they avenged his death.

NOTES

1 THE GOSPEL GENRE

1 Kähler, *The So-Called Historical Jesus and the Historic, Biblical Christ*, Philadelphia: Fortress, 1964, p. 80.

2 London: A. & C. Black, 1910. In reaction to a century of publications on the life of Jesus – popular and influential books by Hermann Reimarus, Ernst Renan, David Strauss, and others – Schweitzer argued that these authors had imposed upon the life of Jesus a reflection of their own ideals. The historical Jesus thus had eluded these romantic authors (as he would also elude Schweitzer).

3 There are still those who maintain that Matthew is the oldest gospel, and has been reedited by Mark and Luke. The so-called "neo-Griesbach hypothesis," named after the eighteenth-century German scholar Johann Jakob Griesbach, has been promulgated in this century by William Farmer, *The Synoptic Problem*, New York: Macmillan, 1964.

4 Perrin, *The New Testament: An Introduction*, New York: Harcourt Brace Jovanovich, 1974, pp. 226–29 (but compare the different wording in *idem* and Dennis Duling, *The New Testament: Proclamation and Parenesis, Myth and History*, 3rd ed., Fort Worth: Harcourt Brace, 1994, p. 415); *idem*, *A Modern Pilgrimage in New Testament Christology*, Philadelphia: Fortress, 1974, pp. 122–28. The views of some of Perrin's students are found in Werner Kelber (ed.), *The Passion in Mark: Studies on Mark 14–16*, Philadelphia: Fortress, 1976. See also Werner Georg Kümmel, *Introduction to the New Testament*, 17th ed., London: SCM, 1975, pp. 202–4; and Burton Mack, *A Myth of Innocence: Mark and Christian Origins*, Philadelphia: Fortress, 1988, p. 324. Others would add that, in addition to Mark, John knew Matthew and/or Luke: C. K. Barrett, *The Gospel According to St John*, 2nd ed., Philadelphia: Westminster, 1978, pp. 15–21, 42–54; M.-E. Boismard and A. Lamouille, *L'Evangile de Jean (Synopse des quatre évangiles*, vol. 3), Paris: Cerf, 1977, pp. 15–59; Frans Neirynck, *et al.*, *Jean et les synoptiques: Examen critique de l'exégèse de M.-E. Boismard*, Leuven: Leuven University Press, 1992 (see other works by Neirynck in the bibliography); Adelbert Denaux (ed.), *John and the Synoptics*, Leuven: Leuven University Press, 1992; Mgr de Solages, *Jean et les synoptiques*, Leiden: Brill, 1979, pp. 67–99; and Ismo Dunderberg, *Johannes und die Synoptiker: Studien zu Joh 1–9*, Helsinki: Suomalainen tiedeakatemia, 1994. Still others argue that John does not know Mark directly, but is influenced by some or all of the synoptic gospels indirectly, by means of oral tradition: Peder Borgen, "John and the Synoptics in the Passion Narrative," *NTS* 5 (1958–59) 246–59; and Anton Dauer, *Die Passionsgeschichte im Johannesevangelium: Eine traditionsgeschichtliche und theologische Untersuchung zu Joh 18,1–19,30*, Munich: Kösel-Verlag, 1972. An excellent summary of the methodological underpinnings of these various suggestions is that of Dwight Moody Smith, "John and the Synoptics and the Question of Gospel Genre," in F. Van Segbroeck, *et al.* (eds), *The Four Gospels* (Festschrift Frans Neirynck), 2 vols, Leuven:

Leuven University Press, 1992, pp. 2.1783–97. Although I do not believe that John was influenced by any of the synoptic gospels, the focus of the present study will be the relation of John to Mark and the structure underlying them. The relation of John to Matthew and Luke must be bracketed here.

5 Edward F. Glusman, Jr., "Criteria for a Study of the Outlines of Mark and John," in Paul J. Achtemeier (ed.), *Society of Biblical Literature 1978 Seminar Papers*, 2 vols, Missoula, Mont.: Scholars, 1978, pp. 2.241–42; on Mark, see Willi Marxsen, *Mark the Evangelist: Studies on the Redaction History of the Gospel*, Nashville: Abingdon, 1969, p. 42.

6 To be sure, John may reflect an older sense of the disciples' misunderstanding, a misunderstanding that will be rectified after the resurrection – cf. John 2: 22; 12: 16; 13: 7, 28; 20: 9 – but not the peculiarly Markan injunction to keep secret the miracles that Jesus has done. See Wilhelm Wrede, *The Messianic Secret*, Cambridge: Clarke, 1971, pp. 184–86; James M. Robinson, *The Problem of History in Mark and Other Studies*, Philadelphia: Fortress, 1980, pp. 20–21.

7 It should also be noted that the obtuseness of the disciples *per se* is not necessarily Markan; it is often a part of the ancient questions-and-answers genre used for esoteric instruction; cf. David E. Aune, *The New Testament in its Literary Environment*, Philadelphia: Westminster, 1987, pp. 55–56, 72–73, 236–37. The theme of the obtuseness of the disciple is quite common, in sources as varied as the *Phaedo* of Plato or the *Corpus Hermeticum*. Jonathan Z. Smith states it even more strongly ("No News is Good News: Aretalogy and Gospel," in Jacob Neusner [ed.], *Christianity, Judaism, and Other Greco-Roman Cults: Studies for Morton Smith at Sixty*, 4 vols, Leiden: Brill, 1975, pp. 1.21–38): "(T)he juxtaposition of the enigma of the son of god with misunderstandings is precisely characteristic of all hellenistic 'gospels'" (p. 35), and "*A 'gospel' is a narrative of a son of god who appears among men as a riddle inviting misunderstanding*" (p. 36, italics his).

8 Smith, review of Dunderberg, *Johannes und die Synoptiker*, *JBL* 115 (1996) 153. Smith's statement is interesting, however, in that he allows, wrongly, I think, some validity to Dunderberg's arguments for Johannine dependence on Mark; see chapter 3.

9 Robinson, *The Priority of John* (London: SCM, 1985); argued also by Raymond Brown, *The Gospel According to John*, 2 vols, Garden City, N. Y.: Doubleday, 1964–70, pp. 1.xli–li.

10 Gardner-Smith, *St. John and the Synoptic Gospels*, Cambridge: Cambridge University Press, 1938. In agreement are Erwin R. Goodenough, "John a Primitive Gospel," *JBL* 64 (1945) 145–82; Rudolf Bultmann, *The Gospel of John*, Philadelphia: Westminster Oxford: Basil Blackwell & Mott, 1971, pp. 6–7; C. H. Dodd, *The Interpretation of the Fourth Gospel*, Cambridge: Cambridge University Press, 1953, pp. 447–51; *idem, Historical Tradition in the Fourth Gospel*, Cambridge: Cambridge University Press, 1963; Brown, *John*, p. 1.xlvii; Rudolf Schnackenburg, *The Gospel According to St John*, 4 vols, London: Burns and Oates, 1982, pp. 1.30–43; Robert T. Fortna, "Jesus and Peter at the High Priest's House: A Test Case for the Question of the Relation Between Mark's and John's Gospels," *NTS* 24 (1977–78) 371–83; Joel B. Green, *The Death of Jesus: Tradition and Interpretation in the Passion Narrative*, Tübingen: Mohr (Paul Siebeck), 1988; and Wolfgang Reinbold, *Der älteste Bericht über den Tod Jesu: Literarische Analyse und historische Kritik der Passionsdarstellungen der Evangelien*, Berlin/New York: de Gruyter, 1994.

11 Bultmann, *John, passim* (note that the introduction [pp. 6–7] to Bultmann's English edition, by Walter Schmithals, is misleadingly ambiguous on Bultmann's views); Koester, *Ancient Christian Gospels: Their History and Development*, (Philadelphia: Trinity Press International, 1990) pp. 250–67; *idem*, "One Jesus and Four Primitive Gospels," in Koester and James M. Robinson, *Trajectories Through Early Christianity*, Philadelphia: Fortress, 1971, pp. 188–89; Robinson, "Johannine Trajectory," in Koester and Robinson, *Trajectories Through Early Christianity*, pp. 266–68; and Aune, "The Gospels as Hellenistic Biography," *Mosaic* 20 (1987) 3–4.

12 Despite the many salutary contributions of Werner H. Kelber, *The Oral and the Written*

Gospel: The Hermeneutics of Speaking and Writing in the Synoptic Tradition, Mark, Paul, and Q, Philadelphia: Fortress, 1983, he worked at that time with a fairly rigid distinction between oral as unfixed and written as fixed; the rigidity of that distinction has since been superseded in the field of folklore studies by a more nuanced approach to discourse in culture. See also L. W. Hurtado, "The Gospel of Mark: Evolutionary or Revolutionary Document?," *JSNT* 40 (1990) 15–32; and Lawrence M. Wills, *The Jewish Novel in the Ancient World*, (Ithaca/London: Cornell University Press, 1995), pp. 32–39.

13 The oral tradition would have continued to coexist with the written unbroken throughout early Christian history; see, for example, Helmut Koester, *Synoptische Überlieferung bei den apostolischen Vätern*, Berlin: Akademie-Verlag, 1957; Joanna Dewey, "The Gospel of Mark as an Oral-Aural Event," in Elizabeth Strothers Malbon and Edgar V. McKnight (eds), *New Literary Criticism and the New Testament*, Sheffield: Sheffield Academic Press, 1994, pp. 145–63; Dennis Ronald MacDonald, *The Legend and the Apostle: The Battle for Paul in Story and Canon*, Philadelphia: Westminster, 1983. It is also important to note that Mark and John are barely "scribal"; compare how they edit their sources to Matthew and Luke. Aune (*New Testament*, pp. 65–66) refers to this process of conforming more closely to elite literary conventions as "literaturization."

On the theoretical issues associated with popular, unfixed written narratives and the comparison with oral transmission, see Wills, *Jewish Novel*, 1–39, and Christine M. Thomas, "Word and Deed: The *Acts of Peter* and Orality," *Apocrypha* 3 (1992) 125–64. The same methods can be brought to bear on Jewish targumic, midrashic, and mystical texts, but here we have fewer controls on whether the changes occurred during the written or oral transmission.

14 Apparent exceptions can arise when translations have occurred after a period of unfixed textual transmission, as is likely the case with the Old Greek and Theodotionic versions of Daniel 4–6, Susanna, and Bel and the Serpent. See Lawrence M. Wills, *The Jew in the Court of the Foreign King: Ancient Jewish Court Legends*, Minneapolis: Fortress, 1990, pp. 75–152; *idem, Jewish Novel*, pp. 235–43.

Note that this lack of agreement in wording is a problem for almost all theories of the relationship between Mark and John. Those who hold, for example, that John read Mark, or even knew Mark, must explain why John so consistently changed almost every word of the source. Matthew and Luke do not change Mark or Q in such a thoroughgoing manner. Although it is possible that John only knew Mark from memory, and did not work directly from a written text, it would still be difficult to explain John's total silence on so many of Mark's redactional themes.

15 Dundes, *The Hero Pattern and the Life of Jesus*, Berkeley: Center for Hermeneutical Studies, 1977, p. 83. See also Albert B. Lord, "The Gospels as Oral Traditional Literature," in William O. Walker (ed.), *The Relationships Among the Gospels: An Interdisciplinary Dialogue*, San Antonio: Trinity University Press, 1978, pp. 39–40; and Gregory Nagy, "Homeric Questions," *Transactions of the American Philological Association* 122 (1992) 17–60.

16 Foley, "Introduction," in *idem* (ed.), *Oral Tradition in Literature: Interpretation in Context*, Columbia: University of Missouri Press, 1986, p. 17.

17 Leach, "Introduction," in M. I. Steblin-Kamenskij, *Myth*, Ann Arbor: Karoma, 1982, pp. 1–20.

18 Jameson, "Magical Narratives: Romance as Genre," *New Literary History* 7 (1975) 135–63. The work of Northrop Frye that is most relevant is *Anatomy of Criticism: Four Essays*, Princeton: Princeton University Press, 1957, and of Vladimir Propp, *The Morphology of the Folktale*, Austin: University of Texas Press, 1968. See also Wills, *Jewish Novel*, pp. 21–22, 232–35.

19 Altman, *The American Film Musical*, Bloomington: Indiana University Press, 1987, esp. 97–102. Altman's approach was also taken up by Ralph Cohen, "Genre Theory, Literary History, and Historical Change," in David Perkins (ed.), *Theoretical Issues in Literary History*, Cambridge, Mass.: Harvard University Press, 1992, pp. 85–113.

NOTES

20 Dundes (*Hero Pattern*) was strongly criticized for applying comparative folklore methods to the narratives of Jesus without taking care, among other things, to differentiate motifs that are found in texts centuries apart, but respondents to his bold hypotheses were often too ready to throw the baby out with the bath water. The hero paradigm *in some form* does apply to the earliest lives of Jesus.

21 Wills, *Jewish Novel*, pp. 142–54, especially pp. 153–54, and the literature cited there.

22 Burridge, *What Are the Gospels? A Comparison with Graeco-Roman Biography*, Cambridge: Cambridge University Press, 1992, esp. pp. 26–81 provides a full and excellent discussion of the issues of genre identification, including bibliography. In addition, see Mary Ann Tolbert, *Sowing the Gospel: Mark's World in Literary-Historical Perspective*, Minneapolis: Fortress, 1989, pp. 55–79; Wills, *Jewish Novel*, pp. 20–25, 232–35.

23 Contractual: Heather Dubrow, *Genre*, London/New York: Methuen, 1982, pp. 31–36; Jonathan Culler, *Structuralist Poetics: Structuralism, Linguistics, and the Study of Literature*, Ithaca: Cornell University Press, 1975, pp. 145–52; Burridge, *What Are the Gospels?*, pp. 34–38; covenantal: Ellen Spolsky (ed.), *Summoning: Ideas of the Covenant and Interpretive Theory*, Albany: State University of New York Press, 1993, especially pp. x–xi; I. Reid, "Genre and Framing," *Poetics* 17 (1988) 28, 34. The covenantal approach to genres insists that there is room in the "contract" for alternative interpretations. See also Steven Kepnes, *The Text as Thou: Martin Buber's Dialogical Hermeneutics and Narrative Theology*, Bloomington: Indiana University Press, 1992.

24 The visible "envelope" of a text is often genre-specific. It is significant that gospels and novels appear to be the first texts in antiquity to circulate in codex rather than scroll form. Likewise, fragments of novelistic literature in Semitic languages found at Qumran were written in distinctive, smaller columns; so J. T. Milik, "Les modèles araméens du livre d'Esther dans la grotte 4 de Qumran," *Revue de Qumran* 59 (1992) 363–65; he refers to them as "'éditions de poche' de l'antiquité."

25 Fowler, *Kinds of Literature: An Introduction to the Theory of Genres and Modes*, Oxford: Oxford University Press, 1982, pp. 40–44; see also Burridge, *What Are the Gospels?*, p. 39.

26 Culler, *Structuralist Poetics*, 154; see also Burridge, *What Are the Gospels?*, pp. 36–38; Dubrow, *Genre*, pp. 37–44; E. D. Hirsch, Jr, *Validity in Interpretation: An Introduction to the Theory of Genres and Modes*, Cambridge, Mass.: Harvard University Press, 1982, pp. 68–126; Wills, *Jewish Novel*, pp. 33–39, 245–56. Hans-Robert Jauss suggests that the distance between the expectations surrounding a work and the demands the author makes upon the readers by introducing challenging and unexpected elements is a means of judging the work's artistic merit ("Literary History as a Challenge to Literary Theory," *New Literary History* 2 (1970) 15). It would be wrong, however, especially at the popular level, to prioritize innovation to the exclusion of tradition. As Oswald Ducrot and Tzvetan Todorov state (*Encyclopedic Dictionary of the Sciences of Language*, Baltimore: Johns Hopkins University Press, 1979, p. 151), "The good detective story . . . does not attempt to be original (if it did, it would no longer deserve the name), but attempts, on the contrary, to apply the formula well."

27 Culler, *Structuralist Poetics*, p. 135; see also Ducrot and Todorov, *Encyclopedic Dictionary*, p. 149; Wills, *Jewish Novel*, p. 20; and Gregory Nagy, *Pindar's Homer: The Lyric Possession of an Epic Past*, Baltimore/London: Johns Hopkins University Press, 1990, pp. 362–63 n. 127.

28 Koester, *Ancient Christian Gospels*, pp. 1–43.

29 Fowler, "The Life and Death of Literary Forms," in Ralph Cohen (ed.), *New Directions in Literary History*, Baltimore: Johns Hopkins University Press, 1974, pp. 77–94; see also *idem*, *Kinds of Literature*, pp. 170–90; Wills, *Jewish Novel*, pp. 233–35.

30 Burridge makes a helpful distinction between genres, modes, and themes in *What Are the Gospels?*, pp. 53–54. Despite the fact that genre, theme, and mode mean different things, particular genres and themes often converge and are inextricably linked; see Dubrow, *Genre*, p. 41.

219

NOTES

31 Guelich, "The Gospel Genre," in Peter Stuhlmacher (ed.), *The Gospel and the Gospels*, Grand Rapids: Eerdmanns, 1991, pp. 173–208. Also excellent as an introduction to the following issues is Aune, *New Testament*, pp. 17–76.

32 Weiss, *Das älteste Evangelium*, Göttingen: Vandenhoeck & Ruprecht, 1903, pp. 6–8, calling to mind Xenophon's *Memorabilia* of Socrates. Cf. Vernon Robbins, "Mark as Genre," in *idem, New Boundaries in Old Territory: Form and Social Rhetoric in Mark*, New York: Peter Lang, 1994, pp. 91–118, esp. pp. 115–16.

33 Votaw, *The Gospels and Contemporary Biographies in the Greco-Roman World*, Philadelphia: Fortress, 1970, esp. pp. 7–11.

34 Perrin, *Modern Pilgrimage*, p. 107 (see also literature cited in Guelich, "Gospel Genre," 176–77); Kelber, *Oral and Written Gospel*, pp. 117–29 (compare also James G. Williams, *Gospel Against Parable: Mark's Language of Mystery*, Sheffield: Almond, 1985; John R. Donahue, *The Gospel in Parable: Metaphor, Narrative, and Theology in the Synoptic Gospels*, Philadelphia: Fortress, 1988; and Paul Ricoeur, "From Proclamation to Narrative," *JR* 64 [1984] 501–12); Carrington, *The Primitive Christian Calendar: A Study in the Making of the Marcan Gospel*, Cambridge: Cambridge University Press, 1952; Goulder, *Midrash and Lection in Matthew*, London: SPCK, 1974; Barr, "Toward a Definition of the Gospel Genre: A Generic Analysis and Comparison of the Synoptic Gospels and the Socratic Dialogues by means of Aristotle's Theory of Tragedy," unpublished Ph.D. dissertation, Florida State University, 1974; Bilezikian, *The Liberated Gospel: A Comparison of the Gospel of Mark and Greek Tragedy*, Grand Rapids: Baker Book House, 1977; Via, *Kerygma and Comedy in the New Testament: A Structuralist Approach to Hermeneutic*, Philadelphia: Fortress, 1975; Fischel, "Studies in Cynicism and the Ancient Near East: The Transformation of a Chria," in Jacob Neusner (ed.), *Religions in Antiquity: Essays in Memory of Erwin Ramsdell Goodenough*, Leiden: Brill, 1968, pp. 372–411.

35 Tolbert, *Sowing the Gospel*, pp. 55–79. Tolbert does mention the more indigenous novels (pp. 63–66), and in conversation has stated that her research is moving increasingly in the direction of the less accomplished novelistic works, including the *Life of Aesop*. See also Pervo, "The Ancient Novel Becomes Christian," in Gareth Schmeling (ed.), *The Novel in the Ancient World*, Leiden: Brill, 1996, p. 689.

36 On the rise of the novel in the Greco-Roman world, see Niklas Holzberg, *The Ancient Novel: An Introduction*, London/New York: Routledge, 1995, pp. 1–42; on the ancient Jewish novel: Wills, *Jewish Novel*; on the apocryphal Acts: Rosa Söder, *Die apokryphen Apostelgeschichten und die romanhafte Literatur der Antike*, Stuttgart: Kohlhammer, 1932; and Richard Pervo, *Profit With Delight: The Literary Genre of the Acts of the Apostles*, Philadelphia: Fortress, 1987.

37 Collins, *The Beginning of the Gospel: Probings of Mark in Context*, Minneapolis: Fortress, 1992, pp. 26–28.

38 Conzelmann, *Acts of the Apostles*, Philadelphia: Fortress, 1987, pp. xl–xli; Hengel, *Acts and the History of Earliest Christianity*, Philadelphia: Fortress, 1980, pp. 13–14, 36–37; Aune, *New Testament*, pp. 138–41.

39 Auerbach, *Mimesis: The Representation of Reality in Western Literature*, Princeton: Princeton University Press, 1953, pp. 40–49. Although Auerbach would distance the gospel from ancient novels, on the grounds that the gospels are more "novelistic," that is, more like modern novels, the similarity of interests and techniques of gospels and ancient novels can still be discerned.

40 Bowersock, *Fiction as History: Nero to Julian*, Berkeley: University of California Press, 1994, pp. 119–43.

41 Merkelbach, *Roman und Mysterium in der Antike*, Munich: Beck'sche, 1962; and Karl Kerényi, *Die griechisch–orientalische Romanliteratur in religionsgeschichtlicher Beleuchtung*, Tübingen: Mohr, 1927.

220

42 Holzberg, *Ancient Novel*, p. 30. See also Tomas Hägg, *The Novel in Antiquity*, Berkeley and Los Angeles: University of California Press, 1983, p. 90; and Pervo, *Profit With Delight*, p. 94.

43 Schmidt, "Die Stellung der Evangelien in der allgemeinen Literaturgeschichte," in H. Schmidt (ed.), *Eucharisterion* (Festschrift Hermann Gunkel), Göttingen: Vandenhoeck & Ruprecht, 1923, pp. 50–134.

44 Dodd, *The Apostolic Preaching and its Developments*, New York: Harper & Row, 1964; Bultmann, *The History of the Synoptic Tradition*, New York: Harper & Row, 1963; Dibelius, *From Tradition to Gospel*, New York: Charles Scribner's Sons, n.d., pp. 9–36. See also Julius Schniewind, "Zur Synoptiker-Exegese," *Theologische Rundschau* n.f. 2 (1930) 129–80, Raymond Brown, *New Testament Essays*, Garden City, N. Y.: Image, 1968, p. 240; Howard Clark Kee, *Jesus in History: An Approach to the Study of the Gospels*, New York: Harcourt, Brace and World, 1970, p. 123; Guelich, "Gospel Genre"; and Philipp Vielhauer, *Geschichte der frühchristlichen Literatur*, Berlin: De Gruyter, 1975, pp. 348–55. An even more radical conclusion is that Mark is the only "real" gospel: Matthew, Luke, and John have evolved in new directions; see Marxsen, *Mark the Evangelist*, p. 150, n. 106; Howard Clark Kee, *Community of the New Age: Studies in Mark's Gospel*, Philadelphia: Westminster, 1977, p. 30; Norman Perrin, "The Literary *Gattung* 'Gospel' – Some Observations," *Expository Times* 82 (1970–71) 7.

45 Burridge, *What Are the Gospels?*, p. 200.

46 Dodd, *Apostolic Preaching*, pp. 47–49.

47 Koester, "One Jesus," pp. 198–204.

48 Kolenkow, "Healing Controversy as a Tie Between Miracle and Passion Material for a Proto-Gospel," *JBL* 95 (1976) 623–38; and *eadem*, "Relationships Between Miracle and Prophecy in the Greco-Roman World and Early Christianity," *ANRW* II 23/2, pp. 1470–1506.

49 Dihle, "The Gospels and Greek Biography," in Peter Stuhlmacher (ed.), *The Gospel and the Gospels*, Grand Rapids: Eerdmanns, 1991, pp. 361–86; Burridge, *What Are the Gospels?*.

50 Talbert, *What Is a Gospel? The Genre of the Canonical Gospels*, Philadelphia: Fortress, 1977, esp. pp. 93–99, 134–35; and Shuler, *A Genre for the Gospels: The Biographical Character of Matthew*, Philadelphia: Fortress, 1982. Talbert also notes the popular biographies listed below, but does not emphasize them sufficiently. In addition, Talbert talks of the gospel as being related to cult, but uses as criteria the linking of the life of the teacher to the collection of the writings, and the existence of lists of successors, neither of which I find compelling concerning "cult."

51 Smith, "Prolegomena to a Discussion of Aretalogies, Divine Men, the Gospels, and Jesus," *JBL* 90 (1971) 174–99; *idem* and Hadas, *Heroes and Gods: Spiritual Biographies in Antiquity*, London: Routledge & Kegan Paul, 1965.

52 Howard Clark Kee, "Aretalogy and Gospel," *JBL* 92 (1973) 402–22; Tiede, *The Charismatic Figure as Miracle Worker*, Missoula, Mont.: Society of Biblical Literature, 1972. See also Carl R. Holladay, *Theios Aner in Hellenistic Judaism: A Critique of the Use of This Category in New Testament Christology*, Missoula, Monk.: Scholars, 1977.

53 See Gregory Nagy, *The Best of the Achaeans*, Baltimore: Johns Hopkins University Press, 1979, pp. 251, 286, 296–97, 304–7; Todd Compton, "The Trial of the Satirist: Poetic *Vitae* (Aesop, Archilochus, Homer) as Background for Plato's *Apology*," *American Journal of Philology* 111 (1990) 330–47; and Adela Yarbro Collins, "Finding Meaning in the Death of Jesus," forthcoming. Also compare Aune's inclusion of some of these works above. We may add here the intriguing traditions about the Jewish miracle workers Hanina ben Dosa and Honi the Circlemaker (see chapter 2).

54 Georgi, *The Records of Jesus in the Light of Ancient Accounts of Revered Men*, Berkeley: Center for Hermeneutical Studies, 1975, especially pp. 15–16. John Dillon, in response to Georgi (pp. 18–19), suggested that he distinguish the "Pythagorean type" of revered person,

the *theios aner* par excellence, and the Socrates/Diogenes type, the *eiron* or jester (or perhaps better, "dissembler").

55 Berger, "Hellenistische Gattungen im Neuen Testament," *ANRW* II 25/2, pp. 1231–45.

56 Aune, "Gospels as Hellenistic Biography," p. 9; also see *idem, New Testament*, p. 63; and "Greco-Roman Biography," in *idem* (ed.), *Greco-Roman Literature and the New Testament*, Atlanta: Scholars, 1988, pp. 107–26.

57 Baltzer, *Die Biographie der Propheten*, Neukirchen-Vluyn: Neukirchener Verlag, 1975; Lührmann, *Das Markusevangelium*, Tübingen: Mohr (Paul Siebeck), 1987, pp. 42–44; Dormeyer, *Evangelium als literarische und theologische Gattung*, Darmstadt: Wissenschaftliche Buchgesellschaft, 1989; *idem* and Hubert Frankemölle, "Evangelium als literarischer und als theologischer Begriff: Tendenzen und Aufgaben der Evangelien Forschung im 20. Jahrhundert, mit einen Untersuchung des Markusevangeliums in seinem Verhältnis zur griechischen Biographie," *ANRW* II 25/2, pp. 1541–1704; Koester, Ancient Christian Gospels, pp. 27–29. Note that Koester had earlier held to the uniqueness of the gospel and its derivation from the early Christian *kerygma* ("One Jesus," p. 162), but has evidently altered his position as a result of the more recent discussions of biography. See also Frankemölle, *Evangelium: Begriff und Gattung: Ein Forschungsbericht*, Stuttgart: Katholisches Bibelwerk, 1988; and Berger, "Hellenistische Gattungen."

58 Lührmann, "Biographie des Gerechten als Evangelium: Vorstellungen zu einem Markus-Kommentar," *Wort und Dienst* 14 (1977) 25–50 esp. p. 37.

59 Guelich, "Gospel Genre," p. 177.

60 Nickelsburg, "Introduction," in *idem* (ed.), *Studies on the Testament of Joseph* (Missoula, Mont.: Scholars, 1975, pp. 11–12. Robert Doran disagreed with Nickelsburg's mixing of the motifs of the persecuted righteous person who lives and the martyr who dies ("The Martyr: A Synoptic View of the Mother and Her Sons," in John J. Collins and George W. E. Nickelsburg [eds], *Ideal Figures in Ancient Judaism: Profiles and Paradigms*, Chico: Scholars, 1980, pp. 189–221), but Green defends Nickelsburg's developmental schema, which assumes a merging of the two (Death of Jesus, p. 167; see also John Dominic Crossan, *The Historical Jesus: The Life of a Mediterranean Jewish Peasant*, San Francisco: HarperCollins, 1991, pp. 383–88). However, although elsewhere Nickelsburg speaks of this as a "genre" ("The Genre and Function of the Markan Passion Narrative," *HTR* 73 (1980) 153–84), I prefer to see it as a thematic development. Nickelsburg's very important contribution was to highlight the relation between the development of the theme of the persecuted righteous and the origins of a new genre. Theme and genre always have a reciprocal relationship, as content and form, but are not the same thing.

61 Aune, "Gospels as Hellenistic Biography," p. 2.

62 Green, *Death of Jesus*, and Burridge, *What Are the Gospels?*; on the latter, see the review by Adela Yarbro Collins, "Genre and the Gospels," *JR* 75 (1995) 241–42.

63 Classic source analyses include Vincent Taylor, *The Gospel According to Mark*, London: Macmillan, 1952, pp. 653–64; Bultmann, *History*, pp. 262–84; Eta Linnemann, *Studien zur Passionsgeschichte*, Göttingen: Vandenhoeck & Ruprecht, 1970; Rudolph Pesch, *Das Markusevangelium*, 2 vols, 3rd ed., Freiburg/Basle/Vienna: Herder, 1980, pp. 2.1–27; Detlev Dormeyer, *Die Passion Jesu als Verhaltensmodell*, Münster: Aschendorff, 1974. A detailed summary of scholarly attempts to divide the passion into sources can be found in Marion L. Soards, "The Question of a Premarcan Passion Narrative," in Raymond Brown (ed.), *The Death of the Messiah*, New York: Doubleday, 1994, pp. 2.1492–1524, and a critical assessment of some recent analyses can be found in Mack, *Myth*, pp. 258–62.

64 Kelber (ed.), *Passion in Mark*; John R. Donahue, *Are You the Christ? The Trial Narrative in the Gospel of Mark*, Missoula: University of Montana Press, 1973; Mack, *Myth, passim*; Frank. J. Matera, *The Kingship of Jesus: Composition and Theology in Mark 15*, Chico, Calif.: Scholars, 1982.

65 Dodd, "The Framework of the Gospel Narrative," in *idem, New Testament Studies*,

Manchester: Manchester University Press, 1953, pp. 1–11; compare the critique by D. E. Nineham, "The Order of Events in St. Mark's Gospel – An Examination of Dr. Dodd's Hypothesis," in *idem* (ed.), *Studies in the Gospels*, Oxford: Basil Blackwell, 1957, pp. 223–39.

66 Koester, *Ancient Christian Gospels*, pp. 220–30, 288–89; Heinz-Wolfgang Kuhn, *Ältere Sammlungen im Markusevangelium* (Göttingen: Vandenhoeck & Ruprecht, 1971); Martin Albertz, *Die synoptischen Streitgespräche* (Berlin: Trowitzsch, 1921), pp. 5–16; Egon Brandenburger, *Markus 13 und die Apokalyptik* (Göttingen: Vandenhoeck & Ruprecht, 1984); Paul J. Achtemeier, "Toward the Isolation of Pre-Markan Miracle Catenae," *JBL* 89 (1970) 265–91; *idem*, "The Origin and Function of the Pre-Markan Miracle Catenae," *JBL* 91 (1972) 198–221.

67 Easton, "A Primitive Tradition in Mark," in S. J. Case (ed.), *Studies in Early Christianity*, New York: Century, 1928, pp. 83–101, followed by Koester, *Ancient Christian Gospels*, p. 287. This is of course possible, but requires a leap beyond what the evidence indicates.

68 Recently this has been argued by Mack, *Myth, passim*. To be sure, it is a matter of degree. Mack allows that some of the traditional materials existed before Mark's redaction, for instance, the catenae of miracles in Mark 5–8 (*Myth*, pp. 216–22).

69 Bultmann, *John*, pp. 6–7. Prior to Bultmann, a Signs Source had been advocated by A. Faure, "Die alttestamentlichen Zitate im 4. Evangelium und die Quellenscheidungshypothese," *ZNW* 21 (1922) 99–121, esp. pp. 107–12. The theory of a passion source is still very much alive, but I do not treat the passion as a source separate from the rest of the narrative source; see chapters 2 and 3. The possibility of a single, distinct Revelation Discourse source has not fared as well, but the process of development of this sort of discourse in general, and in a direction that could logically lead to the Johannine discourses, is demonstrated by Robinson, "Johannine Trajectory," in Koester and Robinson, *Trajectories*, pp. 232–68, and Koester, *Ancient Christian Gospels*, pp. 173–200.

70 Fortna, *The Gospel of Signs: A Reconstruction of the Narrative Source Underlying the Fourth Gospel*, Cambridge: Cambridge University Press, 1970; Nicol, *The Semeia in the Fourth Gospel: Tradition and Redaction* (Leiden: Brill, 1972); Smith, *Johannine Christianity*, Columbia: University of South Carolina Press, 1984; Teeple, *The Literary Origin of the Gospel of John* (Evanston: Religion and Ethics Institute, 1974); and von Wahlde, *The Earliest Version of John's Gospel: Recovering the Gospel of Signs*, Wilmington, Del.: Michael Glazier, 1989. See also Schnackenburg, *The Gospel According to St John*, p. 1.72.

71 Lindars, *Behind the Fourth Gospel*, London: SPCK, 1971, pp. 32–36. Although Teeple's reconstruction is actually closer to mine, he unconvincingly distinguishes too finely between layers, and takes possible stylistic distinctions among layers to be probable. Analysis of stylistic differences still holds out much promise, but the overall project has not been brought successfully to completion.

It is possible, of course, that a Signs Source was used by John, but that it consisted of some other grouping of signs, and did not contain a passion narrative; so Mack, *Myth*, pp. 220–30.

72 Brown, *idem*, *The Community of the Beloved Disciple: The Life, Loves, and Hates of an Individual Church in New Testament Times* (New York: Paulist, 1979); Noack, *Zur johanneischen Tradition: Beiträge zur Kritik an der literarkritischen Analyse des vierten Evangeliums* (Copenhagen: Rosekilde, 1954). Also to be considered as developmental theorists are Boismard and Lamouille, *L'Evangile de Jean*; Mgr de Solages, *Jean et les synoptiques*; Wilhelm Wilkens, *Die Entstehungsgeschichte des vierten Evangeliums* (Zollikon: Evangelischer Verlag, 1958); and Lindars, *Behind the Fourth Gospel*.

2 THE *LIFE OF AESOP* AND THE HERO CULT PARADIGM IN THE GOSPEL TRADITION

1 Early references are found in Eugeon of Samos, Herodotus 2.134–35, Aristophanes, *Wasps* 1446–48, and Plato, *Phaedo* 60b–c. Ben E. Perry, *Studies in the Text History of the Life and Fables of Aesop*, Haverford: American Philological Association, 1936, pp. 25–26, gives the date of the *Life* as first century B.C.E.–second century C.E., while Holzberg, *The Ancient Novel: An Introduction*, London/New York: Routledge, 1995, p. 15, suggests a second-third century C.E. date. The narrative tradition can be dated much earlier, however; Gregory Nagy, *The Best of the Achaeans*, Baltimore: Johns Hopkins University Press, 1979, p. 282, points out that the narrative context of the fables is already mentioned in Aristophanes, *Wasps* 1446–48.

2 Perry, *Studies*, pp. 15–19; *idem*, *Aesopica*, 2 vols, New York: Arno, 1980; A. Wiechers, *Aesop in Delphi*, Meisenheim: Glan, 1961; Francisco R. Adrados, "The 'Life of Aesop' and the Origins of Novel [sic] in Antiquity," *Quaderni urbinati di cultura classica* 30 (1979) 93–112; Cristiano Grotanelli, "Aesop in Babylon," in Hans-Jörg Nissen and Johannes Renger (eds), *Mesopotamia und seine Nachbarn*, 2 vols, Berlin: Reimer, 1982, pp. 2.555–72; Nagy, *Best of the Achaeans*, pp. 279–316; *idem*, *Pindar's Homer: The Lyric Possession of an Epic Past*, Baltimore/London: Johns Hopkins University Press, 1990, pp. 323–26; John J. Winkler, *Auctor & Actor: A Narratological Reading of Apuleius' Golden Ass*, Berkeley: University of California Press, 1985, pp. 279–91; and Niklas Holzberg (ed.), *Der Äsop-Roman: Motivgeschichte und Erzählstruktur*, Tübingen: Gunter Narr Verlag, 1992.

3 Holzberg, "Der Äsop-Roman," in *idem* (ed.), *Der Äsop-roman*, pp. 33–75, esp. 41–42, 71–75.

4 On the "Hellenistic grotesque" in art, see Barbara Hughes Fowler, *The Hellenistic Aesthetic*, Madison: University of Wisconsin Press, 1989, pp. 44–78. The grotesque quality in Aesop or Socrates or in statuary has power in Greco-Roman culture because it is profoundly "Other" to the idealized form of the human figure.

5 Hopkins, "Novel Evidence for Roman Slavery," *Past and Present* 138 (1993) 18–22 (quotation from p. 22).

6 Cambridge: MIT Press, 1968, p. 19.

7 Patterson, *Fables of Power: Aesopian Writing and Political History*, Durham/London: Duke University Press, 1991, pp. 13–15, 24–31.

8 Ibid., pp. 15–16. Patterson herself uses Francis Barlow's 1687 edition of the *Life*, and perhaps because of the differences in the text, states that the *Life* contains a scatological but not a sexual satire. The ancient text of the *Life*, however, as presently reconstructed, contains both.

9 Compare the discussion in Lawrence M. Wills, *The Jewish Novel in the Ancient World*, Ithaca/London: Cornell University Press, 1995, p. 97, on the release of tensions exercised by the reading of the book of Esther and the celebration of Purim.

10 Winkler, *Auctor*, pp. 276–91; Todd Compton, "The Trial of the Satirist: Poetic *Vitae* (Aesop, Archilochus, Homer) as Background for Plato's *Apology*," *American Journal of Philology* 111 (1990) 330–47.

11 MacQueen, *Myth, Rhetoric, and Fiction: A Reading of Longus's "Daphnis and Chloe,"* Lincoln: University of Nebraska Press, 1990, pp. 117–37; Stoneman, "The *Alexander Romance*: From History to Fiction," in *idem* and J. R. Morgan (eds), *Greek Fiction: The Greek Novel in Context*, London: Routledge, 1994, pp. 126–27; and Wills, *Jewish Novel*, pp. 245–56.

12 McKeon, *The Origins of the English Novel, 1600–1740*, Baltimore: Johns Hopkins University Press, 1987.

13 Hopkins, "Novel Evidence," p. 26.

14 Adrados, "Life of Aesop," p. 96. Although Aesop's social criticism is rightly compared to Cynicism, we should note that the fable genre is much older than the Cynic school, and was popular in the ancient Near East as well as in Greece. Wherever we encounter fables, they are satirical, biting, and marked by cruelty; see Albin Lesky, *A History of Greek Literature*,

New York: Crowell, 1966, pp. 154–56; and W. G. Lambert, *Babylonian Wisdom Literature*, Oxford: Clarendon, 1960, pp. 150–220.

15 Note the emendation of the text of chapter 100 by Manolis Papathomopoulos, *Ho vios tou Aisopou: he parallage G*, Ioannina: G. Tsolis, 1990, p. 139, which has been followed by Holzberg, "Der Äsop-Roman," in *idem* (ed.), *Der Äsop-Roman*, p. 65, n. 104, and Richard Pervo, "A Nihilist Fabula: Introducing the *Life of Aesop*," paper read at the American Academy of Religion/Society of Biblical Literature Annual Meeting, Philadelphia, Penn., November 19, 1995, p. 49, n. 143.

16 Nagy, *Best of the Achaeans*, pp. 284–86, 302f, 315f; see also Perry, *Aesopica*, p. 226.

17 Nagy, *Best of the Achaeans*, p. 307. The identification of Aesop with Apollo may appear understated in the *Life*, but it can be seen at the end where Aesop prays by the "leader of the Muses," that is, Apollo. Nagy also argues for this identification from other evidence, aside from the *Life* tradition (pp. 290–91). The parallel drawn in the text with Marsyas (ch. 100) is apt: punished by Apollo, he also became a recipient of cult honors in Phrygia.

18 Nagy, *Best of the Achaeans*, pp. 251, 296–97, 306–7; *idem*, *Pindar's Homer*, *passim*, and esp. pp. 363–64 on the cult of Archilochus and parallels to Aesop.

19 As I am reminded by Kimberley Patton of Harvard Divinity School, the god Hephaistos is equally a grotesque outsider among the gods, a divine parallel to the human figures. Although modern readers sometimes wonder why Jesus is not described as beautiful, on the basis of these parallels, it is more surprising that he is not described as ugly. The *ugly* scapegoat, however, has no place within Jewish tradition because it is specifically a negation of the Greek concept of beauty.

It is also interesting that Aesop's slave status is so central to the definition of the drama. Herakles also began as a slave, but like Aesop spoke to his master with boldness (*parresia*), and acted as if he were free, and even the master of his master! So Philo, *Every Man is Free* 100–104. See Aune, "Heracles and Christ: Heracles Imagery in the Christology of Early Christianity," in David L. Balch, Everett Ferguson, and Wayne A. Meeks (eds), *Greeks, Romans, and Christians: Essays in Honor of Abraham J. Malherbe*, Minneapolis: Fortress, 1990, p. 9. In a different vein, Athenaeus (6.265c–266e) tells the story of the slave Drimacus who escapes and foments a slave revolt. He comes, however, to make peace with his masters, but is then slain for a reward. A cult is established of Drimacus the "gentle hero" (*heros eumenes*), whose spirit gives aid to runaway slaves, but also informs the masters when slaves are about to rebel. The dead benefactor Drimacus restores order and "justice" to the slave system.

20 Nagy, *Best of the Achaeans*, p. 308. Various aspects of the Greek hero tradition, whether the loneliness and death of the heroic warrior or the scapegoating of an outcast, pass over into other periods , and it is important to note some of the ways that it is manifested in literature and popular culture. The theme can be seen equally clearly in *Beowulf* and modern films such as John Ford's classic western *The Searchers*. It can also be found inverted in Shakespeare's *Much Ado About Nothing*, where the young *woman* is named Hero; she is wronged, condemned, "killed," reborn, and receives cult, all over "nothing." One can also detect the first rumblings of a feminist critique of the hero cult in George Eliot's *Middlemarch*, where the ever beneficent heroine Dorothea is at the end memorialized as a counter-model to the typical hero with his tomb cult:

Her finely-touched spirit had still its fine issues, though they were not widely visible. Her full nature, like the river of which Cyrus broke the strength, spent itself in channels which had no great name on the earth. But the effect of her being on those around her was incalculably diffusive: for the growing good of the world is partly dependent on unhistoric acts; and that things are not so ill with you and me as they might have been, is half owing to the number who lived faithfully a hidden life, and rest in unvisited tombs.

(Harmondsworth: Penguin, 1965, p. 896)

21 Quoted in *Best of the Achaeans*, pp. 284–85, from Perry, *Aesopica*, 1.221.

22 Nagy, *Best of the Achaeans*, p. 307.

23 Ibid., p. 303; Adela Yarbro Collins, "Finding Meaning in the Death of Jesus," forthcoming.

24 For other parallels to the Socratic depiction, see Compton, "Trial of the Satirist"; Markus Schauer and Stefan Merkle, "Äsop und Sokrates," in Holzberg (ed.), *Der Äsop-Roman*, pp. 85–96; and Pervo, "Nihilist Fabula." For Cynic associations, see H. Zeitz, "Der Aesoproman und seine Geschichte," *Aegyptus* 16 (1936) 225–56; and Pervo, "Nihilist Fabula," p. 35, n. 92. Compare also Aulus Gellius, *Attic Nights* 2.18.9–10, an anecdote concerning Diogenes the Cynic that is very similar to the individual episodes of *Aesop*. Individual oral anecdotes may have served as building blocks for the composition of the *Life* in much the same way that they did for Mark and John.

25 Nagy, *Best of the Achaeans*, pp. 222–23; *idem*, *Pindar's Homer*, pp. 392–93, following on the work of Georges Dumézil and Marcel Detienne.

26 Holzberg, "A Lesser Known 'Picaresque' Novel of Greek Origin: The *Aesop Romance* and its Influence," in H. Hofmann (ed.), *Groningen Colloquia on the Novel*, 5 vols, Groningen: Egbert Forsten, 1988–93, pp. 5.9–11.

27 It has been judged to be an early church composition, and not an authentic parable of Jesus, by Rudolf Bultmann, *The History of the Synoptic Tradition*, New York: Harper & Row, 1963, pp. 177, 205, and by Charles Carlston, *The Parables of the Triple Tradition*, Philadelphia: Fortress, 1975, pp. 181–89. Mary Ann Tolbert, however, argues (*Perspectives on the Parables: An Approach to Multiple Interpretations*, Philadelphia: Fortress, 1979, pp. 83–89) that it is not as dissimilar from the other parables as at first appears, and the parallel in *Gospel of Thomas* 65 is much less allegorical, indicating that in an earlier form it *may* have been a parable of Jesus; so also Dan Otto Via, Jr., *The Parables: Their Literary and Existential Dimension*, Philadelphia: Fortress, 1967, pp. 132–34. I am still more persuaded by Bultmann and Carlston.

28 Pervo, "Nihilist Fabula," pp. 29, 39.

29 Ibid., pp. 51–52.

30 Examples are: 3: 20–21/22–30/31–35; 5: 21–24/25–34/35–43; 6: 7–13/14–29/30–32; 11: 12–14/15–19/20–26; 14: 1–2/3–9/10–11; 14: 12–16/17–21/22–25; and 14: 54/55 –65/66–72. As a Markan innovation, see John R. Donahue, *Are You the Christ? The Trial Narrative in the Gospel of Mark*, Missoula: University of Montana Press, 1973, p. 42. As an indicator of oral style: Joanna Dewey, "Oral Methods of Structuring Narrative in Mark," *Interpretation* 43 (1989) 32–44. As a typical technique of Greek novels: C. A. Evans, "Peter Warming Himself: The Problem of an Editorial 'Seam,'" *JBL* 101 (1982) 245–49.

31 On popular novelistic techniques during this period in general, see Tomas Hägg, *Narrative Technique in Ancient Greek Romances*, Stockholm: Swedish Institute in Athens, 1971; and Wills, *Jewish Novel*.

32 Nagy, *Best of the Achaeans*, pp. 285–86. The paradigm of the hero has been studied cross-culturally, but generally isolated from any consideration of cult. Classic studies by Otto Rank and Lord Raglan (reprinted in Robert A. Segal [ed], *In Quest of the Hero*, Princeton: Princeton University Press, 1990, along with the essay of Alan Dundes noted below) attempted to isolate the parallel motifs found in the legends of heroes in many different contexts around the ancient Mediterranean. The ambitious treatment of Moses Hadas and Morton Smith (*Heroes and Gods: Spiritual Biographies in Antiquity*, London: Routledge & Kegan Paul, 1965) drew broad parallels between the gospel genre and various aretalogical materials from the ancient world. The comparisons were very suggestive, and Smith proposed that "aretalogical biography" was the genre category that most closely described the range of materials. When Alan Dundes raised the same question, however, he did not address the question of origins of the gospel narrative. The entire first half of the hero's life, especially accounts of the miraculous birth, is of great importance for comparisons with the

later gospel tradition concerning Jesus, but not, it appears, for comparisons with the very early stages, where there is no attention paid to the birth of Jesus, only to his death.

33 Classic studies which draw this conclusion include Martin P. Nilsson, *A History of Greek Religion*, 2nd ed., Oxford: Clarendon, 1956, pp. 103–4; *idem, The Minoan-Mycenaean Religion and its Survival in Greek Religion*, Lund: Gleerup, 1927, pp. 514–17; Erwin Rohde, *Psyche: The Cult of Souls and Belief in Immortality Among the Greeks*, London: Kegan Paul, Trench, Trübner/New York: Harcourt, Brace, 1925, pp. 115–55, esp. p. 139, n. 7, and more recently Ian Morris, "Tomb Cult and the Greek Renaissance," *Antiquity* 62 (1988) 750–61. On popular conceptions of the hero and the hero cults in antiquity, see, in addition to Nagy's two works cited above, Nagy, *Greek Mythology and Poetics*, Ithaca/London: Cornell University Press, 1990; Lewis Richard Farnell, *Greek Hero Cults and Ideas of Immortality*, Oxford: Clarendon Press, 1921; Arthur Darby Nock, "The Cult of Heroes," *HTR* 37 (1944) 141–74; Walter Burkert, *Structure and History in Greek Myth and Ritual*, Berkeley: University of California Press, 1979, esp. pp. 59–77; *idem, Greek Religion*, Cambridge, Mass.: Harvard University Press, 1985, pp. 203–8; Friedrich Pfister, *Der Reliquenkult im Altertum*, 2 vols, Giessen: Töpelmann, 1909–12. In New Testament studies, see especially Wilfred L. Knox, "The 'Divine Hero' Christology in the New Testament," *HTR* 41 (1948) 229–49; Morton Smith, "Prolegomena to a Discussion of Aretalogies, Divine Men, the Gospels, and Jesus," *JBL* 90 (1971) 174–99; Charles H. Talbert, *What Is a Gospel? The Genre of the Canonical Gospels*, Philadelphia: Fortress, 1977, and the lengthy review of this by David Aune, "The Problem of the Genre of the Gospels: A Critique of C. H. Talbert's *What is a Gospel?*" in R. T. France and David Wenham (eds), *Gospel Perspectives II*, Sheffield: JSOT Press, 1981, pp. 9–60. It was argued as early as 1937 by Pfister ("Herakles und Christus," *Archiv für Religionswissenschaft* 34 [1937] 42–60) that the gospels were influenced by the typology of Herakles, but this study has often been judged to be a very simplistic comparison; see, for example, Herbert Jennings Rose, "Herakles and the Gospels," *HTR* 31 (1938) 113–42. Aune, however, has taken up this question again in regard to Herakles parallels in the Letter to the Hebrews ("Heracles and Christ").

34 Nilsson, *Minoan-Mycenaean Religion*, pp. 514–17; Burkert, *Greek Religion*, p. 304; and especially Nagy, *Pindar's Homer, passim*.

35 See W. K. C. Guthrie, *The Greeks and their Gods*, Boston, Mass.: Beacon, 1985, pp. 220–21; D. Roloff, *Gottähnlichkeit, Vergöttlichung und Erhöhung zu seligem Leben: Untersuchungen zur Herkunft der platonischen Angleichung an Gott*, Berlin: de Gruyter, 1970; L. Cerfaux and J. Tondriau, *Le culte des souverains dans la civilization gréco-romaine*, Tournai: Desclée, 1957, pp. 101–21. The discussion in Aune, "Problem of the Genre," is incisive and replete with references to modern scholarship. Talbert's operating distinction in *What Is a Gospel?* between eternals and immortals (i.e., those who are born mortal but become immortal) is sometimes pressed to the exclusion of other categories, and sometimes appears too neatly drawn. Aune reacts particularly sharply to this division (pp. 12–13, 34), and at times Talbert does overdraw it, for example, at p. 30: "Egyptian, Greek, Roman, and Jewish evidence points to the belief in the existence of a certain category of deity, the immortals, alongside the eternals." It is true, however, that though Talbert simplifies the distinctions (but note p. 45, n. 10), notions of heroization and the effective intervention on behalf of the living by those who have died have a general currency in popular religion in this period. Talbert's entire approach, though pointing in the right direction, should simply be rethought in light of the work of Nagy, Compton, and others.

36 On Dionysus, see Nagy, *Pindar's Homer*, pp. 295–97; on Philostratus, see Paul Veyne, *Did Greeks Believe in their Myths?*, Chicago: University of Chicago Press, 1988, pp. 41–42.

37 See Talbert, *What Is a Gospel?*, pp. 31–35. On Alexander see Diodorus Siculus 18.60.5; on Augustus, Dio Cassius, *Roman History* 45.1; on Apollonius of Tyana, Philostratus, *Apollonius of Tyana* 8.30–31; on Empedocles, Diogenes Laertius, *Lives* 8.68; on Cleomenes, Plutarch, "Cleomenes," *Parallel Lives* (and also Hadas and Smith, *Heroes and Gods*, p. 80).

The cult of recently dead kings can be traced to the classical period; compare Herodotus 6.58 and Xenophon, *Constitution of the Lacedaemonians* 15.9 on the honors for Spartan kings as heroes.

38 Talbert, *What Is a Gospel?* pp. 106–7, 113, n. 61; David G. Rice and John E. Stambaugh, *Sources for the Study of Greek Religion*, Missoula, Mont.: Scholars Press, 1979, pp. 65–68. It is surprising that there is so little evidence that Socrates received cult honors after his death, although a small statuette presumably representing him has been found in a room that may have been his jail cell; see Eugene Vanderpool, "The State Prison of Ancient Athens," in Keith DeVries (ed.), *From Athens to Gordion: The Papers of a Memorial Symposium for Rodney S. Young*, Philadelphia: University Museum of University of Pennsylvania, 1980, pp. 17–31 (with photograph of statuette), interpreted positively by John M. Camp, *The Athenian Agora: Excavations in the Heart of Classical Athens*, London: Thames & Hudson, 1986, p. 116. Arthur J. Droge looks to literary evidence to suggest that Socrates might have been venerated in cult ("That Unpredictable Little Beast," paper presented at the American Academy of Religion/Society of Biblical Literature Annual Meeting, Chicago, Ill., November 20, 1994). See also George Hanfmann, "Socrates and Christ," *HSCP* 60 (1951) 205–33; and Compton, "Trial of the Satirist." Note also that according to Diogenes Laertius 2.43, after the death of Socrates the Athenians repented of their verdict, punished his accusers, and erected a bronze statue in the Pompeion.

39 For example, Euripides, *Iphigenia in Aulis* 1378–84. According to Nicole Loraux, *Tragic Ways of Killing a Woman*, Cambridge, Mass.: Harvard University Press, 1987, p. 4, the suicide or slaying of a woman in Greek tragedy was expiatory. On heroine cults, see Jennifer Larson, *Greek Heroine Cults*, Madison: University of Wisconsin Press, 1995; and Gail Patterson Corrington, *Her Image of Salvation: Female Saviors and Formative Christianity*, Louisville: Westminster/John Knox Press, 1992, pp. 71–72. See also below re Jephthah's daughter and Judith.

40 Betz, *Der Apostel Paulus und die sokratische Tradition: Eine exegetische Untersuchung zu seiner "Apologie" 2 Korinther 10–13*, Tübingen: Mohr (Paul Siebeck), 1972, pp. 13–39.

41 Hadas and Smith, *Heroes and Gods*, p. 11.

42 Ibid., p. 52.

43 Burkert, *Structure and History*, pp. 64, 70; see also Jan Bremmer, "Scapegoat Rituals in Ancient Greece," *HSCP* 87 (1983) 299–320; and Dennis D. Hughes, *Human Sacrifice in Ancient Greece*, London/New York: Routledge, 1991.

44 Wendland, "Jesus als Saturnalien-König," *Hermes* 33 (1898) 175–79.

45 Frazer, *The Golden Bough*, Part VI, "The Scapegoat," 3rd ed., London: Macmillan, 1907, pp. 412–23.

46 Theodore J. Lewis, *Cults of the Dead in Ancient Israel and Ugarit*, Atlanta: Scholars Press, 1989; Susan Ackerman, *Under Every Green Tree: Popular Religion in Sixth-Century Judah*, Atanta: Scholars, 1992; Klaas Spronk, *Beatific Afterlife in Ancient Israel and the Ancient Near East*, Kevelaer: Butzon & Bercker/Neukirchen-Vluyn: Neukirchener, 1986; review of Spronk by Marvin Pope, *Ugarit-Forschungen* 19 (1987) 454–55; Elizabeth M. Bloch-Smith, "The Cult of the Dead in Judah: Interpretation of the Material Remains," *JBL* (1992) 213–24; *idem, Judahite Burial Practices and Beliefs about the Dead*, Sheffield: Sheffield Academic Press, 1992; Mark S. Smith and Elizabeth M. Bloch-Smith, "Death and Afterlife in Ugarit and Israel," *JAOS* 108 (1988) 277–84; Mark S. Smith, "The Invocation of Deceased Ancestors in Ps 49: 12c," *JBL* 112 (1993) 105–7; M. Bayliss, "The Cult of the Dead Kin in Assyria and Babylonia," *Iraq* 35 (1973) 115–25; and Saul Olyan, *Asherah and the Cult of Yahweh in Israel*, Atlanta: Scholars, 1988. cf. To b. 4: 17, Let. Jer. 27.

47 Ktziah Spanier, "Rachel's Theft of the Teraphim: Her Struggle for Family Primacy," *Vetus Testamentum* 42 (1992) 404–12.

48 Philip J. King, *Amos, Hosea, Micah – An Archaeological Commentary*, Philadelphia:

Westminster, 1988, pp. 137–61, esp. p. 138; Marvin H. Pope, "Notes on the Ugaritic Rephaim Texts," in Maria de Jong Ellis (ed.), *Essays on the Ancient Near East in Memory of Jacob Joel Finkelstein*, Hamden, Conn.: Archon, 1977, pp. 163–82; and Eric Meyers, *Jewish Ossuaries and Secondary Burials in their Ancient Near Eastern Setting*, Cambridge, Mass.: Harvard University Press, 1969.

49 William Hallo, presentation at Association for Jewish Studies Conference, November 18, 1993, and Wayne T. Pitard, presentation at Society of Biblical Literature Annual Conference, November 21, 1993. Veneration of the dead and necromancy do not necessarily entail worshiping ancestors as gods; so Y. Kaufmann, *Religion of Israel from its Beginnings to the Babylonian Exile*, Chicago: University of Chicago Press, 1960, pp. 311–13; and Roland de Vaux, *Ancient Israel*, 2 vols, New York: McGraw-Hill, 1965, p. 1.98.

50 On the association of Solomon and healing, see Dennis E. Duling, "Solomon, Exorcism, and the Son of David," *HTR* 68 (1975) 235–52; and *idem*, "The Eleazar Miracle and Solomon's Magical Wisdom in Flavius Josephus's *Antiquitates* 8: 42–49," *HTR* 78 (1985) 1–25. In addition, although the motif of god/hero antagonism is not common in the Hebrew Bible, Jacob wrestling with an angel and God's attempt to kill Moses in Exodus 4 may reflect it; see Ron S. Hendel, *The Epic of the Patriarch: The Jacob Cycle and the Narrative Traditions of Canaan and Israel*, Atlanta: Scholars, 1987, p. 108.

51 Blenkinsopp, *A History of Prophecy in Israel*, Philadelphia: Westminster, 1983, pp. 71–2. On the prophetic guilds, see John Gray, *1 & 2 Kings*, 2nd ed., London: SCM, 1970, pp. 371–72.

52 Lester L. Grabbe, "The Scapegoat Tradition: A Study in Early Jewish Interpretation," *JSJ* 18 (1987) 152–67.

53 See especially Girard, *Things Hidden since the Foundation of the World*, Stanford: Stanford University Press, 1987; *idem, The Scapegoat*, Baltimore: Johns Hopkins University Press, 1986; and *idem, Violence and the Sacred*, Baltimore: Johns Hopkins University Press, 1977. An excellent introduction to Girard's theories in regard to the gospel genre is Robert G. Hamerton-Kelly, *The Gospel and the Sacred: Poetics of Violence in Mark*, Minneapolis: Fortress, 1994, and a comparison of Girard's work with others can be found in Hamerton-Kelly (ed.), *Violent Origins: Walter Burkert, René Girard, and Jonathan Z. Smith on Ritual Killing and Social Formation*, Stanford: Stanford University Press, 1987.

Feminist critiques of the category of sacrifice have also appeared recently: Carol Delaney, "The Legend of Abraham," in Rita M. Gross (ed.), *Beyond Androcentrism: New Essays on Women and Religion*, Missoula, Mont.: Scholars, 1977, pp. 217–36; Nancy Jay, *Throughout Your Generations Forever: Sacrifice, Religion, and Paternity*, Berkeley: University of California Press, 1992; and Elisabeth Schüssler Fiorenza, *Jesus, Miriam's Child, Sophia's Prophet: Critical Issues in Feminist Christology*, New York: Continuum, 1994, pp. 97–128.

54 Although Girard's cross-cultural analysis of the scapegoating process contains many compelling observations, he unfortunately retains a passionately held Christian triumphalism that renders some of his conclusions suspect. In simple terms, he praises the Hebrew Bible for at some points taking the point of view of the victim, and thereby uncovering the process by which the violence of scapegoating is transformed into something sacred and constitutional for the foundation of society. However, the Hebrew Bible does not go far enough in his view; the sacrifices are often the will of God, or in the case of Isaac, even demanded by God, and the side of the victim is not always taken. The process of perceiving the sacrifice from the point of view of the victim, in Girard's view, is only completed in the Christian gospels. Here we find the perfect realization of truth-telling concerning the violent origins of scapegoating. Girard thus simplistically recapitulates a common Christian hierarchy of progressive "revelations": pagan is violent and "mythical," the Hebrew Bible is a higher but still incomplete moral vision, and the gospels provide a perfect revelation of a pure moral order. I would reject this notion on two scores. First, pagan hero cults often take the perspective of the victim as much as do the gospels. (I would mention Socrates or

Aesop; note also Burkert's point [*Structure and History*, p. 70] that Greek *narratives* tend to present the victim's point of view, *ritual* the community's.) Second, as Jon Levenson has shown (*The Death and Resurrection of the Beloved Son: The Transformation of Child Sacrifice in Judaism and Christianity*, New Haven: Yale University Press, 1993, esp. pp. 173–219), God's *demand* for a sacrifice is not removed by the gospels – far from it – but is merely transmuted into an intense focus on the victim on the one hand (influenced by the Jewish tradition of the persecuted righteous person), and an equally remarkable silence on the part of God on the other. I shall return to Levenson's analysis in chapter 4.

55 See Wills, *Jewish Novel*, pp. 132–57; and Amy-Jill Levine, "Sacrifice and Salvation: Otherness and Domestication in the Book of Judith," in James C. VanderKam (ed.), *"No One Spoke Ill of Her": Essays on Judith*, Atlanta: Scholars, 1992, pp. 17–27.

56 Joan E. Taylor, *Christians and the Holy Places: The Myth of Jewish-Christian Origins*, Oxford: Clarendon, 1993; Eric Werner, "Traces of Jewish Hagiolatry," *Hebrew Union College Annual* 51 (1980) 39–60; Margaret Schatkin, "Maccabean Martyrs," *Vigiliae Christianae* 28 (1974) 97–113; Marcel Simon, "Les saints d'Israel dans la dévotion de l'Eglise ancienne," in *idem, Recherche d'histoire judéo-chrétienne*, Paris: Mouton, 1962, pp. 154–80; John Wilkinson, "Jewish Holy Places and the Origins of Christian Pilgrimage," in Robert Ousterhout (ed.), *The Blessings of Pilgrimage*, Urbana and Chicago: University of Illinois Press, 1990, pp. 41–53; Joachim Jeremias, *Heiligengräber in Jesu Umwelt (Matt/Luke 23, 29; 11, 47): Ein Untersuchung zur Volksreligion der Zeit Jesu*, Göttingen: Vandenhoeck & Ruprecht, 1958; Julian Obermann, "The Sepulchre of the Maccabean Martyrs," *JBL* 50 (1931) 250–65; Robert Wilken, *The Land Called Holy*, New Haven: Yale University Press, 1992, pp. 101–22; and James W. Parkes, Raphael Posner, and Saul Paul Colbi, "Holy Places," *Encyclopaedia Judaica*, 16 vols, Jerusalem: Keter, 1972, pp. 8.920–940.

57 Jeremias, *Heiligengräber*; Satran, "Biblical Prophets and Christian Legend: The Lives of the Prophets Reconsidered," in Ithamar Gruenwald, Shaul Shaked, and Gedaliahu G. Stroumsa, *Messiah and Christos: Studies in the Jewish Origins of Christianity*, Tübingen: Mohr (Paul Siebeck), 1992, pp. 143–49. Others who have assumed a first-century date include Charles Torrey, *Lives of the Prophets: Greek Text and Translation*, Philadelphia: Society of Biblical Literature and Exegesis, 1946; and D. R. A. Hare in James H. Charlesworth (ed.), *Old Testament Pseudepigrapha*, Garden City, N. Y.: Doubleday, 1985, pp. 380–81. On its character as a guide to grave sites, see also H. A. Fischel, "Martyr and Prophet (A Study in Jewish Literature)," *JQR* 37 (1946–47) 375.

58 Second Chronicles 24: 14–27; 36: 14–16; Neh 9: 26; *Jubilees* 1: 12; see also Louis Ginzberg, *Legends of the Jews*, 7 vols, Philadelphia: Jewish Publication Society, 1946–61, p. 4.295.

59 In favor of the propitiatory theory is André Lacocque, *The Book of Daniel*, Atlanta: John Knox, 1979, p. 230, but John Collins suggests that the *maskilim* make the *rabbim* righteous by instructing them (*Daniel: A Commentary on the Book of Daniel*, Minneapolis: Fortress, 1993, p. 393). On the Prayer of the Three as a sacrifice, see Collins, *Daniel*, pp. 201, 203.

60 See Wills, *Jewish Novel*, pp. 195–201. The death of Onias III is also alluded to at Dan 9: 26. The function of the reappearance motif may be compared to the tradition of the reappearance of Alexander the Great at Diodorus Siculus 18.60.5.

61 See especially Sam K. Williams, *Jesus' Death as Saving Event: The Background and Origin of a Concept*, Missoula, Mont.: Scholars, 1975, along with the works of David Seeley and Martin Hengel cited below.

62 Baruch Bokser, "Wonder Working," *JSJ* 16 (1985) 79.

63 See also Martin Hengel, *The Atonement: The Origins of the Doctrine in the New Testament*, Philadelphia: Fortress, 1981, pp. 4–32. Hengel rightly emphasizes the Greek parallels of the expiatory death of the hero, but draws too sharp a distinction between this and the early Christian cult (pp. 31–32).

64 Sanders, *Jesus and Judaism*, Philadelphia: Fortress, 1985, *passim*, but esp. pp. 61–76. A number of criticisms have been voiced concerning various parts of Sanders's argument. The

two most trenchant are first, that of Craig Evans, who notes that the evidence of an expectation of an imminent destruction and restoration of the temple is weak ("Jesus' Action in the Temple: Cleansing or Portent of Destruction?" *CBQ* 51 [1989] 237–70), and second, that of Bruce Chilton, who argues that Jesus was concerned about aspects of purity in the temple administration (*The Temple of Jesus: His Social Program within a Cultural History of Sacrifice*, University Park, Penn.: Pennsylvania State University Press, 1992, pp. 98–100, 119). I am convinced by the general lines of Sanders's argument, but even if Chilton is correct that the presence of animals is the point on which Jesus' protest hinges, this hardly changes the course of my argument, as the similar Aesop fragment indicates. Although the action in the temple was likely the historical event that precipitated Jesus' execution, in the narratives of Mark and John it is also Jesus' denunciation of opponents in Mark 12 and John 8 that provides this provocation, as noted above in regard to Aesop's fables at the end of the *Life*.

65 Hengel, *Atonement*, pp. 14, 23.
66 C. H. Dodd, "The Prophecy of Caiaphas: John xi 47–53," *Neotestamentica et Patristica*, Festschrift Cullmann, NTSupp. VI, Leiden: Brill, 1962, pp. 134–42.
67 See esp. Krister Stendahl, *Paul among Jews and Gentiles*, Philadelphia: Fortress, 1976.
68 Hengel, *Atonement*, p. 472.
69 Nagy, "Introduction," *The Iliad*, translated by Robert Fitzgerald, Everyman Library, London: Random Century, 1992, p. vii. The term "cult" may also appear problematic in regard to early Christianity. I am referring here to *cultus*, that is, the practice of worship, and not a social organization that might be compared and contrasted with sect. But more to the point, was there a Christian *cultus per se?* Rudolf Bultmann defined the elements of cult practice very specifically, and then denied that it applied to early Christianity. He posits three necessary elements of a cult: (1) human action; (2) fixed, holy rites, conducted at holy times in holy places; and (3) performance by holy people, i.e., priests (*Theology of the New Testament*, 2 vols, New York: Scribner's, 1951–55, p. 1.121). He concludes that these conditions are not met in the earliest Christian groups, although most would not restrict the definition of "cult" to the extent that he has.
70 Bultmann, *History*, pp. 143–44; D. E. Nineham, *Saint Mark*, Harmondsworth: Penguin, 1963, pp. 280–82; and Howard Clark Kee, *Community of the New Age: Studies in Mark's Gospel*, Philadelphia: Westminster, 1977, pp. 47–48, all argue that the last half of this line may have been added to a saying about the Son of Humanity serving others, but I find this unlikely; compare chapter 3.
71 Even though the dating of the trial of Jesus is different in John and Mark, in the former case falling on the day before Passover (John 19: 31), and in the latter, during Passover (Mark 14: 12). Compare also John 18: 28; 19: 14; Exod 12: 46, and see Rudolf Schnackenburg, *The Gospel According to St John*, 4 vols, London: Burns and Oates, 1982, p. 4.292; Levenson, *Death and Resurrection*, pp. 200–19; Anthony J. Saldarini, *Jesus and Passover*, New York: Paulist, 1984, pp. 51–79; and Chilton, *Temple of Jesus*, p. 149. The association of Easter with Passover was kept alive in the early church by the Quartodecimans, but Origen wanted to separate Easter from associations with Passover, rendering it a once-for-all sacrifice, not a yearly reenactment. (In regard to the identification of Jesus with the Passover lamb, we also note an early painting that depicts a ram being sacrificed, identified as Patroklos. See Alan Griffiths, "A Ram Called Patroklos," *Bulletin of the Institute of Classical Studies* 32 [1985] 49–50.)

Several studies have also linked Passover or Exodus with narrative passages in Mark and John: Bertil Gärtner, *John 6 and the Jewish Passover*, Lund: Gleerup/Copenhagen: Munksgaard, 1959; Robert Houston Smith, "Exodus Typology in the Fourth Gospel," *JBL* 81 (1962) 329–42; Etienne Trocmé, *The Passion as Liturgy: A Study in the Origin of the Passion Narratives in the Four Gospels*, London: SCM, 1983, pp. 77–82; Philip Carrington, *The Primitive Christian Calendar: A Study in the Making of the Marcan Gospel*, Cambridge: Cambridge University Press, 1952; and Edward C. Hobbs, "Norman Perrin on

Methodology in the Interpretation of Mark," in Hans Dieter Betz (ed.), *Christology and a Modern Pilgrimage: A Discussion with Norman Perrin*, Missoula, Mont.: Scholars, 1974, pp. 53–60. I find these studies convincing, but cannot treat them here.

72 Compare also Gal 1: 4; 2: 20; 3: 13; 4: 4–5, and see Ernst Käsemann, "The Saving Significance of the Death of Jesus in Paul," in *idem, Perspectives on Paul*, Philadelphia: Fortress, 1971, pp. 32–59, esp. p. 45. At Rom 5: 6–11, one might say that the noble death motif has included within it, perhaps as an older tradition, elements of sacrifice. Other references to Jesus' death as sacrifice are found in the New Testament: Rev 5: 6; Titus 2: 14; 1 Pet 2: 24; and 1 John 1: 7; 2: 2; 4: 10; 5: 6.

The excellent recent study by David Seeley, *The Noble Death: Graeco-Roman Martyrology and Paul's Concept of Salvation*, Sheffield: Sheffield Academic Press, 1990, successfully isolates a martyrological pattern in the New Testament and 4 Maccabees associated with the Greco-Roman philosophical topos of the "noble death." The true philosopher is willing to die for a just cause, and the death is marked by five traits: (1) obedience, (2) overcoming physical vulnerability, (3) military metaphors, (4) vicariousness, and (5) sacrificial metaphors. The tradition I am analyzing is more associated with actual or metaphorical *cultus*, mainly on the popular level, than with a purely philosophical ethos. The first two motifs of the noble death paradigm, obedience and overcoming physical vulnerability, are not particularly associated with the hero. Conversely, sacrificial metaphors, which Seeley asserts are only occasionally found in descriptions of the noble death, are strongly emphasized in hero cults. In the New Testament texts examined here, the hero paradigm is more associated with the gospel tradition and pre-Pauline fragments, and the noble death more with Paul himself and Mark's own redaction. Thus the conclusions of Seeley, which are quite well founded, do not contradict my own. There is a danger, however, in misinterpreting Seeley's conclusions and overemphasizing the pervasiveness of the concept of the "noble death," to the exclusion of notions of sacrifice, which Burton Mack has evidently done (*A Myth of Innocence: Mark and Christian Origins*, Philadelphia: Fortress, 1988, p. 106). See also, in agreement with my position on this question, Adela Yarbro Collins, "From Noble Death to Crucified Messiah," *NTS* 40 (1994) 481–503, and compare Allen Callahan, "Death of a Revolutionary Jesus," unpublished manuscript, read at New England Regional Society of Biblical Literature Conference, March 23, 1995.

73 Levenson, *Death and Resurrection*. Jesus is depicted as the sacrificed Son of God not only in John 1 and John 3: 16, but also in John 10: 11, 17–18, 36.

74 In the cult of Adonis, rites are also performed "in remembrance of his suffering" (*mnemen tou patheos*; Lucian, *The Syrian Goddess* 6). The motif of the disciples "remembering" the words of Jesus after his death, and understanding them in the context of his life (John 2: 17, 22; 12: 16; compare 15: 20; 16: 4), has a different but analogous function in John and, according to Jonathan Z. Smith, also in other Hellenistic "gospels": Philostratus, *Apollonius of Tyana* 3.15, 6.11, 4.24, 5.7, and others ("No News is Good News: Aretalogy and Gospel," in Jacob Neusner (ed.), *Christianity, Judaism, and Other Greco-Roman Cults: Studies for Morton Smith at Sixty*, 4 vols, Leiden: Brill, 1975, p. 1.25). See also Ronald Cameron, *Sayings Traditions in the Apocryphon of James* (Philadelphia: Fortress, 1984), pp. 116–19. On the association of the eucharist with cult meals for the dead, see Bo Reicke, *Diakonie, Festfreude und Zelos in Verbindung mit der altchristlichen Agapenfeier*, Uppsala: Lundequistska/Wiesbaden: Otto Harrassowitz, 1951, pp. 101–49, 257–64. See also Burkert, *Greek Religion*, p. 205, who notes that the hero is often depicted recumbent at a feast: a "cultic feast of living in the company of, and in honor of, the hero." On the theory of Ludger Schenke that there existed cult practices of the first Christians at the tomb of Jesus (*Auferstehungsverkündigung und leeres Grab: eine traditionsgeschichtliche Untersuchung von Mk 16, 1–8*, Stuttgart: Katholisches Bibelwerk, 1968, pp. 93–103), see chapter 3.

75 Helmut Koester, *Introduction to the New Testament*, 2 vols, Philadelphia: Fortress/Berlin and

New York: de Gruyter, 1982, pp. 2.88–89; Joachim Jeremias, *TDNT*, pp. 5.901–4; and Hans Conzelmann, *1 Corinthians*, Philadelphia: Fortress, 1987, pp. 98–99.

76 As we saw above, Bultmann did not apply the word "cult" to early Christianity. So also here some would argue that the Last Supper is not a sacrifice even when it is placed within the gospel setting, and that there is very little in the way of cult here; it is more a memorial of a prior sacrifice. So Nils Alstrup Dahl ("Memorial and Commemoration in Early Christianity," in *idem, Jesus in the Memory of the Early Church*, Minneapolis: Augsburg, 1976, pp. 11–29): "The church of Christ possessed no sacrificial cult. Just as the complete revelation had been given once for all, so also the perfect sacrifice had been offered once for all." This is progressively the case in the early Christian sources (Paul, Mark, Hebrews, Justin Martyr), but not necessarily in the tradition that goes back before the present gospels of Mark and John.

77 Levenson, *Death and Resurrection*, pp. 200–19; Jonathan Z. Smith, *To Take Place: Theory in Ritual*, Chicago: University of Chicago Press, 1987, p. 89; Nagy, *Pindar's Homer*, p. 43.

78 Whether faith follows directly upon the working of miracles is an issue at tension in these works. In the early layers of John, according to W. Nicol (*The Semeia in the Fourth Gospel: Tradition and Redaction*, Leiden: Brill, 1972, pp. 41–46) and Robert T. Fortna (*The Gospel of Signs: A Reconstruction of the Narrative Source Underlying the Fourth Gospel*, Cambridge: Cambridge University Press, 1970, p. 233), faith is a rather mechanical reaction to the witnessing of a miracle, whereas John critiques this limited notion of faith. Mark reverses the order of miracle and faith, and often makes faith a pre-condition of a miracle. The handling of this issue is thus carried out in a very different way.

79 Bickerman, "Das leere Grab," *ZNW* 23 (1924) 281–92, repr. in *idem, Studies in Jewish and Christian History*, 3 vols, Leiden: Brill, 1986, pp. 3.70–81. See also Raymond Brown, *The Gospel According to John*, 2 vols, Garden City, N.Y.: Doubleday, 1964–70, pp. 2.978, 1027–28; Gerd Luedemann, *The Resurrection of Jesus: History, Exposition, Theology*, London: SCM, 1994, p. 171; Adela Yarbro Collins, *The Beginning of the Gospel: Probings of Mark in Context*, Minneapolis: Fortress, 1992, pp. 119–48, esp. pp. 138–43; and Arthur Stan Pease, "Some Aspects of Invisibility," *HSCP* 53 (1942) 1–36.

80 James D. Tabor, "'Returning to the Divinity': Josephus's Portrayal of the Disappearances of Enoch, Elijah, and Moses," *JBL* 108 (1989) 225–38; Christopher Begg, "Josephus's Portrayal of the Disappearances of Enoch, Elijah, and Moses: Some Observations," *JBL* 109 (1990) 691–93.

81 Aune, "Problem of the Genre," pp. 47–48.

82 Nagy, *Pindar's Homer*, p. 178. Compare Diodorus Siculus 4.38.5 on the absence of Herakles' bones in his ashes, Herodian 1.11.2 on Philoctetes and Ganymede, and Diogenes Laertius, *Empedocles* on the missing tomb, and Justin, *Apology* 1.20 on the comparison of the exaltation of Jesus and Greco-Roman figures. Other relevant passages include Herodotus 4.14–15, Ovid, *Fasti* 2.481–509, Livy 1.16, Plutarch, *Romulus* 27–28, Philo, *Life of Moses* 2.51 §288–91, Philostratus, *Apollonius of Tyana* 8.10–11, 30–31, and Eusebius, *Preparation for the Gospel* 9.41.456d–457b. The "missing" body of Jesus may also have been seen in the eucharist, where the body and blood of Jesus "materialize." This occurs in later Christianity, where the eucharistic elements were treated as relics; see Jonathan Sumption, *Pilgrimage: An Image of Mediaeval Religion*, London: Faber & Faber, 1975, pp. 44–48; Patrick J. Geary, *Furta Sacra: Thefts of Relics in the Central Middle Ages*, Princeton: Princeton University Press, 1978, pp. 28–29, 39–40. In the Buddhist tradition, the absence of the Buddha was explored philosophically, which challenges our conceptions of what the presence of the body "must mean" to followers; see Malcolm David Eckel, *To see the Buddha: A Philosopher's Quest for the Meaning of Emptiness*, San Francisco: HarperSanFrancisco, 1992, pp. 49–72.

83 Collins, *Beginning of the Gospel*, p. 141; see also p. 137.

84 Nagy, *Best of the Achaeans*, pp. 189–90, 226.

85 Oscar Cullmann, "The Immortality of Man," in Krister Stendahl (ed.), *Immortality and Resurrection*, New York: Macmillan, 1965, pp. 9–47, but also see George W. Nickelsburg, *Resurrection, Immortality, and Eternal Life in Intertestamental Judaism*, Cambridge, Mass.: Harvard University Press, 1972, pp. 177–80.

86 Greek: Herodotus 4.14–15 (mentioned above), but also faked, 4.95, and Diodorus Siculus 18.60.5 (mentioned above); Jewish: Onias III at 2 Macc 15: 12–16 (also above). An interesting variation in older Israelite tradition is the missing body of the hero coupled with the *succession* of the disciple. Moses and Elijah both leave no body for burial, but have very prominent successors in Joshua and Elisha; see Alan W. Jenks, *The Elohist and Northern Israelite Traditions*, Missoula, Mont.: Scholars, 1977, p. 95.

87 Nagy, *Pindar's Homer*, pp. 66–67, 143, n.40.

88 Martin Hengel's argument ("Christological Titles in early Christianity," in James H. Charlesworth (ed.), *The Messiah: Developments in Earliest Judaism and Christianity*, Minneapolis: Fortress, 1992, pp. 425–48) for a consistent humiliation/exaltation pattern in the hymns of John 1, Philippians 2, and Hebrews 2 is interesting, but only reflects one of the possible patterns found in the New Testament, and is confined to hymns and not narrative materials. His attempts, here and in *Atonement*, to harmonize various traditions within the New Testament are always provocative, but not, to me, fully convincing. See also Nils Dahl, "The Crucified Messiah," in his *Jesus the Christ*, Minneapolis: Fortress, 1991, pp. 27–48.

89 The influence of the Suffering Servant in Isaiah 52–53 on early New Testament christology was already minimized by Morna D. Hooker, *Jesus and the Servant: The Influence of the Servant Concept of Deutero-Isaiah in the New Testament*, London: SPCK, 1959, and even further removed from consideration by Seeley, *Noble Death*, pp. 39–58, although Hengel, Collins, and Koester still affirm the connection of this text to the early development of christology (Hengel, *Atonement*, pp. 59–60; *idem*, "The Expiatory Sacrifice of Christ," *Bulletin of the John Rylands University Library of Manchester* 62 [1980] 470; Collins, "Finding Meaning"; Koester, "The Historical Jesus and the Cult of the *Kyrios Christos*," *Harvard Divinity Bulletin* 24 (1995) 13–18). Matt 8: 17, it should be noted, is likely a Matthean addition to the gospel tradition. The Suffering Son of Humanity has now been ruled out of consideration as an early christology by most scholars. It appears to be an invention of Mark, on which see F. H. Borsch, "Further Reflections on 'The Son of Man': The Origins and Development of the Title," in Charlesworth (ed.), *The Messiah: Developments in Earliest Judaism and Christianity*, Minneapolis: Fortress, 1992, esp. pp. 131–32 (and literature cited there). The evidence for mystery initiations in the first century and their influence on the New Testament has recently been questioned by a number of scholars, on which see Seeley, *Noble Death*, pp. 67–82.

3 A SYNOPSIS OF MARK AND JOHN

1 I have provided a translation of Mark and John that is somewhat literal to make comparisons easier. Where the Greek is the same in the two gospels, I have also tried to use the same English words. The Greek word *Ioudaioi* I have rendered "Judeans" rather than "Jews," in keeping with the recent scholarly attempt not to import later religious issues of the Jewish–Christian schism into the first-century sectarian conflict. See chapter 4 for a discussion of the possible import of the term "Judean."

2 This association of the *arch-* root with the beginning of the gospel recitation of events is noted by James M. Robinson, *The Problem of History in Mark and Other Studies*, Philadelphia: Fortress, 1980, pp. 69–72. Both uses of the noun here also conspicuously lack a definite article. In each case, an explanation lies at hand: in Mark, the lack of an article may reflect a Semitic construct clause; John probably lacks an article because it alludes to Gen 1: 1, where the LXX follows the Hebrew original in having no definite article.

3 In these examples, however, *arche* was not always placed at the very beginning of the recitation of events. In Acts 10: 37 and Ignatius, *Eph.* 19.3 it is introduced later, but these are not strictly historical descriptions. What all of these do have in common is associating the *arche* with the advent or adoption of the Messiah.

4 Polybius 1.5.1, 5.31.1–2; Tacitus, *Histories* 1.1.1; Dionysius of Halicarnassus 1.8.4. See David Aune, *The New Testament in its Literary Environment*, Philadelphia: Westminster, 1987, p. 48.

5 Dennis Duling, "Interpreting the Markan 'Hodology': Biblical Criticism in Preaching and Teaching," *Nexus* 17 (1974) 2–11. In Q (Luke 7: 27/Matt 11: 10), Mal 3: 1 also occurs in relation to John the Baptist. Indeed John also uses *hodos* in a theologically significant way (14: 4–6), but it is probably derived from early Christian usage and owes nothing to Mark's innovations.

6 Here I follow Fortna, *Gospel*, pp. 161–66, but compare also M.-E. Boismard, "Les traditions johanniques concernant le baptiste," *RB* 70 (1963) 5–42 (whose reconstruction at this point is very similar); Brown, *John*, pp. 1.27–28, 68–70, 154–55; Dodd, *Historical Tradition*, pp. 279–87; Barnabas Lindars, *The Gospel of John*, London: Oliphants, 1972, pp. 76, 82; and J. A. T. Robinson, "The Relation of the Prologue to the Gospel of St. John," *NTS* 9 (1962–63) 120–29.

7 Ivor Buse, "St. John and the First Synoptic Pericope," *NT* 3 (1959) 57–61; Marxsen, *Mark the Evangelist*, pp. 35–37, 42, 45–47.

8 John gives voice to the problem of Jesus' birth city ("Can anything good come out of Nazareth?," 1: 46), but this does not result in a new birth narrative as it does in Matthew and Luke.

9 Boismard, "Traditions," pp. 29–30. Fortna, *Gospel*, pp. 179–89, places the short notice at John 3: 23–24 at the beginning of the conversion of the first disciples. His arguments for placing it there do not carry a great deal of conviction, as he concedes by placing these verses in the reconstruction in parentheses. The fact that the two gospels have opposite temporal notices here – after the Baptist's imprisonment in Mark, before in John – can probably be explained by Mark's rearrangement of the timeline to take John the Baptist off the stage and into prison before Jesus' ministry begins.

   Brown, *John*, p. 1.154, and Boismard, "Traditions," pp. 29–30, extend the parallels between chapter 1 and chapter 3 to include 3: 25–30 as well, but this really only applies to parallel Johannine redaction in the two pericopes. The tradition behind John 3: 25–30 is best understood in relation to Mark 2: 18–22, on which see below.

10 Acts 10: 39 also uses a phrase similar to Mark, although in relation to Jesus, not John the Baptist: "We are witnesses of all that he did, both in the countryside of the Jews and also in Jerusalem . . ."

11 The coherence of Bultmann's proposed early layer is not entirely convincing. It is partly achieved by omitting verses based on a clear and plausible (though I think incorrect) criterion, i.e., those phrases parallel to the synoptic traditions. But more worrisome than this, the coherence is also achieved by rearranging verses. Coherence achieved by rearranging verses cannot be used as evidence for a source, which Bultmann would probably have granted. It can only be used as a corollary conclusion about a source which is isolated on other grounds. Although I occasionally advocate rearrangement of sections of the Gospel of John, I do not argue that the coherence thus achieved is evidence of a source. Rearrangements such as this can only be used to illuminate other arguments for sources.

   The strongest argument for Bultmann's theory is the progression from questions to answers in verses 21 and 25. But even here, has he simply pulled out the question and the answer which went together, and perhaps were foremost, in the mind *of the Evangelist?* Bultmann's entire commentary, with its radical rearrangements of the text, is a testament to the belief that the Evangelist wrote with a straightforward progression of ideas which has been disrupted in the textual transmission. Most, however, would see inhering in this gospel not a linear structure, rising steadily, as on a graph, from point A to point B, but a helix, constantly turning back on itself.

As Brown also notes (*John*, p. 1.70), the presence of synoptic traditions here does not accomplish the one thing which would be most expected of a more orthodox Ecclesiastical Redactor: the actual depiction of Jesus being baptized by John the Baptist. In fact, what the synoptic parallels do accomplish could hardly rank as a *coup de grâce* for orthodoxy. For Bultmann, they "canonize" John by harmonizing it with the synoptics, but if once the possibility is considered that the synoptic parallels were from the same source, only to be theologically expanded by the addition of typically Johannine motifs, then an equally if not more plausible picture emerges.

12 Martyn, *History and Theology in the Fourth Gospel*, New York and Evanston: Harper & Row, 1968, pp. 32–42.

13 Some of the material found in chapter 1 of John is paralleled elsewhere in Mark: the three-part question concerning Jesus' messianic identity and the renaming of Simon as Cephas or Peter. These are both found together at Mark 8: 27–29 (see synopsis below). John has placed this combination early on, with the calling of the first disciples, while Mark has associated it with a later, climactic stage in the ministry. If Mark and John have taken this tradition from a common source, then they have treated it quite differently. Mark has created a strong narrative theme of the disciples' misunderstanding. It would be quite believable that Mark moved this material to a more climactic location, looking forward to the very beginning of the passion, but it is difficult (though not impossible) to imagine that John would have undone Mark's evocative drama.

14 Richard A. Edwards, *A Theology of Q*, Philadelphia: Fortress, 1976, pp. 81–82; John Kloppenborg, *Q Parallels*, Sonoma, Calif.: Polebridge Press, 1988, p. 12.

15 Edwards, *Theology of Q*, p. 55.

16 Compare the similar conclusions of Ismo Dunderberg, *Johannes und die Synoptiker: Studien zu Joh 1–9*, Helsinki: Suomalainen tiedeakatemia, 1994, pp. 59–60. However, despite many interesting observations, Dunderberg in general moves too quickly from the *possibility* of Markan redaction to the *probability*. For instance, he assumes (pp. 63, 71) that the heavenly voice in Mark 1: 11 is redactional because the wording is so similar to Mark 9: 7. The voice at John 1: 33 must therefore be dependent upon Mark's redactional innovation. The traditional nature of this kind of motif, however, renders this kind of argument dubious.

17 K. L. Schmidt, *Der Rahmen der Geschichte Jesu: Literarkritische Untersuchungen zur ältesten Jesusüberlieferung*, Berlin: Trowitzsch, 1919, p. 24; Marxsen, *Mark the Evangelist*, pp. 30–53, esp. p. 33; Nineham, *Saint Mark*, pp. 57–59.

18 David Ulansey, "The Heavenly Veil Torn: Mark's Cosmic *Inclusio*," *JBL* 110 (1991) 123–25. In Mark, John the Baptist also baptizes for repentance and the forgiveness of sins. This motif is likely Markan; it is lacking in John, where the Baptist baptizes in order that Jesus be manifested to Israel (John 1: 31).

19 Lührmann, *Markusevangelium*, pp. 37–38, cautions that "adoptionist" is a misleading term in Mark, because a contrast with a theology of pre-existence is not even considered. In comparison with John, however, the term is valid if it is not pushed too far. It is also important to note that early hymnic, non-narrative traditions, for example, Phil 2: 6–11, already posited the pre-existence of Christ.

20 The exact allusions are far from clear. The analysis here reflects the position of, for instance, Nineham, *Saint Mark*, p. 62; Vincent Taylor, *The Gospel According to St. Mark*, 2nd ed., London: Macmillan, 1972, p. 162; Lindars, *Gospel of John*, pp. 139–44; Jack Dean Kingsbury, *The Christology of Mark's Gospel*, Philadelphia: Fortress, 1983, p. 83; and I. Howard Marshall, "Son of God or Servant of Yahweh? – A Reconsideration of Mark I.11," *NTS* 15 (1968–69) 326–36. Some scholars argue that there is no allusion to Ps 2: 7, but that "son" enters the text of Mark from an alternative Greek tradition of translating Hebrew

'*ebed* by *huios*. This view can be found in W. Zimmerli and J. Jeremias, *The Servant of God*, Napierville, Ill.: Allenson, 1957, pp. 81–82; Lührmann, *Markusevangelium*, pp. 37–38; and C. E. B. Cranfield, *The Gospel According to Saint Mark*, Cambridge: Cambridge University Press, 1963, p. 55. However, especially convincing as arguments in favor of an allusion to Ps 2: 7 here are the closeness of the phrasing between the two passages (especially the second-person address), and the fact that Ps 2: 7 is attested elsewhere as a messianic designation by God.

21 Taylor, *Gospel According to St. Mark*, p. 162; Lührmann, *Markusevangelium*, pp. 37–38; and Philipp Vielhauer, "Erwägungen," *Aufsätze zum Neuen Testament* TB 31 (1965) 199–214. The latter traces a redactional pattern in Mark to Egyptian enthronement parallels: adoption and apotheosis, 1: 11; presentation, 9: 7; and enthronement, 15: 39. His suggestion is speculative, but if true, would only strengthen the argument made here. Mark also omits the motif of choosing, which bespeaks a servant christology, in favor of a Son of God christology. This has considerable import for the redaction criticism of Mark, as well as for the immediate question at hand, the relationship between the two gospels.

22 The majority of good ancient witnesses to John read "the Son (*huios*) of God," but *eklektos*, "chosen one," is read by a few early texts (Sinaiticus beneath correction, some Old Latin and Syriac witnesses, and possibly P[5]), and is preferred by many scholars, including Brown, *John*, p. 1.57; Gunter Reim, *Studien zum alttestamentlichen Hintergrund des Johannesevangeliums*, Cambridge: Cambridge University Press, 1974, pp. 163, 250; Zimmerli and Jeremias, *Servant*, p. 61, n. 261; and Fortna, *Gospel*, p. 178. It would be much more likely for a scribe to alter "chosen one" to "son" than vice versa. Bultmann, *John*, pp. 92–93, after assigning this verse to the Evangelist, begs the text-critical question by asserting that *huios* is more typical of the Evangelist and is to be preferred. This half-verse, however, does not likely stem from the Evangelist in my view.

The theological import of the son motif in both Mark and John is addressed provocatively by Jon Levenson, *The Death and Resurrection of the Beloved Son: The Transformation of Child Sacrifice in Judaism and Christianity*, New Haven: Yale University Press, 1993, pp. 200–1, 208–9. Levenson's identification of the chosen one or son with the paschal sacrificial lamb later in John 19: 36 only serves to strengthen the overall approach taken here; see chapter 2 above. See also William R. Stegner, *Narrative Theology in Early Jewish Christianity*, Louisville: Westminster/John Knox, 1989, pp. 13–31; and *idem*, "Baptism of Jesus: A Story Modeled on the Binding of Isaac," in Harvey Minkoff (ed.), *Approaches to the Bible: The Best of Bible Review*, Washington, D. C.: Biblical Archaeological Society, 1994, pp. 66–71, where it is argued that the targumic traditions of the binding of Isaac indicate that the baptism scene is to some extent modeled upon it.

23 Acts 13: 33; Heb 1: 5; 5: 5. The birth image in this psalm – a psalm originally sung to accompany the enthronement of the king of Israel – came to be associated with the resurrection of Jesus, and later, as in Mark, with the baptism of Jesus. The declaration at John 1: 51, "You shall see the heavens open . . ." is paralleled in the *Gospel of Peter*; see the end of the synopsis below for a discussion of this parallel.

24 This list of disciples overlaps a great deal with an early list of disciples in a Papias fragment at Eusebius, *Church History* 3.39.4. John also mentions Thomas in chapter 20.

25 On Mark's redactional timeframe re John the Baptist, see Marxsen, *Mark the Evangelist*, p. 42; on John's different handling of this issue, see Edward F. Glusman, Jr., "Criteria for a Study of the Outlines of Mark and John," in Paul J. Achtemeier (ed.), *Society of Biblical Literature 1978 Seminar Papers*, 2 vols, Missoula, Mont.: Scholars, 1978, pp. 2.241–42.

26 However, since some of the references to Jesus' teaching in Mark are lacking in both Matthew and Luke, it is conceivable that they were added after the original edition; see Helmut Koester, *Ancient Christian Gospels: Their History and Development*, Philadelphia: Trinity Press International, 1990, p. 298. Nevertheless, some of the occurrences of teaching, specifically Mark 1: 22, are picked up; compare Luke 4: 32. John also contains

references to teaching at points where the parallel reference in Mark is attested in Matthew or Luke.

27 The parallel between the first parts of Mark's and John's sections may be even closer than at first appears. David Daube has suggested that the phrase in Mark 1: 22, "he taught them as one who had authority and not as one of their scribes," reflects a Jewish view that the trained rabbi spoke with authority, and could introduce new rulings, while the scribes were mere "paralegal" functionaries ("Exousia in Mark 1 22 and 27," *JTS* o. s. 39 [1938] 45–59). In this light, John 7: 15 can be seen as a similar notion: "How can this man have learning ('know letters'), when he is not educated?" The Hebrew term for scribe, *sofer*, according to Daube, indicated a learned scholar until about the turn of the Christian era, when it developed a whole range of meanings from the highly educated to the lowly copyist. However, intriguing as this suggestion is, Daube's position remains speculative, since the rabbinic evidence derives from later sources, and the translation of *grammateus*, "scribe," cannot be specified precisely.

28 A miracle story is mentioned in John 7: 21, but this refers back to chapter 5; see below.

29 Compare, for instance, the negative judgment on their relationship by Ernst Haenchen, "Johanneische Probleme," *ZTK* 56 (1959) 46–50. Dunderberg, *Johannes und die Synoptiker*, pp. 100–24, comes to conclusions similar to mine: the two narratives should be compared, but no influence of Mark can be found in John.

30 Bultmann, *History*, pp. 14–16; W. E. Beare, *The Earliest Records of Jesus*, Oxford: Basil Blackwell, 1964, pp. 76–77. Joanna Dewey argues that it is not necessary to attribute what appear to be clumsy transitions to interpolations (*Markan Public Debate: Literary Technique, Concentric Structure, and Theology in Mark 2: 1–3: 6*, Chico, Calif.: Scholars, 1980, pp. 100–4); what might be reflected instead is a rhetorical balancing of issues in a concentric pattern, found elsewhere in this section of Mark. Ultimately, however, Dewey does not assert that she has proven that it was composed of a piece, only that it is a possibility.

31 John R. Donahue, *Are You the Christ?, The Trial Narrative in the Gospel of Mark*, Missoula: University of Montana Press, 1973, p. 42; Kee, *Community*, pp. 54–55; Joanna Dewey, "Oral Methods of Structuring Narrative in Mark," *Interpretation* 43 (1989) 32–44.

32 Attridge, "Thematic Development and Source Elaboration in John 7: 1–36," *CBQ* 42 (1980) 160–70. The threads of narrative between chapters 5 and 10 are admittedly very complicated. For example, Attridge looks all the way to 10: 34–36 for the original ending of the story. Compare also Bultmann's complicated restoration in *John*. Focusing on John 5 alone, Jerome Neyrey posits an early miracle (John 5: 1–9), which has a Sabbath controversy redaction (5: 10–16, 30–47), and a further redaction in 5: 17–29 (*An Ideology of Revolt: John's Christology in Social-Scientific Perspective*, Philadelphia: Fortress, 1988, pp. 9–36).

33 We should also note that the opponents' importunate question of verse 20 ("Who is trying to kill you?") is not answered in any way in verse 21. (*Thaumazo* and *ergon* are also both Johannine words.) Between these seams also lies the accusation that Jesus has a demon, which is probably a Johannine insertion from another context. (See Mark 3: 20–30/John 7: 19–20 below.)

34 Smoothing over the disjunction between 5: 16 and 7: 19–23, however, does not eliminate the problem of the abruptness of the introduction of the Sabbath issue at 5: 9b. Although it is quite likely that the Sabbath controversy was already present in John's source material, it is still possible that the miracle circulated originally without this element, and that we must actually contend here with at least three layers in the tradition history, as Attridge also concedes: bare miracle, miracle with Sabbath controversy added (*chreia* elaboration), and finally, miracle, Sabbath controversy and Johannine discourse.

35 Identical words do sometimes crop up in unrelated miracle stories; for example, "Have mercy on me, Son of David!" occurs often in Matthew's healing miracles. However, the use of "Son of David" in these synoptic examples probably derives from a common Christian

and Jewish petitionary prayer form (Dennis Duling, "The Therapeutic Son of David: An Element in Matthew's Christological Apologetic," *NTS* 24 [1978] 392–410). Where we find the same words of *healing*, rather than *petitioning*, we are more likely to be dealing with the same miracle-story tradition.

36 Kolenkow, "Healing Controversy as a Tie Between Miracle and Passion Material for a Proto-Gospel," *JBL* 95 (1976) 623–38; quotation from p. 637.

37 Mack, *Myth*, pp. 188, 380. In addition to the usual clever repartee that we have come to expect in *chreiai*, one should also notice the elegance of construction which places the main verb at one end of the response and the complementary infinitive at the other. Compare with this the redactional verse 19b, where the same verb and infinitive are side by side.

38 The traditional nature of this material may also be indicated by its poetic structure; Brown, *John*, 1.150, places 3: 27, 29–30 in parallel lines. Matthew Black, *An Aramaic Approach to the Gospels and Acts*, 3rd ed., Oxford: Clarendon, 1967, pp. 146–47, also finds evidence of a number of Aramaic plays on words in these verses.

39 Smith, "Mark 6: 32–15: 47 and John 6: 1–19: 42," in Paul J. Achtemeier (ed.), *Society of Biblical Literature Seminar Papers 1978*, 2 vols, Missoula, Mont.: Scholars, 1978, pp. 2.281–87. Others have pointed out the parallel structure of Mark and John, including Edward F. Glusman, Jr., "Criteria for a Study of the Outlines of Mark and John," a companion presentation to Smith's in the same volume, pp. 239–49, but Smith presents the most convincing case. See also Joachim Jeremias, "Johanneische Literaturkritik," *Theologische Blätter* 20 (1941) 42; C. H. Dodd, *The Interpretation of the Fourth Gospel*, Cambridge: Cambridge University Press, 1953, pp. 448–49; Brown, *John*, p. 1.238–39. To be sure, those scholars who argued for the dependence of John upon Mark have always emphasized the parallel order of Mark and John in the middle section of the gospels; see, for example, Barrett, *Gospel According to St. John*, pp. 42–54; Arthur H. Maynard, "Common Elements in the Outlines of Mark and John," in the same volume with Smith and Glusman, pp. 2.251–60; René Kieffer, "Jean et Marc: Convergences dans la structure et dans les détails," in Adelbert Denaux (ed.), *John and the Synoptics*, Leuven: Leuven University Press, 1990, pp. 109–25; and John Dominic Crossan, *The Historical Jesus: The Life of a Mediterranean Jewish Peasant*, San Francisco: HarperCollins, 1991, pp. 310–13, 429.

40 Achtemeier, "Toward the Isolation of Pre-Markan Miracle Catenae," *JBL* 89 (1970) 265–91, and *idem*, "The Origin and Function of the Pre-Markan Miracle Catenae," *JBL* 91 (1972) 198–221.

41 Mack, *Myth*, pp. 216–22; and also Helmut Koester, *Introduction to the New Testament*, 2 vols, Philadelphia: Fortress/Berlin and New York: de Gruyter, 1982, p. 2.167. Note Smith's brief remarks rejecting Achtemeier's theory in his response in Howard Clark Kee, *Aretalogies, Hellenistic "Lives," and the Sources of Mark*, Berkeley: Center for Hermeneutical Studies, 1975, p. 34, and compare with my arguments below.

42 But note Mack's argument (*Myth*, pp. 220–22) that the first and last of the signs (the water changed to wine and the raising of Lazarus) are not "typical" gospel miracles: the former is too minor and insignificant, indeed barely noticed except as a "sign," while the latter is essentially overwrought and laden with significance for Jesus' own resurrection. They both figure as important interpretations of miracles as signs, and were perhaps added to the other more typical miracles when the enumeration of miracles as signs was undertaken. If that is the case, then the original collection would have consisted of five miracles, just as in the two Markan catenae, with two of them closely parallel. Appealing as this is, however, I prefer a different hypothesis of the relationship of John's and Mark's miracles.

43 An equally interesting parallel is found in the Talmud concerning the healing at a distance by the Jewish sage Hanina ben Dosa, *bBer* 34b. Dodd, *Historical Tradition*, pp. 188–95, emphasizes instead the relationship of John 4: 46–54 to Mark 7: 24–30, but the parallels adduced may be attributed to typical story-telling techniques; it is not clear that they have

239

any traditional elements in common. Note also the variant of Mark 5: 21–23, 35–43 at Acts 10: 36–43. On the relation of this miracle in John to the Q parallel, see Stefan Landis, *Das Verhältnis des Johannesevangeliums zu den Synoptikern*, Berlin/New York: de Gruyter, 1994. Landis sees no dependence of John upon Matthew or Luke or on Q, and indeed sees the Johannine miracle as more primitive than the others.

44 Franz Schnider and Werner Stenger, *Johannes und die Synoptiker*, Munich: Kösel, 1971, pp. 79–80.

45 Mark 1: 21–28 does not turn negative even though Jesus heals on a Sabbath! That only becomes a problem at 3: 1–6. Some note the discrepancy between the positive astonishment at 6: 2 and the negative turn in the next verse, and suggest that the astonishment has been added; so W. L. Knox, *The Sources of the Synoptic Gospels*, 2 vols, Cambridge: Cambridge University Press, 1953–57, pp. 1.48–49, and Bultmann, *History*, p. 31.

46 Theissen, *Sociology of Early Palestinian Christianity*, Philadelphia: Fortress, 1977, pp. 7–30. At several points Mark contains passages which seem to reflect this sort of early Christian experience, but a number of scholars question Theissen's "wandering prophets" explanation; see Richard Horsley, *Sociology and the Jesus Movement*, New York: Crossroad, 1989, p. 111; and William E. Arnal, "The Rhetoric of Marginality: Apocalypticism, Gnosticism, and Sayings Gospels," *HTR* 88 (1995) 480–92 (with a good summary of recent literature). It is very significant that the Gospel of John apparently does not reflect any interest in this motif, however it is to be interpreted in Mark. This, then, creates another difficulty for those who believe that John may have used Mark as a source: one would have to suppose that John deleted every such reference found in Mark – not modified these concerns, as *Didache* and Matthew have done, but deleted the references without a trace (unless John 2: 4 and 7: 5 are interpreted in this light).

47 Kelber, *The Oral and the Written Gospel: The Hermeneutics of Speaking and Writing in the Synoptic Tradition, Mark, Paul, and Q*, Philadelphia: Fortress, 1983.

48 Robbins, "*Dunameis* and *Semeia* in Mark," in *idem, New Boundaries in Old Territory: Form and Social Rhetoric in Mark*, New York: Peter Lang, 1994, pp. 59–72, esp. p. 66.

49 This would be clearer still if, as some have suggested, the Samaritan interlude of 4: 4–42 has been added, and the text originally connected from 4: 3 to 4: 43: "When Jesus learned that the Pharisees had heard that he was baptizing more disciples than John . . . he left Judea and went to Galilee." The Samaritan interlude betrays a number of Johannine redactional themes, while the verses before and after it are mainly traditional. Jesus' pronouncement in verse 44 (no honor in his own country) would in that case be uttered after he emerged from Judea, not Samaria.

50 Jouette Bassler, "The Galileans: A Neglected Factor in Johannine Community Research," *CBQ* 43 (1981) 243–57; Seán Freyne, *Galilee, Jesus and the Gospels: Literary Approaches and Historical Investigations*, Dublin: Gill and Macmillan, 1988, p. 122.

51 Even the words of John from this section that are found in Mark show a peculiarity: they are sometimes paralleled in the feeding of the 5,000 in Mark 6, and at other times in the feeding of the 4,000 in Mark 8. Brown notes (*John*, 1.239): "Even if it is proposed that the evangelist blended details from [the two accounts], one must admit that there is no recognizable scheme or pattern to the borrowing."

52 Because of the mention of rough seas, Brown (*John*, p. 1.254) takes John's version to be a mixing of the walking on the water narrative and the stilling of the storm (Mark 4: 35–40). It is not necessary to postulate this, however; the motif is germane to the story as a whole, as the similarity at this point to Mark's version here indicates. Udo Schnelle asserts that it is Mark who has enriched the walking on the water miracle with motifs from the stilling miracle (*Antidoketische Christologie im Johannesevangelium*, Göttingen: Vandenhoeck & Ruprecht, 1987, pp. 128–30). If that were the case, then this would constitute evidence that John is familiar with the Markan tradition, but his arguments for Markan redaction are unconvincing. Compare also the arguments for Markan redaction

appearing in John's narrative found in Dunderberg, *Johannes und die Synoptiker*, pp. 156–64; they are sometimes intriguing, as when the time designation in John 6: 16 is presumed to be influenced by Mark (who uses similar time designations often), but they are never fully convincing. Dunderberg also argues (pp. 124–74) that Mark is responsible for the connection of the feeding miracle and the walking on the water, but this remains only a possibility.

53 It is interesting that Mark and John also follow up on these stories with similar motifs: Mark immediately connects this miracle with the miracle of the multiplication of loaves (verse 52), while John creates an entire discourse on bread later in chapter 6.

54 The word "way" (*hodos*) figures prominently in each, emphasizing the "way" the disciples must travel. Ironically, each prediction is followed by a narrative that shows up the disciples' lack of understanding. See Dennis Duling, "Interpreting the Markan 'Hodology,'" 2–11, and Elizabeth Struthers Malbon, *Narrative Space and Mythic Meaning in Mark*, Sheffield: JSOT Press, 1991, pp. 68–71, 104–5.

55 Matthew's fuller version is better known, and interestingly, Brown (*John*, pp. 1.301–2) and Bultmann (*History*, pp. 138–39) have argued that Matthew knew, in addition to Mark's account, a separate primitive tradition. Compare also Dodd, *Historical Tradition*, pp. 219–21. Matt 16: 13–23 contains both the confession of Simon and his renaming as Peter (Cephas in Aramaic). The latter event is not recounted in Mark, but it is found in another context in John (1: 40–42). In addition, Matthew has other elements that are not present in Mark but are in John, for example, the original name of Peter as "Simon Barjona" (verse 17), which is Aramaic for "Simon son of John" (compare John 1: 41). Compare also the independent traditions at John 20: 22–23. Brown (p. 1.302) goes so far as to say that "almost every element of the peculiarly Matthean material is found elsewhere in John."

56 Compare *Gospel of Thomas* 13 on the questions and answers and confession motif, and see Bultmann, *History*, pp. 82–83, 257–59; Ferdinand Hahn, *The Titles of Jesus in Christology: Their History in Early Christianity*, New York and Cleveland: World, 1969, pp. 223–26; Erich Dinkler, "Peter's Confession and the 'Satan' Saying: The Problem of Jesus' Messiahship," in James H. Robinson (ed.), *The Future of Our Religious Past: Essays in Honour of Rudolf Bultmann*, New York: Harper & Row, 1971, pp. 169–202; Ron Cameron, *Sayings Traditions in the Apocryphon of James*, Philadelphia: Fortress, 1984, pp. 86–88.

57 It is here also in John that we find the intriguing statement that "he said this in order to indicate by what sort of death he was about to die" (John 12: 33). This complex in John 12 could be seen by some as a vestigial trace of Mark's great passion predictions, bereft now of their former power, but I prefer to see them as a reflection of an earlier tradition that Mark has expanded. In this context it is probably also significant that the word for "indicate" in John 12: 33, *semaino*, is related to the noun *semeion*, and may have appeared in the pre-Johannine tradition.

58 Nineham, *Saint Mark*, pp. 282–83, Norman Perrin and Dennis C. Duling, *The New Testament: Proclamation and Paraenesis, Myth and History*, 3rd ed., Fort Worth: Harcourt Brace, 1994, pp. 304–5, 309–12; Norman R. Petersen, *Literary Criticism for New Testament Critics*, Philadelphia: Fortress, 1978, pp. 60–68.

59 Whether or not the word "Satan" is older than *diabolos*, as Joachim Jeremias maintains (*Parables of Jesus*, 2nd ed., New York: Scribner, 1972, p. 81, n. 49). Compare also Mark 14: 4 and John 12: 4 for what may be a similar substitution of other disciples for Judas. The background of Mark's "He rebuked (*epitimao*) Peter, 'Get thee behind me, Satan!'" is perhaps influenced by God's intercession for the high priest Joshua (Jesus in Greek) before Satan in Zech 3: 2: "The Lord rebuke (*epitimao*) you, O Satan!" *Epitimao* is a key word in Mark to describe Jesus rebuking the demons; so Cameron, *Sayings Traditions*, p. 87. Yet it is not, *per se*, a *Markan* invention; one must consider here the enormous influence of Zechariah on the gospel tradition. Whether "ruler of this world" in John 12: 31 is related to the Satan/devil motif is unclear.

Other elements in Mark may also be redactional. Mark 8 places the location of the exchange between Jesus and his disciples in Caesarea Philippi, a city north of Galilee, while John places Jesus in Capernaum of Galilee. Jesus' movements describe a well-defined arc in Mark, from Galilee, to the region to the north, and back again toward a resolution of the drama in Jerusalem. John presents a rather confused back-and-forth movement between Galilee and Jerusalem, with no foray to the north. Whether Mark's plan derives from a source or is redactional, it is not found in John. The liminal significance of Caesarea Philippi, however, may express a cultic concern: the area was known as a prominent place for revelations. George W. E. Nickelsburg notes ("Enoch, Levi, and Peter: Recipients of Revelation in Upper Galilee," *JBL* 100 [1981] 575–600) that *1 Enoch* 12–16 is set in Dan, about three miles from Caesarea Philippi. But Mark's injunction to keep silence at verse 30 (a substitution for the renaming of Peter) is likely redactional, and is also lacking in John.

60 To judge from the wide attestation of these sayings independently in early Christianity, however, they were probably not originally grouped. Mark 9: 1 is also paralleled at John 8: 51–52, but this saying may have been transmitted independently of any of these narrative contexts. On the independent circulation of these sayings, see Bultmann, *History*, pp. 82–83; Cameron, *Sayings Traditions*, pp. 87–88.

61 At the same time, each passage has a possible parallel elsewhere in the other gospel: "my words" at Mark 8: 38 finds echoes at John 5: 24; 8: 31, 51; and 14: 23–24. Likewise, the wisdom saying at John 12: 24 has a parabolic quality on its own, quite similar to the parables in Mark 4. See Dodd, *Historical Tradition*, pp. 366–69, 338–43; Brown *John*, pp. 1.471–73. Thus the argument that Mark and John both knew these sections connected in the tradition is made somewhat weaker by the independent attestation of the sayings.

62 Smith, *Clement of Alexandria and a Secret Gospel of Mark*, Cambridge, Mass.: Harvard University Press, 1973. There is some controversy over the text, since western scholars other than Smith have not seen the manuscript. It is reportedly under the protection of officials of the Mar Saba monastery, where it was found. However, the possibility of a forgery has been raised gratuitously, and is highly unlikely. See the discussion in John Dominic Crossan, *Four Other Gospels: Shadows on the Contours of Canon*, Minneapolis: Winston, 1985, pp. 91–121.

The English translation used here is my own, based on the Greek text as provided by Smith. The numbering follows the translation of Stephen J. Patterson, in Robert J. Miller (ed.), *The Complete Gospels*, San Francisco: Polebridge, 1992, p. 411. Another translation with introduction is found in Ron Cameron, *The Other Gospels: Non-Canonical Gospel Texts*, Philadelphia: Westminster, 1982, pp. 67–71.

63 Crossan, *Four Other Gospels*, pp. 104–10; Koester, *Ancient Christian Gospels*, pp. 293–303. Arguing less assuredly for the independence from John is Raymond Brown, "The Relation of 'The Secret Gospel of Mark' to the Fourth Gospel," *CBQ* 36 (1974) 466–85.

64 Other passages in canonical Mark that are parallel to *Secret Mark* include 4: 11; 9: 25–27; and 10: 21. Koester notes, however (*Ancient Christian Gospels*, pp. 297–98), that some of these parallels in Mark are not taken up by Matthew and Luke, and may not have been in the texts of Mark that they used. See Koester's complicated but ultimately convincing discussion (pp. 298–303) of the probable stages of Mark and *Secret Mark*. Crossan, *Four Other Gospels*, pp. 107–10, assumes more simply that *Secret Mark* is the earliest version of Mark for which we have evidence, and that canonical Mark arises as a result of the elimination of this and other passages. For our present purposes, it is only necessary to argue that *Secret Mark* is early, and occurred in some form at this point in the literary structure of the early gospel narrative tradition.

65 So, rightly, Brown, *John*, p. 1.423, though Bultmann, *John*, p. 304, n. 6 disagrees. The difficult emotional response of Jesus in verses 33 and 38 may also parallel Jesus' anger in *Secret Mark*. Do both cases reflect a story in which the miracle worker is angry at the demonic realm? Compare Mark 1: 43 and the variant reading at Mark 1: 41, and see also Barnabas

Lindars, "Rebuking the Spirit: A New Analysis of the Lazarus Story of John 11," *NTS* 38 (1992) 89–104.

66 It is possible that Lazarus was to be understood as the "disciple whom Jesus loved" of 13: 23; 19: 26; 20: 2, etc., through an esoteric reading of the text; so Floyd Filson, "Who Was the Beloved Disciple?," *JBL* 68 (1949) 83–88, but Brown, *John*, p. 1.xcv, disagrees. Marvin W. Meyer has recently pressed Filson's argument further ("The Youth in *Secret Mark* and the Beloved Disciple in John," in James E. Goehring, *et al.* (eds), *Gospel Origins and Christian Beginnings*, Sonoma, Calif.: Polebridge, 1990, pp. 94–105): the youth in *Secret Mark*, Lazarus, and the disciple whom Jesus loved in John all have many similar traits. Meyer suggests that they all derive from a tradition of the ideal disciple who is initiated into Jesus' teaching.

67 Brown, *John*, pp. 1.442–4, has suggested that this section of John is parallel to the parable of the wicked tenants who kill the son of the master of the vineyard (Mark 12: 1–11), but this parallel is tenuous. He sees a similarity partly in that both passages describe the death of Jesus and God's choice of a new people, but the Caiaphas oracle is primitive, and speaks, I believe, of a redemption of the people of Israel through the death of Jesus.

68 Dibelius, *Message of Jesus Christ*, New York: Scribner's, 1939, p. 138.

69 Q contained a version of this exchange, still visible in Luke 22: 24–27 (Matt 20: 20–23 is influenced more by Mark). Here we also see the political overtones of the challenge to worldly hierarchies, and the first response of Mark 10: 38–40 is not present. Therefore, the evidence of Q would also indicate that the second response is older.

70 Dodd, "The Prophecy of Caiaphas: John xi 47–53," *Neotestamentica et Patristica*, Festschrift Cullmann, NTSupp. VI, Leiden: Brill, 1962, pp. 134–42; compare also Till Arend Mohr, *Markus- und Johannespassion: Redaktions- und traditionsgeschichtliche Untersuchung der Markinischen und Johanneischen Passionstradition*, Zurich: Theologischer Verlag, 1982, pp. 125–28, on the traditional nature of this passage. According to Martin Hengel, *The Atonement: The Origins of the Doctrine in the New Testament*, Philadelphia: Fortress, 1981, pp. 14, 23, the motif of the prediction of the death of the hero is common in hero legends. The difficult problems concerning the existence of prophecy and attitudes toward prophecy in the first century need not be addressed here, if we allow that it is an important *literary* motif. This question will be taken up again in chapter 4.

71 Contra Brown, *John*, p. 1.440, who believes that the in-gathering of Gentiles must be meant.

72 R. H. Lightfoot, *The Gospel Message of St. Mark*, Oxford: Clarendon, 1950, p. 61, followed by Nineham, *Saint Mark*, pp. 289–90. Compare also Bultmann, *History*, pp. 275–84.

73 Compare "astounded at his teaching" at Mark 1: 22, which forms an *inclusio* with Mark 11: 18 that encompasses the period of Jesus' ministry. John's parallel to Mark 11: 18 has the people astounded at Jesus' *learning*, not his *teaching*. The former was probably present in the tradition, but the latter is Mark's own redaction. Joachim Jeremias, expanding on some of these same points, also asserted that one early version of the passion narrative began with the triumphal entry (*Eucharistic Words of Jesus*, 3rd ed., New York: Scribners, 1966, pp. 89–96). He noted that from chapter 11 onward Mark presents a very cogent narrative, with clear geographical and temporal markers, which is unlike the somewhat episodic nature of the rest of Mark. Jeremias then proceeds, however, to argue that behind this long passion account there existed a shorter passion account, which began with the arrest of Jesus and went through the crucifixion. Jeremias points out that the passion predictions in Mark 8: 31; 9: 31; and 10: 33–34 all refer to the events in this short account, and never to the events which precede it in the long account. However, even if a short source behind the passion narrative can be reconstructed, it is irrelevant to the isolation of an earlier narrative, since the latter would likely have contained the longer passion account, as John indicates.

74 Vernon K. Robbins, "Last Meal: Preparation, Betrayal, and Absence (Mark 14: 12–25)," in Werner Kelber (ed.), *The Passion in Mark: Studies on Mark 14–16*, Philadelphia: Fortress,

1976, p. 36; Elisabeth Schüssler Fiorenza, *In Memory of Her: A Feminist Theological Reconstruction of Christian Origins*, New York: Crossroads, 1983, pp. 319–21; Nineham, *Saint Mark*, pp. 370–73, who also notes that Mark 14: 1–2 connects more smoothly with verses 10–11.

75 Bultmann, *History*, pp. 261–64; Robbins ("Last Meal," p. 23) argues that this section is redactional because it is constructed as a preparation for the Last Supper.

76 Nineham, *Saint Mark*, pp. 291–92. John 7: 27 introduces the issue of a hidden Messiah, but expressed in a very different way.

77 John 12: 16 interrupts the narrative and informs us that the disciples did not remember and understand this until later. It seems likely here that an earlier prophecy/fulfillment motif has been reinterpreted as remembering and understanding the fulfillment, under the influence of the tradition of remembering the words of Jesus found elsewhere in John.

It is interesting that Ismo Dunderberg (*Johannes und die Synoptiker*, pp. 28–29) takes this verse as evidence that John is dependent upon Mark, because the seemingly insignificant reference to the disciples here in John appears to depend upon the more logical and integrated role of the disciples in Mark 11: 1–11. This example is significant because D. Moody Smith (review of Dunderberg, *JBL* 115 [1996] 151), who had formerly argued for John's independence of Mark, followed Dunderberg in this conclusion. However, John 12: 16 does not indicate influence of the text of Mark; it is simply another example of the common Johannine theme of apostolic remembering, on which see Cameron, *Sayings Traditions*, pp. 116–19.

78 Brown, *John*, pp. 1.117–18, Bultmann, *John*, pp. 128–29. Bultmann notes that by placing the temple expulsion early, John associates the *arche* with the *telos*, the beginning with the end, in that the *semeion* is presented at the temple, which will bring the Jews who have disbelieved into judgment. Compare, however, the balanced discussion of Wolfgang Reinbold, *Der älteste Bericht über den Tod Jesu: Literarische Analyse und historische Kritik der Passionsdarstellungen der Evangelien*, Berlin/New York: de Gruyter, 1994, pp. 112–18, who finally decides that the Markan order is not original.

79 Wilhelm Wilkens (*Die Entstehungsgeschichte des vierten Evangeliums*, Zollikon: Evangelischer Verlag, 1958) postulates that the three Passovers in John that do not have synoptic parallels, 2: 13; 6: 4; and 11: 55, were created when material formerly in the passion was moved earlier in the gospel. This is not likely true in all three cases, but probably does account for 2: 13.

80 Chilton, *The Temple of Jesus: His Social Program within a Cultural History of Sacrifice*, University Park, Penn.: Pennsylvania State University Press, 1992. A more general eschatological condemnation is more likely, and the belief in a new eschatological temple was known before the time of Jesus; compare *1 Enoch* 90: 28f, Tobit 13: 16; 14: 5. Jesus' utterance in John is similar to Zeph 1: 9: "On that day I shall punish all (the worshippers of the god Dagon), who fill their master's house with violence and fraud." In the case of Zephaniah there is a particular theological abuse in mind, but John is simply not clear. The provoking condemnation is *generalized*, just as it is in *Life of Aesop*.

81 Mark 11: 17 was probably added by Mark; so Kee, *Community*, p. 52.

82 Bultmann, *History*, p. 20; Dodd, *Historical Tradition*, pp. 156–62.

83 Vernon K. Robbins, "*Dunameis* and *Semeia* in Mark," in *idem*, *New Boundaries in Old Territory: Form and Social Rhetoric in Mark*, New York: Peter Lang, 1994, pp. 59–72.

84 Sanders, *Jesus and Judaism*; Crossan, *Historical Jesus*, pp. 355–60; Mohr, *Markus- und Johannespassion*, pp. 106–108. Despite Craig A. Evans' objections ("Jesus' Action in the Temple: Cleansing or Portent of Destruction?," *CBQ* 51 [1989] 237–70), Sanders is essentially correct in his argumentation. Compare also Adela Yarbro Collins, "The Influence of Daniel on the New Testament," in John J. Collins (ed.), *Daniel: A Commentary on the Book of David*, Minneapolis: Augsburg Fortress, 1993, p. 92.

85 Although it has been mentioned once before at 3: 6, where it is the "Pharisees and

Herodians," not the "chief priests and scribes," who conspire. See the concluding chapter on this question of Jewish opponents.

86 The Mount of Olives appears as a location of a discourse at John 8: 1, but this is likely a later addition to the gospel. On Mark/John parallels here in general, see Brown, *John*, p. 2.595, and Dale C. Allison, *The End of the Ages Has Come*, Philadelphia: Fortress, 1985.

87 Robbins, "*Dunameis* and *Semeia*." John's use of *semeion* in general reflects the same background-tradition, but John alters the use of the term in a way ignorant of and foreign to Mark's usage: John de-eschatologizes *semeion* at the same time that Jesus is identified as the one sent from above.

88 There has been a good deal of source analysis of this section. Vincent Taylor (*The Gospel According to Mark*, London: Macmillan, 1952, pp. 653–64) provides a very ambitious and clearly argued source division of Mark 14–15, dividing it into two strands, A and B, using both thematic and linguistic criteria. A is the connected narrative which was the basis of Mark's passion account, written in a somewhat better Greek style than is the norm in Mark. Among the themes associated with A are the use of *paradidomi* ("to betray"), reference to the twelve, and attention to prophecy and fulfillment of Jewish scriptures. The B strand lacks these themes and is marked by Semitisms. Ivor Buse ("St John and the Marcan Passion Narrative," *NTS* 4 [1957–58] 215–19) argues that of Taylor's two suggested layers, only one, the "B" layer, contains significant parallels to John's passion account, but Brown, *John*, p. 2.914 disagrees. Brown does suggest that Bultmann's division produces a closer relation between one of Mark's sources and John.

   A detailed summary of scholarly attempts to divide the passion into sources can be found in Marion L. Soards, "The Question of a Premarcan Passion Narrative," in Raymond Brown (ed.), *The Death of the Messiah*, 2 vols, New York: Doubleday, 1994, pp. 2.1492–1524. A critical survey of some recent analyses can also be found in Mack, *Myth*, pp. 258–62. Important scholarly analyses include Eta Linnemann, *Studien zur Passionsgeschichte*, Göttingen: Vandenhoeck & Ruprecht, 1970; Rudolph Pesch, *Das Markusevangelium*, 2 vols, 3rd ed., Freiburg/Basle/Vienna: Herder, 1980, pp. 2.1–27; Detlev Dormeyer, *Die Passion Jesu als Verhaltensmodell*, Münster: Aschendorff, 1974. The studies of Joel B. Green, *The Death of Jesus: Tradition and Interpretation in the Passion Narrative*, Tübingen: Mohr (Paul Siebeck), 1988, pp. 187–217, and Reinbold, *Der älteste Bericht*, both assume that John is independent of Mark. Anton Dauer, *Die Passionsgeschichte im Johannesevangelium: Eine traditionsgeschichtliche und theologische Untersuchung zu Joh 18,1–19,30*, Munich: Kösel-Verlag, 1972, does not posit any direct influence of Mark on John, but argues instead that Matthew and Luke have influenced the oral traditions about the death of Jesus, with which John is familiar. Because the present study is limited to the relations of Mark and John, Dauer's study will not be as relevant as the other works.

89 The relation of the three passages is unclear. In Luke, the woman wipes Jesus' feet as in John, but the nard appears to have been added secondarily to a story about a woman who anoints Jesus' feet with her tears. Mack believes (*Myth*, pp. 199–204, 384) that a *chreia* challenge/response lies behind all three passages. An objection is raised to Jesus' being anointed by a woman, and the original response is "She has done a beautiful thing to me." If this was the case, then the *chreia* response was likely elaborated before Mark and John made use of it.

90 Robbins argues ("Last Meal: Preparation, Betrayal, and Absence [Mark 14: 12–25]," in Kelber [ed.], *Passion*, p. 36) that the emphasis on the memorial to Jesus is moved by Mark from the Last Supper to the anointing precisely in order to avoid the making of a cult ritual for the dead hero. If this is so, then it only serves to bolster my general thesis that the pre-Markan narrative is concerned with the cult of the dead hero, and that Mark and John begin to move in new directions that obscure the earlier theme.

91 Schüssler Fiorenza, *In Memory of Her*, pp. 319–21. It is interesting that the figures in Secret Mark are unnamed as well, while their counterparts in John are, as here, Mary, Martha, and Lazarus.

92 Compare the discussion by Green, *Death of Jesus*, pp. 106–11, which comes to similar conclusions about the independence of John here.

93 See, for example, Brown, *John*, pp. 2.555–56; Anthony J. Saldarini, *Jesus and Passover*, New York: Paulist, 1984, pp. 56–57. Green, *Death of Jesus*, pp. 111–25, argues that John is independent of Mark throughout this section, rebutting the arguments to the contrary by M. Sabbe, "The Footwashing in Jn 13 and its Relation to the Synoptic Gospels," *Ephemerides theologicae lovanienses* 58 (1982) 279–308.

94 Koester, "The Historical Jesus and the Cult of the *Kyrios Christos*," *Harvard Divinity Bulletin* 24 (1995) 13–18.

95 Michael Cook's very intriguing analysis (*Mark's Treatment of the Jewish Leaders* [Leiden: Brill, 1978]) comes to conclusions similar, but not identical to my own. See chapter 4 below for a discussion of his theory.

96 So Brown, *John*, p. 1.470, but compare Kelber, "The Hour of the Son of Man and the Temptation of the Disciples," in Kelber (ed.), *Passion*, p. 56, who asserts that Mark's quotation is of Ps 42: 6, 12; 43: 5, and John's of Ps 6: 4–5.

97 Brown, *John*, p. 1.475, probably overemphasizes the "suffering" Jesus in John at this point. The source of John may have included this motif, but the redactor limits it.

98 Kelber, "Hour of the Son of Man." Compare the treatment by Mohr, *Markus- und Johannespassion*, pp. 245–48, which posits a traditional garden narrative behind both Mark and John here.

99 With Glusman, "Criteria," pp. 243–44. Dauer, *Passionsgeschichte im Johannesevangelium*, pp. 51–56, argues that John is here indebted to the oral tradition that was created by the texts of Matthew and Luke, a sort of "secondary orality," and not by the text of Mark, but Raymond Brown's review (*JBL* 92 [1973] 608–10) rightly points out that these motifs are likely traditional, and not the creations of Matthew or Luke.

100 John R. Donahue, "Temple, Trial and Royal Christology (Mark 14: 53–65)," in Kelber (ed.), *Passion*, pp. 61–79. The summary of the difficulties of the text given here is based on Donahue's article and Linnemann, *Studien zur Passionsgeschichte*, pp. 109–10. See also above re Mark 14: 1.

101 Donahue ("Temple," p. 65, and *idem, Are You the Christ?*, pp. 53–102) would see less that is traditional here in Mark than I would, but he makes a very interesting point in suggesting that the actual elements that emphasize a *trial* are Markan. We note, however, that they are lacking in John, as Glusman, "Criteria," p. 244, also points out. See also Green, *Death of Jesus*, pp. 125–27, who argues for the independence of John in this section.

102 The location of the Sanhedrin deliberation remains a difficulty. Was it parallel to Mark 10: 35–45, as it is now in John, or later, as a prelude to the high priest's interrogation? The senseless transitions at John 18: 24, 28 indicate that an interrogation before Caiaphas may have been eliminated there, but it is perhaps more likely that the Sanhedrin deliberation was earlier in the narrative.

103 The fact that John has *eutheos* here does not mean that it is taken from Mark's very typical *euthus*. Although Mark does use the latter often, it is not exclusively "Markan." The constant use of both Greek words in Mark and John is probably derived from Aramaic *'adayin*, which can mean "immediately," but is also often used as a transitional adverb in narrative.

104 Perrin, *A Modern Pilgrimage in New Testament Christology*, Philadelphia: Fortress, 1974, pp. 122–28; Donahue, *Are You the Christ?*, pp. 58–63. Treated in Donahue's study are the following pericopes, divided here into frame narrative/core narrative/frame narrative: 3: 20–21/22–30/31–35; 5: 21–24/25–34/35–43; 6: 7–13/14–29/30–32; 11: 12–14/15–19/20–26; 14: 1–2/3–9/10–11; 14: 12–16/17–21/22–25; 14: 53–54/55–65/66–72.

105 See also C. A. Evans, "Peter Warming Himself: The Problem of an Editorial 'Seam,'" *JBL* 101 (1982) 245–49, who notes this technique in Achilles Tatius, *Leucippe and Clitophon*

2.2.1 (resumes in 2.3.1), and 2.11.1 (resumes in 2.12.1). See also Wills, *The Jewish Novel in the Ancient World*, Ithaca/London: Cornell University Press, 1995, on the general question of popular novelistic literature in the milieu of the gospels. Joanna Dewey, "Oral Methods of Structuring Narrative in Mark," 32–44, would see this technique as oral and not novelistic in its use. Although I would see it as both, if she were right, then certainly it could not be claimed that John borrowed the structuring principle from Mark; it would have been in the public domain of oral story telling.

106 So Evans, "Peter," p. 247.

107 Auerbach, *Mimesis: The Representation of Reality in Western Literature*, Princeton: Princeton University Press, 1953, p. 42.

108 As noted in chapter 2, the Barabbas episode has parallels in the installation of a mock-king or the scourging of a substitute sacrifice, a scapegoat. It is interesting that in *Gospel of Peter* 3 this theme is, if anything, even more concentrated.

109 Brown, *John*, pp. 2.858–59; *idem, Death*, p. 1.757–59.

110 On Paul's defense of himself as the true philosopher, see Hans Dieter Betz, *Der Apostel Paulus und die sokratische Tradition: Eine exegetische Untersuchung zu seiner "Apologie" 2 Korinther 10–13*, Tübingen: Mohr (Paul Siebeck, 1972).

111 Matera, *The Kingship of Jesus: Composition and Theology in Mark 15*, Chico, Calif.: Scholars, 1982, esp. pp. 57–66.

112 Even some apparent influences of Mark's redaction in John disappear on closer inspection. John's hour designation in 19: 14 is parallel to one of Mark's five time designations in chapter 15, but John's timing of the crucifixion on the day before the Passover is usually considered a more primitive tradition, and unlike Mark's time designations, it actually makes sense: the sixth hour on the day of Preparation is the time when the Passover lambs were slaughtered. Mark has likely expanded this or a similar time designation into the present schema.

113 Adela Yarbro Collins, "Finding Meaning in the Death of Jesus," forthcoming.

114 Many scholars have postulated a separate early source for the crucifixion scene, which may have become the core of an elongated passion narrative. The special exegetical nature of this section should be noted, and is treated fully by Koester, *Ancient Christian Gospels*, pp. 216–40, on which see below. If it is true, as Koester argues, that *Barnabas* 7.7–11 reflects an earlier exegetical tradition that "generates" passion motifs, then that would indicate some independence of the passion from the larger narrative. Nevertheless, it is my view that such a crucifixion narrative would have been incorporated into the larger narrative that runs the length of the gospel.

115 For example, Alfred Suhl, *Die Funktion der alttestamentlichen Zitate und Anspielungen im Markusevangelium*, Gütersloh: Gütersloher/Gerd Mohn, 1965, pp. 46–47. Douglas Moo (*The Old Testament in the Gospel Passion Narratives*, Sheffield: Almond, 1983, pp. 358–59, and D. Moody Smith ("The Use of the Old Testament in the New," in James M. Efird (ed.), *The Use of the Old Testament in the New and Other Essays*, Durham, N. C.: Duke University Press, 1972, p. 42) have tried to refute Suhl, but unconvincingly. Despite some examples of the more primitive form of prophecy/fulfillment (Mark 14: 27), Mark's general tendency is as Suhl has suggested. Compare also George W. E. Nickelsburg, "The Genre and Function of the Markan Passion Narrative," *HTR* 73 (1980) 153–84.

116 Koester, *Ancient Christian Gospels*, pp. 222–30, shows convincingly that the crucifixion scene is developed from an exegetical tradition that explores motifs found in the scapegoat ritual of Leviticus 16, elaborated with reference to Isa 50: 6; Ps 69: 21; and Zech 12: 10 (see chapter 2 above). *Gospel of Peter* is dependent on this pre-Markan exegetical tradition (found also in *Barnabas* 7.7–11), not on the canonical gospels. We also see in Mark what is likely a development beyond John in multiplying the correspondences to scripture and separating them into separate scenes.

Mark's extension of the mocking in 15: 29–32 has also rightly been attributed to

Mark's redaction (Bultmann, *History*, p. 271; Ernest Best, *The Temptation and the Passion: The Markan Soteriology*, Cambridge: Cambridge University Press, 1965, pp. 96–97), and is similarly not found in John. See Brown, *Death*, pp. 1.568–86 for a comparison of the mocking scenes, which Brown would trace back to a historical event; this goes beyond the evidence.

117 A different expression is used at John 19: 13, 17, 20 (*hebraisti*); the second of these is parallel to Mark 15: 22.

118 On the economy of John here, note the intriguing theory expressed by Alexander Rofé some years ago ("The Classification of the Prophetical Stories," *JBL* 89 [1970] 427–40), that the Deuteronomistic history contains written summaries or skeletal outlines of much longer oral traditions about the prophets, which are now, of course, lost to us. This explains the economy of those accounts, and their lack of detail. The same phenomenon may be reflected here.

Koester also notes (*Ancient Christian Gospels*, p. 230) that although "completed" becomes a very "Johannine" term in John's Gospel (compare 4: 34; 5: 36; 17: 4), in John's passion source it may have referred to the completion of the biblical testimonies.

119 Dodd, "The Appearances of the Risen Christ: An Essay in Form-Criticism of the Gospels," in *idem, Studies in the Gospels*, Oxford: Basil Blackwell, 1957, pp. 9–35, esp. 33; Brown, *John*, pp. 2.967, 1003. Paul Mirecki, "Mark 16: 9–20: Composition, Tradition, and Redaction," unpublished Th.D. dissertation, Harvard Divinity School, 1987.

120 Contrast Mark 9: 3; Matt 28: 2–3; Luke 24: 4; John 20: 12; *Gospel of Peter* 13.55. It was noted above that Meyer ("Youth in *Secret Mark*") connects this "young man" with the one found in Secret Mark, as well as with Lazarus and "the disciple whom Jesus loved" in John.

121 Andreas Lindemann, "Die Osterbotschaft des Markus: Zur theologischen Interpretation von Mark 16.1–8," *NTS* 26 (1980) 298–317.

122 Crossan, *The Cross That Spoke: The Origins of the Passion Narrative*, San Francisco: Harper & Row, 1988, pp. 15–30, believes that while part of the *Gospel of Peter* is early, certain sections, including the parallel to Mark 16: 1–8, are late and dependent upon the canonical gospels. Koester has argued, however (*Ancient Christian Gospels*, pp. 216–40, esp. p. 231), that aside from occasional later harmonizations with the canonical gospels, the *Gospel of Peter* represents an old, independent tradition, even here in the empty tomb scene. See also Arthur Dewey, "'Time to Murder and Create': Visions and Revisions in the *Gospel of Peter*," *Semeia* 49 (1990) 101–27, who discerns stages in the development of the *Gospel of Peter*, but does not posit any influence of the canonical gospels, and Brown, *Death*, 2.1332–36, who argues that the *Gospel of Peter* is indirectly dependent upon the canonical gospels.

A further problem is the parallel between the end of the *Gospel of Peter*, which is broken off, and John 21, which most scholars believe was added to John (see below). My own view is that the material in the *Gospel of Peter* that is parallel to John 21 is late, as argued by Dewey, but the question is enormously complicated. The main question is the presence of a commissioning scene in the earliest tradition. John 21 includes such a scene ("Feed my sheep"), as does the Longer Ending and John 20, but the variety of early Christian commissioning scenes and appearances to Peter make it difficult to posit any early connection among them. See Koester, *Introduction*, 2.161.

Without reference to the *Gospel of Peter*, Ludger Schenke also reconstructs an early tradition within Mark 16: 1–8 consisting of Mark 16: 2, 5–6, 8a (*Auferstehungsverkündigung und leeres Grab: eine traditionsgeschichtliche Untersuchung von Mk. 16, 1–8*, Stuttgart: Katholisches Bibelwerk, 1968, pp. 11–30, esp. pp. 29–30), but some of the verses that he excludes from the source are present in the *Gospel of Peter*. His reconstruction is thus contradicted by the evidence of the latter. He also argues, however, that the source (whatever verses are included) was a cult legend of the early Christians in Jerusalem who worshiped at the site of the empty tomb. As much as this latter suggestion would reinforce my thesis in chapter 2 it is probably incorrect to imagine an actual cult at the tomb of Jesus. The criticisms of Hans Dieter Betz ("Zum Problem der Auferstehung Jesu," in *idem*, *Hellenismus und Urchristentum*, 3 vols, Tübingen: Mohr [Paul Siebeck], 1990, pp. 1.245–47), to the effect that early Christians show no evidence of any interest in the tomb of Jesus until the fourth century, is considerably blunted if we view the hero cult as a literary topos, a "cult of remembrance," which may have lacked any actual tomb cult, *or if* we look to Galilee as a locus of the resurrected Jesus.

123 Bickerman, "Das leere Grab," *ZNW* 23 (1924) 281–92, repr. in *idem*, *Studies in Jewish and Christian History*, 3 vols, Leiden: Brill, 1986, pp. 3.70–81. See also Brown, *John*, pp. 2.978, 1027–28; Gerd Luedemann, *The Resurrection of Jesus: History, Exposition, Theology*, London: SCM, 1994, p. 171; and Martin Hengel, "Maria Magdalena und die Frauen als Zeugen," in *idem*, Otto Betz, and Peter Schmidt (eds), *Abraham Unser Vater: Jüden und Christen im Gespräch über die Bibel*, Leiden: Brill, 1963, pp. 243–56, who also asserts that the appearance to Mary Magdalene is a separate tradition from the empty tomb.

124 Though some, for example, Luedemann (*Resurrection*, pp. 119–21), have argued that Bickerman may have overdrawn the distinction and the relative ages of the traditions. Luedemann considers, for example, the fascinating parallel from Herodotus 4.14–15, where the poet Aristeas disappears from the site of his death and reappears later. A "mirror" account is told of a charlatan who fakes his disappearance and reappearance, Herodotus 4.94–95.

125 This is the only point at which the *Gospel of Peter* also agrees with the Longer Ending and John over against canonical Mark; it is likely an early tradition that has been expanded to include other women in the synoptic gospels.

126 The break between the end of chapter 20 and the beginning of chapter 21 is very awkward, and the latter introduces episodes which seem anticlimactic, and may in some cases have been based on incidents in the life of Jesus, now transferred to a post-resurrection setting. The disjunction is simply too great to reconcile chapter 21 to the rest of the gospel; the verses at 20: 30–31 were thus at one time probably the conclusion of the whole gospel, but may also have been the conclusion of the Signs Source. It has also been argued, however (Fortna, *Gospel*, pp. 7–8, 87–88), that 20: 30–31 sounds like the conclusion of the gospel only because it was originally the conclusion to the Signs Source, and that the break between chapter 20 and 21 is no greater than some of the other awkward disjunctions in John. See also P. S. Minear, "The Original Functions of John 21," *JBL* 102 (1983) 85–98.

127 Brown, *John*, pp. 2.995–96, 999. It is possible, however, that the race to the tomb is a reworking of an early tradition in which Jesus appears to two men. The order of events in the Longer Ending and John 20 is almost parallel at this point when the race to the tomb is included:

John 20	Longer Ending
Mary	Mary
two disciples	two disciples
Mary	
the eleven	the eleven

The repetition of Mary in John 20 may result from the reworking process. The difficulty with this hypothesis is that John 20: 11 re Mary appears at one time to have followed directly upon 20: 1. Be that as it may, the parallel structure of John 20 and the Longer Ending at this point is still intriguing.

4 CONCLUSION

1 Boismard (with A. Lamouille), *L'Evangile de Jean* (*Synopse des quatre évangiles*, vol. 3), Paris: Cerf, 1977; Fortna, *The Gospel of Signs: A Reconstruction of the Narrative Source Underlying the Fourth Gospel*, Cambridge: Cambridge University Press, 1970; and

Teeple, *The Literary Origin of the Gospel of John*, Evanston: Religion and Ethics Institute, 1974.

2 Rebecca Gray, *Prophetic Figures in Late Second Temple Jewish Palestine: The Evidence from Josephus*, New York: Oxford University Press, 1993, pp. 7–34; Josephus, *Antiquities* 4.8.44 §§313–14, *Jewish War* 3.8.3 §§352–54, *Against Apion* 1.41, and see Louis H. Feldman, "Prophets and Prophecy in Josephus," *JTS* 41 (1990) 386–422, esp. 404–5, and the review of Gray by Steve Mason, *JBL* 114 (1995) 308–12.

3 Dodd, *Historical Tradition in the Fourth Gospel*, Cambridge: Cambridge University Press, 1963, p. 214; Gray, *Prophetic Figures*, p. 124.

4 Sommer, "Did Prophecy Cease? Evaluating a Reevaluation," *JBL* 115 (1996) 31–47.

5 Horsley, "'Like One of the Prophets of Old': Two Types of Popular Prophets at the Time of Jesus," *CBQ* 47 (1985) 435–63.

6 See David E. Aune, *Prophecy in Early Christianity and the Ancient Mediterranean World*, Grand Rapids, Mich.: Eerdmans, 1983; M. Eugene Boring, *Sayings of the Risen Jesus: Christian Prophecy in the Synoptic Tradition* (Cambridge: Cambridge University Press, 1982); David Hill, *New Testament Prophecy*, Atlanta: John Knox Press, 1979, pp. 48–69; and Antoinette Clark Wire, *The Corinthian Women Prophets: A Reconstruction through Paul's Rhetoric*, Minneapolis: Fortress, 1990.

7 If we accept John Kloppenborg's division of Q into two main layers (*The Formation of Q: Trajectories in Ancient Wisdom Collections*, Philadelphia: Fortress, 1987, pp. 173, 227–29), then the prophetic passages are found only in the second, apocalyptic overlay. Note below, however, the challenges to Kloppenborg's division of Q put forward by Adela Yarbro Collins and Horsley.

8 Horsley also points out ("Like One of the Prophets of Old," p. 453) that there is a strong association of the prophets with the rural areas, and that they were considered by Josephus to be unlearned.

9 *Antiquities* 12.4.3 §173; *Apollonius* 6.34; Herodotus 1.27.

10 Raymond Brown, *The Gospel According to John*, 2 vols, Garden City, N. Y.: Doubleday, 1964–70, p. 1.246; J. Louis Martyn, *History and Theology in the Fourth Gospel*, New York and Evanston: Harper & Row, 1968; Howard M. Teeple, *The Mosaic Eschatological Prophet*, Philadelphia: Society of Biblical Literature, 1957; and M.-E. Boismard, *Moses or Jesus: An Essay in Johannine Christology*, Minneapolis: Fortress/Leuven: Peeters, 1993. Roughly contemporary evidence for the existence of an expectation of a prophet like Moses can also be seen in 1QS 9: 11 and 4QTest from Qumran, and Acts 3: 22.

11 Karl Kertelge, *Die Wunder im Markusevangelium: Eine redaktionsgeschichtliche Untersuchung*, Munich: Kösel, 1970, pp. 23–27; Gray, *Prophetic Figures*, pp. 123–44, esp. 125–30; E. P. Sanders, *Jesus and Judaism*, Philadelphia: Fortress, 1985, pp. 172–73; Ferdinand Hahn, *The Titles of Jesus in Christology: Their History in Early Christianity*, New York: World, 1969, pp. 352–406; and Brown, John, p. 1.529.

12 Draper, "The Development of 'The Sign of the Son of Man' in the Jesus Tradition," *NTS* 39 (1993) 1–21.

13 Meeks, *The Prophet-King: Moses Traditions and Johannine Christology*, Leiden, Brill: 1967; Aune, *Prophecy in Early Christianity*, pp. 153–57; Brown, *John*, p. 1.485; André Feuillet, *Johannine Studies*, Staten Island: Alba House, 1965, pp. 58–66; Boismard, *Moses or Jesus*, p. 66; and J. A. T. Robinson, "The Most Primitive Christology of All?," *JTS* 7 (1956) 177–89. Compare the paraclete as prophet: Bruce Vawter, "Ezechiel and John," *CBQ* 26 (1964) 451–58. According to Meeks and T. Francis Glasson, *Moses in the Fourth Gospel*, London: SCM, 1963, p. 31, the references to Jesus as king in John are not likely a "Davidic" christology, but a Mosaic one.

14 Smith, "Exodus Typology in the Fourth Gospel," *JBL* 81 (1962) 329–42. Douglas K. Clark, "Signs in Wisdom and John," *CBQ* 45 (1983) 201–9, also argues that the signs in John are parallel to Wisdom of Solomon 11–19, which contrasts the seven *semeia* of Moses

that give benefits with the punishments against Pharaoh.

15 Brown, *John*, pp. 1.234–35 notes that John 6: 14–15 could have been an independent saying, and in that case the prophet to come would not have referred to Moses, but more likely Elijah. Still, Moses is never out of sight in the Johannine tradition.

16 For example, Howard Clark Kee's *Community of the New Age: Studies in Mark's Gospel*, Philadelphia: Westminster, 1977, pp. 45–46, 78, 87–88, 148; Aune, *The New Testament in its Literary Environment*, Philadelphia: Westminster, 1987, pp. 54, 153–57, 171–83; and Vernon Robbins, *Jesus the Teacher: A Socio-Rhetorical Interpretation of Mark*, Philadelphia: Fortress, 1984, pp. 185–86.

17 W. E. Beare, *The Earliest Records of Jesus*, Oxford: Basil Blackwell, 1964, pp. 142–43; Hobbs, "The Gospel of Mark and the Exodus" unpublished Ph.D. dissertation, University of Chicago, 1958.

18 Baltzer, Die Biographie der Propheten (Neukirchen-Vluyn: Neukirchener Verlag, 1975), pp. 184–89.

19 Smith (responding to Kee) in Kee, *Aretalogies, Hellenistic "Lives," and the Sources of Mark*, Berkeley: Center for Hermeneutical Studies, 1975, pp. 32–35.

20 Robbins, "*Dunameis* and *Semeia* in Mark," in *idem, New Boundaries in Old Territory: Form and Social Rhetoric in Mark*, New York: Peter Lang, 1994, pp. 59–72. See also Gray, Prophetic Figures, pp. 125–33.

21 Peter Riga, "Signs of Glory: The Use of 'Semeion' in St. John's Gospel," *Interpretation* 17 (1963) 402–10. On the importance of the kingdom in Mark, see below.

22 One need not posit Rudolf Bultmann's Revelation Discourse source as the basis of John's discourse material to see here a pre-Johannine development of the sayings tradition. See Helmut Koester, *Ancient Christian Gospels: Their History and Development*, Philadelphia: Trinity Press International, 1990, pp. 173–200, 256–67.

23 Fortna. See p. 231 on the lack of exorcisms in John.

24 Mack, *A Myth of Innocence: Mark and Christian Origins*, Philadelphia: Fortress, 1988, pp. 221–22.

25 Kolenkow, "Healing Controversy as a Tie Between Miracle and Passion Material for a Proto-Gospel," *JBL* 95 (1976) 623–38.

26 Fortna, *Gospel*, pp. 41, 233.

27 Bultmann, *The History of the Synoptic Tradition*, New York: Harper & Row, 1963, pp. 11–69; Dibelius, *From Tradition to Gospel*, New York: Charles Scribner's Sons, n.d., pp. 37–69.

28 Tannehill, "Varieties of Synoptic Pronouncement Stories," *Semeia* 20 (1981) 101–19. See also *Semeia* volume 64; Ronald F. Hock and Edward N. O'Neil, *The Chreia in Ancient Rhetoric*, vol. 1, Atlanta: Scholars, 1986; and Mack, *Myth*, pp. 172–207.

29 Bultmann, *History*, pp. 19–20.

30 Kolenkow, "Healing Controversy"; Williams, "Parable and Chreia: From Q to Narrative Gospel," *Semeia* 43 (1988) 85–114.

31 Mack, *Myth*, pp. 208–45. Mack, of course, differs greatly from me in thinking that these two sets of controversies have no role in a pre-Markan gospel narrative.

32 Adela Yarbro Collins, "Finding Meaning in the Death of Jesus," forthcoming.

33 Two excellent yet very different attempts to explain the offense that caused the execution of Jesus are Sanders, *Jesus and Judaism*, and Bruce Chilton, *The Temple of Jesus: His Social Program Within a Cultural History of Sacrifice*, University Park, Penn.: Pennsylvania State University Press, 1992.

34 Wills, *The Jew in the Court of the Foreign King: Ancient Jewish Court Legends*, Minneapolis: Fortress, 1990, pp. 29–32.

35 This conflict and the one following in the list were probably originally separate, and have now been interwoven by Mark; see synopsis.

36 I take the question of authority to have been associated originally with the prophetic action in the temple, as it is in John 2 (see synopsis).

37 The threat of death is implied in the content of the parable.

38 On the connection of John 5: 1–18 and 7: 14–31, see synopsis. It is likely that a separate tradition is found in John 7: 14–18 (compare Mark 1: 21–22), now incorporated by John into a longer discourse.

39 For example, Nicolaus of Damascus (90, frag. 103i in Felix Jacoby (ed.), *Die Fragmenta der griechischen Historiker*, 14 vols, Leiden: Brill, 1961, p. 3.385); Diogenes Laertius 8.22; Josephus, *Jewish War* 2.8.6 §135; Matt 5: 33–37.

40 Cook, *Mark's Treatment of the Jewish Leaders*, Leiden: Brill, 1978.

41 Saldarini, *Pharisees, Scribes, and Sadducees in Palestinian Society: A Sociological Approach*, Wilmington, Del.: Michael Glazier, 1988, pp. 103–5, 187–96, 277–97. Saldarini notes (p. 193) that neither scribes nor elders appear in John; both blend into the Pharisees (or were perhaps never added to the lists of officials, as Mark has done). On the historical issues concerning the Galilean region at the time of Jesus, see Horsley, *Galilee: History, Politics, People*, Valley Forge, Penn.: Trinity Press International, 1995; and Sean Freyne, *Galilee, Jesus and the Gospels: Literary Approaches and Historical Investigations*, Dublin: Gill and Macmillan, 1988.

42 On Galilean wonder workers, see Geza Vermes, *Jesus the Jew: A Historian's Reading of the Gospels*, London: Collins, 1973, pp. 79–80; on Galilean visions, see George W. E. Nickelsburg, "Enoch, Levi, and Peter: Recipients of Revelation in Upper Galilee," *JBL* 100 (1981) 575–600.

43 Lohmeyer, *Galiläa und Jerusalem*, Göttingen: Vandenhoeck & Ruprecht, 1936.

44 Marxsen, *Mark the Evangelist*, pp. 93, 107. Elizabeth Struthers Malbon, "Galilee and Jerusalem: History and Literature in Marcan Interpretation," *CBQ* 44 (1982) 242–55, rightly emphasizes that it is not simply a question of the sociological origins, but also of the role of Galilee in the narrative.

45 Wilhelm Wilkens, *Die Entstehungsgeschichte des vierten Evangeliums*, Zollikon: Evangelischer Verlag, 1958, pp. 92–93; see also Jürgen Becker, "Wunder und Christologie," *NTS* 16 (1969–70) 130–48, esp. p. 135. Wilkens also argues the intriguing but ultimately unconvincing hypothesis that three episodes originally from the Passover week (2: 13–25; 6: 51–58; and 12: 1–7) have been placed back into the Galilee period, thus cementing a connection between the Passover sacrifice and the previous ministry.

46 Bassler, "The Galileans: A Neglected Factor in Johannine Community Research," *CBQ* 43 (1981) 243–57; see also Meeks, "Galilee and Judea in the Fourth Gospel," *JBL* 85 (1966) 159–69.

47 Dodd, *Historical Tradition*, pp. 244–47; Freyne, *Galilee*, pp. 61–62.

48 Aune, *New Testament*, p. 49; Dennis C. Duling, "Interpreting the Markan 'Hodology': Biblical Criticism in Preaching and Teaching," *Nexus* 17 (1974) 2–11.

49 Theissen, *Sociology of Early Palestinian Christianity*, Philadelphia: Fortress, 1977, pp. 8–30, esp. pp. 24–30. Theissen also believes that the Son of Humanity christology was the ideology of the wandering preachers who carried the Christian message from place to place. Not only does John lack the suffering Son of Humanity, but John also seems ignorant of some of these other motifs that Mark and Q associate with the Son of Humanity.

50 Perrin, *A Modern Pilgrimage in New Testament Christology*, Philadelphia: Fortress, 1974, pp. 122–28.

51 Kloppenborg, *Formation of Q*, pp. 159–70, 240–42.

52 Collins, "The Son of Man Sayings in the Sayings Source," in Maurya P. Horgan and Paul J. Kobelski (eds), *To Touch the Text: Biblical and Related Studies in Honor of Joseph A. Fitzmyer, S.J.*, New York: Crossroad, 1989, pp. 369–89; Collins's review of Kloppenborg, *CBQ* 50 [1988] 720–22; and Horsley, "Q and Jesus: Assumptions, Approaches, and Analyses," *Semeia* 55 (1991) 175–209.

53 Brown, *John*, p. 1.130.

54 Meeks, "The Man from Heaven in Johannine Sectarianism," *JBL* 91 (1972) 44–72; see also Douglas R. A. Hare, *The Son of Man Tradition*, Minneapolis: Fortress, 1990, pp. 79–112.

On the background of John's Son of Humanity sayings as eschatological judgment passages, see Rudolf Schnackenburg, *The Gospel According to St John*, 4 vols, London: Burns and Oates, 1982, p. 1.531–32.

55 Brown, *John*, p. 1.84, believes that John's three predictions regarding the Son of Humanity at 3: 14; 8: 28; and 12: 34 touch on the theme of suffering. If that is the case, which I found doubtful, it is still not present in the way that Mark would emphasize it.

56 Adela Yarbro Collins, "The Influence of Daniel on the New Testament," in John J. Collins, *Daniel: A Commentary on the Book of Daniel*, Minneapolis: Augsburg Fortress, 1993, pp. 97–98. Compare also Mark 8: 38; 13: 26; 14: 62; and Acts 7: 56.

57 Collins, "Influence of Daniel," pp. 100–2; Brown, *John*, p. 1.220, contra Gunter Reim, *Studien zum alttestamentlichen Hintergrund des Johannesevangeliums*, Cambridge: Cambridge University Press, 1974, pp. 186, 252–56; and F. H. Borsch, *The Son of Man in Myth and History*, London: SCM, 1967, p. 294.

58 Many scholars believe that in the Christian tradition, the Son of Humanity was not originally identified with the earthly Jesus or the risen Christ, even if preached by the historical Jesus; so Bultmann, *History*, pp. 112, 122, 128; H. E. Tödt, *The Son of Man in the Synoptic Tradition*, London: SCM, 1965, pp. 46–56; and more recently, Collins, "The Origin of the Designation of Jesus as 'Son of Man,'" *Harvard Theological Review* 80 (1987) 391–407.

59 Philipp Vielhauer, "Erwägungen zur Christologie des Markusevangeliums," in Erich Dinkler (ed.), *Zeit und Geschichte: Dankesgabe an Rudolf Bultmann zum 80. Geburtstag*, Tübingen: Mohr (Paul Siebeck), 1964, pp. 155–69. The term "Son of God" also appears in some exorcisms (Mark 3: 11; 5: 7). Baltzer, *Biographie der Propheten*, also emphasized these designations as key for his comparison of Mark with the biography of the prophet in the Hebrew Bible.

Norman Perrin has argued (*Modern Pilgrimage*, pp. 92–93) that the high, Son of God christology in Mark was derived from tradition, and that Mark's new interpretation of the Son of Humanity, that he must *suffer*, betrays an attempt to correct a false Son of God christology. If this is the case, John is certainly ignorant of it, but Perrin's theory of the relationship of the two christologies in Mark has been challenged by others: Jack Dean Kingsbury, *The Christology of Mark's Gospel*, Philadelphia: Fortress, 1983, pp. 157–79; Collins, "Influence of Daniel," pp. 97–98.

60 Mack, *Myth*, pp. 285–86; Vielhauer, "Erwägungen."

61 Mack, *Myth*, p. 231.

62 On the common motif of the obtuseness of the disciple: Jonathan Z. Smith, "No News is Good News: Aretalogy and Gospel," in Jacob Neusner (ed.), *Christianity, Judaism, and Other Greco-Roman Cults: Studies for Morton Smith at Sixty*, 4 vols, Leiden: Brill, 1975, pp. 1.21–38; on the Markan disciples: Robert C. Tannehill, "The Disciples in Mark: The Function of a Narrative Role," *JR* 57 (1977) 386–405; and on the supplanting of the disciples at the end of Mark by the women: Elisabeth Schüssler Fiorenza, *In Memory of Her: A Feminist Theological Reconstruction of Christian Origins*, New York: Crossroads, 1983, pp. 319–21.

63 Levenson, *The Death and Resurrection of the Beloved Son: The Transformation of Child Sacrifice in Judaism and Christianity*, New Haven: Yale University Press, 1993.

64 Mack, *Myth*, pp. 96–97. Werner Kelber ties the oral gospel traditions to a "living" Christ who speaks by means of the spirit of prophecy in the community, and the written text to the cult of a dead Christ (*The Oral and the Written Gospel: The Hermeneutics of Speaking and Writing in the Synoptic Tradition, Mark, Paul, and Q*, Philadelphia: Fortress, 1983, pp. 185–207). I would agree that sayings gospels such as Q and the *Gospel of Thomas* were associated with a "living" Christ and the narratives of Mark and John were cult narratives of a "dead" Christ, but it is not certain that the distinction was also between oral and written.

65 Edwin K. Broadhead, *Teaching With Authority: Miracles and Christology in the Gospel of Mark*, Sheffield: Sheffield Academic Press, 1992, p. 194.

66 Smith, "No News is Good News."

67 On charter myths, see Edmund Leach, "Introduction," in M. I. Steblin-Kamenskij, *Myth*, Ann Arbor: Karoma, 1982, pp. 1–20.

APPENDIX ENGLISH TRANSLATION OF THE *LIFE OF AESOP*

1 Perry, *Studies in the Text History of the Life and Fables of Aesop*, Haverford: American Philological Association, 1936, p. 2.

2 Daly, *Aesop Without Morals*, New York: T. Yoseloff, 1961, pp. 31–90.

3 Perry, *Aesopica*, Urbana, Ill.: University of Illinois Press, 1952, pp. 1.35–77.

4 Papathomopoulos, *Ho vios tou Aisopou: he parallage G*, Ioannina: G. Tsolis, 1990, pp. 37–177. See also his *Aesopus revisitatus: recherches sur le texte des vies ésopiques*, Ioannina: G. Tsolis, 1989.

5 Except for this passage, the adjective *mystakon*, as far as I can discern, is unattested in ancient Greek literature. *Mystax* means "mustache" or "upper lip," which by itself would hardly imply a deformity or negative description, so I have merely speculated as to a possible meaning. Daly, *Aesop*, p. 31, translates it "liver-lipped," whatever that might mean in English. In his modern Greek translation, Papathomopoulos, *Ho vios*, p. 36, gives *mystakias*.

6 Or perhaps "is worth a bull," *taurou axion* for *staurou axion*. The text of G has *tarou*, which most recent scholars have emended to *staurou*, although Perry, *Aesopica*, p. 1.41 prefers *taurou*.

7 Nagy, *The Best of the Achaeans*, Baltimore: Johns Hopkins University Press, 1979, p. 302, notes that the raven was considered the bird of Apollo.

8 Nagy, ibid., p. 316, suggests that this odd collection of insults may match characters from the Aesop's fables tradition.

9 The exact sense of the Greek is unclear, but note the parallels with Jewish wisdom.

10 With Perry, *Aesopica*, p. 1.63, who deletes 88a, since it repeats much of 88. Note the arguments of Papathomopoulos, *Aesopus*, pp. 69–70, on including this passage.

11 Reading with Papathomopoulos, *Aesopus*, p. 73, but against his later reconstruction in *Ho vios*, p. 135, and against Perry, *Aesopica*, p. 1.65. Note the parallel to the speech of Achior in Judith 5.

12 Nagy notes here the intended contrast of locusts, which are destructive, to cicadas, which are both harmonious-sounding and creatures of the Muses (*Pindar's Homer: The Lyric Possession of an Epic Past*, Baltimore/London: Johns Hopkins University Press, 1990, pp. 323–24; *Best of the Achaeans*, p. 302). This contrast was obscured in Perry's edition of the G text (and thus in Lloyd Daly's translation), but restored by Papathomopoulos.

13 Marsyas, a satyr who, like Aesop, was identified with Phrygia, had challenged Apollo to a fluting contest. Apollo won the contest, but angry at Marsyas' effrontery, hung him on a tree and flayed him. This resulted in a cult of Marsyas in Phrygia.

14 Note the discussion in Papathomopoulos, *Aesopus*, p. 85.

15 The passage is obscure here. See ibid., pp. 92–93.

16 With W text, against G; compare above, para. 105.

17 The thrust of the insult is unclear. *Lachanois . . . homochroas* could conceivably mean "as colorless as vegetables," in the sense of dull and uninteresting, or perhaps pale, unlike Aesop (compare para. 1) – so Daly, "as pale as potherbs." Papathomopoulos, *Ho vios*, p. 164, takes the more literal sense I have given. Note that these lines seem to be an intrusion into the story, perhaps motivated by the desire to insert the "relevant" line from the *Iliad*.

18 Papathomopoulos, *Aesopus*, p. 100, conjectures that there should be added here the clause "and condemn him as a temple-robber," but I find this unwarranted.

19 As Nagy notes (*Best of the Achaeans*, p. 283), there is a play on words here between *onos*, donkey, and *noos*, mind or sense, but the pun is only effective in the older Ionic version of the story, before the word *noos* has been contracted to *nous*. Thus this narrative fragment can be dated to a relatively early period.

BIBLIOGRAPHY

Achtemeier, Paul J., "Toward the Isolation of Pre-Markan Miracle Catenae," *JBL* 89 (1970) 265–91.

—— "The Origin and Function of the Pre-Markan Miracle Catenae," *JBL* 91 (1972) 198–221.

Ackerman, Susan, *Under Every Green Tree: Popular Religion in Sixth-Century Judah*, Atlanta: Scholars, 1992.

Adrados, Francisco R. "The 'Life of Aesop' and the Origins of Novel [sic] in Antiquity," *Quaderni urbinati di cultura classica* 30 (1979) 93–112.

Attridge, Harold, "Thematic Development and Source Elaboration in John 7: 1–36," *CBQ* 42 (1980) 160–70.

Aune, David, "The Problem of the Genre of the Gospels: A Critique of C. H. Talbert's *What is a Gospel?*" in R. T. France and David Wenham (eds), *Gospel Perspectives II*, Sheffield: JSOT Press, 1981, pp. 9–60.

—— *Prophecy in Early Christianity and the Ancient Mediterranean World*, Grand Rapids, Mich.: Eerdmans, 1983.

—— "The Gospels as Hellenistic Biography," *Mosaic* 20 (1987) 1–11.

—— *The New Testament in its Literary Environment*, Philadelphia: Westminster, 1987.

—— (ed.), *Greco-Roman Literature and the New Testament*, Atlanta: Scholars, 1988, pp. 107–26.

—— "The Gospels: Biography or Theology?," *Bible Review* 6 (1990) 14–37.

—— "Heracles and Christ: Heracles Imagery in the Christology of Early Christianity," in David L. Balch, Everett Ferguson, and Wayne A. Meeks (eds), *Greeks, Romans, and Christians: Essays in Honor of Abraham J. Malherbe*, Minneapolis: Fortress, 1990, pp. 3–19.

Badian, Ernst, *The Deification of Alexander the Great*, Berkeley: Center for Hermeneutical Studies in Hellenistic and Modern Culture, 1976.

Bailey, J. A., *The Traditions Common to the Gospels of Luke and John*, Leiden: Brill, 1963.

Baltzer, Klaus, *Die Biographie der Propheten*, Neukirchen-Vluyn: Neukirchener Verlag, 1975.

Barr, James, "Toward a Definition of the Gospel Genre: A Generic Analysis and Comparison of the Synoptic Gospels and the Socratic Dialogues by means of Aristotle's Theory of Tragedy," unpublished Ph.D. dissertation, Florida State University, 1974.

Barrett, C. K., *The Gospel According to St John*, 2nd ed., Philadelphia: Westminster, 1978.

Bassler, Jouette, "The Galileans: A Neglected Factor in Johannine Community Research," *CBQ* 43 (1981) 243–57.

Bayliss, M., "The Cult of the Dead Kin in Assyria and Babylonia," *Iraq* 35 (1973) 115–25.

Beare, W. E., *The Earliest Records of Jesus*, Oxford: Basil Blackwell, 1964.

Berger, Klaus, "Hellenistische Gattungen im Neuen Testament," *ANRW* II 25/2, pp. 1231–45.

Bertram, Georg, *Die Leidensgeschichte und der Christuskult: Eine formgeschichtliche Untersuchung*, Göttingen: Vandenhoeck & Ruprecht, 1922.

Best, Ernest, *The Temptation and the Passion: The Markan Soteriology*, Cambridge: Cambridge University Press, 1965.

Betz, Hans Dieter, *Der Apostel Paulus und die sokratische Tradition: Eine exegetische Untersuchung zu seiner "Apologie" 2 Korinther 10–13*, Tübingen: Mohr (Paul Siebeck), 1972.

—— "Zum Problem der Auferstehung Jesu," in *idem, Hellenismus und Urchristentum*, 3 vols, Tübingen: Mohr (Paul Siebeck), 1990, pp. 1.245–47.

Bickerman, Elias, "Das leere Grab," *ZNW* 23 (1924) 281–92, repr. in *idem, Studies in Jewish and Christian History*, 3 vols, Leiden: Brill, 1986, pp. 3.70–81.

Bilezikian, Gilbert G., *The Liberated Gospel: A Comparison of the Gospel of Mark and Greek Tragedy*, Grand Rapids: Baker Book House, 1977.

Blenkinsopp, Joseph, "Biographical Patterns in Biblical Narrative," *Journal for the Study of the Old Testament* 20 (1981) 27–46.

Blinzler, Josef, *Johannes und die Synoptiker: Ein Forschungsbericht*, Stuttgart: Verlag Katholisches Bibelwerk, 1965.

Bloch-Smith, Elizabeth M. "The Cult of the Dead in Judah: Interpretation of the Material Remains," *JBL* (1992) 213–24.

Boismard, M.-E. "Les traditions johanniques concernant le baptiste," *RB* 70 (1963) 5–42.

—— *Moses or Jesus: An Essay in Johannine Christology*, Minneapolis: Fortress/Leuven: Peeters, 1993.

Boismard, M.-E., and A. Lamouille, *L'évangile de Jean* (*Synopse des quatre évangiles*, vol. 3), Paris: Cerf, 1977.

Borgen, Peder, "John and the Synoptics in the Passion Narrative," *NTS* 5 (1958–59) 246–59.

Bousset, Wilhelm, *Kyrios Christos: A History of the Belief in Christ from the Beginnings to Irenaeus*, Nashville: Abingdon, 1970.

Bowersock, G. W., *Fiction as History: Nero to Julian*, Berkeley: University of California Press, 1994.

Bremmer, Jan, "Scapegoat Rituals in Ancient Greece," *HSCP* 87 (1983) 299–320.

Broadhead, Edwin K., *Teaching With Authority: Miracles and Christology in the Gospel of Mark*, Sheffield: Sheffield Academic Press, 1992.

Brown, Raymond, *The Gospel According to John*, 2 vols, Garden City, N. Y.: Doubleday, 1964–70.

—— "The Relation of 'The Secret Gospel of Mark' to the Fourth Gospel," *CBQ* 36 (1974) 466–85.

—— *The Community of the Beloved Disciple: The Life, Loves, and Hates of an Individual Church in New Testament Times*, New York: Paulist, 1979.

—— (ed.), *The Death of the Messiah*, 2 vols, New York: Doubleday, 1994.

Bultmann, Rudolf, *Theology of the New Testament*, 2 vols, New York: Scribner's, 1951–55.

—— *The History of the Synoptic Tradition*, New York: Harper & Row, 1963.

—— *The Gospel of John*, Philadelphia: Westminster/Oxford: Basil Blackwell & Mott, 1971.

Burkert, Walter, *Structure and History in Greek Myth and Ritual*, Berkeley: University of California Press, 1979.

—— *Greek Religion*, Cambridge, Mass.: Harvard University Press, 1985.

Burridge, Richard A., *What Are the Gospels? A Comparison with Graeco-Roman Biography*, Cambridge: Cambridge University Press, 1992.

Buse, Ivor, "St John and the Marcan Passion Narrative," *NTS* 4 (1957–58) 215–19.

Cameron, Ron (ed.), *The Other Gospels: Non-Canonical Gospel Texts*, Philadelphia: Westminster, 1982.

—— *Sayings Traditions in the Apocryphon of James*, Philadelphia: Fortress, 1984.

Carrington, Philip, *The Primitive Christian Calendar: A Study in the Making of the Marcan Gospel*, Cambridge: Cambridge University Press, 1952.

Carroll, John T., and Joel Green, *The Death of Jesus in Early Christianity*, Peabody, Mass.: Hendrickson, 1995.

Cartlidge, David R., and David L. Dungan, *Documents for the Study of the Gospels*, Philadelphia: Fortress, 1980.

Cerfaux, L., and J. Tondriau, *Le culte des souverains dans la civilization gréco-romaine*, Paris and Tournai: Desclée, 1957.

Chance, J. Bradley, "Fiction in Ancient Biography: An Approach to a Sensitive Issue in Gospel Interpretation," *Perspectives in Religious Studies* 18 (1991) 125–42.

Charlesworth, James H. (ed.), *The Messiah: Developments in Earliest Judaism and Christianity*, Minneapolis: Fortress, 1992.

Chilton, Bruce, *The Temple of Jesus: His Social Program within a Cultural History of Sacrifice*, University Park, Penn.: Pennsylvania State University Press, 1992.

Collins, Adela Yarbro, "The Origin of the Designation of Jesus as 'Son of Man,'" *Harvard Theological Review* 80 (1987) 391–407.

—— *The Beginning of the Gospel: Probings of Mark in Context*, Minneapolis: Fortress, 1992.

—— "The Genre of the Passion Narrative," *Studia Theologica: Scandinavian Journal of Theology* 47 (1993) 3–28.

—— "The Influence of Daniel on the New Testament," in John J. Collins, *Daniel: A Commentary on the Book of Daniel*, Minneapolis: Augsburg Fortress, 1993, pp. 90–123.

—— "From Noble Death to Crucified Messiah," *NTS* 40 (1994) 481–503.

—— "Genre and the Gospels" (review of Burridge, *What Are the Gospels?*), *JR* 75 (1995) 239–46.

—— "Finding Meaning in the Death of Jesus," forthcoming article.

Compton, Todd, "The Trial of the Satirist: Poetic *Vitae* (Aesop, Archilochus, Homer) as Background for Plato's *Apology*," *American Journal of Philology* 111 (1990) 330–47.

Cook, Michael, *Mark's Treatment of the Jewish Leaders*, Leiden: Brill, 1978.

Corrington, Gail Patterson, *Her Image of Salvation: Female Saviors and Formative Christianity*, Louisville: Westminster/John Knox Press, 1992.

Crossan, John Dominic, *Four Other Gospels: Shadows on the Contours of Canon*, Minneapolis: Winston, 1985.

—— *The Cross That Spoke: The Origins of the Passion Narrative*, San Francisco: Harper & Row, 1988.

—— *The Historical Jesus: The Life of a Mediterranean Jewish Peasant*, San Francisco: HarperCollins, 1991.

Dahl, Nils Alstrup, "Memorial and Commemoration in Early Christianity," in *idem*, *Jesus in the Memory of the Early Church*, Minneapolis: Augsburg, 1976, pp. 11–29.

Daly, Lloyd, *Aesop Without Morals*, New York: T. Yoseloff, 1961.

Dauer, Anton, *Die Passionsgeschichte im Johannesevangelium: Eine traditionsgeschichtliche und theologische Untersuchung zu Joh 18,1–19, 30*, Munich: Kösel-Verlag, 1972.

Davies, Philip R., and Bruce Chilton, "The Aqedah: A Revised Tradition History," *Catholic Biblical Quarterly* 40 (1978) 514–46.

Delaney, Carol, "The Legend of Abraham," in Rita M. Gross (ed.), *Beyond Androcentrism: New Essays on Women and Religion*, Missoula, Mont.: Scholars, 1977, pp. 217–36.

Denaux, Adelbert (ed.), *John and the Synoptics*, Leuven: Leuven University Press, 1992.

Derrett, J. Duncan M., *The Victim: The Johannine Passion Narrative Reexamined*, Shipston-on-Stowe, Warwickshire: P. Drinkwater, 1993.

Dewey, Arthur, "'Time to Murder and Create': Visions and Revisions in the *Gospel of Peter*," *Semeia* 49 (1990) 101–27.

Dewey, Joanna, "Oral Methods of Structuring Narrative in Mark," *Interpretation* 43 (1989) 32–44.

—— "The Gospel of Mark as an Oral-Aural Event," in Elizabeth Strothers Malbon and Edgar V. McKnight (eds), *New Literary Criticism and the New Testament*, Sheffield: Sheffield Academic Press, 1994, pp. 145–63.

Dihle, Albrecht, "The Gospels and Greek Biography," in Peter Stuhlmacher (ed.), *The Gospel and the Gospels*, Grand Rapids: Eerdmanns, 1991, pp. 361–86.

Dodd, C. H., "The Framework of the Gospel Narrative," in *idem, New Testament Studies*, Manchester: Manchester University Press, 1953, pp. 1–11.

—— *The Interpretation of the Fourth Gospel*, Cambridge: Cambridge University Press, 1953.

—— "The Prophecy of Caiaphas: John xi 47–53," *Neotestamentica et Patristica* (Festschrift Cullmann), NTSupp. VI, Leiden: Brill, 1962, pp. 134–42.

—— *Historical Tradition in the Fourth Gospel*, Cambridge: Cambridge University Press, 1963.

—— *The Apostolic Preaching and its Developments*, New York: Harper & Row, 1964.

Donahue, John R., *Are You the Christ? The Trial Narrative in the Gospel of Mark*, Missoula: University of Montana Press, 1973.

—— *The Gospel in Parable: Metaphor, Narrative, and Theology in the Synoptic Gospels*, Philadelphia: Fortress, 1988.

Dormeyer, Detlev, *Die Passion Jesu als Verhaltensmodell*, Münster: Aschendorff, 1974.

—— *Evangelium als literarische und theologische Gattung*, Darmstadt: Wissenschaftliche Buchgesellschaft, 1989.

Dormeyer, Detlev, and Hubert Frankemölle, "Evangelium als literarischer und als theologischer Begriff: Tendenzen und Aufgaben der Evangelien Forschung im 20. Jahrhundert, mit einen Untersuchung des Markusevangeliums in seinem Verhältnis zur griechischen Biographie," *ANRW* II 25/2, pp. 1541–1704.

Droge, Arthur J., and James D. Tabor, *A Noble Death: Suicide and Martyrdom among Christians and Jews in Antiquity*, San Francisco: HarperSan Francisco, 1992.

Duling, Dennis, "Interpreting the Markan 'Hodology': Biblical Criticism in Preaching and Teaching," *Nexus* 17 (1974) 2–11.

Dunderberg, Ismo, *Johannes und die Synoptiker: Studien zu Joh 1–9*, Helsinki: Suomalainen tiedeakatemia, 1994.

Dundes, Alan, *The Hero Pattern and the Life of Jesus*, Berkeley: Center for Hermeneutical Studies, 1977.

Evans, Craig, "Peter Warming Himself: The Problem of an Editorial 'Seam,'" *JBL* 101 (1982) 245–49.

—— "Jesus' Action in the Temple: Cleansing or Portent of Destruction?," *CBQ* 51 (1989) 237–70.

Farnell, Lewis Richard, *Greek Hero Cults and Ideas of Immortality*, Oxford: Clarendon Press, 1921.

Faure, A., "Die alttestamentlichen Zitate im 4. Evangelium und die Quellenscheidungshypothese," *ZNW* 21 (1922) 99–121.

Feldman, Louis H., "Prophets and Prophecy in Josephus," *JTS* 41 (1990) 386–422.

Feuillet, André, *Johannine Studies*, Staten Island: Alba House, 1965.

Fischel, H. A., "Martyr and Prophet (A Study in Jewish Literature)," *JQR* 37 (1946–47) 265–80, 363–86.

—— "Studies in Cynicism and the Ancient Near East: The Transformation of a Chria," in Jacob Neusner (ed.), *Religions in Antiquity: Essays in Memory of Erwin Ramsdell Goodenough*, Leiden: Brill, 1968, pp. 372–411.

Foley, John Miles, "Introduction," in *idem* (ed.), *Oral Tradition in Literature: Interpretation in Context*, Columbia: University of Missouri Press, 1986, pp. 10–19.

Fortna, Robert T., *The Gospel of Signs: A Reconstruction of the Narrative Source Underlying the Fourth Gospel*, Cambridge: Cambridge University Press, 1970.

—— "Jesus and Peter at the High Priest's House: A Test Case for the Question of the Relation Between Mark's and John's Gospels," *NTS* 24 (1977–78) 371–83.

—— *The Fourth Gospel and its Predecessors: From Narrative Source to Present Gospel*, Philadelphia: Fortress, 1988.

Fowler, Barbara Hughes, *The Hellenistic Aesthetic*, Madison: University of Wisconsin Press, 1989.

Frankemölle, Hubert, *Evangelium: Begriff und Gattung: Ein Forschungsbericht*, Stuttgart: Katholisches Bibelwerk, 1988.

Freyne, Seán, *Galilee from Alexander the Great to Hadrian, 323 B.C.E. to 145 C.E.: A Study of Second Temple Judaism*, Notre Dame, Ind.: University of Notre Dame Press, 1980.

—— *Galilee, Jesus and the Gospels: Literary Approaches and Historical Investigations*, Dublin: Gill and Macmillan, 1988.

Gardner-Smith, Percival, *Saint John and the Synoptic Gospels*, Cambridge: Cambridge University Press, 1938.

Gärtner, Bertil, *John 6 and the Jewish Passover*, Lund: Gleerup/Copenhagen: Munksgaard, 1959.

Georgi, Dieter, *The Records of Jesus in the Light of Ancient Accounts of Revered Men*, Berkeley: Center for Hermeneutical Studies, 1975.

Gill, Christopher, and T. P. Wiseman, *Lie and Fiction in the Ancient World*, Exeter: University of Exeter Press, 1993.

Girard, René, *Violence and the Sacred*, Baltimore: Johns Hopkins University Press, 1977.

—— *The Scapegoat*, Baltimore: Johns Hopkins University Press, 1986.

—— *Things Hidden Since the Foundation of the World*, Stanford: Stanford University Press, 1987.

Glasson, T. Francis, *Moses in the Fourth Gospel*, London: SCM, 1963.

Glusman, Edward F., Jr., "Criteria for a Study of the Outlines of Mark and John," in Paul J. Achtemeier (ed.), *Society of Biblical Literature 1978 Seminar Papers*, 2 vols, Missoula, Mont.: Scholars, 1978, pp. 2.239–249.

Goodenough, Erwin R., "John a Primitive Gospel," *JBL* 64 (1945) 145–82.

Grabbe, Lester L., "The Scapegoat Tradition: A Study in Early Jewish Interpretation," *JSJ* 18 (1987) 152–67.

Gray, Rebecca, *Prophetic Figures in Late Second Temple Jewish Palestine: The Evidence from Josephus*, New York: Oxford University Press, 1993.

Green, Joel B., *The Death of Jesus: Tradition and Interpretation in the Passion Narrative*, Tübingen: Mohr (Paul Siebeck), 1988.

Grotanelli, Cristiano, "Aesop in Babylon," in Hans-Jörg Nissen and Johannes Renger (eds), *Mesopotamia und seine Nachbarn*, 2 vols, Berlin: Reimer, 1982, pp. 2.555–72.

Guelich, Robert, "The Gospel Genre," in Peter Stuhlmacher (ed.), *The Gospel and the Gospels*, Grand Rapids: Eerdmanns, 1991, pp. 173–208.

Gundry, Robert H., "Recent Investigations into the Literary Genre 'Gospel,'" in Richard N. Longenecker and Merrill C. Tenney (eds), *New Dimensions in New Testament Study*, Grand Rapids, Mich.: Zondervan, 1974, pp. 97–114.

Hadas, Moses, and Morton Smith *Heroes and Gods: Spiritual Biographies in Antiquity*, London: Routledge & Kegan Paul, 1965.

Haenchen, Ernst, "Johanneische Probleme," *ZTK* 56 (1959) 46–50.

—— *John*, 2 vols, Philadelphia: Fortress, 1984.

Hägg, Tomas, *Narrative Technique in Ancient Greek Romances*, Stockholm: Swedish Institute in Athens, 1971.

—— *The Novel in Antiquity*, Berkeley and Los Angeles: University of California Press, 1983.

—— "Callirhoe and Parthenope: The Beginnings of the Historical Novel," *Classical Antiquity* 6 (1987) 184–204.

Hamerton-Kelly, Robert G. (ed.), *Violent Origins: Walter Burkert, René Girard, and Jonathan Z. Smith on Ritual Killing and Social Formation*, Stanford: Stanford University Press, 1987.

—— *The Gospel and the Sacred: Poetics of Violence in Mark*, Minneapolis: Fortress, 1994.

Harris, William V., *Ancient Literacy*, Cambridge, Mass.: Harvard University Press, 1989.

Hengel, Martin, "Maria Magdalena und die Frauen als Zeugen," in *idem*, Otto Betz, and Peter

Schmidt (eds), *Abraham Unser Vater: Jüden und Christen im Gespräch über die Bibel,* Leiden: Brill, 1963, pp. 243–56.

—— *Judaism and Hellenism: Studies in their Encounter in Palestine During the Early Hellenistic Period,* Philadelphia: Fortress, 1974.

—— *Acts and the History of Earliest Christianity,* Philadelphia: Fortress, 1980.

—— "The Expiatory Sacrifice of Christ," *Bulletin of the John Rylands University Library of Manchester* 62 (1980) 454–75.

—— *The Atonement: The Origins of the Doctrine in the New Testament,* Philadelphia: Fortress, 1981.

Hobbs, Edward Craig, "The Gospel of Mark and the Exodus," unpublished Ph.D. dissertation, University of Chicago, 1958.

Hock, Ronald F., "The Greek Novel," in David Aune (ed.), *Greco-Roman Literature and the New Testament,* Atlanta: Scholars, 1988, pp. 132–41.

Hock, Ronald F., and Edward N. O'Neil, *The Chreia in Ancient Rhetoric,* vols, Atlanta: Scholars, 1986.

Holladay, Carl R., *Theios Aner in Hellenistic Judaism: A Critique of the Use of This Category in New Testament Christology,* Missoula, Mont.: Scholars, 1977.

Holzberg, Niklas "A Lesser Known 'Picaresque' Novel of Greek Origin: The *Aesop Romance* and its Influence," in H. Hofmann (ed.), *Groningen Colloquia on the Novel,* 5 vols, Groningen: Egbert Forsten, 1988–93, pp. 5.1–16.

—— (ed.), *Der Äsop-Roman: Motivgeschichte und Erzählstruktur,* Tübingen: Gunter Narr Verlag, 1992.

—— *The Ancient Novel: An Introduction,* London/New York: Routledge, 1995.

Hooker, Morna D., *Jesus and the Servant: The Influence of the Servant Concept of Deutero-Isaiah in the New Testament,* London: SPCK, 1959.

—— *Not Ashamed of the Gospel: New Testament Interpretations of the Death of Christ,* Grand Rapids, Mich.: Eerdmans, 1995.

Hopkins, Keith, "Novel Evidence for Roman Slavery," *Past and Present* 138 (1993) 3–27.

Horsley, Richard, "'Like One of the Prophets of Old': Two Types of Popular Prophets at the Time of Jesus," *CBQ* 47 (1985) 435–63.

—— *Sociology and the Jesus Movement,* New York: Crossroad, 1989.

—— *Galilee: History, Politics, People,* Valley Forge, Penn.: Trinity Press International, 1996.

Horsley, Richard, and John S. Hanson, *Bandits, Prophets, and Messiahs: Popular Movements at the Time of Jesus,* Minneapolis: Winston, 1985.

Hughes, Dennis D., *Human Sacrifice in Ancient Greece,* London/New York: Routledge, 1991.

Hurtado, L. W., "The Gospel of Mark: Evolutionary or Revolutionary Document?," *JSNT* 40 (1990) 15–32.

Jay, Nancy, "Sacrifice as Remedy for Having Been Born of Woman," in Clarissa W. Atkinson, Constance H. Buchanan, and Margaret R. Miles (eds), *Immaculate and Powerful: The Female in Sacred Image and Social Reality,* Boston, Mass.: Beacon, 1985, pp. 283–309.

—— *Throughout Your Generations Forever: Sacrifice, Religion, and Paternity,* Berkeley: University of California Press, 1992.

Jeremias, Joachim, "Johanneische Literaturkritik," *Theologische Blätter* 20 (1941) 42.

—— *Heiligengräber in Jesu Umwelt (Mt. 23, 29; Lk. 11, 47): Ein Untersuchung zur Volksreligion der Zeit Jesu,* Göttingen: Vandenhoeck & Ruprecht, 1958.

Juel, Donald, *Messianic Exegesis: Christological Interpretation of the Old Testament in Early Christianity,* Philadelphia: Fortress, 1987.

Käsemann, Ernst, "The Saving Significance of the Death of Jesus in Paul," in *idem, Perspectives on Paul,* Philadelphia: Fortress, 1971, pp. 32–59.

Kee, Howard Clark, *Jesus in History: An Approach to the Study of the Gospels,* New York: Harcourt, Brace and World, 1970.

—— "Aretalogy and Gospel," *JBL* 92 (1973) 402–22.

—— *Aretalogies, Hellenistic "Lives," and the Sources of Mark*, Berkeley: Center for Hermeneutical Studies, 1975.

—— *Community of the New Age: Studies in Mark's Gospel*, Philadelphia: Westminster, 1977.

Kelber, Werner, *The Kingdom in Mark: A New Place and a New Time*, Philadelphia: Fortress, 1974.

—— (ed.), *The Passion in Mark: Studies on Mark 14–16*, Philadelphia: Fortress, 1976.

—— *The Oral and the Written Gospel: The Hermeneutics of Speaking and Writing in the Synoptic Tradition, Mark, Paul, and Q*, Philadelphia: Fortress, 1983.

Kertelge, Karl, *Die Wunder Jesu im Markusevangelium: Eine redaktionsgeschichtliche Untersuchung*, Munich: Kösel, 1970.

Kingsbury, Jack Dean, *The Christology of Mark's Gospel*, Philadelphia: Fortress, 1983.

Koester, Helmut, *Introduction to the New Testament*, 2 vols, Philadelphia: Fortress/Berlin and New York: de Gruyter, 1982.

—— *Ancient Christian Gospels: Their History and Development*, Philadelphia: Trinity Press International, 1990.

—— "The Historical Jesus and the Cult of the *Kyrios Christos*," *Harvard Divinity Bulletin* 24 (1995) 13–18.

Koester, Helmut, and James M. Robinson, *Trajectories Through Early Christianity*, Philadelphia: Fortress, 1971.

Kolenkow, Anitra Bingham, "Healing Controversy as a Tie Between Miracle and Passion Material for a Proto-Gospel," *JBL* 95 (1976) 623–38.

—— "Relationships Between Miracle and Prophecy in the Greco-Roman World and Early Christianity," *ANRW* II 23/2, pp. 1470–1506.

Kuhn, Heinz-Wolfgang, *Ältere Sammlungen im Markusevangelium*, Göttingen: Vandenhoeck & Ruprecht, 1971.

Larson, Jennifer, *Greek Heroine Cults*, Madison: University of Wisconsin Press, 1995.

Leach, Edmund, "Introduction," in M. I. Steblin-Kamenskij, *Myth*, Ann Arbor: Karoma, 1982, pp. 1–20.

Lefkowitz, Mary R., *The Lives of the Greek Poets*, Baltimore: Johns Hopkins University Press, 1981.

Levenson, Jon, *The Death and Resurrection of the Beloved Son: The Transformation of Child Sacrifice in Judaism and Christianity*, New Haven: Yale University Press, 1993.

Levine, Amy-Jill, "Sacrifice and Salvation: Otherness and Domestication in the Book of Judith," in James C. VanderKam (ed.), *"No One Spoke Ill of Her": Essays on Judith*, Atlanta: Scholars, 1992, pp. 17–27.

Lewis, Theodore J., *Cults of the Dead in Ancient Israel and Ugarit*, Atlanta: Scholars, 1989.

Lindars, Barnabas, *New Testament Apologetic: The Doctrinal Significance of the Old Testament Quotations*, Philadelphia: Westminster, 1961.

—— *Behind the Fourth Gospel*, London: SPCK, 1971.

—— *John*, Sheffield: JSOT Press, 1990.

Linnemann, Eta, *Studien zur Passionsgeschichte*, Göttingen: Vandenhoeck & Ruprecht, 1970.

Lohmeyer, Ernst, *Galiläa und Jerusalem*, Göttingen: Vandenhoeck & Ruprecht, 1936.

Lohse, Eduard, *Märtyrer und Gottesknecht: Untersuchungen zur urchristlichen Verkündigung vom Sühntod Jesu Christi*, 2nd ed., Göttingen: Vandenhoeck & Ruprecht, 1963.

Lord, Albert B., "The Gospels as Oral Traditional Literature," in William O. Walker (ed.), *The Relationships Among the Gospels: An Interdisciplinary Dialogue*, San Antonio: Trinity University Press, 1978, pp. 39–40.

Luedemann, Gerd, *The Resurrection of Jesus: History, Exposition, Theology*, London: SCM, 1994.

Lührmann, Dieter, "Biographie des Gerechten als Evangelium: Vorstellungen zu einem Markus-Kommentar," *Wort und Dienst* 14 (1977) 25–50.

—— *Das Markusevangelium*, Tübingen: Mohr (Paul Siebeck), 1987.

Mack, Burton, *A Myth of Innocence: Mark and Christian Origins*, Philadelphia: Fortress, 1988.

MacRae, George W., "Messiah and Gospel," in Jacob Neusner, William Scott Green, and Ernest S. Freirschs (eds), *Judaisms and their Messiahs at the Turn of the Christian Era*, Cambridge: Cambridge University Press, 1987, pp. 169–85.

Malbon, Elizabeth Struthers, *Narrative Space and Mythic Meaning in Mark*, Sheffield: JSOT Press, 1991.

Martyn, J. Louis, *History and Theology in the Fourth Gospel*, New York and Evanston: Harper & Row, 1968.

Marxsen, Willi, *Mark the Evangelist: Studies on the Redaction History of the Gospel*, Nashville: Abingdon, 1969.

Matera, Frank J., *The Kingship of Jesus: Composition and Theology in Mark 15*, Chico, Calif.: Scholars, 1982.

Maynard, Arthur H., "Common Elements in the Outlines of Mark and John," in Paul J. Achtemeier (ed.), *Society of Biblical Literature Seminar Papers 1978*, 2 vols, Missoula: Scholars Press, 1978, pp. 2.251–60.

Meeks, Wayne, *The Prophet-King: Moses Traditions and Johannine Christology*, Leiden: Brill, 1967.

—— "The Man from Heaven in Johannine Sectarianism," *JBL* 91 (1972) 44–72.

Merkelbach, Reinhold, *Roman und Mysterium in der Antike*, Munich: Beck'sche, 1962.

Meyer, Marvin W., "The Youth in *Secret Mark* and the Beloved Disciple in John," in James E. Goehring, *et al.* (eds), *Gospel Origins and Christian Beginnings*, Sonoma, Calif.: Polebridge, 1990, pp. 94–105.

Meyers, Eric, *Jewish Ossuaries and Secondary Burials in their Ancient Near Eastern Setting*, Cambridge, Mass.: Harvard University Press, 1969.

Miller, Robert J. (ed.), *The Complete Gospels*, San Francisco: Polebridge, 1992.

Mirecki, Paul Allan, "Mark 16: 9–20: Composition, Tradition, and Redaction," unpublished Th.D. dissertation, Harvard Divinity School, 1987.

Mohr, Till Arend, *Markus- und Johannespassion: Redaktions- und traditionsgeschichtliche Untersuchung der Markinischen und Johanneischen Passionstradition*, Zurich: Theologischer Verlag, 1982.

Moo, Douglas, *The Old Testament in the Gospel Passion Narratives*, Sheffield: Almond, 1983.

Morgan, J. R., and Richard Stoneman (eds), *Greek Fiction*, London: Routledge, 1994.

Morris, Ian, "Tomb Cult and the Greek Renaissance," *Antiquity* 62 (1988) 750–61.

Nagy, Gregory, *The Best of the Achaeans*, Baltimore: Johns Hopkins University Press, 1979.

—— *Greek Mythology and Poetics*, Ithaca/London: Cornell University Press, 1990.

—— *Pindar's Homer: The Lyric Possession of an Epic Past*, Baltimore/London: Johns Hopkins University Press, 1990.

—— "Homeric Questions," *Transactions of the American Philological Association* 122 (1992) 17–60.

Neirynck, Frans, *Duality in Mark: Contributions to the Study of the Markan Redaction*, Leuven: Leuven University Press, 1972.

—— *Evangelica. Gospel Studies – Études d'évangile: Collected Essays*, Leuven: Leuven University Press, 1982.

—— *Evangelica III. 1982–1991: Collected Essays*, Leuven: Leuven University Press, 1991.

Neirynck, Frans, *et al.*, *Jean et les synoptiques: Examen critique de l'exégèse de M.-E. Boismard*, Leuven: Leuven University Press, 1992.

Neyrey, Jerome, *An Ideology of Revolt: John's Christology in Social-Scientific Perspective*, Philadelphia: Fortress, 1988.

Nickelsburg, George W. E., *Resurrection, Immortality, and Eternal Life in Intertestamental Judaism*, Cambridge, Mass.: Harvard University Press, 1972.

—— (ed.), *Studies on the Testament of Joseph*, Missoula, Mont.: Scholars, 1975.

—— "The Genre and Function of the Markan Passion Narrative," *HTR* 73 (1980) 153–84.

—— "Enoch, Levi, and Peter: Recipients of Revelation in Upper Galilee," *JBL* 100 (1981) 575–600.

Nicol, W., *The Semeia in the Fourth Gospel: Tradition and Redaction*, Leiden: Brill, 1972.

Nilsson, Martin P., *The Minoan-Mycenaean Religion and its Survival in Greek Religion*, Lund: Gleerup, 1927.

—— *A History of Greek Religion*, Oxford: Clarendon, 1956.

Nineham, D. E., "The Order of Events in St. Mark's Gospel – An Examination of Dr. Dodd's Hypothesis," in *idem* (ed.), *Studies in the Gospels*, Oxford: Basil Blackwell, 1957, pp. 223–39.

—— *Saint Mark*, Harmondsworth: Penguin, 1963.

Noack, Bent, *Zur johanneischen Tradition: Beiträge zur Kritik an der literarkritischen Analyse des vierten Evangeliums*, Copenhagen: Rosekilde, 1954.

Nock, Arthur Darby, "The Cult of Heroes," *HTR* 37 (1944) 141–74, repr. in Zeph Stewart (ed.), *Essays on Religion and the Ancient World*, 2 vols, Cambridge, Mass.: Harvard University Press, 1972, pp. 2.575–602.

Obermann, Julian, "The Sepulchre of the Maccabean Martyrs," *JBL* 50 (1931) 250–65.

O'Neill, J. C., "Did Jesus Teach that his Death would be Vicarious as well as Typical?," in William Harbury and Brian McNeil, *Suffering and Martyrdom in the New Testament: Studies Presented to G. M. Styler by the Cambridge New Testament Seminar*, Cambridge: Cambridge University Press, 1981, pp. 9–27.

Overbeck, Franz , "Über die Anfänge der patristischen Literatur," *Historische Zeitschrift* 12 (1882) 417–72.

Painter, John, "Tradition and Interpretation in John 6," *NTS* 35 (1989) 421–50.

Papathomopoulos, Manolis, *Aesopus revisitatus: recherches sur le texte des vies ésopiques*, Ioannina: G. Tsolis, 1989.

—— *Ho vios tou Aisopou: he parallage G*, Ioannina: G. Tsolis, 1990.

Patterson, Annabel, *Fables of Power: Aesopian Writing and Political History*, Durham/London: Duke University Press, 1991.

Perkins, Judith, *The Suffering Self: Pain and Narrative Representation in the Early Christian Era*, London and New York: Routledge, 1995.

Perrin, Norman, *The Kingdom of God in the Teaching of Jesus*, Philadelphia: Westminster, 1963.

—— *A Modern Pilgrimage in New Testament Christology*, Philadelphia: Fortress, 1974.

Perry, Ben Edwin, *Studies in the Text History of the Life and Fables of Aesop*, Haverford: American Philological Association, 1936.

—— *The Ancient Romances*, Berkeley: University of California Press, 1967.

—— *Aesopica*, 2 vols, New York: Arno, 1980.

Pervo, Richard, *Profit with Delight: The Literary Genre of the Acts of the Apostles*, Philadelphia: Fortress, 1987.

—— "A Nihilist Fabula: Introducing the *Life of Aesop*," paper read at the American Academy of Religion/Society of Biblical Literature Annual Meeting, Philadelphia, Penn., November 19, 1995.

Pesch, Rudolph, *Das Markusevangelium*, 2 vols, 3rd ed., Freiburg/Basle/Vienna: Herder, 1980.

Pfister, Friedrich, *Der Reliquenkult im Altertum*, 2 vols, Giessen: Töpelmann, 1909–12.

—— "Herakles und Christus," *Archiv für Religionswissenschaft* 34 (1937) 42–60.

Reardon, B. P., *The Form of the Greek Romance*, Princeton: Princeton University Press, 1991.

Reicke, Bo, *Diakonie, Festfreude und Zelos in Verbindung mit der altchristlichen Agapenfeier*, Uppsala: Lundequistska/Wiesbaden: Otto Harrassowitz, 1951.

Reim, Gunter, *Studien zum alttestamentlichen Hintergrund des Johannesevangeliums*, Cambridge: Cambridge University Press, 1974.

Reinbold, Wolfgang, *Der älteste Bericht über den Tod Jesu: Literarische Analyse und historische Kritik der Passionsdarstellungen der Evangelien*, Berlin/New York: de Gruyter, 1994.

Reiser, Mark, "Der Alexanderroman und das Markusevangelium," in Hubert Cancik (ed.),

Markus-Philologie: Historische, literargeschichtliche und stilistische Untersuchungen zum zweiten Evangelium, Tübingen: Mohr (Paul Siebeck), 1984, pp. 131–61.

Riga, Peter, "Signs of Glory: The Use of 'Semeion' in St. John's Gospel," *Interpretation* 17 (1963) 402–10.

Robbins, Vernon, *Jesus the Teacher: A Socio-Rhetorical Interpretation of Mark*, Philadelphia: Fortress, 1984.

—— *New Boundaries in Old Territory: Form and Social Rhetoric in Mark*, New York: Peter Lang, 1994.

Robinson, James M., *The Problem of History in Mark and Other Studies*, Philadelphia: Fortress, 1980.

Robinson, J. A. T., "The Most Primitive Christology of All?," *JTS* 7 (1956) 177–89.

—— *The Priority of John*, London: SCM, 1985.

Rohde, Erwin, *Psyche: The Cult of Souls and Belief in Immortality Among the Greeks*, London: Kegan Paul, Trench, Trübner/New York: Harcourt, Brace, 1925.

Rose, Herbert Jennings, "Herakles and the Gospels," *HTR* 31 (1938) 113–42.

Sanders, E. P., *Jesus and Judaism*, Philadelphia: Fortress, 1985.

Schatkin, Margaret, "Maccabean Martyrs," *Vigiliae Christianae* 28 (1974) 97–113.

Schenk, Wolfgang, *Der Passionsbericht nach Markus: Untersuchungen zur Überlieferungsgeschichte der Passionstraditionen*, Leiden: Brill/Gütersloh: Gerd Mohn, 1974.

Schenke, Ludger, *Auferstehungsverkündigung und leeres Grab: eine traditionsgeschichtliche Untersuchung von Mk. 16, 1–8*, Stuttgart: Katholisches Bibelwerk, 1968.

—— *Studien zur Passionsgechichte des Markus: Tradition und Redaktion in Markus 14,1–42*, Würzburg: Echter/Stuttgart: Katholisches Bibelwerk, 1971.

—— *Der gekreuzigte Christus: Versuch einer literarkritischen und traditionsgeschichtlichen Bestimmung der vormarkinischen Passionsgeschichte*, Stuttgart: Katholisches Bibelwerk, 1974.

Schmidt, Karl Ludwig, *Der Rahmen der Geschichte Jesu: Literarkritische Untersuchungen zur ältesten Jesusüberlieferung*, Berlin: Trowitzsch, 1919.

—— "Die Stellung der Evangelien in der allgemeinen Literaturgeschichte," in H. Schmidt (ed.), *Eucharisterion* (Festschrift Hermann Gunkel), Göttingen: Vandenhoeck & Ruprecht, 1923, 50–134.

Schnackenburg, Rudolf, *The Gospel According to St John*, 4 vols, London: Burns and Oates, 1982.

Schneider, Gerhard, *Die Passion Jesu nach den drei älteren Evangelien*, Munich: Kösel-Verlag, 1973.

Schniewind, Julius, "Zur Synoptiker-Exegese," *Theologische Rundschau* n.f. 2 (1930) 129–80.

Schnider, Franz and Werner Stenger, *Johannes und die Synoptiker*, Munich: Kösel, 1971.

Schreiber, Johannes, *Die Theologie des Vertrauens: Eine redaktionsgeschichtliche Untersuchung des Markusevangeliums*, Hamburg: Furche, 1967.

—— *Die Markuspassion: Wege zur Erforschung der Leidensgeschichte Jesu*, Hamburg: Furche, 1969.

Schweitzer, Albert, *The Quest of the Historical Jesus: A Critical Study of its Progress from Reimarus to Wrede*, London: A. & C. Black, 1910.

Seeley, David, *The Noble Death: Graeco-Roman Martyrology and Paul's Concept of Salvation*, Sheffield: Sheffield Academic Press, 1990.

Segbroeck, F. van *et al.* (eds), *The Four Gospels 1992 I–III* (Festschrift Frans Neirynck), Leuven: Leuven University Press, 1992.

Shuler, Philip L., *A Genre for the Gospels: The Biographical Character of Matthew*, Philadelphia: Fortress, 1982.

Smith, Dwight Moody, *The Composition and Order of the Fourth Gospel: Bultmann's Literary Theory*, New Haven: Yale University Press, 1965.

—— *Johannine Christianity*, Columbia: University of South Carolina Press, 1984.

—— *John Among the Gospels: The Relationship in Twentieth-Century Research*, Minneapolis: Fortress, 1992.

—— "John and the Synoptics and the Question of Gospel Genre," in F. Van Segbroeck, *et al.* (eds), *The Four Gospels* (Festschrift Frans Neirynck), 2 vols, Leuven: Leuven University Press, 1992, pp. 2.1783–97.

Smith, Jonathan Z., "No News is Good News: Aretalogy and Gospel," in Jacob Neusner (ed.), *Christianity, Judaism, and Other Greco-Roman Cults: Studies for Morton Smith at Sixty*, 4 vols, Leiden: Brill, 1975, pp. 1.21–38.

—— *To Take Place: Theory in Ritual*, Chicago: University of Chicago Press, 1987.

Smith, Mark S., "The Invocation of Deceased Ancestors in Ps 49: 12c," *JBL* 112 (1993) 105–7.

Smith, Mark S., and E. M. Bloch-Smith, "Death and Afterlife in Ugarit and Israel," *JAOS* 108 (1988) 277–84.

Smith, Morton, *Palestinian Parties and Politics that Shaped the Old Testament*, New York: Columbia University Press, 1971.

—— "Prolegomena to a Discussion of Aretalogies, Divine Men, the Gospels, and Jesus," *JBL* 90 (1971) 174–99.

—— *Clement of Alexandria and a Secret Gospel of Mark*, Cambridge, Mass.: Harvard University Press, 1973.

—— Response in Howard Clark Kee, *Aretalogies, Hellenistic "Lives," and the Sources of Mark*, Berkeley: Center for Hermeneutical Studies, 1975, pp. 32–35.

—— *Jesus the Magician*. New York: Harper & Row, 1978.

—— "Mark 6: 32–15: 47 and John 6: 1–19: 42," in Paul J. Achtemeier (ed.), *Society of Biblical Literature Seminar Papers 1978*, 2 vols, Missoula, Mont.: Scholars, 1978, pp. 2.281–87.

Smith, Robert Houston, "Exodus Typology in the Fourth Gospel," *JBL* 81 (1962) 329–42.

Soards, Marion L., "The Question of a Premarcan Passion Narrative," in Raymond Brown (ed.), *The Death of the Messiah*, New York: Doubleday, 1994, pp. 2.1492–1524.

Solages, Mgr (Bruno) de, *Jean et les synoptiques*, Leiden: Brill, 1979.

Spronk, Klaas, *Beatific Afterlife in Ancient Israel and the Ancient Near East*, Kevelaer: Butzon & Bercker/Neukirchen-Vluyn: Neukirchener, 1986.

Stegner, William Richard, *Narrative Theology in Early Jewish Christianity*, Louisville: Westminster/John Knox, 1989.

Stuhlmacher, Peter (ed.), *The Gospel and the Gospels*, Grand Rapids: Eerdmanns, 1991.

Suhl, Alfred, *Die Funktion der alttestamentlichen Zitate und Anspielungen im Markusevangelium*, Gütersloh: Gütersloher/Gerd Mohn, 1965.

Talbert, Charles H., *What Is a Gospel? The Genre of the Canonical Gospels*, Philadelphia: Fortress, 1977.

Tannehill, Robert C., "The Disciples in Mark: The Function of a Narrative Role," *JR* 57 (1977) 386–405.

—— "Varieties of Synoptic Pronouncement Stories," *Semeia* 20 (1981) 101–19.

Taylor, Joan E., *Christians and the Holy Places: The Myth of Jewish-Christian Origins*, Oxford: Clarendon, 1993.

Taylor, Vincent, *The Formation of the Gospel Tradition*, 2nd ed., London: Macmillan, 1933.

Teeple, Howard M., *The Mosaic Eschatological Prophet*, Philadelphia: Society of Biblical Literature, 1957.

—— *The Literary Origin of the Gospel of John*, Evanston: Religion and Ethics Institute, 1974.

Theissen, Gerd, *Sociology of Early Palestinian Christianity*, Philadelphia: Fortress, 1977.

Tiede, David L., *The Charismatic Figure as Miracle Worker*, Missoula, Mont.: Society of Biblical Literature, 1972.

Tolbert, Mary Ann, *Sowing the Gospel: Mark's World in Literary-Historical Perspective*, Minneapolis: Fortress, 1989.

Trocmé, Etienne, *The Passion as Liturgy: A Study in the Origin of the Passion Narratives in the Four Gospels*, London: SCM, 1983.

Vermes, Geza, "Redemption and Genesis xxii – The Binding of Isaac and the Sacrifice of Jesus," in *idem*, *Scripture and Tradition in Judaism: Haggadic Studies*, Leiden: Brill, 1961, pp. 193–227.

——— *Jesus the Jew: A Historian's Reading of the Gospels*, London: Collins, 1973.

Vernant, Jean-Pierre, "Ambiguity and Reversal: On the Enigmatic Structure of *Oedipus Rex*," in *idem* and Pierre Vidal-Naquet, *Tragedy and Myth in Ancient Greece*, Brighton, Sussex: Harvester, 1981.

Vielhauer, Philipp, "Erwägungen zur Christologie des Markusevangeliums," in Erich Dinkler (ed.), *Zeit und Geschichte: Dankesgabe an Rudolf Bultmann zum 80. Geburtstag*, Tübingen: Mohr (Paul Siebeck), 1964, pp. 155–69.

——— *Geschichte der frühchristlichen Literatur*, Berlin: De Gruyter, 1975.

Votaw, C. W., *The Gospels and Contemporary Biographies in the Greco-Roman World*, Philadelphia: Fortress, 1970.

Wahlde, Urban C. von, *The Earliest Version of John's Gospel: Recovering the Gospel of Signs*, Wilmington, Del.: Michael Glazier, 1989.

Weeden, Theodore J., *Mark: Traditions in Conflict*, Philadelphia: Fortress, 1971.

Weiss, Johannes, *Jesus' Proclamation of the Kingdom of God*, Philadelphia: Fortress, 1971.

Werner, Eric, "Traces of Jewish Hagiolatry," *Hebrew Union College Annual* 51 (1980) 39–60.

Wiechers, Anton, *Aesop in Delphi*, Meisenheim: Glan, 1961.

Wilkens, Wilhelm, *Die Entstehungsgeschichte des vierten Evangeliums*, Zollikon: Evangelischer Verlag, 1958.

Wilkinson, John, "Jewish Holy Places and the Origins of Christian Pilgrimage," in Robert Ousterhout (ed.), *The Blessings of Pilgrimage*, Urbana and Chicago: University of Illinois Press, 1990, pp. 41–53.

Williams, James G., *Gospel Against Parable: Mark's Language of Mystery*, Sheffield: Almond, 1985.

Williams, Sam K., *Jesus' Death as Saving Event: The Background and Origin of a Concept*, Missoula, Mont.: Scholars, 1975.

Wills, Lawrence M., *The Jewish Novel in the Ancient World*, Ithaca/London: Cornell University Press, 1995.

Windisch, Hans, *Johannes und die Synoptiker: Wollte der vierte Evangelist die älteren Evangelien ergänzen oder ersetzen?*, Leipzig: Hinrichs'sche Buchhandlung, 1926.

Winkler, John J., *Auctor & Actor: A Narratological Reading of Apuleius' Golden Ass*, Berkeley: University of California Press, 1985.

Wrede, Wilhelm, *The Messianic Secret*, Cambridge: Clarke, 1971.

Young, Frances M., *Sacrifice and the Death of Christ*, London: SCM/Philadelphia: Westminster, 1975.

Zeitz, H., "Der Aesoproman und seine Geschichte," *Aegyptus* 16 (1936) 225–56.

INDEX OF ANCIENT SOURCES

HEBREW BIBLE

Genesis
1:1	234
22	178
23	38
25:7–10	39
31:19	38
32	229
35:4	38–39
35:20	38–39
35:27–29	38–39
49:31	39
50:13	39

Exodus
3:13–15	168
4	229
7:14–24	162
7:25–8:32	162
9:1–7	162
9:8–12	162
9:13–35	162
10:1–20	162
10:21 29	162
11:1–12:32	162
12:10	142
12:46	142, 231
34:20	178

Leviticus
14:6–7	40
16	247
16:20–22	40
17:7	40
19:28, 31	38
21:1–5	38
21:10–11	38

Numbers
6:6–7	38
19:11–22	38
21:4–9	161

Deuteronomy
4:34	161
6:22	161
7:19	161
11:3	161
18:11	38
18:15	57, 162
18:15–18	161, 163

Joshua
24:33	41

Judges
2:17–18	39
8:32	39
10:2, 5	39
11	39, 228
12:7–15	39
16:31	39

1 Samuel
1–3	39
2:1–10	27
12	39
19:13	38
28	38

28:13	38	69	141, 143
		69:10	111
1 Kings		69:21	142, 145, 246
2:10	41	88:11–12	38
17–2 Kgs 10	40, 77	109:25	142
17:1	40	110:1	167–68
17:2–7	40	118:25–26	108, 141
17:8–16	40, 57		
17:17–24	40, 57	**Ecclesiastes**	
18:12, 46	40	9:10	38
19:5–8	40		
		Isaiah	
2 Kings		6:1	142
1:8	55, 162	29:4	38
2:1–12	40	40:3	54–55
2:9–12	40	42:1	60–61
2:16	40	42–53	17, 40, 178
4:42–44	88	50:6	142, 247
9:13	108	50:6–7	139
13:20–21	40	52–53	40, 234
		53:1	142
2 Chronicles		53:3	139
24:14–27	230	53:5	139
36:14–16	230	53:7	142
		56:7	111
Nehemiah			
3:16	41	**Jeremiah**	
9:26	230	7:11	111
		16:5–9	38
Esther	5, 7, 11		
		Ezekiel	
Job		43:7–9	41
14:22	38		
		Daniel	5, 11
Psalms	17	4–6	218
2:7	60–61, 236–37	7:13	167–68, 176
6:4–5	142, 245	9:26	230
22	45, 141, 143	11:33	42
22:1	142, 145	12:3	42
22:2	143		
22:7–8	142	**Amos**	
22:18	142	6:7	38
22:19	143		
27:12	142	**Micah**	
34:21	142	5:1	139
35:11	142		
41:9	121, 142	**Zephaniah**	
42:5	124, 142	1:9	244
42:6	142, 246		
42:11	142	**Zechariah**	
42:12	246	3:2	241
43:5	142, 246	9:9	108, 141, 143

12:10	142, 247	Joseph and Aseneth	5, 11
13:7	142		
14:4	108, 113, 157	Josephus	
14:21	111, 127, 137	Antiquities	
		1.3.4 §85	48
Malachi		3.5.7 §96	48
3:1	54–55, 235	4.8.44 §§313–14	250
		4.8.48 §326	42
		5.1.29 §119	41
		9.2.2 §28	48

OLD TESTAMENT APOCRYPHA

		12.4.3 §173	160
3 Kingdoms (1 Kings)		13.6.1 §§211–12	41
14:6	161	14.2.1–2 §§22–28	43
		20.5.1 §97	157
Tobit	5, 11	20.8.6 §§167–70	157
13:16	244	Jewish War	
14:5	244	2.8.6 §135	252
		2.13.4 §259	157
Judith	7, 11, 228	3.8.3 §§352–4	250
5	254	4.9.7 §532	41
8:11–27	41	6.5.2 §285	157
16:25	40	6.5.3 §§300–9	158–60
		6.5.3 §301	44
Wisdom of Solomon	17	Against Apion	
6:24	42	1.41	250
11–19	250–51		
		Jubilees	
Prayer of Azariah		1.12	230
16–17	42		
		Lives of the Prophets	41–42
Song of the Three Jews	230		
		4 Maccabees	232
Susanna	218	6:29	42–43
		17:21–22	42–43
Bel and the Dragon	218		
		Manual of Discipline	
1 Maccabees		1QS 8.3, 10	42
13:51	108	1QS 9.4	42
		1QS 9.11	250
2 Maccabees			
3–4	17, 42, 164	Philo	
10:7	108	Every Man is Free	
15:12–16	234	100–4	225
		Life of Moses	16
		2.51.2 §288–91	42, 49, 233

ANCIENT JEWISH LITERATURE

		Against Flaccus	
bBerachot		6.36–39	37
34b	239		
		bTaanit	
1 Enoch		23a	43
12–16	242		
90:28–9	244	Testament of Abraham	26

Testament of Joseph   17

Testament of Moses
9.7   41

Testimonia (4QTest)   250

Yoma
6:6   40

GRECO-ROMAN AUTHORS

Achilles Tatius, *Leucippe*
  and Clitophon   26
2.2.1–2.3.1   247
2.11.1–2.12.1   247

Apollodorus, *Library*
"Herakles"
2.4.6–2.7.8   16

Apuleius, *Golden Ass*   26, 30

Archilochus   30

Aristophanes, *Wasps*
1446–8   224

Arrian
Anabasis of Alexander
4.11.2–4   32
Discourse of Epictetus   11

Athenaeus
6.265c–266e   225

Aulus Gellius, *Attic Nights*
2.18.9–10   226

(Pseudo-) Callisthenes,
  Alexander Romance   5, 11, 26

Diodorus Siculus
4.38.5   233
18.60.5   227, 230, 234

Diogenes Laertius, *Lives*
"Chilo"   27
"Empedocles"   15
8.22   252
8.68   227, 233

Dionysius of Halicarnassus
1.8.4   235

Eugeon of Samos   224

Euripides, *Iphigenia in Aulis*
1378–84   228

Herodian
1.11.2   233

Herodotus
1.27   160
2.134–35   224
4.14–15   233, 234, 249
4.94–95   234, 249
6.58   228

Hesiod, *Theogony*   29

Homer   30
Iliad   26, 28, 45, 50
16.791–92   45
18.28–31   45
18.175–77   45
Odyssey   50
3.447–55   45

Life of Aesop   5, 10, 16, 22,
   23–50, 51, 66,
   74, 160, 177,
   178, 179, 220,
   226, 229–30,
   244, 254
1   26, 254
6–7   29
13–14   30
21   30
25   30
25–26   31
26   30
37   66
57–64   30
65   31
66   30
99   30, 31, 34
100   225
124   31, 43
124–42   231
127   31
129–33   30
132   168

Life of Archilochus 16, 28–29

Life of Hesiod 16

Life of Homer 16

Life of Pindar 16
Life of Secundus 16

Livy
1.16 233

Longus, *Daphnis and Chloe*
26

Lucian 24
Passing of Peregrinus 33–34, 50, 160, 179
The Syrian Goddess
6 232

Nicolaus of Damascus
90 252

Ninus Romance 11

Ovid, *Fasti*
2.481–509 233

Pausanius
9.17.1 39

Petronius, *Satyricon* 26

Pindar, *Nemean Odes*
6 32
9.23–26 49

Philostratus
Heroicus 227
9.141.6 33
Life of Apollonius of Tyana 11
3.15 232
4.24 232
5.7 232
6.11 232
6.34 160
8.7 137
8.10–11 233
8.30–31 227, 233

Plato 11, 35, 229–30
Apology 11, 160
Laws
828c 32
Phaedo
60b–c 224

Plautus 26

Plutarch, *Parallel Lives*
"Cleomenes" 227
"Romulus"
27–28 233

Polybius
1.5.1 235
5.31.1–2 235

(Pseudo-) Seneca, *Apokolokyntosis*
9 33

Quintus Curtius, *History of Alexander*
8.5.15–19 32

Sophocles
Oedipus Rex 24
Oedipus at Colonus 49

Strabo
9.2.11 48

Tacitus
Annals
4.34–35 36
Histories
1.1.1 235

Xenophon
Constitution of the Lacedaemonians
15.9 228
Cyropaedia 11, 16
Memorabilia 11

NEW TESTAMENT

Matthew 1–7, 10, 19, 29, 156, 216, 217, 218, 237–38, 240
3:3 54–55
3:11–12 59
5:33–37 252

Matthew – *contd*

7:22	158
8:17	234
16:13–23	241
20:20–23	243
20:28	45
23:27	42
24:29–31	161
26:26–29	46
28	155
28:2–3	248

Mark

1:1	52–53
1:2–6	53–57
1:6	162
1:7–11	57–61
1:9–11	30
1:11	17, 176, 236, 237
1:14–20	61–64
1:15	162
1:20	162
1:21–22	252
1:21–28	19, 64–66, 84, 73, 240
1:22	111, 237, 238, 243
1:27	111
1:41	242
1:43	242
2:1–12	14, 66–71, 164, 168, 173
2:1–3:6	19
2:11	4
2:15–17	168, 171
2:18–22	72–74, 166, 168, 171, 235
2:23–28	168, 171
2:28	174
3:1–6	14, 71–74, 169, 171, 240
3:6	244–45
3:11	25
33:20–21	162
3:20–30	74–76
3:20–35	226, 246
3:21	168
3:22	56
3:22–30	166, 168, 169, 171
3:31–35	162, 169
4	16, 19, 242
4:10–12	163
4:11	242

4:11–12	1
4:35–40	240
4:35–8:26	76–78
5	76
5–8	19, 223
5–10	78–80
5:1–20	19
5:7	253
5:21–43	81–83, 164, 166, 173, 226, 240, 246
6	83, 164, 240
6:1–6	84–86, 166, 169, 174
6:2	240
6:4	162, 164
6:7–32	226, 246
6:15	162
6:17	173
6:24	173
6:32–44	86–88
6:45–52	88–90
6:52	91
6:59	173
7:1	56, 172
7:1–2	71–74
7:1–15	166, 169, 171
7:5	71–74
7:14–15	71–74
7:24–30	19, 77, 239
8	174, 240, 242
8–10	77, 95
8:11–13	137, 162, 164, 169
8:11–21	90–92
8:14–15	169
8:27	55
8:27–29	236
8:27–33	63–64
8:27–38	92–96
8:28	162
8:30	242
8:31	93–95, 243
8:31–33	169
8:33	3, 117, 177
8:38	242, 253
8:38–9:1	60
9	174
9:1	242
9:2	63
9:2–8	16
9:3	248
9:4	162

9:7	162, 176, 236, 237	14–15	117, 245
9:11–13	162, 171	14:1	31, 246
9:14–29	19	14:1–2	105, 114–15, 169, 244
9:25–27	242		
9:30–32	96–99	14:1–11	246
9:31	93–95, 174, 243	14:1–25	226
9:33	55, 173	14:3–9	105, 115–17
10	174	14:4	241
10:1	96–99	14:7	4
10:2–9	169	14:10–11	105, 169, 244
10:13–16	117	14:10–21	118–22, 127
10:21	242	14:12	231
10:28–30	162	14:12–16	105
10:32–34	31, 93–99, 101, 169, 243	14:12–25	246
		14:17–20	105
10:35–45	102–104, 130, 246	14:18	142, 143
10:38–40	243	14:21	105
10:41	117	14:22–25	46, 105
10:45	43, 45, 174	14:26	113
10:52	55	14:26–31	105, 122–23
11:1	113	14:27	127, 142, 247
11:1–8	121, 141, 143	14:32–41	105, 123–25
11:1–11	105–109, 244	14:33	63
11:9–10	141	14:34	142
11:12–14	109	14:36	127
11:12–26	226, 246	14:42	105
11:15–19	43, 105, 108–12, 113, 166–67, 169	14:42–50	125–28, 169
		14:43–15:52	105
		14:51–52	101
11:17	244	14:53–65	128–30, 142, 169
11:18	65–66, 167, 243	14:53–15:5	105
11:19	109	14:53–72	226, 246
11:20–25	109	14:56–58	112
11:27	109	14:57–58	142
11:27–33	105, 109–12, 167, 169	14:57–59	113
		14:58	167
12	31, 231	14:61	142
12–13	105	14:61–64	167
12:1–12	169, 243	14:64	167
12:13–17	169, 171	14:65	142
12:18–27	169, 171	14:66–72	131–33
12:28–34	171	15	152, 247
12:35–40	169, 171	15:1–15	133–37
13	16, 19, 125, 163	15:5	142
13:1–2	112	15:6–47	105
13:3	123	15:9	4
13:3–13	112–14	15:16–20	137–39
13:4	163	15:19	142
13:6	168	15:20–27	139–44
13:22	163	15:22	64, 145, 248
13:24	145	15:23	142
13:26	253	15:24	142

Mark – contd

15:25	145
15:29–30	142
15:29–32	247
15:33–39	144–46
15:34	45, 142, 143–44
15:35–36	142, 143
15:36	143
15:38	60
15:39	17, 176, 237
15:40	153
15:40–41	146
15:42	145
15:42–47	147–48
16:1–8	47–49, 105, 148–55, 248
16:9–20	47, 148–55, 172, 249
16:17	163
16:20	163

Luke

	1–7, 10, 12–13, 19, 29, 156, 216, 217, 218, 221, 237–38, 240
1:46–55	27
3:4–6	54–55
3:16	59
4:32	237
7:36–38	117
7:50	117
9:51	31
22:19	46
22:27	45
23:46	45
24	155
24:4	248
24:47	52

Q

	2, 4, 6, 51, 84, 156, 158, 163, 164, 167, 174–75, 218, 240, 250, 252, 253

(listed according to Luke)

3:7–8	167
3:16	59–60
7:1–10	167
7:18–23	167
7:24–25	167

11:14–26	75–76, 167
11:47	42
22:24–27	243

John

1	30, 144, 145, 232, 234, 235, 236
1:1	52–53
1:1–18	55
1:6–8	53–57
1:19	172
1:19–23	53–57
1:19–28	169
1:21	161–62, 160–61, 235
1:24	56, 172
1:25	56, 235
1:25–34	57–61
1:31	236
1:33	236
1:34	176
1:35–50	61
1:40	3
1:40–42	241
1:41	57
1:45	55, 57, 161–62
1:46	235
1:49	176
1:51	30, 57–61, 237
2	83, 105
2:1–12	20, 57, 162, 165, 239
2:4	240
2:11	19–20, 154, 161, 172
2:12	173
2:13	244
2:13–17	166–67
2:13–22	43, 108–12, 251, 252
2:17	232
2:18–19	163–64
2:22	217, 232
2:23	20
3	175, 235
3:3–21	91
3:13	175
3:14–15	161, 94, 253
3:16	232
3:18	176
3:23–24	53–57, 63, 235
3:25	166

John – *contd*
3:25–30   71–74, 166, 169, 235
3:27–30   239
4   76
4–6   77–78
4–11   78–80
4:1–3   169
4:3   240
4:4–42   240
4:9   69
4:10–15   91
4:19   160–61
4:34   248
4:43   240
4:43–45   84–86, 166, 173, 174
4:44   164
4:46–54   20, 57, 77, 81–83, 162, 164–66, 173, 239
4:48   20
4:53   154
4:54   20, 172
5   170, 238
5–7   57
5:1–9   20, 162, 165
5:1–16   66–71, 164, 165
5:1–18   14, 169, 252
5:1–47   238
5:8   4
5:16   167
5:17–25   176
5:18   167, 168, 176
5:24   242
5:25–29   175–76
5:36   248
5:46   161–62
6   83, 161, 164, 241
6:1–15   20, 162, 165
6:4   244
6:14   162, 154, 160–61
6:14–15   251
6:16   241
6:16–21   20, 88–90, 162, 165
6:22   91
6:22–59   169
6:26–34   90–92
6:41   91
6:41–42   170
6:51–59   56, 252

6:60–71   63
6:62   175
6:66–71   92–96
6:70–71   117
7   161
7:1   96–99, 170
7:5   240
7:10   69, 96–99
7:14   128
7:14–18   64, 252
7:14–20   166
7:14–31   252
7:15   238
7:16–17   161
7:19–20   74–76
7:19–23   66–71, 164, 165, 238
7:20   238
7:21   238
7:21–30   66
7:27   244
7:31–59   91
7:32–36   170
7:28   128
7:40   160–62
7:52   160–61, 173
8   31, 231
8:1   245
8:12–20   169
8:15   168
8:24   114, 168
8:28   94, 114, 168, 253
8:28–29   161
8:31   242
8:48–49   173
8:48–52   74–76, 166
8:51–52   242
8:58   114
9   57, 170
9:1–8   20
9:1–34   165
9:1–41   162
9:13–34   169
9:14   70
9:17   160–61
9:22   114
9:35   175
9:35–41   169
10   238
10:11   232
10:17–18   232
10:19–21   74–76

John – *contd*

10:22–39	170
10:31–33	167, 168
10:31–39	176
10:33	176
10:34–36	238
10:36	232
10:40–41	96–99
11	110, 239
11:1–3	99–102
11:1–45	20, 162, 165
11:4	176
11:7–8	96–99
11:11–16	96–99
11:20–22	99–102
11:27	176
11:32–41	99–102
11:43–46	99–102
11:45–53	102–4, 130, 170
11:45–57	105
11:48	167
11:50	44
11:51	158
11:52	44, 121
11:55	244
11:55–57	114–15
12	241
12–17	124
12:1	101
12:1–7	252
12:1–11	105, 107, 115–17
12:4	241, 242
12:8	4
12:9–11	102, 170
12:12–19	105, 106–109, 169
12:13	141
12:15	141
12:16	217, 232, 244
12:21–22	88
12:23	124, 175
12:23–34	92, 94–95
12:27	142
12:27–28	105, 123–25
12:31	241
12:31–33	161
12:33	241
12:34	253
12:37	154
12:38	142
12:40	142
12:42	114

12:42–43	169
12:48–50	161
13–17	113, 117
13:1–2	105
13:1–11	118–22
13:2	127
13:2–20	105
13:7	217
13:18	143, 142
13:18–31	118–22
13:19	114, 168
13:21	142
13:21–30	105
13:23	21, 243
13:27	127
13:28	217
13:31–32	105
13:36–38	105, 122–23
14:4–6	235
14:10	161
14:11	20
14:23–24	242
14:30–31	125–28
14:31	4, 105, 124
15–17	105
15:18–16:4	112–14
15:20	232
16:2	114
16:4	232
17:1	176
17:4	248
17:6–26	161
18:1	123–25
18:1–11	170
18:1–19:11	105
18:2	124
18:2–11	125–28
18:3	170
18:12–14	128–30, 142
18:12–24	170
18:12–19:16	105
18:15–18	131–33
18:19–24	128–30, 142
18:22–23	142
18:24	246
18:25–27	131–33
18:28	231, 246
18:28–40	133–37, 148
18:35	173
18:39	4
19:1	142
19:2–12	137–39

John – *contd*

19:3	45, 142
19:7	168, 176
19:9	142
19:13	248
19:13–25	139–44
19:14	231, 247
19:17	248
19:17–42	105
19:20	248
19:24	142
19:25–27	146
19:26	243
19:28	142
19:28–29	142
19:28–30	144–46
19:30	45
19:31	136–37, 146, 147–48, 231
19:36	142, 237
19:37	142
19:38–42	147–48
20	49, 237, 248, 249
20–21	48
20:1	249
20:1–10	105
20:1–31	148–55
20:2	243
20:2–10	63
20:4	3
20:9	217
20:11	249
20:11–21:25	105
20:12	248
20:22–23	241
20:30–31	47, 249
20:31	176
21	47, 154–55, 172, 248, 249
21:1–14	20
21:20–22	63

Acts

	5, 12–13
1:22	52–53
2:22–36	13
3:13–21	13
3:22	161, 250
7:37	161
8:4–40	132
10:36–43	240
10:37	52–53, 235
10:37–43	13
10:38	55
10:39	235
13:23–33	13
13:33	237

Romans

1:3–4	13
3:25	43
5:6–11	232
8:31–34	13

1 Corinthians

4:13	45
5:7	43, 45
11:23	122
11:24	46
15	49
15:1–3	94
15:1–5	13
15:3	43
15:3–5	141
15:20	49

2 Corinthians

12	161

Galatians

1:4	232
2:20	232
3:13	232
4:4–5	232

Philippians

2	234
2:6–11	236

Titus

2:14	232

Hebrews

	233
1:5	237
2	234
2:17	43
5:5	237

1 Peter

2:24	232

1 John

1:7	232
2:2	232

1 John – *contd*
4:10   232
5:6   232

Revelation
1:3   157
5:6   232
19:10   157
22:10   157

EARLY CHRISTIAN LITERATURE

Apocryphal Acts   5, 11

Barnabas
7.7–11   247

Didache
9–10   88, 104, 121
9–11   47
16.6–8   161

Eusebius
Church History
3.39.4   237
Preparation for the Gospel
9.41.456d–457b   233

Gospel of Peter   146, 247, 248, 249
5.15   136–37, 148
5.19   145–46
9.35–11.49   155
12–13   155
12.50–14.60   148–55, 237
13.55   248

Gospel of Thomas   6, 9, 13, 51, 241, 253
65   226

Ignatius, *Ephesians*
19.3   52, 235

Justin Martyr   10–11, 233
Apology
1.20   233
1.54   33
Dialogue
69   33

Martyrdom of Polycarp
12.2–3   137

Secret Mark   19, 99–102, 110, 242

SUBJECT INDEX

apocalypses 11, 19, 106, 112–14
aretalogy 15–16, 24, 35–6, 156, 160, 177

baptism of Jesus 1–2, 7, 17, 30, 176, 236
beloved disciple 21, 47, 100–2, 118–22, 131–3, 146–55, 243
biography 1, 4, 11–18, 23–4, 156, 177, 179, 221

Carabas/Barabbas 37, 134–9
chief priests and high priest 7, 31, 92–6, 102–5, 115–22, 125–30, 133–44, 166–74
chreia (including apophthegm and pronouncement story) 11, 69–71, 73–4, 166–71, 245
controversies and conflicts 7, 14, 16, 19, 23, 31, 69–71, 73–4, 105, 122, 164–71, 178–9
crucifixion 2, 66, 92–7, 102–5, 111–12, 133–7, 166–71, 176
cult of Jesus 12, 17–18, 21, 23–50, 104, 156, 177–9, 221, 231, 232, 233, 248–9
Cynics 24–5, 30, 34

disciples 3, 16, 45, 71–4, 86–9, 92–7, 107–22, 132, 147–55, 168–9, 177, 179, 217
discourses in John 3, 19

Elijah and Elisha 40, 48, 53, 55, 57, 58, 77, 88, 92–6, 144–6, 162
empty tomb 48–9, 105, 147–55, 233–4
eschatology 11–13, 15, 47, 88, 104, 111–14, 122, 157–64, 174–6
Exodus 77, 161–2
expiation of sin 28, 38, 40–6

eucharist and Lord's Supper 46–7, 88, 105, 118–22, 177, 233

faith and believing (*pistis, pisteuo*) 20, 47–8, 67, 69, 83, 94, 100–2, 165–6, 233

Galilee (including Cana, Capernaum, Nazareth) 20, 31, 48–50, 55, 58, 60, 61, 62, 64–6, 81–2, 84–90, 96–8, 122–3, 131–3, 146–55, 171–4, 241–2
genre 1, 8–10
gospel genre 1–22, 29–32, 34, 46, 104, 179, 219

Hebrew Bible and scripture quotation 3, 17, 108–9, 109–12, 119–28, 139–44, 167–8, 175–6, 247–8
Hebron (Kiriath-arba, Cave of Machpelah) 38–9
hero cult 21, 23–50, 53, 219, 226–8; in Judaism 37–43

infancy narrative (includes birth) 1, 4, 6, 14, 29, 52–3, 55
irony 3, 24, 26, 28, 69, 91, 136–7, 148

John the Baptist 1–3, 7, 53–63, 71–4, 92–8, 110, 168–9, 236
Jews, Judeans, and Judaism 3, 7, 18, 31, 37–46, 53, 56, 61, 64–6, 68–76, 85–6, 96–8, 100–2, 104, 110–12, 116–22, 134–44, 147–55, 166–71, 234
Judas 45, 92–6, 105, 116–22, 126–8, 241

kerygma 10–14, 18, 21, 23

law 3, 68–71, 74, 138–9, 166–71
Lazarus 97–102, 105–10, 115–17

messianic secret 3, 83, 217
miracles 2–3, 7, 14, 16, 19–21, 38–43, 65–71, 76–8, 81–3, 86–90, 99–102, 164–6, 172–3, 178–9, 233, 238–40, 242–3
Moses 39, 42, 48, 57, 68–71, 91, 94, 157–64
myth 6, 37, 53, 179

novels 5, 11–13, 16, 23–4, 26–8, 31, 42, 219, 220, 246–7

oral and written tradition 4–6, 21, 51, 85, 89, 217–18, 246, 253

parables 1, 11, 14, 19, 31
passion narrative 1–2, 14, 18–21, 30, 92–8, 104–9, 117
Passover 45–7, 86–8, 105–22, 133–44, 231, 252
persecuted righteous person (*dikaios*) 17, 23
Peter 3, 45, 62–4, 82, 92–6, 105, 112, 119–28, 131–3, 147–55, 241
Pharisees 7, 45, 71–4, 90–2, 100, 102–9, 130, 166–74, 252
pharmakos 36–7, 40
philosopher 15–16, 24, 30, 31, 33, 35, 136–7, 157–64, 178–9, 217, 228, 232

prophet, prophecy 17–18, 39–44, 57, 61, 84–6, 105, 109–14, 129–30, 157–64, 174, 244, 250, 251

resurrection 2, 4, 7, 16, 48–9, 92–7, 100–2, 105, 117, 123, 172–3, 249

Sabbath 67–71, 84, 164–71, 238, 240
sacrifice 15–16, 28, 36–7, 44–7, 102–4, 122, 174, 178, 229–30, 233
scapegoat 36–7, 40
scribes 67–9, 72, 74, 92–6, 115, 128–30, 133–7, 168–74
signs 3, 19–20, 47–8, 88, 90–2, 97, 102, 109–14, 152–5, 157–65, 172, 245
Son of Humanity 16, 45, 50, 60, 67, 90–9, 103–5, 120–2, 124–30, 174–6, 234, 252–3
suffering 16–17, 23, 50, 139–46, 174–6, 234, 253

teaching 7, 14, 16, 20–1, 23, 30, 64–6, 84–8, 92–7, 106, 111, 126–8, 132, 164, 178, 217, 237–8, 243
theios aner (divine man) 16, 32
therapon (ritual substitute) 16, 28, 36

way (*hodos*) 55, 93–6, 107, 235, 241
women at tomb 45, 146–8, 177, 249

INDEX OF MODERN SCHOLARS

Achtemeier, Paul 76–7, 217, 223, 239
Ackerman, Susan 228
Adrados, Francisco 27, 224
Albertz, Martin 223
Allison, Dale 245
Altman, William 240
Attridge, Harold 70, 238
Auerbach, Erich 12, 133, 220, 247
Aune, David 4, 12, 16, 17, 48, 217, 218, 220, 222, 225, 227, 233, 235, 250, 251, 252

Bakhtin, Mikhail 25
Baltzer, Klaus 17, 162–3, 222, 251, 253
Barr, David 11, 220
Barrett, C. K. 216, 239
Bassler, Jouette 173, 240, 252
Bayliss, M. 228
Beare, F.W. 238, 251
Becker, Jürgen, 252
Begg, Christopher 233
Berger, Klaus 16, 222
Best, Ernest 248
Betz, Hans Dieter 33, 228, 232, 247, 249
Bickerman, Elias 48, 153, 233, 249
Bilezikian, Gilbert 11, 220
Black, Matthew 239
Blenkinsopp, Joseph 229
Bloch-Smith, Elizabeth 228
Boismard, M.-E. 56, 156–7, 216, 223, 235, 249, 250
Bokser, Baruch 230
Borgen, Peder 216
Boring, M. Eugene 250
Borsch, F. H. 234, 253
Bowersock, G. W. 12, 220
Brandenberger, Egon 223
Bremmer, Jan 228

Broadhead, Edwin 253
Brown, Raymond 21, 56–7, 60, 63, 85, 88, 91, 102, 109, 110, 145, 152, 154, 217, 221, 222, 223, 233, 235, 236, 237, 239, 240, 241, 242, 243, 244, 245, 246, 247, 248, 249, 250, 251, 252, 253
Bultmann, Rudolf 4, 13, 14, 19, 56–7, 63, 65, 73, 75, 94–5, 108, 110, 121, 127, 130, 153, 166–7, 217, 221, 222, 223, 226, 231, 233, 235, 236, 237, 238, 241, 242, 243, 244, 245, 248, 251, 253
Burkert, Walter 37, 227, 228, 229, 230, 232
Burridge, Richard vi, 14–18, 219, 221, 222
Buse, Ivor 235, 245

Callahan, Allen vi, 232
Cameron, Ronald 232, 241, 242
Camp, John 228
Carlston, Charles 226
Carrington, Philip 11, 220, 231
Case, Shirley Jackson 223
Cerfaux, L. 227
Charlesworth, James 230, 234
Chilton, Bruce 111, 231, 244, 251
Clark, Douglas 250
Cohen, Ralph 218, 219
Colbi, Saul Paul 230
Collins, Adela Yarbro vi, 11–13, 49, 175–6, 220, 221, 222, 226, 232, 233, 234, 244, 247, 250, 251, 252, 253
Collins, John 222, 230, 253
Compton, Todd 221, 224, 226, 228
Conzelmann, Hans 12, 220, 233
Cook, Michael 170–1, 246, 252
Corrington, Gail Patterson 228
Cranfield, C. E. B. 237
Crossan, John Dominic 222, 239, 242, 248
Culler, Jonathan 9, 219

Cullmann, Oscar 234

Dahl, Nils Alstrup 233, 234
Daly, Lloyd 180, 254
Daube, David 238
Dauer, Anton 216, 245, 246
de Vaux, Roland 229
Delaney, Carole 229
Denaux, Adelbert 216, 239
Detienne, Marcel 226
Dewey, Arthur 248
Dewey, Joanna vi, 218, 226, 238, 246
Dibelius, Martin 103, 166, 221, 243, 251
Dihle, Albrecht 14–15, 221
Dillon, John 221
Dinkler, Erich 241
Dodd, C. H. 13–14, 18–19, 21, 104, 152, 217, 221, 222, 223, 231, 235, 239, 241, 242, 243, 244, 248, 250, 252
Donahue, John 132, 220, 222, 226, 238, 246
Doran, Robert 222
Dormeyer, Detlev 17, 222, 245
Draper, Jonathan 161, 250
Droge, Arthur 228
Dubrow, Heather 219
Ducrot, Oswald 219
Duling, Dennis 216, 229, 235, 239, 241, 252
Dumézil, Georges 226
Dunderberg, Ismo 216, 217, 236, 238, 241, 244
Dundes, Alan 5, 218, 219, 226

Easton, B. S. 19, 223
Eckel, Malcolm David 233
Edwards, Richard 236
Eliot, George 225
Evans, Craig 226, 231, 244, 246, 247

Farmer, William 216
Farnell, Lewis Richard 227
Faure, A. 223
Feldman, Louis 250
Feuillet, André 250
Filson, Floyd 243
Fischel, H. A. 11, 220, 230
Foley, John Miles 5–6, 218
Ford, John 225
Fortna, Robert 19–21, 69–70, 132, 157, 164–6, 217, 223, 233, 235, 237, 249, 251

Fowler, Alastair 8, 10, 219
Fowler, Barbara Hughes 224
France, R. T. 227
Frankemölle, Herbert 222
Frazer, James 37, 228
Freyne, Seán 240, 252
Frye, Northrop 6, 218

Gärtner, Bertil 231
Gardner-Smith, Percival 4, 217
Geary, Patrick 233
Georgi, Dieter, 16, 221
Ginzberg, Louis 230
Girard, René 40, 229
Glasson, T. Francis 250
Glusman, Edward, 217, 237, 239, 246
Goehring, James 243
Goodenough, Erwin 217
Goulder, Michael 11, 220
Grabbe, Lester 229
Gray, John 229
Gray, Rebecca 250, 251
Green, Joel 18, 217, 222, 245, 246
Griesbach, Johann Jakob 216
Griffiths, Alan 231
Gross, Rita 229
Grotanelli, Cristiano 224
Guelich, Robert 10, 17, 220, 221, 222
Guthrie, W. K. C. 227

Hadas, Moses 15, 35–6, 221, 226, 227, 228
Hägg, Tomas 221, 226
Haenchen, Ernst 238
Hahn, Ferdinand 241, 250
Hallo, William 229
Hamerton-Kelley, Robert 229
Hanfmann, George 228
Hare, Douglas R. A. 230, 252
Hendel, Ronald 229
Hengel, Martin 12, 44–5, 220, 230, 231, 234, 243, 249
Hill, David 250
Hirsch, E. 219
Hobbs, Edward 231, 251
Hock, Ronald 251
Hofmann, H. 226
Holladay, Carl 221
Holzberg, Niklas vi, 12, 24, 30, 220, 221, 224, 225, 226
Hooker, Morna 234
Hopkins, Keith 25, 27, 224

Horsley, Richard vi, 158, 175, 240, 250, 252
Hughes, Dennis 228
Hurtado, Larry 218

Jacoby, Felix 252
Jameson, Frederic 6, 218
Jauss, Hans-Robert 219
Jay, Nancy 229
Jenks, Alan 234
Jeremias, Joachim 41, 115, 230, 233, 237, 239, 241, 243
Jonas, Hans 48

Kähler, Martin 1, 104, 216
Käsemann, Ernst 232
Kaufmann, Y. 229
Kee, Howard Clark 15, 221, 231, 238, 239, 244, 251
Kelber, Werner 11, 85, 125, 216, 217, 220, 222, 240, 243, 245, 246, 253
Kepnes, Steven 219
Kerényi, Karl 12, 220
Kertelge, Karl 250
Kiefer, René 239
King, Philip 228
Kingsbury, Jack Dean 236, 253
Kloppenborg, John 174–5, 236, 250, 252
Knox, Wilfred 227, 240
Koester, Helmut 4, 14, 17, 80, 98, 145, 217, 218, 219, 221, 222, 223, 232, 234, 237, 239, 242, 246, 247, 248, 251
Kolenkow, Anitra Bingham 14, 71, 165, 167, 221, 239, 251
Kümmel, Werner Georg 216
Kuhn, Heinz-Wolfgang 223

Lacocque, André 230
Lambert, W. G. 225
Lamouille, A. 216, 223, 249
Landis, Stefan 240
Larson, Jennifer 228
Leach, Edmund 6, 218, 254
Lesky, Albin 224–5
Levenson, Jon vi, 178, 230, 231, 232, 233, 237, 253
Levine, Amy-Jill 230
Lewis, Theodore 228
Lightfoot, R. H. 105, 243
Lindars, Barnabas 21, 223, 235, 236, 243
Lindemann, Andreas 248
Linnemann, Eta 222, 245, 246

Lohmeyer, Ernst 172, 252
Loraux, Nicole 228
Lord, Albert 218
Luedemann, Gerd 233, 249
Lührmann, Dieter 17, 145, 222, 236, 237

MacDonald, Dennis vi, 218
Mack, Burton 73–4, 165, 176–8, 216, 222, 223, 232, 239, 245, 251, 253
McKeon, Michael 26, 224
McKnight, Edgar 218
MacQueen, Bruce 26, 224
Malbon, Elizabeth Strothers 218, 241, 252
Marshall, I. Howard 236
Martyn, J. Louis 57, 236, 250
Marxsen, Willi 172, 217, 221, 235, 236, 237, 252
Mason, Steve 250
Matera, Frank 137, 222, 247
Maynard, Arthur 239
Meeks, Wayne 92, 161, 175, 250, 252
Merkelbach, Reinhold 12, 220
Merkle, Stefan 226
Meyer, Marvin 243, 248
Meyers, Eric 229
Milik, J. 219
Miller, Robert 242
Minear, Paul 249
Mirecki, Paul vi, 152, 248
Mohr, Till Arend 243, 244, 246
Moo, Douglas 247
Morgan, J. R. 224
Morris, Ian 227

Nagy, Gregory vi, 27–30, 35–6, 45, 218, 219, 221, 224, 225, 226, 227, 231, 234, 254
Neirynck, Frans 216
Neusner, Jacob 217, 220, 232
Neyrey, Jerome 238
Nickelsburg, George 17, 222, 234, 242, 247, 252
Nicol, W. 19, 223, 233
Nilsson, Martin 227
Nineham, D. E. 108, 113, 121, 145, 148, 223, 231, 236, 241, 243, 244
Nissen, Hans-Jörg 224
Noack, Bent 21, 223
Nock, Arthur Darby 227

Obermann, Julian 230
Olyan, Saul 228

O'Neil, Edward 251

Papathomopoulos, Manolis 180, 225, 254
Parkes, James 230
Patterson, Annabel 25, 224
Patterson, Stephen, 242
Patton, Kimberley vi, 225
Pease, Arthur Stan 233
Perkins, David 218
Perrin, Norman 2, 11, 132, 174, 216, 220, 221, 231–2, 241, 246, 252, 253
Perry, Ben 23, 27, 180, 224, 225, 226, 254
Pervo, Richard vi, 31, 220, 221, 225, 226
Pesch, Rudolph 222, 245
Petersen, Norman 241
Pfister, Friedrich 227
Pitard, Wayne 229
Pope, Marvin 228, 229
Posner, Raphael 230
Propp, Vladimir 6–7, 218

Raglan, Lord (Fitzroy) 39, 48, 226
Rank, Otto 226
Reicke, Bo 232
Reid, I. 219
Reim, Gunter 237, 252
Reinbold, Wolfgang 217, 244, 245
Renger, Johannes 224
Rice, David 228
Ricoeur, Paul 220
Riga, Peter 251
Robbins, Vernon 220, 240, 243, 244, 245, 251
Robinson, James 4, 80, 98, 217, 223, 234
Robinson, John A. T. 3, 217, 235, 250
Rofé, Alexander 248
Rohde, Erwin 227
Roloff, D. 227
Rose, Herbert Jennings 227

Sabbe, M. 246
Saldarini, Anthony 172, 231, 246, 252
Sanders, E. P. 43, 111, 141, 230, 231, 244, 250, 251
Satran, David 41, 230
Schatkin, Margaret 230
Schauer, Markus 226
Schenke, Ludger 232, 248
Schmidt, H. 221
Schmidt, Karl Ludwig 13, 236
Schmithals, Walter 217

Schnackenburg, Rudolf 217, 223, 231, 253
Schnelle, Udo 240
Schnider, Franz 240
Schniewind, Julius 221
Schüssler Fiorenza, Elisabeth 117, 229, 244, 245, 253
Schweitzer, Albert 1, 216
Seeley, David 230, 232, 234
Shakespeare, William 225
Shaw, George Bernard 30
Shuler, Philip 15, 221
Simon, Marcel 230
Smith, Dwight Moody ii, 3, 19, 216, 217, 223, 244, 247
Smith, Jonathan Z. 179, 217, 229, 232, 233, 253
Smith, Mark 228
Smith, Morton 15, 35–6, 76, 78–80, 87, 98, 101, 163, 221, 226, 227, 228, 239, 242, 251
Smith, Robert Houston 162, 231, 250
Soards, Marion 222, 245
Söder, Rosa 220
Solages, Mgr (Bruno) de 216, 223
Sommer, Benjamin 157, 250
Spanier, Ktziah 228
Spolsky, Ellen 219
Spronk, Klaas 228
Stambaugh, John 228
Steblin-Kamenskij, M. 218, 254
Stegner, William 237
Stendahl, Krister 231, 234
Stenger, Werner 240
Stoneman, Richard vi, 26, 224
Stuhlmacher, Peter 220, 221
Suhl, Alfred 247
Sumption, Jonathan 233

Tabor, James 233
Talbert, Charles 221, 227, 228
Tannehill, Robert 166–7, 251, 253
Taylor, Joan 230
Taylor, Vincent 222, 236, 237, 245
Teeple, Howard 19, 157, 223, 250
Theissen, Gerd 85, 174, 240, 252
Thomas, Christine 218
Tiede, David 15, 221
Todorov, Tzvetan 219
Tödt, H. E. 253
Tolbert, Mary Ann 11–12, 219, 220, 226
Tondriau, J. 227

Torrey, Charles 230
Trocmé, Etienne 231

Ulansey, David 236

Van Segbroeck, F. 216
VanderKam, James 230
Vanderpool, Eugene 228
Vawter, Bruce 250
Vermes, Geza 252
Veyne, Paul 227
Via, Dan 11, 220, 226
Vielhauer, Philipp 176–7, 221, 237, 253
Votaw, Clyde Weber 11, 13, 14, 220

Wahlde, Urban C. von 19, 223
Walker, William 218
Weiss, Johannes 10–11, 220

Wendland, Paul 37, 228
Wenham, David 227
Werner, Eric 230
Wiechers, Anton 224
Wilken, Robert 230
Wilkens, Wilhelm 223, 244, 252
Wilkinson, John 230
Williams, James 167, 220, 251
Williams, Sam K. 230
Wills, Lawrence 218, 219, 220, 224, 226,
    230, 247, 251
Winkler, John 26, 224
Wire, Antoinette Clark 250
Wittgenstein, Ludwig 8
Wrede, Wilhelm 217

Zeitz, H. 226
Zimmerli, Walther 237